POVERTY, WEALTH, AND WELL-BEING

Poverty, Wealth, and Well-Being

Experiencing Penia *in Democratic Athens*

CLAIRE TAYLOR

OXFORD
UNIVERSITY PRESS

OXFORD
UNIVERSITY PRESS

Great Clarendon Street, Oxford, OX2 6DP,
United Kingdom

Oxford University Press is a department of the University of Oxford.
It furthers the University's objective of excellence in research, scholarship,
and education by publishing worldwide. Oxford is a registered trade mark of
Oxford University Press in the UK and in certain other countries

First Edition published in 2017

Published in the United States of America by Oxford University Press
198 Madison Avenue, New York, NY 10016, United States of America

British Library Cataloguing in Publication Data
Data available

ISBN 978-0-19-878693-1

To YF and YM,
with deepest thanks.

Preface

This book is about poverty and well-being in Athens during the period of Athenian democracy, with the greatest emphasis placed on the century between *c*.420 and *c*.320 BCE. It investigates ancient discourses about poverty side by side with approaches derived from contemporary social-science research in order to ask what it meant to be poor in the radical participatory democracy of the late fifth and fourth centuries. This was a world in which (some of) those categorized as poor had real political power, but also one in which ideas about poverty were shaped by elitist ideologies; indeed, our source material is, for the most part, heavily weighted towards those who were not at all poor. This complicates our understanding of poverty, but also raises important questions for discussion.

There is, however, a danger involved in writing about poverty and the poor as an outsider distanced from the daily struggles of the people whom you describe: it can be easy to reify the poor, to highlight the stereotypes and then create new ones yourself, to assimilate dissimilar groups of people and their various experiences together for want of a better way to describe them. It is easy to consider vastly divergent groups as homogenous, to default to concepts that should be unpicked, or to use terminology that is anachronistic or problematic in one way or another. It is easy to overlook the differences, the changes over time, and the ways in which those who were categorized as 'poor' contested their social roles, and overlook the processes that create and reproduce poverty. I have strived to address these faults, but am sure that other historians will place emphasis in different places to those I have chosen.

It is also, to be sure, a privilege to write about poverty from a position of relative security. Over the years in which this book was conceived, written, and rewritten, the modern state of Greece (like the UK) has seen a horrendous increase in poverty and hardship, and a decrease in living standards the likes of which have not been seen for generations—a shameful consequence of un- (even anti-)democratic decision-making of political and economic elites. Writing this book whilst large numbers of people are paying the price for so-called austerity measures has solidified in my mind the importance of reframing our understanding of ancient economies from the point of view of those who were deprived, marginalized, or socially excluded in various ways.

This book would not have been produced without the support of a number of people and institutions which at various points in my career provided a (literal and metaphorical) lifeline. I was fortunate to have been part of the last cohort to have attended university in the UK before tuition fees were introduced, to have received a small, but at the time much-needed, grant from the British state to start my undergraduate studies, to have graduated with minimal debt—an experience sadly taken away from large numbers of young people today. I am deeply thankful that my education was considered important enough to invest in, and for the institutions and teachers who encouraged me along the (sometimes bumpy) way.

More recently, this book has taken shape with financial support from the Leverhulme Trust, who supported an Early Career Fellowship at the University of Manchester where this project was begun, a Tytus summer fellowship at the University of Cincinnati, a residential fellowship at the Center for Hellenic Studies in Washington, DC, and the Office of the Vice Chancellor for Research and Graduate Education with funding from the Wisconsin Alumni Research Foundation at the University of Wisconsin-Madison. Each of these institutions provided congenial places to work, the intellectual space to develop as a historian, as well as time to write. I am also immensely grateful to a number of people who provided debate, discussion, criticism, as well as hospitality during these years: Jen Baird (first alphabetically, but truly just first), Kate Bayley, Paul Cartledge, Federica Carugati, Christy Constantakopoulou and family, James Kierstead, Marc Kleijwegt, Polly Low, Josiah Ober, Robin Osborne, Lene Rubinstein, Dan Stewart, as well as the anonymous readers for the press. There will still be disagreements, of that I am sure; I remain, nevertheless, most thankful.

In addition, participants at the Stanford 'Wealthy Hellas' seminar put me through my paces and forced me to rethink (as well as defend) a number of my assumptions; audiences in Florida, Vienna, Bangor, Gregynog, and Manchester helped me sharpen various parts of my argument and discard other parts; Claudia Tiersch's conference ('Die athenische Demokratie im 4. Jh.: zwischen Modernisierung und Tradition') provided much-needed encouragement at a time when the project was lagging, and the Department of History at UW-Madison has provided a superbly stimulating environment to finish this book. Last but not least, Thanasi Papapostolou provided far more encouragement than he ever realized, as well as welcome distraction. I am grateful to you all.

Contents

List of Figures

List of Tables

List of Abbreviations

For ancient authors and works I have used the abbreviations of the *Oxford Classical Dictionary* fourth edition for the most part (so Isoc. rather than Isok.), even though I have preferred to transliterate Greek names (rather than used Latinized forms). I trust this will not be too confusing to the reader. Unless stated otherwise, translations of literary texts are from the Loeb Classical Library.

Additional abbreviations are as follows:

Agora XVI	A. G. Woodhead 1997. *The Athenian Agora XVI. Inscriptions: The Decrees.* Princeton: American School of Classical Studies at Athens
Agora XVII	D. W. Bradeen 1974. *The Athenian Agora XVII. Inscriptions: The Funerary Monuments.* Princeton: American School of Classical Studies at Athens
Agora XIX	G. V. Lalonde, M. K. Langdon, and M. B. Walbank 1991. *The Athenian Agora XIX. Inscriptions: Horoi, Poletai Records, Leases of Public Lands.* Princeton: American School of Classical Studies at Athens
APF	J. K. Davies 1971. *Athenian Propertied Families.* Oxford: Clarendon Press
AR	*Archaeological Reports*
CAT	C. W. Clairmont 1993–5. *Classical Attic Tombstones.* Kilchberg, Switzerland: Akanthus
CEG	P. A. Hansen 1983. *Carmina Epigraphica Graeca: Saeculorum VIII–Va. Chr. n.* Berlin: de Gruyter
DT	A. Audollent (ed.) 1904. *Defixionum Tabellae.* Paris: Fontemoing
IEleusis	K. Clinton 2008. *Eleusis. The Inscriptions on Stone: Documents of the Sanctuary of the Two Goddesses and Public Documents of the Deme.* 2 vols. Athens: The Archaeological Society at Athens
IG	1873– . *Inscriptiones Graecae.* Berlin: de Gruyter
LGPN	M. J. Osborne and S. G. Byrne 1994. *A Lexicon of Greek Personal Names, II: Attica.* Oxford: Oxford University Press
SEG	1971– . *Supplementum Epigraphicum Graecum.* Leiden: Brill

Note on money: classical Athens used the following monetary system: 6 obols = 1 drachma; 100 drachmas = 1 mina; 60 minai = 1 talent.

1

Poverty and *Penia*

Approaching the Lives of the Poor in the Ancient World

At some point during the first half of the fourth century BCE, a cobbler in Athens named Dionysios made a dedication on behalf of himself and his family to the hero Kallistephanos. After seeing a vision in a dream, the dedication tells us, Dionysios honoured Kallistephanos and his sons with a votive stele depicting a cobbler's workshop (Fig. 1.1). In return, he explicitly asked the god for wealth and happy health.[1] As a cobbler—a skilled workman who earned his living through labour, rather than a member of the leisured elite—Dionysios would likely have been considered by his contemporaries in Athens as 'poor'. His labour categorized him as a *penes*—a 'poor' man—in contrast to the *plousioi* (the rich), but the fact of his dedication demonstrates that his poverty was understood as being rooted in the social roles he inhabited as much as it was defined by his economic condition. Indeed, it is clear that those described as *penetes* (the 'poor', though perhaps more precisely, 'those who worked for a living') encompassed a broad range of people, from the moderately well-off though not permanently leisured to those living on the borders of subsistence.

[1] *SEG* 55.307 (Agora I 7396): 'Dionysios the cobbler, son of [. . .]onos, and his children dedicate this to the hero Kallistephanos. Having seen a divine vision in his sleep, Dionysios honours the hero and the children of Kallistephanos; do you give in return for these things wealth and happy health (πλοῦτόν τε καὶ εὐαίων' ὑγίειαν).' Little is known about Kallistephanos, but Parker 2005: 449–50 suggests he is a cobbler himself. On the dedication see Camp 1986: 147; Löhr 2000 no. 81.

Figure 1.1. Dedication of the cobbler Dionysios to Kallistephanos (Agora I 7396)

We cannot tell from this dedication how 'poor'—in economic terms—Dionysios and his family actually were and so where we might place him on a sliding scale of well-off to subsisting. We do not know in a drachma-and-obol sense the financial resources Dionysios had access to, nor whether this dedication was the result of years of saving or easily purchased without significant economic hardship. The dedication does, however, raise questions about how we might approach *penia* (poverty) in Athens and how we might consider the lives of the *penetes* because it reveals the contours of well-being among groups of people who were not part of the elite: Dionysios maintained a family life as well as his workshop, he participated in a cultic community, and he had aspirations not only of wealth, but also of health and happiness.[2] It also reveals the gap between the ancient category of *penia* and the modern category of poverty, leading to questions about how poverty in the ancient world should be analysed. Should we view it as predominantly an economic condition—that is, in terms of how much wealth Dionysios had or did not have—or in terms of its non-material elements too? These are the questions which form the basis for this book.

Until recently historians' views of poverty in the ancient Greek world have been fairly pessimistic. Drawing, for example, from Herodotus' famous observation that 'in Hellas poverty is always endemic', commentators have tended to view the Greek world and its peoples as poor, reading this statement as a factual assessment of available resources and typical lifestyles in the classical period.[3] But, as others have pointed out, these words are spoken by the exiled Spartan king Demaratos who, in 480, was addressing Xerxes as the Persians were invading the Greek mainland. In this conversation Demaratos explains to Xerxes the characteristics and attitudes that

[2] See also the fragmentary *IG* I[3] 824, a dedication by Euphronios the potter (*kerameus*) to Athena, late sixth or early fifth century: Raubitschek 1949: no. 225.

[3] Hdt 7.102.1: *τῇ Ἑλλάδι πενίη μὲν αἰεί κοτε σύντροφος ἐστί*. See Cartledge 2002 [first published 1978]: 21: 'the overall picture of classical Greece . . . is of a generally rocky, infertile and poor country'. Ste. Croix 1981: 117: 'even in their great days, in the fifth and fourth centuries BC, the Greeks of the mainland inhabited a very poor country, with little natural wealth, agricultural or mineral, and . . . the predominance of the great states, Sparta and Athens, was due to military or naval strength, resting upon an organised system of alliances . . . It is of mainland Greece that Herodotus was thinking when he made Demaratus say that Greece and poverty had always been foster-sisters (VII.102.1).' Desmond 2006: 1: 'In antiquity, mainland Greece and its Aegean islands were poor places.'

the Persians would come across during the invasion.[4] It is in this context that he describes Hellas as poor, describing poverty and Greece as being so intricately intertwined that they are like foster-children, brought up together (*syntrophoi*). However, in the same breath Demaratos also emphasizes that poverty can be overcome through courage (*arete*), a moral quality which is acquired through wisdom (*sophia*) and strong laws (*nomoi*)—precisely the qualities the Spartans possessed.

Herodotus does not intend to describe here the complexities of poverty in the Greek world, and we should be cautious about reading this passage as a statement of socioeconomic fact, especially one that is valid for all places and all times in a diverse and changing economic landscape, not least because it is explicitly moralizing. It is through proper use of *arete*, Demaratos exclaims, that Hellas not only keeps poverty but also tyranny at bay. Poverty here, therefore, functions as a contrast to Persian wealth and as a catalyst for action, and it is understood in terms of moral or ethical behaviour. It is, in Demaratos' characterization, something not only to avoid, but also something that can be avoided with the correct values and proper behaviour. Poverty in this passage is not value-free; we should not read it as if it were.

Indeed, Demaratos' statement is more an observation that Hellas was considerably poorer than the Persian Empire than any comment on the Greeks themselves. It is a comparative poverty that Herodotus has in mind here and one that is in no way controversial—the independent city-states of Hellas, small in scale, could indeed not match the gold of the vast Persian Empire. Frequently the Greeks contrasted the wealth and luxury of the Persians to their own austere way of life, an austerity which was itself shaped by the comparison.[5] However, we should not take this picture as the end of debate about poverty and simply state that because the Greek world (taken as a whole) was poorer than the Persian ruling class that poverty and Hellas go hand-in-hand, that the Greek world was irreducibly poor. Where would Dionysios and his family fit in here?

[4] Hdt 7.101–2. On this scene see Balot 2014: 81–4, and with particular emphasis on the role of poverty here see Ober 2010: 243–7; 2015: 76–8.

[5] Hdt. 1.131–40. See Hall 1989.

Decontextualized, Herodotus' comment appears to equate Hellas and poverty for all time (*aiei*). But in recent years historians have sought to overturn the previous orthodoxy that saw the ancient Greek world as poor and its people as living predominantly in poverty. New models have emphasized long-term economic growth over the course of the archaic and classical periods and relatively high standards of living, at least in comparison with other historical societies, both ancient and modern.[6] The cities of the Greek world in the fifth and fourth centuries, in particular, appear to have undergone a period of efflorescence, with the development of institutions, a rise in consumption, and steady improvement in standards of living with larger numbers of people living above (rather than at or below) subsistence than previously thought. These new accounts paint a much more optimistic picture of the economic history of the Greek world, but they also beg the question: how should we factor in the lives of the poor and the marginalized within interpretations that are otherwise fairly positive? We need to ask who did, and who did not, gain from these processes of change which have been increasingly highlighted. We need to investigate how ideas about poverty—and ideas about the role, behaviour, and lifestyles of those described as poor—developed in the context of this long-term economic growth and changing standards of living. That is, what is missing in such accounts is an exploration of poverty or investigation of the lives of those, like Dionysios, who were deemed to be poor.

This book seeks to do just that. It is a book that seeks to build on this recent literature to investigate not only how poverty was an ideological vehicle for the shaping of moral behaviour, as we see in Demaratos' speech, but also how these discourses of poverty affected the strategies employed by the *penetes* to define their own well-being in Athens during the late fifth and fourth centuries. It does so by refocusing attention on the discourses surrounding poverty as well as highlighting the diverse experiences of it, and therefore seeks to expand our understanding of what it meant to be poor in a world in which *penia* is understood as the need to work for a living. It is vital, if we are interested in the economic history of the ancient world—especially when the main emphasis in recent years has been

[6] See e.g. Morris 2004; 2005; Ober 2010; 2014; 2015; Kron 2014; Bresson 2015.

on economic growth, markets, and long-term institutional change—to consider the role of poverty too (however poverty is defined). In fact, we need to place ideas about, and experiences of, poverty at the centre of these debates, as an integral part of these trends, and investigate the contours of well-being and hardship among the *penetes* and other groups who might be categorized as poor. Doing so is more than a simple contrast of material deprivation with material riches. Instead it is a study in the social relations that shaped and defined the city of Athens in the fifth and fourth centuries. Framed in this way this book acts as a counterweight to discussions of long-term abstract processes—important though these are—because it seeks to bring people back into our analysis; history is nothing if we ignore the lived experience of people in the past.

The approach of this book, therefore, is not simply to investigate how poverty was discussed within philosophical circles or among other elite groups, or how it was depicted on the Athenian stage; this forms, of course, an interesting part of a picture of poverty but necessarily downplays, or even ignores, other (arguably more important) aspects. Instead, it is necessary to read these texts as part of a multifaceted series of poverty discourses which frame the experience of *penia* in Athens. By drawing explicitly on social science methodologies, particularly the capabilities approach of Amartya Sen (on which more below), this book seeks to interrogate not only (some of) the discourses of poverty in Athens, but also the multidimensional, complex, and sometimes competing ways it was experienced. By doing so it questions standard assumptions about the distribution of wealth in the late fifth and fourth centuries, suggesting that this likely underwent change at various points in time, and that we can point to times when the gap between rich and poor shrank or grew.

This introductory chapter is, therefore, divided into two parts. First I will explore some of the methodological difficulties that occur when studying poverty and the lives of the poor in the ancient world, as well as some problems of evidence, before turning to the theoretical framework which underlies the chapters ahead. Throughout I will suggest that debates within contemporary social sciences have a lot to offer ancient historians thinking about poverty, well-being, and the distribution of wealth in Athens, but that also the Athenian experience provides an important case study for social scientists too.

WHO ARE THE POOR?

Investigating poverty and the lives of the poor in ancient societies is no easy task. This is not because there were no people in Athens who were 'poor' (there were), nor because finding evidence for this group is difficult (though this is also true), but because poverty is rooted within a variety of complex and competing social, economic, political, and cultural factors that affect how it is experienced and perceived. In Athens, wealth and poverty were placed at the centre of a number of contemporary debates about how to run a city, how to avoid *stasis*, or how to be virtuous.[7] This provides a great deal of information about how poverty was perceived, but also muddies the water somewhat, because most of these debates took place within elite circles which deliberately disengaged from the actual lives of the poor.

To some extent the study of poverty and the poor in past societies is troublingly elusive. There is, of course, a difficulty with accessing evidence which details the everyday lives of those outside the various groups of elites which dominate the sources; we are viewing through a lens which refracts our vision away from these experiences.[8] On the one hand it is true enough to say that our evidence is skewed towards those who had more wealth and away from those who had less: there are few—if any—literary texts written by (or, more contentiously, for) the 'poor', and even fewer which do not present them in an unproblematic fashion: see the figure of Chremylos in Aristophanes' *Wealth*, for example, or the fragments of fourth-century comedies which paint the poor as gluttons. These are not particularly sympathetic, nor, arguably, realistic portrayals of the lives of the *penetes*. Although it may be argued that theatre audiences were relatively broad (they certainly did not only consist of wealthy elites)—and therefore these are not simply mocking depictions of the poor doled out from on high—these portrayals show a world in which *penia* touched a nerve, where poor lifestyles provided a great deal of comic, even hostile, material, and where jokes about wealth were frequently politicized.

[7] See e.g. Arist. *Pol.* 1279b5–1280a7, 1332a19–25, Thuc. 3.82, Pl. *Rep.* 551b–552e, 556c–557a.

[8] We might argue here about what constitutes 'the elite(s)' in Athens—see the discussions of Davidson 1997; Fisher 1998; Duplouy 2006—but the point stands: however fluid, however constituted, however contested or reined in, the source tradition is dominated by those who we can legitimately think of as 'elite' in one way or another.

We cannot simply read the character of Chremylos as a matter-of-fact 'poor' man and take Aristophanes' portrayal of his (comic) world as a straight depiction of what life was really like for the *penetes* in Athens.[9] Rather, we need to look, as argued in Chapter 2, behind these portrayals (as well as others) to see what discourses these create, react against, shape, or contest.

Aside from the real difficulties of the literary sources, there are also important issues to consider with the non-literary evidence. Whilst we might expect the material objects used, and buildings lived in, by the poor to be smaller, perhaps less well constructed, or more ephemeral than those used by the better-off, this assumption is often questionable in general terms, nor is it easy to see in the archaeological record in Athens (or elsewhere in the Greek world).[10] It might well be argued that the poor did not live in the types of houses, commission the types of funerary monuments and dedications, or use the types of painted pottery that survive (or are collected), because they were too busy trying to subsist, or had too few resources to spend on such items. However, we should be cautious here. By removing the poor wholesale from these activities we remove them from the communities in which they lived, imply that they have no role to play in them, desocialize them, and marginalize them. The fact is, though, we should question whether—rather than assume that—poverty permanently excluded large numbers of people from activities such as commemorating the dead, religious practice, or the preparation or consumption of food. Should we, as outside observers, whose reading of the past is shaped by a historical tradition that favours certain groups of people over others, automatically write them out of these activities based on our assumptions about what being poor meant? Consideration of the materiality of poverty, or rather of *penia*, demands that we confront our expectations of what we think we should find and question the relationship between poverty and the evidence that survives.

In a positivistic sense, it is probably true to say that the poor tend to leave less of a trace in the historical record.[11] We know little, for

[9] In this context the approach of Forsdyke 2012 is particularly useful and should be applied more broadly to the literary material.

[10] See e.g. Orser 2011b; Barnes 2011; Richard 2011 with some specific difficulties outlined by Ault 2005; Villanueva-Puig 2013 or Rougier-Blanc 2014.

[11] On the invisibility of the poor in the ancient world see the cogent comments of Morley 2006: 30–2. That this should not necessarily be an insurmountable problem is

example, about property ownership (or any quantifiable form of wealth or income) of those outside of the group of liturgists whose property portfolios are catalogued by Davies.[12] Those who were the poorest would have had little property to quantify in the first place, and finding records of this is harder simply because of the nature of the evidence that does survive, because it favours liturgists and other groups of relatively wealthy citizens (though this does not mean that we cannot model this information to suggest parameters of plausibility, as I will argue in Chapter 3). More profoundly, however, this statement also raises serious questions—like Dionysios' dedication—about who is categorized as 'poor' and why they are described so. Is 'poor' to be understood, following much ancient discourse, as those who were simply not wealthy: the *penetes* in contrast with the *plousioi*, or the *aporoi* in contrast with the *euporoi*? Are the 'poor' to be seen as those who did not, or who did not always, live a 'leisured' lifestyle?[13] As those who subsisted rather than lived the Aristotelian good life?[14] As those who were destitute or on the brink of starvation?[15] As those who were free but went hungry, or those who were enslaved but were well fed by their masters?[16] These options cover an enormous range of the Athenian population and a massive variety of different types of experiences, and might well be chronologically and temporally distinct.

The idea that the poor are those who leave no trace, who need to be imagined into the gaps left by other evidence, is therefore problematic in Athens for two reasons. First it ignores the breadth of—and possible distinctions between—the groups of people who were described as *penetes*, *aporoi*, or *ptochoi*; and second it disguises an important and ongoing phenomenon that is related to evidence survival. One difficulty is that framing poverty in terms of gaps creates problems of attestation: what evidence *can* we use, and for what kinds of questions?[17] More seriously, it deflects attention from

demonstrated by the historiography of women or slavery in the ancient world: see e.g. DuBois 2008: 6–7. A similar argument might be made about children, for which there is much recent research. On some of the methodological issues see Baxter 2005.

[12] Indeed our knowledge of liturgists has large gaps, is chronologically weighted towards the second half of the fourth century, and undoubtedly excludes those who were not politically active. See Davies 1971; 1981.

[13] Ste. Croix 1981: 114–5.

[14] Gallant 1991.

[15] Scheidel and Friesen 2009: 91.

[16] See Brown 2002: 61–3.

[17] See e.g. the difficulties raised by the study of Baumer 2014.

the historical processes that create the uneven production and/or survival of our evidence in the first place. Patterns of evidence survival are only in a certain sense accidental. To a large degree they reproduce the relations of power which dominated the ancient world, assigning—or removing—value to, or from, the lives and experiences of certain groups of people. In doing so they privilege the past as has been created by the wealthiest and most powerful in Athens, and elites since then, who chose what to preserve and what to ignore or discard. When we simply fill these 'gaps' with an amorphous block of 'the poor', without further investigation or further comment, we risk reproducing, rather than critiquing, this nexus of power. We risk simply redescribing poverty as seen through the eyes of those who were not poor, or those who were hostile to the poor, rather than analysing it as a social reality or as a lived experience.

Instead of reproducing the silence of the 'gaps', we need to interrogate a range of different types of evidence—literary, archaeological, epigraphic—to see where, how, and in what contexts they reproduce, as well as contest, the social categories and identities formed by those who dominate the historical or archaeological record. We cannot 'discover' the poor through analysis of one type of evidence without reference to other material.[18] We need, instead, to strive to hear alternative narratives from the dominant discourses of elite (or quasi-elite) texts and everyday objects, to see how poverty is a product of social relations of power, where (during the almost two centuries of Athenian democracy) this changes and where it remains the same, and identify different types and different experiences of poverty in the ancient world. We need to question the narratives that equate the poor with *kakia* (badness or evilness), that paint them as dirty, or living in squalor, or that associate manual labour, certain physical attributes, or types of activities with poverty or servitude.[19] This book aims to suggest one way in which we can do just this.

[18] Chicone 2011b.

[19] Dirt: Eupolis F 280, see also Eur. *El.* 182. Roughness/squalor: Eur. *Hel.* 1540 (Menelaos' men clad in rags after a shipwreck), Pl. *Symp.* 203d (Eros as *skleros* and *auchmeros*), Kratinos F 215, Plato Com. F 265 (*auchmeros*, *auchmerobios* as an insult), Ar. *Plut.* 84 (Ploutos as *auchmeros*), Xen. *Mem.* 2.1.31 (old age brings *auchmeria* and hardship). Sunburn: Men. *Dys.* 754, Pl. *Rep.* 556d. Clothes: *tribon* (woollen, or often, threadbare cloak): Lys. 32.16, Ar. *Ach.* 184, 343, *Vesp.* 1131, Pherekrates F 124; *tribon* and *embadas* (felt shoes): Is. 5.11; Ar. *Plut.* 842–9; *exomis* (one-shouldered chiton) and *pilos* (hat): Pipili 2000 with the cautious remarks of

POVERTY AND THE ANCIENT WORLD

The topic of poverty has not been completely ignored by ancient historians, but a greater amount of research has focused on the Roman (compared with the Greek) world, with particular interest in recent years directed to late antiquity. Here debate has focused on the social changes brought about by the increasing power of the Christian church and how Christianity shaped attitudes to, and conceptions of, poverty which were different from those of the ancient city.[20] In addition, different aspects of the condition of poverty have been investigated by both Greek and Roman historians, for example almsgiving, food shortage, and subsistence strategies, as well as depictions of the poor in various kinds of evidence.[21]

Recent work with a focus on Athens has subjected texts to increasingly sophisticated readings and investigated various aspects of material evidence with a view to reconstructing not only representations of the poor in our sources but different aspects of their lifestyles.[22] Reacting in particular to histories of the ancient world which either prioritize discussion of elites (of various descriptions), or view the poor in the context of social conflict, these studies provide a fruitful way forward. Collectively they emphasize that we can do more not only to assess the discourses of poverty, but also to understand the ways in which they shape how *penia* was experienced in Athens. Fundamental here is the need to focus not just on the exploitation or oppression of the poor,[23] but to see how they negotiated their own roles in society, ways of belonging to the community, and how they defined their own world—that is, we need to emphasize, wherever possible, questions of agency, the diverse experiences of poverty as well as the conditions that produced it, and how it is (varyingly) represented. Elsewhere, historians

Osborne 2011: 107–8. Rags or other poor-quality clothes: Ar. *Plut.* 540, *Eccl.* 408–10. See further the discussion of Coin-Longeray 2014b: 157–64.

[20] See e.g. Patlagean 1977; Brown 2002; Atkins and Osborne 2006; Finn 2006; P. Allen 2009.

[21] Almsgiving: Hands 1968. Subsistence: Garnsey 1988; 1998; Gallant 1991. Depictions of the Athenian poor in various literary sources: Rosivach 1991; Lévy 1997; Knoch 2010; in material evidence: Villanueva-Puig 2013; Rougier-Blanc 2014; Jacquet-Rimassa 2014.

[22] In addition to the works cited in n. 21, see Roubineau 2010; 2012; 2013; Lenfant 2013; Galbois and Rougier-Blanc 2014c.

[23] Cf. Fuks 1974 or Ste. Croix 1981.

have made considerable strides in detailing aspects of the lives of non-elite groups of different kinds and in different contexts.[24] This book seeks to bring together these strands of research by exploring questions of poverty and well-being side by side.

Part of the difficulty that previous work on poverty has rightly demonstrated is the problem of reconciling modern ideas about poverty with ancient understandings of *penia*. It is all too easy, for example, to dismiss evidence like that of Dionysios' dedication (Fig. 1.1) by reasoning that because he commissioned a votive stele he cannot have been *that* poor. The problem is conceptualized partly as one of degrees and partly one of definition: poverty marks the very bottom of a wide spectrum of wealth in the modern world, whereas *penia* was frequently seen in the ancient world as a contrasting position to *ploutos* and therefore encompassing a much larger proportion of the population.[25] This encourages historians to partially disassociate (the modern category of) poverty from (the ancient category of) *penia*—there are too many moderately well-off *penetes* for this to map on exactly—but to view poverty instead as the worst forms of *penia*, overlapping with *ptocheia* (beggary, destitution).[26]

To a large extent this distinction is perfectly sensible, not least because it reveals a tension between how we as historians talk about poverty and the way the Athenians did. One of the disadvantages, however, is that it places rather a lot of weight on poverty being understood as an economic condition, whilst playing down its social and ideological roles (poverty is implicitly defined, in this sense, by the presence or absence of wealth—that is, Dionysios is too rich to be poor). But, as already mentioned, we do not know and cannot know how much wealth Dionysios had: did he save for years to make this dedication? Was it easy to pay for from the fruits of his labours? In effect, these questions reduce Dionysios' dedication to a series of simple economic transactions, when there is considerable social and ideological (and even religious) complexity surrounding this votive. The way forward is to recognize that poverty is a social condition too, and one which is variously stigmatizated. This means that *ptocheia* can be conceptualized not just as a worse form of poverty, but in

[24] Vlassopoulos 2007b; Gottesman 2014; Sobak 2015.
[25] See Lenfant 2013: 48; Roubineau 2013: 17–18 and discussion on pp. 36–8.
[26] See e.g. Ste. Croix 1981; Christesen 2013.

terms of social exclusion that can align with, but is often constructed in a highly distinct way from, that of *penia*.[27]

These definitional problems highlight the fact that poverty is a category which is not ahistorical, that is, it is not the same across time and space, but is shaped by, and the product of, social relations within a historical context, and that this categorization is often politicized and contested. The differences between *penia* and/or *ptocheia* as ancient categories and poverty as a modern one should prompt us to consider not only absolute measures of deprivation in Athens, but also why that label is applied to a larger group of people than we might apply it to today, as well as the strategies that were used to negotiate or ameliorate it, and the ways in which it was reproduced.

Indeed, other terminology used by the Athenians to describe those who were poor—and those who were not—highlight further problems. Take the thetes, for example. In Athens the term not only meant 'hired labourers', as it had done in the Homeric poems (and referred to those who were therefore 'poor' in the sense of needing to work for a living), but also was used in a technical sense to denote the lowest of the Solonian property classes (therefore poor in comparison with other citizens).[28] These property classes were devised to divide up political responsibilities during a crisis at the beginning of the sixth century, but by the mid-fifth century thetes were still actively excluded from office-holding. Presumably because of this, *Ath. Pol.* tells us, still no one admitted to being a *thes* in fourth-century *dokimasia* trials (though clearly some office-holders were).[29] Indeed, by the mid–late fourth century the Solonian property classes are rather poorly documented, subject to numerous controversies, and were considered by at least one contemporary writer to be 'old-fashioned'.[30] Even the author of the *Athenaion Politeia* himself, writing in the 330s or 320s (and our best source for the property classes in general), was not entirely sure about the details of them: the discussion makes it clear that he does not know for sure whether the resources of the *hippeis* and *zeugitai* were measured according to

[27] Roubineau 2013; Coin-Longeray 2014a; Galbois and Rougier-Blanc 2014b.

[28] On the thetes in general see Jacquemin 2013. On the property classes, see e.g. Foxhall 1997; van Wees 2001; Rosivach 2002a; 2002b; 2012; Ste. Croix 2004.

[29] *Ath. Pol.* 7.4, 26.2.

[30] Theophrastos Vat. Gr. 2306, F B, ll. 19–20: they are ἀρχαικώτερος. See Keaney and Szegedy-Maszak 1976.

agricultural produce or on the basis of ownership of draught animals, the measures required for membership in each class are different to that recorded elsewhere, and Aristotle in the *Politics* seems to imply that *hippeis* were the third (rather than the second) highest class.[31] What's more, *pentakosiomedimnoi* holding office could be represented in the 330s not as amongst the richest Athenians, as they had been at the beginning of the sixth century, but as being by contrast 'rather poor'.[32] 'Rather poor compared to whom?' we should ask. The confusion highlights that we should think about the processes of categorization, who they benefit and who they constrain, as well as the fact of it.

The numerous controversies surrounding the military activities of the thetes shows the disconnect between the civic expectations of this group and their economic status. Hoplite armour was traditionally supplied by soldiers themselves, which suggests a *de facto* wealth barrier to service, but as others have pointed out, armour need not be expensive, nor new, and it could be provided by friends and relatives. It is, therefore, likely that some thetes also served as hoplites too.[33] What is more, rowing in the fleet was recognized as being the backbone of Athenian power from the mid-fifth century on, which provided poorer citizens with a mechanism for serving the polis.[34] Such service led to reward: pay for military service of course, but also preferential treatment in receiving land overseas on at least one occasion, as the Brea decree of the 430s attests.[35] By the 330s the polis not only provided political pay for a broad range of activities, but provided armour too for citizens enlisted in the *ephebeia*.[36]

Whilst some historians view the thetes as being 'outsiders in their own community', others view the same evidence as indicating inclusion and participation.[37] It is, to some degree, a glass-half-full or glass-half-empty question. As an author, it is Aristotle who most

[31] Cf. *Ath. Pol.* 7.3 with [Dem.] 43.54 and Arist. *Pol.* 1274a 18–21.

[32] *Ath. Pol.* 47.1: πάνυ πένης. Rhodes 1993: 141–8.

[33] On this question see the discussions of Christ 2001; van Wees 2001; Ste. Croix 2004.

[34] [Xen.] *Ath. Pol.* 1.2. Strauss 1996.

[35] *IG* I^3 46. On the down-dating of the Brea decree to the 430s, but still pre-war, see Mattingly 1996: 381–5; Rhodes 2008: 505.

[36] *Ath. Pol.* 42.4.

[37] Cf. Raaflaub 1996: 146 (the quote here) and Liddel 2007: 312: thetes on the 'fringes of the citizen body', with Ober 1998: 76: 'in the fifth and fourth centuries . . . Athenian thetes believed they deserved a full share in the *politeia* and seem not to have

frequently mentions the thetes, and he uses the term to distinguish a particular type of labour related to, but ultimately distinct from, that of the *banausoi* (craftsmen).[38] This distinction essentially comes down to earning power (and therefore perhaps different levels of skill): many of the latter group, he says, are in fact rich (*ploutousi*) and are therefore not necessarily excluded from citizenship in an oligarchy.[39] Here he implies that the thetes were, in contrast, poor (or at least poorer), but predominantly when he writes of thetes he seems to have in mind those for whom their economic activity is problematic in some way, rather than their poverty per se.[40] Fundamentally, however, the controversies over the property classes shows that using a classification system devised before coined money was invented to understand the complex (and monetized) economy of the fourth century is unwise, especially when that system and the economic and political world for which it was invented had changed considerably. It also shows how the language of poverty used by historians today sometimes collides with that used in the ancient world.

In a similar way, the so-called 'middling' tradition of Greek thought also raises questions about how the poor are categorized. Ideologically, the 'middling' tradition disguises differences of wealth, emphasizing equality rather than difference. However, this discourse is rooted in the self-presentation of predominantly elite sources;[41] it deliberately elides economic differences in ways which no doubt benefited those elites more than they benefited the poor, and excludes both the rich and the poor in the process of emphasizing moderation.[42] The removal of the poor shows that the category of poverty is

doubted that this state of affairs was quite "natural" ', and Strauss 1996: 317, 320: the thetes as a 'disciplined community' which 'taught poor men how to be free'.

[38] Arist. *Pol.* 1278a12–13: *banausoi* and thetes are similar in that they perform services for the community (*koinon*), and this marks them as different from slaves; both are excluded from citizenship in an aristocracy, but only the thetes are in an oligarchy (*Pol.* 1278a15–25). In a democracy both *banausoi* and thetes can be included, but this affects—negatively for Aristotle—the type and quality of the constitution (*Pol.* 1317a24–9, 1319a26–31).

[39] Arist. *Pol.* 1278a24–25: πλουτοῦσι γὰρ καὶ οἱ πολλοὶ τῶν τεχνιτῶν.

[40] See Arist. *Pol.* 1337b21, where he equates thetes with slaves, but note also *Pol.* 1329a35–9, where the thetes, *technitai*, and farmers are all described as being indispensable to the polis.

[41] Foxhall 2007: 28–33.

[42] Morris 1996: 22, but see also Raaflaub 1996: 158: 'there may have been noticeable discrepancies between the ideology and the reality of democratic equality.'

a powerful one; it can be used to render people powerless, it is a tool of exclusion.[43] As such it reduces the poor to a homogeneous, though not equal, group, when there is in fact a considerable diversity of experience, and recategorizes them as socially distant. We need to be aware of when we are led by our sources to do the same in Athens.

WHAT IS POVERTY?

As is clear from the discussion so far, defining poverty is more complex than at first appears. On its most basic level poverty is a material condition in which resources are lacking; it is the state of having no (or perhaps very minimal) wealth or income. But this bare-bones definition does not begin to touch on the complexities of poverty or its place within a social structure, nor on the discourse(s) surrounding it, its impact on different social groups or on society as a whole, or the relationship between poverty and exclusion (to name just a few avenues of research). As soon as we define poverty in this way, the following questions immediately arise. What resources do we mean? What are they needed for?

Teasing apart these nuances highlights some fundamental concepts in poverty research. As is clear from the difficulties highlighted already, although we might be tempted to view poverty primarily as an economic condition—as having little or no money or being on the borders of subsistence—it is better conceptualized as (i) a socially constructed category, which has (ii) both a material and a non-material element—that is, it is a social relationship as well as an economic condition—and (iii) it is created and maintained by structural inequalities (for example, status, gender, class) reinforced through (iv) a socially embedded discourse which often seeks to exclude, marginalize, or otherwise portray the poor as different from other members of society.[44] Poverty, then, is the outcome of a process that is shaped by social relations and therefore manifests itself

[43] See e.g. Eur. *Supp.* 238–45, Arist. *Pol.* 1295b6–1296a22. On the importance of categorization: Green 2007.

[44] See e.g. Lister 2004 for an accessible introduction to the field of poverty research. Laderchi, Saith, and Stewart 2003 or Misturelli and Heffernan 2010 provide discussions of the concept of poverty in social-science literature.

differently in different times and places.[45] Conceptualizing poverty as being the absence of wealth or a lack of income simply will not do.

This means a number of things for an analysis of poverty in Athens. For starters, a basic distinction to make is that between absolute and relative poverty.[46] Absolute poverty is the lack of sufficient resources to provide for basic needs, for example, food for subsistence. Absolute measures of poverty provide a baseline measure for comparisons across place and time, but they raise serious questions about how those basic needs are defined and how they are socially and culturally constituted.[47] In a society like Athens, which was otherwise relatively affluent, where—as has recently been argued (and this is a position I will assume in Chapter 3)—a large proportion of the population was living above subsistence, then absolute measures become less useful outside of a comparative context. We can use new research on skeletal material to understand why.

Stable isotope analysis on material drawn from three cemeteries in Athens and Attica shows that the classical Athenian diet was not lacking in nutrients, but instead consisted of a relatively high level of animal protein (meat and/or dairy), supplemented by marine resources, vegetables, and fruits. Diets were varied and nutrition was relatively good during the classical and early hellenistic periods, better than before or after.[48] Incidences of severe malnutrition are absent from the classical sample (though not from other time-periods) and the average height of skeletons was as tall as would be the case until the twentieth century, which implies relatively good childhood nutrition in particular.[49] The patterns of the Athenian cemeteries analysed are similar to other classical and hellenistic Greek sites, suggesting this is not a localized phenomenon but one that is replicated across the Greek world. Athens in particular, however, compares favourably to samples from southern Italy during the Roman imperial period, which suggests that nutrition here amongst non-elite groups was significantly worse than among similar groups in Athens. The picture derived from the skeletal evidence therefore shows that—on a population level—basic needs were

[45] Green and Hulme 2005; Chicone 2011a; 2011b.
[46] Townsend 1979: 32–9, 50–3. [47] Lister 2004: 20–28; Brady 2009: 32–4.
[48] Lagia 2014; 2015a; 2015b.
[49] Lagia 2015a; Kron 2005. For further discussion see Chapter 6, pp. 198–9.

broadly being met in classical Athens, at least in comparison with other times and places.

Studies like these provide strong evidence for arguing that standards of living in cities like Athens were relatively good by pre-modern standards: the population, broadly speaking, appears to have had enough to eat. This is not to deny that there may well have been periodic short-term food shortages in the late fifth and fourth centuries, but famine only seems to have occurred in connection with the siege that ended the Peloponnesian War.[50] Using nutrition as an indicator of the presence or absence of poverty therefore becomes difficult to reconcile with the discussions of *penia* which permeate our written evidence—are we to suggest that because nutrition was relatively good, poverty did not exist? This seems untenable. First of all, it is possible that the samples only contain the bodies of those who could afford funerals or had families to perform these rites for them. Those who were the most marginalized arguably were not buried in these cemeteries but their remains might have been disposed of elsewhere, and more cheaply.[51] Whilst the sample provides a reasonable cross-section of Athenian society, it is up for debate whether the poorest are included at all. More importantly, however, the main difficulty here is that absolute measures can be misleading because they ignore the social norms and values that shape how resources were distributed and therefore how poverty was experienced. In effect they reduce the complexity of poverty to a question of subsistence and survival. Having enough to eat may seem like a crucial indication of being poor or not-poor (in some contexts it is *the* most important aspect), but this in itself is conditioned by a multitude of social, cultural, and historical factors.[52]

The fact that a very large section of the Athenian population, including some of those who had real political power within Athenian

[50] Garnsey 1988: 35–6. On one of these shortages see pp. 118–19.

[51] The sample derives from three cemeteries: the Kerameikos, Plateia Kotzia, and Laurion (Thorikos), which Lagia 2015a: 122 schematizes as representing the 'upper social strata', 'ordinary people from demes of the urban center', and 'slaves who worked in the numerous silver and lead mines of the locality'. This might be an over-schematization, but religious and civic practices would have maximized the provision of funerary rites for a wide group (see [Dem.] 43.57–8 on the demarch's responsibility to provide burials for slaves if masters did not—'at the lowest possible price'). Some, however, may have slipped through the net. See further comments on pp. 167–8.

[52] Townsend 1979: 38. See also Chicone 2011b.

democracy, could be described as 'poor' demonstrates that Athenian ideas about, and responses to, poverty were absolutely shaped by social practices. This means that in order to understand more clearly how poverty both functioned and was perceived within Athenian society, we should conceptualize it not only in absolute terms but in relative ones too. Relative poverty means not just that the Athenians recognized differentials in wealth (though this is important in itself), but that poverty is seen in relation to socially approved behaviours, customs, and lifestyles among society at large.[53] The basic terminology used by Athenians to refer to the poor (that is, *penetes*, *aporoi*, *ptochoi*) suggests that they conceptualized poverty precisely in relative terms; these are used less as purely economic designations than as a comment on the relative social or moral position of those groups, as we will see further in Chapter 2.

WELL-BEING, CAPABILITIES, AND SOCIAL EXCLUSION: THE CONTOURS OF POVERTY

One way in which to reconcile absolute and relative conceptions of poverty is through the capability approach of Amartya Sen. This is useful for a number of reasons. Instead of focusing on wealth solely as a financial resource which one either has or lacks, Sen argued that it is necessary to consider the ways in which its presence or absence affects the quality of life. Influenced by the work of Aristotle and John Rawls, he argued that wealth is only good for a purpose, because it provides the freedom to live the kind of lives that people have reason to value.[54] Wealth, therefore, may of course contribute to a better quality of life, and lack of wealth frequently denotes a lower one (that is, he does not deny that absolute measures of deprivation are useful to an understanding of poverty), but many other aspects also contribute to well-being (for example, health, family life, freedom, or political autonomy), and economic resources may not be considered the most

[53] Townsend 1979: 31–9; Lister 2004: 20–3.

[54] See Arist. *NE* 1096a7–8 (and on *eudaimonia* more broadly: *NE* 1097a15–1098b9), *Rhet.* 1360b19–24. On Aristotle as a 'conversation partner' see principally Nussbaum 1988; 2000a, who develops Sen's capability approach.

important of these at all times.[55] In place of viewing wealth merely as the sum of financial resources and poverty as the lack of them, it is preferable to ask what someone is able to do or to be with those resources. This sets wealth (or its absence) within its social context. Indeed, poverty—as well as wealth—cannot be sufficiently understood if they are divorced from this context.

Sen's work was a reaction to the branches of poverty research which emphasized utility in terms of desire-fulfilment and basic needs usually conceptualized (unsurprisingly for economists working in the contemporary world) in terms of income or the possession of commodities.[56] He aimed to reconcile absolute and relative views on poverty by considering instead 'capabilities' and 'functionings', that is, what a person is able to do or be with the resources available to them and what that person can actually achieve. Financial resources, of course, are important here—perhaps they are even in some contexts *the* most important thing—but social position, freedom, health, education, political involvement, gender, family, nourishment, and so on are also crucial and are variable. Capabilities and functionings are therefore configured differently depending on the convergence of a variety of factors. What one chooses to do or to be (that is, how capabilities are turned into functionings) reveals much about what is valued, either by the person herself or by society at large, as well as about the constraints placed on different groups. The capability approach therefore places the ability to function in society as a central concept in understanding poverty, or more precisely, well-being.

One of the criticisms of the capabilities approach is its conceptualization of well-being in terms of individual attainment.[57] This is particularly problematic for the ancient world, because it is questionable whether the individual—as opposed to the family or the community—is the most appropriate unit of analysis.[58] Even in modern contexts a significant problem with explanations of poverty which focus on individual behaviour is that they run the risk of ascribing to the poor certain behaviours, characteristics, or lifestyles which divorce them from the social structures in which they operate and effectively blame them for their own poverty. This is clearly reductive. However, these discourses of poverty in themselves are

[55] Sen 1987; 1991; 1999b. [56] Sen 1987.

[57] See e.g. the discussions of Jackson 2005; Robeyns 2005.

[58] Allen and Sitzler 2009: 26–7; in general: Cartledge 2009: 18; Balot 2014: 312–16.

revealing because through them we can interrogate patterns of social exclusion.

Sen, in fact, views social exclusion (the lack of ability to function in society) in terms of capabilities—it is both a part of capability deprivation and a cause of different capability failures—and therefore it is an important factor that shapes well-being.[59] Belonging to groups and maintaining social relationships (affiliation) is seen not only as an essential capability affecting well-being, but also forms a way in which to move away from individualist understandings of poverty and place greater emphasis on social structures and the way these are intertwined with individual and cultural capacities to act.[60] Recognizing social exclusion as an important feature of poverty foregrounds the processes through which social relations shape deprivation and marginalization. This is valuable for highlighting how people interact with social structures in a variety of changing ways, emphasizes the dynamism of these interactions, and raises questions about the agency of the social actors involved.[61] Of course, there is a great deal of literature responding to and critiquing different aspects of this research,[62] but for our purposes there are a number of important conclusions from these approaches on which we can draw when looking at Athens. These are the following.

(i) Poverty is best understood not simply as the lack of wealth, but as a condition shaped by, contingent on, and a product of social

[59] Sen 2000: 5, although this was in response to developments elsewhere in the field. On the development of the concept of social exclusion see principally Silver 1994.

[60] Nussbaum 2003; Stewart 2005; Jackson 2005.

[61] Lister 2004: 74–98. See esp. Galbois and Rougier-Blanc 2014c, where a number of the papers are influenced by the work of Serge Paugam (a leading proponent of the concept of social exclusion).

[62] Criticism tends to converge around the following points. (i) The approach is not 'operational', or assumes an 'abstract universalism'; i.e. it is difficult to identify which capabilities are valuable and isolate the extent to which these are culturally specific or universal. Nussbaum's (2000b, 2003) list of fundamental human entitlements receives criticism for e.g. prioritizing western liberal values and viewing them as universal. See in general Menon 2002; Green and Hulme 2005: 873. (ii) Well-being is subjective and therefore a theoretically weak concept that is difficult to measure. However, well-being as a concept places emphasis on what is valued (and how this might be culturally specific and, indeed, contested). The subjectivity of well-being is therefore a strength, which focuses attention on individual or group welfare. See Narayan et al. 2000 or Clark 2005 for discussion. It is worth stating also that subjectivities are inherent in every historical endeavour, whether we admit this to ourselves or not. (iii) The capabilities approach presents too rosy a picture of poverty, overemphasizing individual agency rather than social structures. See comments on p. 22.

relations. Prioritizing capabilities rather than commodities provides a means through which to contextualize not only the presence or absence of those commodities which contribute to wealth but to ask what wealth is used for. As Sen outlines: 'the role of income and wealth—important as it is along with other influences—has to be integrated into a broader and fuller picture of success and deprivation.'[63]

(ii) Poverty is multidimensional in terms of its causes, how it is experienced, and its impact. This recognizes that wealth and poverty are not static conditions but dynamic states, the products of processes that are continually reshaped by the social and historical context, and subject to different temporalities (such as within an individual life-cycle, inter-generationally, or over the longer term). This approach therefore goes further than assessing basic needs (or absolute poverty) by asking in addition what those needs are for. The upshot is that poverty is viewed not just in terms of subsistence but in terms of well-being, that is, 'as an index of a person's functionings', which might change over time or over the life-course.[64] Social exclusion is a constituent part of this.

(iii) Viewing poverty in terms of capabilities and social exclusion creates a theoretical space in which to consider questions of social agency. That is, rather than viewing poverty and the poor through the lens of the wealthy or the elite (or extrapolated from the gaps in the evidence as mentioned earlier), we can interrogate the experiences of the poor themselves by framing the question as one of well-being as much as one of poverty. This approach sets out to view the poor not as the Other, but starts from the assumption that their lives are positively valued, and provides a means through which to assess this.[65] Rather than being a rose-tinted or romantic view of poverty, it deliberately positions itself as an approach which is pro-poor, that is, it privileges accounts of how the conditions of poverty were constructed, perceived, negotiated, experienced, and contested, whilst acknowledging the structural inequalities and circumstances which shape those conditions.

[63] Sen 1999b: 20. [64] Sen 1999a: 17. [65] See Chapters 4 and 6.

Capabilities, Slavery, and the Dependent Poor

A central part of Sen's formulation of the capability approach is freedom, in that capabilities refer to the opportunities one has to lead a valued life, and freedom is a key part of that dynamic. Poverty is, therefore, viewed by Sen as a form of unfreedom.[66] How, then, can we reconcile this with the presence of slavery in the ancient world? At first sight this appears to be problematic: it is certainly true that assessing poverty in Athens is complicated by the peculiarities of citizenship and slavery and the oppressive nature of the master–slave relationship. However, material deprivation and social deprivation as distinct categories do not necessarily map onto one another; social exclusion is not necessarily a product of material poverty as opposed to social status in the ancient world, although in some circumstances, of course, these categories aligned closely. It cannot be denied that many slaves would have had few material possessions and were socially marginalized with a low quality of life, with masters who controlled their economic resources and social interactions. In this sense, then, slaves form one category of dependent poor.[67]

However, slaves should not be seen as an undifferentiated mass, and we know of a number who had access to considerable material resources.[68] This problematizes assessments of the relationship between poverty and slavery. Recent research argues for the importance of viewing slavery in terms of social relations (rather than regarding slaves as passive objects of exploitation), and suggests that the experience of slavery across the Mediterranean world ought to be nuanced with a greater emphasis placed on slave agency.[69] This is entirely compatible—indeed, aligns well—with the approach here. In the terms of the capability approach we can recognize that slaves certainly had a restricted set of capabilities compared to citizens, and were in many cases less able to convert these into functionings. Some capabilities were shaped pretty closely by a slave's legal status (for example, freedom, political participation), but others were not—or not necessarily (for example, education or income). This prompts us to consider the lives of slaves in a multidimensional way, and provides a mechanism for cutting across legalistic status boundaries. A female slave, for sure, had comparatively restricted capabilities

[66] Sen 1999b. [67] See also Brown 2002: 61–3. [68] E. Cohen 1998.
[69] See Vlassopoulos 2009; 2011a.

and functionings. She was not entitled to participate in political life, since little value was placed on the political opinions of women or slaves, but she may have been able to sell goods in the market, develop useful social networks, take part in the religious life of the polis, have a family, and perhaps save up for her freedom.[70] A male citizen would have had a wider range of capabilities and more opportunity to turn these into functionings, but may not have been able to achieve economic prosperity, may have been maimed in war, failed to marry well, and lived a life of relative hardship; that is, he may have been comparatively less able to convert those capabilities into functionings.

Thinking in terms of capabilities and functionings, therefore, provides a tool with which to consider poverty and well-being from a wider perspective than that based on economic factors alone.[71] It allows us to model the relationships between citizens and non-citizens, acknowledge gender differences (see Chapter 4), and consider the impact of both freedom and slavery (see Chapter 6). Doing so allows poor and marginalized groups—those who were constructed as such—to be viewed as active agents in controlling what they were able to do and be, rather than as passive and undifferentiated blocks to whom poverty was something which just happened to them.

Viewing poverty in terms of capabilities, social exclusion, and well-being, then, allows us to direct our focus onto how people in Athens lived their lives, what opportunities were available to them, and whether they were able to put these to use, rather than reducing them to the sum of their property-holdings, for which evidence is, in any case, lacking. It places importance on the agency of those in the ancient world to determine their own life-course, as well as the ways in which they were constrained in doing so. It shows how they might be active participants in the creation and contestation of poverty discourses, and allows us to take into account a wide variety of human experience and aspects of well-being.

[70] See e.g. *IG* II^2 12073, a grave marker for Melitta, a salt-seller (*halopolis*); *IG* II^2 1553 (ll. 13–16), Soteris, probably a market trader (*kapelis*) in Alopeke freed along with a man named Sosias (ll. 4–7: a relative?); *SEG* 60.181 (ll. 112–22), the family of Malthake, a wool-worker (*talasiourgos*) in Keiriadai freed presumably with her three children, Plangon, Moschos, and Aristonike. On slave families see further pp. 230–1. Approximately 44% of the surviving names recorded on the *phialai exeleutherikai* inscriptions are of women.

[71] See also Taylor 2015.

EXPERIENCING *PENIA*

Understanding poverty in Athens, therefore, requires us not only to assess the extent to which the population was malnourished, destitute, or lacking in material goods, but also to investigate the ways in which poverty was socialized and the social roles it played. In order to do this we need to think about two related but distinct issues. First, how did Athenian society talk about poverty? And second, how did the Athenian population experience *penia*? This requires us to integrate study of the discourses of poverty with analysis of how it was experienced by different groups at different times.

With that in mind, Chapter 2 discusses how poverty was socially constructed in Athens by examining the multiple discourses surrounding *penia* within the surviving literary evidence. Through this we will see in more detail how the Athenians thought about and wrote about poverty and the poor. Here we will investigate how poverty was used as an ideological vehicle for certain types of behaviour, but also see that ideas about poverty and the poor were actively debated and contested. However, whilst literary texts are very revealing about the potential contestation of poverty in Athenian life, this on its own does not necessarily reveal very much at all about how poverty was experienced on a day-to-day basis, at least not directly. To understand this the remaining chapters will recast the ancient evidence—literary, epigraphic, and material—with a view to examining poverty in terms of social relations.

Chapter 3, therefore, turns to the 'hard surfaces' of poverty, posing the question: was poverty experienced by many or by few in Athens? By employing—and critiquing—a range of quantitative techniques for evaluating poverty, this chapter adapts existing models of the distribution of wealth and income in Athens to interrogate what poverty looks like within them. Essentially, this exercise questions whether large proportions of the Athenian population can be considered as poor (as is implied by the dichotomous rhetoric of the literary sources), and what this means in broader terms. By deliberately eschewing ancient categories of poverty, and using instead modern sociological ones, I explore here questions of economic inequality by asking also how poor were the poor, how big was the gap between the richest and poorest, and how this might have changed over time. Quantitative tools are useful for certain types of historical questions, for modelling (within suitable parameters) what

Athens might have looked like if we assume certain things to be true. For a study of poverty and well-being, where one of the principal difficulties, as discussed already, is the survival of source material which pertains to those who were not wealthy, this provides an essential reframing of the issues at stake.

There are dangers, however, in this endeavour, and these are as follows. First, just as when we examine texts and objects, when using statistical tools we also risk reproducing relations of power rather than evaluating or criticizing them.[72] It is true to say that a model is only as good as its data, and our 'data' are frequently problematic. However, as has been recently argued, quantitative techniques should not be considered as a 'straw man' set up in opposition to qualitative ones, but as another tool that historians can use to test our assumptions about the past and critique them.[73] The value here, then, lies as much in raising questions and testing outcomes as it does in categorically stating that large numbers of Athenians were or were not poor. Second, difficult data aside, there are judgements involved in each of the different mechanisms used for measuring poverty. Some techniques, for example, draw an arbitrary 'poverty line' under which people fall, dichotomizing a society into the poor and not-poor based on assessments of their wealth or income, whilst others emphasize how poor some groups are in relation to others. Whilst these measurements frame different aspects of poverty in novel ways, none of these can be used in isolation, nor do they purport to provide a full picture of the complexities of a diverse set of experiences (notably, they envision poverty in an absolute sense and only take into account economic criteria). Poverty cannot be reduced to a single figure, although aspects of it can be interrogated through quantitative tools.

Chapters 4, 5, and 6, therefore, set out to explore these diverse experiences and multidimensional aspects of poverty, concentrating in turn on its dynamism and temporalities, the ways in which it was reproduced or alleviated, and ultimately focusing on how the *penetes* defined their own well-being. Chapter 4 starts from the premise that poverty is dynamic, and investigates this in three distinct ways: in

[72] du Toit 2009: 238.

[73] Morley 2014. See also de Callataÿ 2014 on the history of quantification as part of ancient history, and Addison, Hulme, and Kanbur 2009b for a social-science perspective.

terms of the duration of poverty experiences, in terms of the depth of poverty, and in terms of gender. Separating out these aspects emphasizes, first, the conjunctural nature of some aspects of poverty by exploring the temporal and transitory dimension of (some) poverty experiences. This highlights the types of events which are described as precipitating factors in hardship. Caution needs to be exercised here, though, because these events describe the world of those who predominantly have resources to start with, and they are presented in terms of misfortune.

Second, although many episodes of poverty that appear in our literary sources are presented as temporary, Chapter 4 argues that persistent, or chronic, poverty should be seen not only in terms of economic deprivation but as social reordering. By contrasting subsistence approaches to poverty with those which foreground social norms and values, it is possible to see how social relations shaped destitution as much as economic deprivation did. Here we return to the idea, suggested in Chapter 2, that *ptocheia* is as much a social status as an economic one. Finally, Chapter 4 investigates gendered poverty, arguing that poor women attempted to recast their economic activities (which were necessary for the survival of the family) not as low-status markers of servility, but as being positively valued. These activities linked networks of women and show how important it is to view poverty in the ancient world through a gendered lens, despite (or rather, because of) the fact that women, for the most part, are marginalized from the poverty discourses of the literary sources. Together these case studies show that poverty is dynamic and heterogeneous, embedded within a complex network of social relations and social values.

Chapter 5 explores the processes and institutions within the Athenian social structure that shaped the reproduction of poverty, and those which allowed it to be ameliorated. Central here is political pay and other civic distributions, which undoubtedly provided much-needed additional resources to citizens. However, these measures were never really viewed as poverty relief, and it is misleading to describe them in such terms. In fact, they were conceived in terms of maintaining political, rather than economic, equality, fostering civic unity, and supporting good citizenship. Civic status, therefore, can be seen as a major factor in alleviating, or reproducing, poverty in Athens. It is status, rather than economic need, which shaped access to a wide range of resources, directly or indirectly.

Other features, too, show a similar picture. We might expect local political institutions such as demes (or even phratries)—because of their small size and hereditary nature—to provide assistance to their members, but the epigraphic evidence suggests that economic support of the poorer members of the group was not central to the corporate mission of these bodies. In contrast, the patterning of social networks appears to be more important, not least because these cut across civic status. By examining the role social networks played in fostering social capital, we can explore how voluntary associations provided resources to their members, investigate differential structures of credit, and examine the impact of distributions of sacrificial meat. What we see is that social networks, like political pay and other civic distributions, might have served to alleviate hardship and expand capabilities for some, but they likely reinforced such hardship for others.

Perhaps the most important factor in the reproduction of poverty, however, was the economic structures which allowed the wealthy to consolidate their resources over the course of the fourth century. By examining changes in the organization of public finance, mining, landownership, and the grain trade, it is possible to marshal a great deal of evidence which suggests that the rich were getting richer and wealth was becoming increasingly concentrated into fewer hands during this period. This means that the face of poverty was changing over the course of the fourth century (and into the third).

Chapter 6, in contrast, shines a spotlight onto the world of the *penetes* by viewing them as active agents in shaping their own well-being. It argues for an expansion of the standards-of-living debate, so it is not solely framed by questions of subsistence and consumption but also includes measures of functioning. Appearing without shame, then, forms the backbone of the investigations here, and I argue that we can use Sen's capability approach to interrogate the quality of life of those who we might consider as low-status, marginalized, or economically deprived. By analysing three central aspects of well-being—affiliation, social connectivity, and the creation and maintenance of emotional bonds—we can consider how those who were categorized as poor (citizen and non-citizen) were able to function within Athenian society and negotiate their well-being.

As we shall see over the course of these discussions, by viewing poverty in terms of social relations rather than simply as an economic condition (or, indeed, as a philosophical position), we are able to refocus our attention on the lives of those who experienced it, highlight the structural inequalities which constrained (or aided) different groups at different times, as well as contextualize ideas about poverty within Athenian society. One of the aims of this book, then, is to isolate and identify different types of poverty and deprivation in the ancient world, to see how these connect, contrast, and influence one another, and how they shape—and are shaped by—social constructions of poverty. By investigating where these differential experiences overlap, it is possible to illuminate the constituent parts of the most chronic forms of poverty, but it is also possible to place greater emphasis on the means through which poverty was reproduced and through which those who are categorized as poor shaped their own well-being.

2

Poverty and Poverty Discourses

For among the best people there is minimal wantonness and injustice but a maximum of scrupulous care for what is good, whereas among the demos there is a maximum of ignorance, disorder, and wickedness; for poverty (*penia*) draws them rather to disgraceful actions, and because of a lack of money some men are uneducated and ignorant.

[Xen.] *Ath. Pol.* 1.5

SOKRATES: What kind of men do you call poor and rich respectively?

EUTHYDEMOS: The poor (*penetes*), I imagine, are those who have not enough to pay for what they want; the rich (*plousioi*) those who have more than enough.

SOKRATES: Have you observed, then, that some who have very little not only find it enough, but even manage to save out of it, whereas others cannot live within their means, however large?

EUTHYDEMOS: Yes, certainly—thanks for reminding me—I know, in fact of some tyrants even who are driven to crime by need, just like the poorest (*aporotatoi*).

Xen. *Mem.* 4.2.37–8

It is easy to view wealth and poverty in Athens as dichotomous or as contrasting conditions—one *either* has resources *or* lacks them—because literary sources like these frequently define poverty through its relationship with wealth or otherwise juxtapose the two ideas.[1] The different terms used to refer to the poor (*penetes*, *aporoi*, *ptochoi*), however, cover a large and varied group of people, with a variety of

[1] On wealth and poverty in Xenophon see Roubineau 2010.

social roles. These include some who might not be considered to be particularly 'poor' in an economic sense at all, but whose relative position is noted or whose moral behaviour is under scrutiny, as is clear in the texts above. Words for (and ideas about) poverty and the poor, therefore, are bound up with social and political ideologies and moral qualities as much as they denote the lack of economic wealth.[2]

This chapter will explore the way discourses of poverty in Athens were created and contested in order to highlight how ancient ideas about poverty contrast with modern definitions. The *penetes*, for example, were not necessarily poor financially; they were 'poor' in the sense that they were compelled to work for a living, that is, they are implicitly—and often explicitly—contrasted with the wealthy (*plousioi*) who did not.[3] Whether the *penetes* were financially 'poor' as a result of their work would naturally vary: it would depend on the type of work performed, on the success of the worker, on perceptions of what was considered enough. All of these topics were actively considered, debated, and questioned by contemporary Athenian thinkers,[4] but this also means that attempts to align ancient Greek categories of poverty with modern ones can be problematic.

Poverty in Athens had a significant impact on the social, political, and intellectual life of the city.[5] Since wealth was commonly linked with virtue, poverty could be configured as moral inferiority as readily as it was considered an economic condition.[6] This had two effects: first, it was easy to use the language of poverty as an insult or to attack opponents and imply that they were wicked (regardless of their actual wealth)—the language of poverty equated the poor with the bad or

[2] Rosivach 1991; Galbois and Rougier-Blanc 2014b, Ste. Croix 1981: 283–93, but see also Desmond 2006: 33–4, who argues in addition for the importance of economic markers of wealth—at least for the wealthy. For Aristotle, wealth and poverty constituted political categories, in that oligarchy was, in fact, the rule of the 'rich' and democracy the rule of the 'poor' (rather than rule in the interests of these groups): Arist. *Pol.* 1279b35–1280a7.

[3] See Rosivach 1991; Markle 1985: 268–71; Knoch 2010: 306–7.

[4] See e.g. Xen. *Oik.* 2.17–18: Sokrates discusses the relationship between hard work and wealth. Arist. *Pol.* 1278a24–5 acknowledges that craftsmen (*technites*) can become rich.

[5] For wealth as 'qualitative', i.e. associated less with material possessions and more with moral virtue, see Desmond 2006: 34–40. Desmond (pp. 33–4) also emphasizes that this view did not necessarily correspond with 'popular attitudes', which focused much more readily on quantitative measures (i.e. how much property one owned). Further discussion by Lenfant 2013: 48.

[6] Rosivach 1991; Coin-Longeray 2014a: 53–61; Lenfant 2013.

the base (*kakoi*), after all.[7] And second, it allowed the rhetoric of poverty to become politicized by blurring the lines between the poor (as an economic group) and the demos (as a political group).[8] When Aristotle, for example, argues that democracy was in fact the rule of the poor rather than the rule of the demos (and, in contrast, that oligarchy was the rule of the rich rather than the few), his aim was not to engender feelings of pride by associating the poor with political power.[9] Instead he is trying to demonstrate the dangers of democratic and oligarchic constitutions respectively: these are, after all, deviant forms of more virtuous *politeiai* which wealth (or the lack of it) corrupts.[10] The Old Oligarch had gone further, however: he conceptualized the *penetes*, the *poneroi*, and the demos as a power bloc opposed to the noble and rich whose contributions to the polis he valued much more.[11]

Comic ridicule of demagogues frequently suggested they were lowborn and derived their income from manual labour (albeit that of others), thereby claiming that these political leaders were *penetes*, when in fact the majority were liturgists and therefore part of the economic elite.[12] In addition, comic poets as well as orators attacked one another with jokes about their opponents' poverty.[13] The slippage between poverty, the demos, and moral inferiority positioned *penetes* in direct contrast to *plousioi*. It is a narrative which serves to socially isolate the non-wealthy many from the wealthy few by differentiating behaviour, attitudes, or virtue, and in doing so attempted

[7] See e.g. Ar. *Eq.* 1272, Pl. *Gorg.* 478a, Isoc. 7.45, Dem. 57.36 with n. 7.

[8] This is not to imply that the poor identified themselves as an economic group as such; merely to point out that the *penetes* and the demos are not synonymous, despite the claims of democratic critics. See e.g. Morris 2000: 114–16 on the ideological importance of citizens identifying with *hoi mesoi*, or Lenfant 2013: 45–8 on the conflation of the terms 'demos' and '*penetes*' by the Old Oligarch. Lenfant (pp. 49–50) argues that the Old Oligarch is (or, at least, given the survival of evidence, appears) innovative in this regard, an idea which was picked up, refined and recast by later authors (i.e. Plato and Aristotle).

[9] Arist. *Pol.* 1279b19–1280a7, 1290a34–1290b4. See Ste. Croix 1981: 71–3.

[10] Arist. *Pol.* 1279b5–9.

[11] [Xen.] *Ath. Pol.* 1.2–4. See also Pl. *Gorg.* 477c: Sokrates views poverty, disease, and injustice as the three *poneriai* of property, the body, and the soul respectively.

[12] Kleon as tanner: Ar. *Eq.* 136 (but see *APF*: 318–19); Hyperbolos as lyre-maker: Schol. Ar. *Ran.* 681 (but see *APF*: 517); Androkles as a hired labourer: Kratinos F 281; in general: Ar. *Eq.* 128–45. The struggle for leadership in fifth-century Athens was an intra-elite one which employed the language of poverty and labour to insult opponents, rather than a struggle between rich and poor. See Rosenbloom 2004a; 2004b.

[13] Schol. Ar. *Vesp.* 1187, Dem. 18.257.

to create and/or reinforce a binary conception of Athenian society. However, this is not the only way to view poverty in Athens, as we will see in this chapter.

POVERTY, LEISURE, AND WORK

As has been demonstrated by previous studies, the conception of poverty which views those who were not *plousioi* as 'poor' is related to the dynamics of labour and leisure within the polis and the requirements for citizens to have a political stake in the community.[14] Aristotle, for example, discusses the relationship between leisure and political activity in different kinds of democracies, concluding that the availability (or otherwise) of leisure enables (or constrains) political participation for non-elite groups: farmers, those with moderate property, and the poor.[15] Even when wealthy Athenians celebrated work, which they did through placing great emphasis on the ideal of *ponos* (toil), they differentiated themselves from the labour (*ergon*) which characterized the activities of the poor, as Johnstone has convincingly shown.[16] Aristocratic *ponos* was located instead within elite ideas of self-definition; it involved self-sufficiency, overseeing others, and virtue. Even if work was sometimes viewed in a positive light, the elite were keen to disassociate their work from the work which was undertaken by the *penetes*; doing so emphasized their goodness, and by extension, the inferiority of others.

However, as Desmond argues, the association between poverty and work is an idea particularly grounded within philosophical thinking of the Sokratic tradition, which is not entirely reflected in other forms of discourse.[17] As we will see throughout this chapter, there are some ideas about poverty and the poor which are aired in terms unrelated to work and leisure, but there are also other narratives which reclaim

[14] Markle 1985: 269–71; Austin and Vidal-Naquet 1977: 16; Ste. Croix 1981: 116–17, 183–4.

[15] Arist. *Pol.* 1292b22–1293a13: *τὸ γεωργικὸν, τὸ κεκτημένον μετρίαν οὐσίαν, τὸ τῶν ἀπόρων πλῆθος.*

[16] Johnstone 2010. See also Desmond 2006: 32–3, who discusses positive attitudes towards work.

[17] Desmond 2006: 33–4.

(non-elite) labour as providing a positive contribution to, as opposed to symbolizing a negative strand of, Athenian society. Indeed, when philosophers like Aristotle discuss the relationship between leisure, work, and politics they naturally place the polis—and its political community of citizens—centre-stage, and historians have not unreasonably followed suit.[18] But if we frame poverty in terms of having leisure or lacking it, we construct a sociological category which (because it is focalized through the lifestyles of a relatively small, relatively elite group of citizens) becomes excessively large and unwieldy and which necessarily defines poverty primarily as being not-wealthy. Leisure is, in itself, a fairly fluid category, shaped as much by behaviour as by economics.[19] Indeed, those who were leisured could style themselves as 'poor', even though their wealth was considerable; here 'poor' is not an absolute but a relative position, judged in juxtaposition with the richest members of the liturgical elite.[20] A similar problem presents itself for those whose resources were much less extensive. Although various Athenians at different times may have had relative leisure provided by political pay or other types of economic activity, or may have performed certain types of behaviours often associated with elites, they did not become part of the *euporoi* as a result.[21]

This means that it is exceedingly difficult to talk meaningfully about this group (that is, those who were not *euporoi*), with their diverse and often competing interests, as if they are one. By viewing the leisured rich and the working poor as dichotomous we neglect to recognize the gradations and nuances within and between these groups, but these definitely existed: some *penetes* and some *aporoi* would have had enough resources to work only sporadically, some would have benefited massively from measures designed to provide leisure to those who did not have it, and others would have been near-destitute.[22] We also ignore the different entitlements of this diverse group of people (and the political debates surrounding these), and we leave no conceptual space for those who were not citizens. In addition,

[18] For the historiography of the polis-centred approach, and suggestions for new directions, see Vlassopoulos 2007c; Taylor and Vlassopoulos 2015a. See also ideas about civic unity on pp. 151–3.

[19] Fisher 1998; 2000. [20] See e.g. Dem. 18.108.

[21] Arist. *Pol.* 1293a3–7. See Ste. Croix 1981: 114–17.

[22] See also Roubineau 2013: 17–18.

the social relationships and social structures which created and maintained poverty within sections of the Athenian population, or protected others from it, are glossed over. The leisure/work ideal is certainly a part of the history of poverty in Athens, but it is not the only lens through which to view these poverty discourses.

The Rich, the Poor, and the *Ptochoi*

One of the difficulties in categorizing Athenians as *either* rich *or* poor is that it overlooks the differentiations which existed within this necessarily large and diverse group, thereby glossing over how ideas about being poor were created and contested. One problem is the gap between the contemporary conceptualizations of 'rich' and 'poor' and ancient ones: as Lenfant rightly points out, we tend to think of these as extremes of a wide spectrum, whereas in the ancient world they were frequently viewed in a dichotomous way.[23] Frequently the *penetes* or *aporoi* are rhetorically (and sometimes analytically) contrasted with the *plousioi* or the *euporoi*.[24] This can be seen, for example, in terms of their political views: Aristophanes parodies not only the generation gap, but also the economic differences between Philokleon and his son, aligning the older man with a more radical version of democracy than his son. In the *Ekklesiazousai*, the poor support the launching of a fleet, whereas the rich and the farmers do not.[25] The Old Oligarch argues that the poor do not claim for themselves the same responsibilities as they place on the rich.[26] For Aristotle the rich and the poor not only favoured different constitutions but had different conceptions of equality, and therefore justice.[27]

On the other hand, as Rosivach shows, *ptochoi* cause difficulties within this binary classification because, whilst it is clear that they were thought of differently from *penetes*, if poverty is considered as being the opposite of wealth they are placed within the same

[23] Lenfant 2013: 48. See also pp. 12–13.

[24] On Aristotle's analysis of democracy as rule of the poor see p. 32, n. 2, with Ste. Croix 1981: 284.

[25] Cf. also Ar. *Vesp.* 340–1 with 1003–8; Ar. *Eccl.* 198–9. See further ll. 185–8: those who draw political pay praise Agyrrhios, whereas those who do not wish for the death penalty for those who do.

[26] [Xen.] *Ath. Pol.* 1.2–4, 1.13, 2.9–10.

[27] Arist. *Pol.* 1279b40–1280b9. Further (selective) examples: Eur. *El.* 367–400, Isoc. 5.89–90, Dem. 24.112. On equality see Harvey 1965; Cartledge 1996.

conceptual space.[28] The clearest statement that *penetes* and *ptochoi* were considered different is Aristophanes' *Wealth*: even though Chremylos gives a long list of criteria by which poverty should be defined (rags as clothing, little food or fuel, lack of furniture, and so on), Penia is at pains to distinguish herself from her 'sister' Ptocheia (Beggary). The life of the *penetes*, she argues, is 'thrifty and hard-working', whereas a *ptochos* 'has nothing'.[29] It is difficult to tell, however, whether the joke hits home because Penia's distinction is ridiculous or whether it sets up a situation in which the majority of the audience would recognize themselves in the *penetes* on stage.

One response to these difficulties is to recast the *penetes* as not-poor, emphasizing their prosperity (as opposed to their poverty) in contrast with the social exclusion of the *ptochoi*.[30] In this way we switch the point of view from a top-down bifurcation of wealthy/not-wealthy to a position which acknowledges the economic resources of (some) *penetes* and recognizes their economic, social, and political contributions to the city. The category of 'poor', then, is reserved for the *ptochoi*, those for whom frequent labour was absolutely necessary because the outlay on slaves or hired workers was too great.[31] However, by grounding the prosperity of the *penetes* and *ptochoi* in the leisure/work ideal, even when we flip it around we maintain the dichotomous framework dictated to us by the *plousioi*; the terms are changed (which might allow for nuance and perhaps even new questions), but the bifurcation remains. Instead of wealthy/not-wealthy, we are left with the categories of leisured/not-leisured, and economic measures are contextualized with parallel socio-political criteria. We are also left with a paradox: the Athenians used the language of poverty to talk

[28] Rosivach 1991: 196, n. 5: 'it is not quite correct [to say that *ptochoi* were] . . . a distinct under-class . . . beneath the *penetes* . . . since properly speaking, all non-wealthy, including beggars, were *penetes*.'

[29] Ar. *Plut*. 535–47. See also discussion by Roubineau 2013: 16–18.

[30] On social exclusion see Roubineau 2013; Coin-Longeray 2014a.

[31] See e.g. Christesen 2013: 213: '*penetes* were people from households prosperous but not rich enough that their adult male citizens were entirely free from labor . . . [they] worked hard on their farms for part of the year, but also had enough labor at their disposal from women, slaves, and dependents to enjoy a considerable amount of leisure during slack periods', whereas *ptochoi* 'ranged from those who made a decent but not spectacular living to outright beggars'. Roubineau 2013 and Coin-Longeray 2014a: distinguish (in social terms) between *penetes* and *ptochoi*, with emphasis on the latter as socially excluded. This view of the *penetes* is undoubtedly correct, but see also the discussion that follows (pp. 38–42) for the rhetorical impact of the term *ptochoi*.

about the lives of those who were not *plousioi*, but who were not (in absolute terms) poor, creating a set of discourses which distanced the *penetes* and/or *ptochoi* from them and which very much emphasized aspects of their social and economic position. This is a strategy of social differentiation rather than an observation of a complex social reality.[32] In order to view the *penetes* as not-poor, then, we need to understand the multiple narratives which constructed them in this way as well as examining how the experience of *penia* or *ptocheia* was shaped by these discourses. That is, we need to think through how categories of poverty are created and contested. Some of the complexities are highlighted by examining depictions of *ptochoi*.

When *ptochoi* appear in the literary record, they usually elicit a strong emotional response. In tragedy this is often sympathy: role-reversal devices transform elites (often temporarily) into beggars, creating pity—or perhaps more precisely, self-pity—for their plight.[33] In oratory, on the other hand, it is to provoke outrage by casting an opponent as degenerate.[34] In both cases, *ptocheia* intensifies the emotions evoked in the theatre audience or jury.[35] That ideas about beggars evidently have this function speaks to a series of interwoven assumptions about their position within Athenian society: that they are foreign, that they are social outcasts, and that they are effeminate. These resonances not only demonstrate how *ptochoi* were constructed as characters on stage or in the courtroom, but shape how *ptocheia* was perceived within Athenian society.[36]

[32] For a similar mechanism in a different historical context see Orser 2011a.

[33] Aesch. *Ag.* 1270–4, Soph. *OC* 440–5 (see also *OT* 449–56 for the prophecy), *OT* 1478–1513, Eur. *Hel.* 408–434, *Med.* 509–15, *Heraclid.* 314–20. There is also a comic play *Ptochoi*, attributed to Chionides or Gnesippos, but only four fragments survive (these all mention food, which is perhaps not surprising given they are preserved by Athenaios): Athen. 638d, 119e, 137e.

[34] Dem. 21.185, 199, 23.209, Lys. 30.27, 32.10, 17, F 1.5. When Plato uses the language of poverty and wealth metaphorically he does not significantly depart from these ideas. Even though he stresses that money is not necessarily a signifier of virtue, and constructs an ideal city in which there is no excessive wealth or excessive poverty, he presents *ptochoi* as the antithesis of those living a 'good, intelligent life', and the city they (hypothetically) lead as beset by *stasis* (Pl. *Rep.* 521a).

[35] This is in contrast to the use of *aporotatoi*, which rarely appears (with the sense of meaning the poorest) in a dramatic or forensic context, but is used more commonly in philosophical texts. Cf. Dem. 14.17 with Xen. *Mem.* 4.2.39 (quoted earlier), *Symp.* 4.36.2, Pl. *Phdr.* 233d.

[36] Roubineau 2013: 19–20 argues similarly how *ptocheia* can be used to modify *penia* and present it as more extreme.

There is a long history in Greek literature of depicting *ptochoi*, and this is drawn upon by classical authors.[37] However, there are few actual references to real *ptochoi*. As Kloft has demonstrated, since the archaic period *ptocheia* had been associated with wandering or exile.[38] Typically without the protection of polis or family, *ptochoi* fell outside the developing institutions of authority; they were *apolis*. This rich history, reimagined in and reinforced through tragedy, must have resonated within contemporary Athens, making real-life *ptochoi* seem like foreigners even if they were Athenian-born or had never been exiled.[39] Their 'foreignness' is underscored by depictions of both their dress and their habits. When Dikaiopolis in the Aristophanic parody of Euripides' *Telephos* borrows the costume of the beggar-king, he not only has rags and carries a staff, but also wears a Mysian *pilidion*.[40] As the scene develops, it is clear there is an expectation that those who appear as *ptochoi* are unable—and unwelcome—to speak in the Assembly, that is, their attempts are met with considerable hostility, which means they cannot function as normal (Athenian) citizens.[41] Although this scene is a comic parody of the *Telephos*, not being able to speak is a pattern repeated elsewhere.[42] *Ptochoi* are outsiders.

We do not know what percentage of *ptochoi* in Athens, if any, came from elsewhere, but given the political disruption and warfare across the Greek world during the classical period and the large non-Athenian free population in Athens, it would not be too much of a stretch to imagine that men (perhaps, but not necessarily) exiled from other poleis might have made their way to the city. Isokrates almost says as much when he implies that the Greek world in the 380s was overrun with 'vagrants, beggars, and the poor'.[43] Not all migrants to Athens were exiles,

[37] Coin-Longeray 2014a.

[38] Kloft 1988: 85–92, also Roubineau 2013: 23–8. See too the walking-staff carried by Euripides' beggar-kings and parodied by Aristophanes (Ar. *Ach.* 448).

[39] The speaker of Antiphon *Tetralogy* I connects exile, displacement, and *ptocheia*: 'if... I go into exile, I shall become a beggar in a strange land, an old man without a country,' (I 2.9). The use of the *hapax legomenon* ἀγύρτρια ('wanderer', fem.) by Aeschylus when describing Kassandra's *ptocheia* underscores her otherness too (Aesch. *Ag.* 1270–4). See Galbois and Rougier-Blanc 2014b: 42.

[40] Ar. *Ach.* 439. Telephos is a Mysian himself, but nevertheless the costume must have been seen as having 'foreign' connotations for Athenians.

[41] Ar. *Ach.* 497–9, 557–9, 578–80.

[42] Eur. *Tel.* F 703, 706, 712a; Eur. *Hel.* 448–9. Kassandra is unheard: Aesch. *Ag.* 1256–94.

[43] Isoc. 14.46: ἀλῆται, πτωχοὶ... ἀποροῦντες.

certainly, but it is possible that some of those who did make their way to the city might have fallen into destitution if they were not well connected or otherwise well resourced. This may well have reinforced the tragic idea yet further. It may have been easy for Athenians to view *ptochoi* en masse as foreign, regardless of whether this was the reality.

Secondly, *ptochoi* could be viewed as social outcasts, a perception which stands apart from depictions of *penetes*.[44] In Demosthenes 21, for example, Demosthenes accuses Meidias of acting hubristically. Meidias, Demosthenes claims, has treated people as if they were *ptochoi*, outcasts (*katharmata*), and inhuman (*oud' anthropous*).[45] Here it is clear how Demosthenes ratchets up the charge, intensifying the outrage of the jury for Meidias' behaviour by associating *ptocheia* with other distasteful characteristics in a man who was very far from destitute.[46] *Katharmata* are ritually impure, scapegoats for the city, and socially repellent; they were considered criminals, especially thieves.[47] In other examples, too, *ptochoi* were associated with slavery, dishonour, and criminal activity.[48]

Ptochoi appear to have found succour at sanctuaries, however; at least Aristotle, when writing about logical fallacies, provides the following example: '*ptochoi* sing and dance in the sanctuaries, [and] exiles can live where they please.'[49] We do not need to assume this was true to recognize that these were common enough prejudices to deserve such a refutation. Begging priests occupied an important space within the rituals of Greek religion and perhaps can be seen in a broad sense as a mechanism to ameliorate poverty, since they demonstrate a (mostly) socially accepted way of providing resources to those outside the family or community.[50] They cover a range of

[44] See also the discussions of Roubineau 2013 and esp. Coin-Longeray 2014a.

[45] See also Ar. *Plut.* 454, Men. *Sam.* 481, Pl. *Rep.* 552d, 554c. Subhuman actions of *ptochoi* include eating animal fodder: Ar. *Thesm.* 387. Those 'begging for subsistence' do not fall in love: Eur. F 322. For discussion see Kloft 1988: 91–2.

[46] Meidias was a liturgist with properties in the silver-mining region at the time: see *APF*: 385–7. Throughout the speech Demosthenes employs the language of wealth and poverty to characterize Meidias as suspicious.

[47] Rosenbloom 2002; 2004b: 336–7. Demosthenes is called a *katharma* in his corruption trial before being cast as a beggar before the demos (τὸν δῆμον αἰτήσας δωρεὰς): Dein. 1.16–17.

[48] See p. 48, n. 87. Also Schol. Ar. *Vesp.* 1187. Further: Kloft 1988: 82, with n. 3.

[49] Arist. *Rhet.* 1401b25.

[50] On the role of strong social ties for providing resources see Chapter 5. In general, Parker 2005; Dickie 2001: 65–7.

practices and deities, but are frequently associated with childbirth cults and women.[51] As Dickie shows, these wandering priests were common enough to be noted fairly frequently with the assumption that they were familiar to the general population.[52] If this is the case, it implies that the act of begging in a non-ritual context may well have been seen as effeminizing, thus reinforcing the outsider status of *ptochoi*.[53] Xenophon also links *ptochoi* with effeminate behaviour: Sokrates compares the unrestrained behaviour of (male) lovers with *ptochoi* who beg and follow around the objects of their affection. This behaviour is described as servile and unbefitting for a man of status.[54]

Gorgias, in Menander's *Dyskolos*, is one of the few non-elite characters who identifies himself as a *ptochos* (as opposed to a *penes*), in a play performed in 317/16, that is, after the end of democracy.[55] He gives a warning to the wealthy Sostratos, who is in love with his stepsister: do not assume your wealth will last, and 'do not trample on us *ptochoi*'.[56] A *ptochos*, he goes on to say, is the most grumpily misanthropic (*dyskolotatos*) man of all when crossed, because his injuries are interpreted as an act of *hybris*.[57] Lape interprets this scene as an analogue for a democratic discourse which ameliorates inequalities across class groups, but if a *ptochos* is defined as someone who has nothing, Gorgias is certainly no *ptochos*.[58] He is the stepson of a wealthy, though mean, father, who will one day inherit a fortune; he has a small farm (that is, he is not homeless or in exile), he works hard (that is, he does not derive his income through begging), and he supports his mother and a slave (so is not destitute). Menander might be arguing in a general sense for compassion for the poor in this play,

[51] Robertson 1983. [52] Dickie 2001: 65.

[53] See Kassandra as an *agyrtria* in Aesch. *Ag.* 1273 (p. 39, n. 39); Hector accuses Odysseus of the same in Eur. *Rh.* 503.

[54] Xen. *Mem.* 1.2.29: οὐ πρέπον ἀνδρὶ καλῷ κἀγαθῷ. See also Xen. *Sym.* 8.23. Further: Halperin 1990: 99.

[55] See also the (presumably) Olynthian family in Alexis' fragmentary play *The Olynthians* (F 167): Ἔστιν ἀνήρ μοι πτωχός, κἀγώ γραῦς ('My husband is a beggar and I am an old woman'). Aristophanes' Dikaiopolis is another, but the nature of the scene as a parody of Euripides' *Telephos* adds a further layer of complexity. Telephos is, after all, a beggar-king. See discussion p. 39.

[56] Men. *Dys.* 285–6.

[57] Men. *Dys.* 295–8. Note, however, that *hybris* is restored here. For bibliography see Lape 2004: 177, n. 19.

[58] Lape 2004: 115–17. See also Roubineau 2013: 18 on *penia* and *ptocheia* in the play.

but he does so by using *ptocheia* as an emotional intensifier, much like Demosthenes.[59]

By highlighting the emotional resonances of *ptocheia*, I do not intend to imply that chronic poverty did not exist, nor to imply that it was only a problem for non-Athenians in Athens. If it did indeed conjure up the web of associations suggested above, then it was a familiar enough concept, and a powerful one too. Many in Athens (citizen or otherwise) may have been precariously close to *ptocheia* at various times in their lives, but whereas citizens had various institutional means through which to avoid or ameliorate chronic poverty (such as political pay, military service, family and deme structures), non-citizens would have had a much-reduced set of options, as I will argue in Chapter 5. Considering the temporality of both poverty and chronic poverty is an important way to understand poverty experiences.[60] However, it is also important to note that the ancient sources do not portray poverty, chronic or otherwise, in an unfiltered way. Real, as opposed to dramatic, destitution is rarely, if ever, mentioned, and no writer directly reflects on the causes, conditions, or lifestyles of those who suffer from it without some other agenda. This means that historians should be sensitive to the differences between the discourses of poverty and the experience of it. Regardless of where *ptochoi* were actually from, whether they actually behaved like criminals, or whether they actually sang or danced in sanctuaries, the discourses surrounding *ptocheia* portrays them as socially isolated, lacking social relations, and being actively deprived of any sustained and significant voice in Athenian society.[61] *Ptocheia*, therefore, plays a very specific role within the rhetoric of poverty in Athens. This marks *ptochoi* out from *penetes*.

POVERTY AND WEALTH, THE POOR AND THE RICH

The discourses of poverty are important not only for understanding how Athenians thought and wrote about poverty and the poor, but

[59] See also Theog. 277–8, Alexis F 78. [60] See further Chapter 4.

[61] See also Chapter 4, pp. 125–8. Christesen 2013 discusses the social isolation of *ptochoi* in terms of athletics, marginalized by both *plousioi* and *penetes*. See also Roubineau 2013: 21, 36; Coin-Longeray 2014a: 61.

also because they shape our response to Athenian poverty as historians; what we think we know, or cannot know, how we interpret what survives or does not survive, is framed by these ideas. In pulling apart these discourses, therefore, it is useful to separate ideas about poverty from those about the poor. Distinguishing the two is important, not necessarily because the Athenians always maintained a sharp distinction (they did not), but because it allows us to interrogate different ideas surrounding poverty and the poor in order to highlight some nuances. Whilst both reveal concerns about appropriate behaviour and both can be ideologically driven, examining the condition of poverty frames it as a situation which is structured by social, political, and economic institutions and processes. This is useful because it allows us to interrogate the competing claims made about poverty and to assess how it was perceived as a phenomenon within society in general. Viewing the poor as people, on the other hand, reveals how these poverty discourses shaped the experience of life through, for example, associating specific characteristics with being poor. This shifts the emphasis from poverty as a concept viewed at arm's length to a position which recognizes the agency—or rather the constrained agency—of this group of people over their lives.[62] What follows, then, is an exploration of these aspects of poverty discourses in Athens.

THE POOR

In 2014 a controversial television programme was broadcast on the UK network Channel 4. In it, a camera crew visited what they billed as 'one of Britain's most benefit-dependent streets'—James Turner Street in Winson Green, Birmingham—and produced a reality-show-style documentary. Over five episodes, they aimed to show 'the reality of life on benefits' at a time when austerity measures had begun to bite on the very poorest in British society through government-imposed cuts to the welfare support provided to those both in and out of work.

[62] Bastiaensen, de Herdt, and D'Exelle 2005. On the relationship between structure and agency in poverty studies see Lister 2004: 126–57; Sen 1999b: 18–34, with Chapters 5 and 6 here.

The series, titled *Benefits Street*, was designed to provoke, depicting the residents, critics argued, as criminal, racist, dysfunctional, and work-shy layabouts, 'scrounging' off the state, whereas defenders of the programme emphasized the sense of community shown by the residents, their self-reliance in adversity, and entrepreneurialism.[63] It caused a huge outcry in Britain, leading to much comment in the media as well as public petitions targeting the production company, and discussion in parliamentary debates.[64] Both reactions played into existing narratives about the poor and the working class in twenty-first century Britain: that they are either feckless, lazy, and refuse to work, or salt-of-the-earth types upholding traditional British values (whatever they are).[65]

The controversy surrounding the show might seem a million miles away from democratic Athens, but it demonstrates how the discourses of poverty are built up around competing and deeply embedded narratives which characterize the poor in distinct and often contrasting ways. Likewise in the ancient world. Of course, it is important to remember, just as in *Benefits Street*, that we are looking into a world which has been framed for us by outsiders. In this case, instead of a television production team it is the literary evidence, mostly—though not entirely—created, and preserved, by and for the wealthy elite.[66] As in *Benefits Street*, there are multiple views of the poor, their characteristics, and behaviour—not all negative—which suggest that this formed part of a discourse which was, or could be, contested. It is necessary, however, to be aware that often these portrayals represent the poor as a foil against which to show the

[63] Cf. Jones 2014 with Nelson 2014. The series was criticized not only for portraying the residents in a negative light, but also for being exploitative ('poverty porn'), i.e. providing a voyeuristic experience for viewers.

[64] *Hansard*, 13 Jan. 2014, *Welfare Reforms and Poverty*: column 671 (John McDonnell; Hayes and Harlington; Labour): 'The question was asked earlier about how we pay off the deficit. There was a choice when the economic crisis hit: should those who created the economic crisis pay for it, or should the others? This Government decided that the poorest in our society would pay. To enable that to happen there had to be some form of ideological attack on the poorest—the latest example is the programme "Benefits Street"—that identifies a group of people and demonstrates that they somehow stand for all those people who are dependent on benefits. That is then used as a justification to cut benefits overall.'

[65] Charlesworth 2000; Jones 2011.

[66] There are few depictions of poverty in the visual arts in the classical period; see Villanueva-Puig 2013; Jacquet-Rimassa 2014.

desirable moral behaviour of the wealthy.[67] Rarely are classical authors interested in the actual lived experience of poverty within Athens, and this shapes how they depict poverty and the poor. Nevertheless, it is possible to use these to sketch the contours of poverty discourses and gain an insight into how the Athenians thought about poverty and the poor.

Deficiencies, Material and Moral

It is noteworthy in the literature of fifth- and fourth-century Athens that the language of deficiency pervades the way the poor are depicted. Perhaps this is no surprise, given the term *aporoi* ('men who lack resources'), but nevertheless, being deficient is one of the most striking characteristics associated with being poor in Athens. Not only did the poor lack material goods, such as food, clothes, and furniture, as made clear by Chremylos (see p. 37), but they also lacked moral qualities.[68] To the Old Oligarch, for example, being poor was equated with *ataxia*, *apaideusia*, *amathia*, and *adikia*.[69] The repeated use of the negative-force prefix α- is not only a literary alliteration but symbolizes the way in which the poor were defined in contrast to the rich, lacking the characteristics which made the rich worthy members of society. Other authors write in a similar way.[70] The poor not only lacked moral qualities such as *eutaxia* (good order, discipline), they suffered from *adoxia*, *atimia*, and were *apragmosyne*.[71] They were associated with *amathia* and *ascholia*, but they also

[67] Roubineau 2010 shows how Xenophon is not interested in the poor as a social or economic group, but instead about the behaviour of the wealthy.

[68] Rosivach 1991: 196. The hungry poor: Eur. F 915, Ar. *Plut.* 253, 283, Eupolis F 77. For clothes see p. 10, n. 19. Furniture: Eupolis F 307, Ar. *Plut.* 540–7.

[69] [Xen.] *Ath. Pol.* 1.5: i.e. lacking order (being chaotic, unruly, ill-disciplined), lacking education, learning, or culture (being ignorant), lacking justice (being unjust). See also *adikia*: Arist. *Pol.* 1285a14–16; *amathia*: Eur. *Supp.* 420–1 (and for the reverse, i.e. the rich are ignorant: Eur. F 235). On the language of poverty in general see Coin-Longeray 2014b.

[70] See further Galbois and Rougier-Blanc 2014b: 39–40.

[71] *Adoxia* (lack of reputation, disgrace): Isoc. 5.89, Dem. 57.52; *atimia* (lack of honour): Eur. *Erech.* F 362, (see also Tyrtaios F 64); *apragmosyne* (the opposite of *polypragmosyne*, meddlesome; i.e. lazy, uncurious, not as involved in political life as one should be): Plut. *Nic.* 4.5 (describing the depiction of Hyperbolos in Eupolis' *Marikas*). On the association of poverty with disrespectability see Demosthenes' characterization of Aeschines' youth: Dem. 18.256–66.

lacked awareness of their condition and place in society.[72] Standing outside social and political norms, they could be described as *apolis* and *aoikos*.[73] They lacked physical strength: they were *asthenes* and *adynatos*.[74] They lacked property and food: they were *adoulos*, *achrematos*, *aboutes*, *anaristos*, *anupodetos*, and *astrotos*.[75] Not all descriptors of the behaviour of the poor used this lexical construction, certainly (sometimes the poor are described as unwashed and dirty),[76] but the examples above make the point: the poor were frequently characterized as lacking the necessities of life as defined by the non-poor.[77] The implication is that elites considered the poor as not quite living up to the necessary standards—material or moral.

Need and Dissatisfaction

Another side to the characterization of the poor as deficient is that they are also portrayed as needy and covetous: the lives of the poor are shaped by *endeia* and *chreia*. Plato's Eros, the son of Penia (Poverty) and Poros (Resource), 'forever lives with want (*endeia*)', and it is *chreia* that compels the poor to work, according to Aristophanes' personification of Penia.[78] *Chreia* and *endeia* are seen as catalysts, propelling the poor into behaviours which underscore their servility or submissiveness: Demosthenes accuses Aeschines of

[72] *Ascholia* (lack of time/leisure): [Dem.] 44.4 (here used in an apologetic way); lacking awareness: Eur. *Bellerophon* F 285 (the 'absolute nobody' does not even know he is deprived).

[73] *Apolis*: Antiph. *Tetr.* I 2.9; *aoikos*: Diog. Laer. 6.38, Pl. *Symp.* 203d.

[74] *Astheneia* (lack of strength/influence): Eur. *Supp.* 433, *El.* 39, 267, Xen. *Cyr.* 8.1.30, [Dem.] 44.3; *adynamia* (lack of power, i.e. bodily power): Lys. 24, Aeschin. 1.103, (lack of power, i.e. resources or influence): Dem. 19.186, 44.28, Xen. *Oik.* 20.22.

[75] *Adoulos* (lack of slaves): Men. *Dys.* 328–32; *achrematos* (lack of money): Arist. *Pol.* 1271b16 (on Sparta), Aesch. *Ag.* 167; *aboutes* (lack of oxen): Hes. *WD* 451; *anaristos* or *anaristetos* (without breakfast): Eupolis F 77, Pollux 292, citing Menander; *anupodetos* (lack of shoes), *astrotos* (lack of shelter, i.e. homeless): Pl. *Symp.* 203d. See also *aktemon* (without property): Plut. *Sol.* 14; *amechanos* (impotent, helpless): Hes. *WD* 496–7, Hdt 8.3.3, *argia* (without work, i.e. idle): Isoc. 7.44–5, 8.75 (but see also Dem. 57.32: a *nomos* against *argia*).

[76] Eur. *El.* 1107 (also 182), Eupolis F 280. See also *autolekythos* (self-oil-flasked, i.e. 'too poor to have a slave to carry your oil-flask when visiting the baths', although perhaps also an obscene joke): Harp. s.v. *autolekythoi*, citing Dem. 54.14, Men. *Daktylios*.

[77] Eur. *Supp.* 238–45 characterizes the poor as σπανίζοντες βίου in contrast to both the rich who are greedy and useless and the *mesoi* who save the city.

[78] Pl. *Symp.* 203d: ἀεὶ ἐνδείᾳ σύνοικος. Ar. *Plut.* 534: διὰ τὴν χρείαν καὶ τὴν πενίαν.

doing disgraceful things 'because of want'—unlike Demosthenes himself—whereas Xenophon's Antisthenes states that *endeia* leads to theft, burglary, and kidnap.[79] Xenophon's Euthydemos, in his discussion with Sokrates, states that tyrants—just like the poorest (*aporotatoi*)—are compelled to injustice through *endeia*, which reveals the basic expectation that want and need detract from appropriate behaviour in sometimes criminal ways.[80] Isokrates has a slightly different view: he implies that the poor, compelled by *penia* and *endeia*, simply complain too much, whereas a character in Euripides' fragmentary play *Archelaos* associates *endeia* with lowliness.[81]

On the other hand, Xenophon in particular is very clear in saying, through the mouth of Sokrates, that although need and want are central aspects of poverty, they do not (or rather, *should* not) define the behaviour of the poor. Sokrates, in his conversation with Euthydemos in the *Memorabilia*, points out that being poor did not necessarily depend on how much a person owns but on what he needs; that is, he is arguing for thrift, frugality, and not coveting others' wealth.[82] Sokrates pities Kritoboulos in the *Oikonomikos* for the same reason: he (Sokrates) has wealth enough for his needs, whereas Kritoboulos continuously desires more to maintain his social position.[83] Roubineau rightly argues that Xenophon's portrayal of the poor here betrays more of an interest in social position than being concerned with material conditions; that is, being poor is equated to being dissatisfied with one's position in life (rather than the material

[79] Dem. 18.257: *αἰσχρὸν ποιήσοντα δι' ἔνδειαν*. Xen. *Symp*. 4.36: *δι' ἔνδειαν μὲν γὰρ δήπου οἱ μὲν κλέπτουσιν, οἱ δὲ τοιχωρυχοῦσιν, οἱ δὲ ἀνδραποδίζονται.*

[80] Xen. *Mem*. 4.2.38 (see p. 31). See also Arist. *NE* 1163a–b: *endeia* can be remedied by gain (*kerdos*) but those in need necessarily lack honour: 'Both parties [in friendship] should receive a larger share from the friendship, but not a larger share of the same thing: the superior should receive the larger share of honour, the needy one the larger share of profit; for honour is the due reward of virtue and beneficence, while need obtains the aid it requires in pecuniary gain.' Cf. Arist. *Pol*. 1267a13–14, where he argues that 'the greatest transgressions spring from a desire for superfluities, not for bare necessaries (*διὰ τὰς ὑπερβολάς, ἀλλ' οὐ διὰ τὰ ἀναγκαῖα*).'

[81] Isoc. 8.128: *οἱ μὲν γὰρ τὰς πενίας καὶ τὰς ἐνδείας ἀναγκάζονται διεξιέναι καὶ θρηνεῖν πρὸς σφᾶς αὐτούς* ('some are compelled to complain and lament among themselves their poverty and need'). Eur. *Archelaos* F 249: *ἐνδεέστερος γὰρ ὢν ταπεινὸς ἔσται.* See also Ar. *Eq*. 803–4 where the Sausage-seller links 'necessity, want, and jury pay (*ἀνάγκης . . . καὶ χρείας καὶ μισθοῦ*).'

[82] Xen. *Mem*. 4.2.37–9, *Symp*. 4.42. Arist. *Pol*. 1295b29–33 also assumes the *penetes* covet the lives of the *plousioi* (and therefore the polis based on the rule of the *mesoi* is best).

[83] Xen. *Oik*. 2.2, 2.7.

conditions of it).[84] What this means is that the portrayal of the poor in these passages is not really about the poor themselves and their way(s) of life, but is much more deeply concerned with relative and highly subjective views related to fulfilling the moral obligations of being rich. The role reversal which constructs Sokrates as rich and Kritoboulos as poor, then, is very much rooted in elite concerns, a strand of poverty thinking which we will return to again. This is reinforced by other writers too: 'lowly' (*tapeinos*) is a word frequently used to describe the poor; a term which refers to their social position rather than their material condition.[85]

Is to be Poor to be Bad?

On the one hand, being poor was to be obscure, friendless, or submissive.[86] In archaic poetry in particular, to be poor was to be bad (*kakos*).[87] However, it is misleading to suggest that this is the full picture. These negative characterizations frequently go hand in hand with ideas that prize frugality, moderation, or acknowledge the changeability of wealth.[88] In the conversations of Sokrates just discussed, Xenophon is keen to emphasize that the behaviours associated with being poor (even if these are refracted through the moral universe of being rich) are actually non-deterministic. Indeed, it is the lack of want which is key to living the good life within philosophical circles, and this opens the door to the poor being viewed not simply as grasping parasites, but as models for virtue.[89] Lysias 24, a speech in

[84] Roubineau 2010.

[85] Isoc. 5.64, 89 (the poor are *adoxos* and *tapeinos*, whereas the rich are *lampros* (illustrious) and *despotes* (masters [of many lands and cities]); Antiphanes F 165, Dem. 57.45 (being a nurse is lowly), Pl. *Rep.* 553c, Dem. 8.67, Heraclid. Pont. F 55. For the association between *tapeina* and slavery see Pl. *Laws* 791d, Xen. *Mem.* 3.10.5, Dem. 57.45.

[86] Friendlessness: Dem. 21.131, Eur. F 462, but see also Arist. *Rhet.* 1385a25, who acknowledges that the poor and exiles receive help from others. Submissiveness: Eur. F 249.

[87] Hes. *WD* 638, Theog. 315–22, 393–400, 525–6; Solon F 15. The contrast here, however, is with the *aristoi*, that is, the aristocratic elite. On poverty being an excuse for criminal behaviour see p. 40, n. 48.

[88] e.g. Theog. 903–4, Ar. *Plut.* 553–4, Pl. *Rep.* 553c, Isoc. 7.4–5.

[89] Sokrates, although materially poor, did not strive for more possessions (Xen. *Oik.* 2.3–4, 2.9). In Dem. 18.102–9 Demosthenes presents himself as protector of the poor (but see also Dem. 18.256–64: his scathing criticisms of Aeschines' poverty).

which a disabled man (*adynatos*) argues for the retention of his 1-obol-per-day pension, provides a means in which to explore the virtues (or otherwise) of being poor. It presents a complex picture of poverty which plays with different characteristics of being poor, but allows us to interrogate some competing ideas. Presented to the Boule as part of a *dokimasia* trial, the speaker is addressing a charge that he no longer qualifies for the pension.[90] Given that the *Athenaion Politeia* states property worth less than 3 minai and disability were the qualifying limits, it is necessary for the speaker to imply that his resources were limited.[91] Whether or not the speaker was actually poor (that is, whether he really should have received the dole) is not particularly relevant here, but the assumptions that he makes in the course of the speech, and the ideas he puts in the minds of the *bouleutai* about his opponent, reveal details about expectations of the behaviour of the poor.

The speaker presents himself as a good son supporting his mother until her death, sharp-witted and humorous, and committed to democracy (he left the city under the Thirty). That is, he is as good and normal a citizen as one could find; he even states this outright himself.[92] The effect of this is to normalize his behaviour, to present the activities of those who receive the dole as being much like everyone else; that is, he emphasizes inclusivity.[93] This strategy underscores the idea that men like himself (the poor) are a useful part of Athenian society through arguing that they are moderate in their behaviour, lack *hybris*, and are not meddlesome. They put into action Aristotle's description of virtue: 'the virtuous man will use even poverty, disease, and other forms of bad fortune in a noble manner.'[94]

The speaker's presentation could not have been effective unless the poor could be seen as virtuous rather than detestable, as a valued part of the citizen body, not separate from it.[95] The argument in this

[90] See Dillon 1995: 37–9 for discussion of the question of authenticity. On the speech see Edwards and Usher 1985; Carey 1990.

[91] *Ath. Pol.* 49.4 with Rhodes 1993: 570–1. The rate of pay was presumably increased at some point during the fourth century to the 2 obols of *Ath. Pol.* 49.4. As noted by Todd 2000: 252–3, the speaker never actually itemizes his property: surely the easiest way to demonstrate that he falls within the criteria.

[92] Lys. 24.3.

[93] That his behaviour is perhaps unusual is emphasized by the charge that he rides (or, in his words, 'borrows') a horse: Lys. 24.11–12.

[94] Arist. *Pol.* 1332a19.

[95] See also Dein. 1.36: accusations against Demosthenes of 'living in luxury during the city's misfortunes, travelling down the road to the Piraeus in a litter and

speech, as has been pointed out by other commentators, is based on humour and the trivialization of the charge in question, that is, the speaker takes a position which assumes the *bouleutai* will identify with him rather than against him.[96] Whilst historians have noted a sense of pathos in the presentation of his affairs, he does not beg the Boule to aid him, nor is he ashamed of his circumstances.[97] In this way it taps into a counter-discourse to that which presents the poor in purely negative or detestable terms. Indeed, the raising of the dole from 1 to 2 obols at some point during the course of the fourth century also implies the same. His strategy, then, could not have been thought to be effective unless he could reasonably assume that the Boule would be broadly sympathetic to his plight.

However, the charges he seeks to answer also betray other perceptions of the poor. For example, that the poor do not (or cannot) socialize with the wealthy, that they keep bad company because of their trade, they are misfortunate, and powerless.[98] The fact that cases like these were heard at all hints that Athenians had a keen sense of who ought to receive help from the city and who ought not. That is, there is a hint here that some Athenians were considered deserving of the dole whereas others were not. Although it is difficult to read through the rhetorical positioning of the speaker's presentation to see his opponent's argument, it seems that the speaker's virtue is under scrutiny here (he claims his opponent describes him as insolent, violent, and licentious).[99] For his opponent the defendant's behaviour makes him undeserving of the dole because it proves he is too rich. This might be the case—we simply cannot tell—but the fact that these things are singled out as proof are telling: these are behaviours that place the defendant outside the expected norms of being poor. Regardless of the facts (or otherwise) of the speaker's poverty, what is at stake here is that his opponent views him as undeserving of the dole.

This debate surrounding the virtue of the poor is echoed elsewhere, and I shall return to the question in due course. Here, it is sufficient to

reproaching the poor for their poverty'. On the partisan equation of *penetes* and *demos* see Lenfant 2013.

96 On the social composition of the Boule see Sinclair 1988.

97 Lys. 24.10. Carey 1990: 46–9.

98 Lys. 24.5, 19, 8, 18 respectively. See also Aeschin. 1.104: the uncle of Timarchos, blind Arignotos, also had his pension successfully challenged.

99 Lys. 24.15.

note that frequently the poor were not blamed for their circumstances and that being poor was not always to be bad.[100] Rosivach suggests that attitudes like these do not betray sympathy for the plight of the poor, but form instead part of a demeaning narrative because they show the poor to be morally inferior, not held to the same standards as the rich.[101] It therefore represents them as having less agency over their lives and being less powerful. This is undoubtedly the case; it is made clear by reading such discourses within the context of competing claims about poverty and the poor in Athens.

The fact that unashamedly presenting oneself as poor in court could be an effective rhetorical strategy at all suggests that poverty occupied a place within the Athenian imaginary which was contestable. However, more frequently than not such claims were made by men whose wealth we can reasonably reconstruct as having been extensive.[102] So, Apollodoros, Demades, Andokides, and Aristodemos all claim poverty, yet they either came from liturgical families or paid liturgies themselves.[103] In each case such pleas play into their arguments: they are positioning themselves as relatively poor in comparison with their opponents. All of these men use a similar rhetoric as the speaker of Lysias 24, which plays down their wealth and instead positions their (wealthier) opponent as morally inferior. Apollodoros asks the jurors to imagine their slaves behaving as Phormion has done whilst calling him a thief, a liar, and a barbarian.[104] Demades uses his 'humble position' to juxtapose his honesty and democratic credentials to those of his opponents who, he implies, are sykophants and bribe-takers.[105] Andokides equates the jurors with his own family, appealing to their sense of kinship, whilst casting

[100] Dover 1974: 109–10. See further Roubineau 2013: 18, who argues that there was no social indignity in being a *penes*—this was reserved for *ptochoi*.

[101] Rosivach 1991: 190–1.

[102] On poverty in the lawcourts see Cecchet 2013. More frequently it is a fear tactic: speakers accuse their opponents of poverty (Dem. 18.263) or claim their opponent will 'play the poverty card', by saying they were compelled to crime because of poverty (see e.g. Lys. 7.14, 22.13, Isoc. 18.35, Is. 5.43).

[103] [Dem.] 45.75, 85, Demades 1.8, Andoc. 1.144, [Dem.] 44.4. See *APF*: 100–2 (Demades), 194–6 (Aristodemos). Although Andokides claims poverty, he was nonetheless—in the four years between returning to Athens and his trial—able to outbid Agyrrhios for the grain-tax concession (Andoc. 1.134) as well as own some ships (Andoc. 1.137). Apollodoros was the son of the wealthy Pasion: *APF*: 427–42.

[104] Cf. [Dem.] 45.68 with [Dem.] 45.34, 47, 30 respectively.

[105] Demades 1.8, 10, 21.

Kallias as dissolute.[106] Aristodemos (and his grandfather Meidyllos) are reasonable folks, whereas their opponents Leostratos and Leochares are fraudulent cheats.[107] These are role reversals which operate much like that of Sokrates and Euthydemos: they seek to flip the script by associating the rich with moral dissolution and the poor with moderation.

This positioning might be explained in part by recourse to arguments about the composition of juries, in that it is suggested that 'poorer' men made up a significant proportion of those in attendance.[108] However, Lysias 24 was heard by the Boule, which alerts us to the possibility that such arguments were located within a broader democratic discourse rather than simply being a reflection of who was expected to be on a jury. Despite the need for arbitration in these cases, the speakers are concerned with presenting themselves as part of a united and harmonious civic body and to position their opponents outside of this. That is, if it is part of a democratic discourse for the rich to identify with the poor, this suggests that the poor were not as lacking in power as might sometimes be seen to be the case.[109]

Indeed, occasionally in court speakers make it clear that mockery of, or bad behaviour towards, the poor is unacceptable. Dinarchos sharply criticizes Demosthenes for his luxurious living and accuses him of 'reproaching the *penetes* because of their poverty'.[110] Demosthenes himself accuses Meidias of corruption and *hybris* in his behaviour towards the arbitrator Straton, 'a poor man, but certainly not wicked (*poneros*)'.[111] Dikaiogenes is severely criticized for his treatment of his orphaned nephews and accused of deliberately impoverishing them, and Euxitheos presents Euboulides' discussion of his mother's situation as a slander.[112] Reproaching the poor for their circumstances, or otherwise treating them in a high-handed way, did not play well in court. Such portrayals were designed to provoke anger or pity.

Being poor, therefore, was associated with a range of behaviours and characteristics, but this picture was also a contested one, emphasizing

[106] Cf. Andoc. 1.148 with Andoc. 1.124–31.

[107] [Dem.] 44.36, 48.

[108] See Todd 1990 for discussion of the difficulty of such a reconstruction.

[109] See further Lenfant 2013, who equates poverty-talk with anti-democratic sensibilities.

[110] Dein. 1.36.

[111] Dem. 21.95.

[112] Is. 5.10–11, Dem. 57.30–1. On these examples see discussion by Rubinstein 2013.

that the experience of poverty was both dynamic and complex. This opens the door for a more detailed exploration of *penia* in the following chapters which draws on these multiple narratives, but first it is necessary to examine Athenian ideas about poverty.

POVERTY

Examining Athenian ideas about the poor is useful because it emphasizes how the Athenians associated certain characteristics and behaviours with poverty. But it is also useful to examine the discourses of poverty themselves. Certainly, ideas about poverty and the poor overlap as well as mutually reinforce one another, but there is value in sketching them separately because it allows us to focus on both the structures of power and the agency (or otherwise) of different sections of Athenian society. That is, it allows us to shine a light on the discourses of poverty in terms of both moral expectations and relationships of power, and move away from the idea that being poor is some kind of personal quality.[113] See, for example, Athenian ideas about the condition of poverty: these are closely related to ideas about citizenship and therefore tend to be grounded in (male) citizen concerns; there is little interest in the poverty of slaves, beyond general entreaties not to deny them food in order that they work more efficiently. Women are only considered to be suffering (or escaping) from poverty in the context of their relationships with citizen men.[114] The characteristics of the poor sketched out above are exclusively the characteristics of poor citizen men.

That poverty is conceptualized in purely citizen terms is made clear by numerous examples. Even Plato's ideal state, in which relative economic equality is highly prized and the rich are prevented from owning more than four times the land of the poor, relies on slave labour for its existence.[115] Xenophon's scheme to 'alleviate the poverty of the masses' described in the *Poroi* is only concerned with the

[113] See Harriss 2009: 216–7.

[114] [Arist.] *Oik.* 1344a29–30, 35–1344b5, Dem. 57.45. Philemon, the slightly earlier contemporary of Menander, wrote a comic play called *Πτωχή* or *The Rhodian Woman*, but the feminine form of πένης, ἡ πένησσα, does not appear until late antiquity.

[115] Pl. *Laws* 742a, 936d–e.

poverty of citizens; like Plato, his answer is to increase citizen-dependency on/exploitation of slaves.[116] When slaves are mentioned otherwise it is to emphasize the blurring effect poverty has on citizenship status or as part of a general expectation that they will steal from their masters.[117] Although the slave Karion does benefit from the beneficence of the god Ploutos in Aristophanes' *Wealth*, this is only in his capacity as a member of Chremylos' household.[118]

When Poverty is personified she is depicted as the 'vilest of deities'.[119] In Aristophanes' *Wealth*, Penia is imagined as a hideous old woman, pale and frightening.[120] She argues (unsuccessfully) to maintain a clear distinction between the rich and poor, is eventually expelled, and Chremylos' plan to cure Ploutos of his blindness so he can free the good from her clutches is realized.[121] Penia's arguments in the agon are not only dismissed by Chremylos within the dramatic context of the play, but are also presented as faintly ludicrous by Aristophanes; as the drama unfolds it is clear that even though Penia associates poverty with good honest toil, it actually leads to an effeminizing dependence on women, impiety, and want.[122] In this sense *penia* is little better than *ploutos*: wealth also inspires wickedness, neglect of the gods, and greed.[123]

Plato's Penia echoes that of Aristophanes. She is ugly, wily, and persistent, lying with Poros (Resource) to conceive a child, Eros, without his permission.[124] She passes her nature onto Eros: rough and unkempt, he lacks even the basics of normal life (clothes, shelter, friends).[125] In contrast, the traits inherited from his father include

[116] Xen. *Por.* 4.1–52 (see further pp. 151–2 here). Plato is concerned with reducing wealth inequality between citizens, but is ready to expel *ptochoi* from his ideal city in order to ensure the balance between rich and poor (Pl. *Laws* 936b). See Knoch 2010: 7–8.

[117] Eur. *El.* 1004–6, Dem. 57.45, Ar. *Plut.* 1139–46.

[118] Ar. *Plut.* 802–22.

[119] Eur. *Archelaos* F 248: αἰσχίστης θεοῦ. See also Theog. 267–70, 351–4.

[120] Ar. *Plut.* 422–4.

[121] Ar. *Plut.* 415–22, 604–7.

[122] Cf. Ar. *Plut.* 975–1026, 665–83, 706, 614–19. On the effeminizing nature of poverty see Halperin 1990: 99, and pp. 40–1 on *ptochoi*, though note that Cartledge 1998: 63–5 argues for a 'thetic riposte . . . to counteract the dominant hoplite ideology', in terms of a discourse on masculinity (quote from p. 64). Martin 2001: 63–74 emphasizes the feminine natures of Penia and Limos (Famine) through the 'female "voicing"' given to these personification in lyric poetry. Penia in the sympotic context represents 'poverty of thought, being "at a loss", . . . just as much to be avoided as the real thing' (p. 73).

[123] Ar. *Plut.* 502–4, 1112–16, 398–400 respectively.

[124] Pl. *Symp.* 203b–c.

[125] Pl. *Symp.* 203d.

beauty and bravery: Poros—and therefore Eros—is clever in thought, speech, and actions.[126]

These personifications do not of course present poverty (that is, poverty of citizens) in a good or noble light, and it was often portrayed as a 'most hateful evil', which acted as a catalyst for certain types of shameful behaviour.[127] But even the Old Oligarch admits that only 'some people' (*eniois*) are led into shame through poverty, and although Euripides says that 'poverty . . . teaches men to be base (*kakon*) in his need', there is a sense here that such baseness can be avoided: *penia* teaches (*didaskei*) *kakon* rather than compels (*anagkazei*) or forces (*biazetai*) it.[128] Other voices strike back at the idea: Perikles in the funeral speech claims that poverty was not shameful in itself, it was not trying to escape from it that was.[129] Demades, in explaining to a jury that he comes from a humble background, acknowledges that poverty may bring inconvenience and hardship, but denies outright that it is shameful.[130] Euxitheos positively promotes the idea that his family is poor, mainly by pointing out that (citizen) poverty is better than being foreign and/or servile, whilst anticipating that Euboulides will accuse him of being wealthy.[131] Effectively capturing this ground is particularly important for Euxitheos. Had he failed in his trial, he would have lost his citizen rights and been sold into slavery.

Poverty is often associated with fear, but different kinds of fears pervaded ideas about poverty.[132] First, poverty was something to fear falling into, but what is meant is that there were concerns for the

[126] Pl. *Symp.* 203e. Pébarthe 2014 views this scene as a reference to Sokrates.

[127] Poverty as *kakon*: Eur. *Archelaos* F 230: κακὸν ἔχθιστον, Arist. *NE.* 1115a10 (and references in p. 48, n. 87). For Sokrates it was a wickedness on a par with disease and injustice (Pl. *Gorg.* 477c) and Aeschines describes it as 'the greatest evil of mankind' (Aeschin. 1.88). Poverty as shameful: [Xen.] *Ath. Pol.* 1.5, Isoc. 14.50. See further Dover 1974: 239–40; Rosivach 1991: 190–1, 197, n. 7; Lape 2004: 156–9.

[128] [Xen.] *Ath. Pol.* 1.5; Eur. *El.* 376. This implies a sense of agency for the poor; as Dover 1974: 110 says, 'a poor man can transcend his limitations'. When Isoc. 14.50 (see n. 127) discusses shame and poverty, it is the poverty which comes about through exile rather than poverty in general. For poverty and compulsion or force see Isoc. 8.128, Dem. 57.45, Xen. *Por.* 1.1.

[129] Thuc. 2.40.1.

[130] Demades 1.8: ἡ πενία . . . κεχώρισται δ' αἰσχύνης.

[131] Dem. 57.35–6, 45, 52–3.

[132] Typically it is poverty which is to be feared, rather than the poor themselves. See Arist. *NE* 1115a10–12.

wealthy falling into poverty, rather than for the poor themselves.[133] Xenophon exemplifies this thinking when he claims that it was 'harder to become poor after being rich than never being rich at all'.[134] Within philosophical circles, writers discussed ways in which they might avoid this misfortune through good management: the starting-point for Sokrates' and Kritoboulos' conversation about running an estate is the observation that some farmers are more effective than others with the same-sized parcel of land.[135] No doubt there was some truth to this, but these hypothetical farmers had land—and therefore assets—to begin with. Even Menander's Knemon, the comically misanthropic *dyskolos*, who labours hard on his farm without any help, actually has an estate worth 2 talents.[136] He is not without economic resources, he is socially isolated through his meanness of character. Constructing poverty as something to fear is a politicizing strategy. It is a distancing tactic on behalf of those who do not experience it which serves to distinguish their behaviour from that of others and implies that they are somehow morally superior. Poverty can be overcome, in this view, simply by good estate management; in contrast, the implication is that poor management, laziness, or bad character is at the root cause of poverty.

Second, there were fears surrounding the types of behaviour associated with poverty and, in particular, poverty-escapes. It is an assumption repeated frequently that those who have risen from poverty to wealth have done so as a result of bribery, theft, or other criminal activity.[137] Creating a sense of moral outrage by associating poverty and criminality not only generated mistrust of the accused, but encouraged fears of social disruption.[138] Orators actively, for reasons which will be discussed presently, stoked up a sense of social instability by emphasizing that wealth and poverty were not fixed states, casting suspicion on those who appeared to have become wealthy

[133] e.g. Isoc. 14.50. See also the characteristics of the poor (pp. 51–2) and esp. Roubineau 2010 on Xenophon. Ideally, philosophers were exempt from these fears: Pl. *Phd.* 82c.

[134] Xen. *Anab.* 7.7.28. A similar idea is expressed in Eur. *Hel.* 417–19.

[135] Xen. *Oik.* 3.5. See also Xen. *Symp.* 4.35–6. This echoes Pl. *Rep.* 564e: 'those naturally best organized generally become the richest.'

[136] Men. *Dys.* 327–8.

[137] Isoc. 8.124, Lys. 25.26, 30.27, Dem. 23.209, Dein. 1.45. See Dover 1974: 109–10.

[138] Lys. 12.93 even links wealth acquisition with oligarchic rule and the loss of wealth with upholding democratic values.

without explanation and usually at the expense of the demos, thus creating a climate of fear surrounding their unpredictable actions.[139]

Third, there were fears that poverty might lead to political instability or *stasis*. Both Plato and Aristotle regarded excessive poverty, like excessive wealth, to be a negative feature of a polis community. For Plato, poverty led to servility (*aneleutheria*), bad workmanship (*kakoergia*), and revolution (*neoterismos*).[140] Plato's solution was not, however, to redistribute property to those with less, but to avoid disharmony: fix people within their class—or drive them out of the city.[141] It is an answer to the problem of instability rather than an answer to the problem of poverty. Although Aristotle departs from Plato in his analysis of the causes of political change, he nevertheless assumes that poverty is a driving force for *stasis* and evil-doing (*kakourgia*), and assumes the characters of those who recently have acquired wealth to be defective in the same way that those of the poor are.[142] For Isokrates, poverty threatened the political order because it unbalanced relations within the polis. As a result he presents the poor as desperate, envious, and dependent, and as vagabonds (*aletai*) and evil-doers (*kakourgoi*).[143] Instability permeates the way poverty was written about.

However, fear could also provoke courage in adversity. Misfortune—whether newly acquired or longstanding—required courage to overcome; as Balot argues, 'courage is [a way to] . . . reinvent luck', to reverse misfortune. Viewed like this, it is possible to unpick the apparent contradiction between the ideas of poverty and shame in Perikles' funeral speech and in the orators. For Perikles, endeavouring to escape poverty is part of the idealized Athenian character, an example of courage-in-action not unlike fighting in war.[144] This is not too different

[139] See e.g. Dem. 17.24 on *neoploutoi* as treacherous and poor decision-makers. This is reflected in other genres (see p. 33, n. 12). Thucydides' description of the oligarchic revolution of 411 might be seen in this light: the climate of fear described vividly by him in this episode (8.66) related not only to the *stasis* that it brought with it, but is a comment on the causes of the revolution and the demands of the navy for pay. As Greenwood 2006: 94–7 demonstrates, 'economic language' (e.g. *poros*, *misthos*, *kerdos*) pervades this episode, as does mistrust or lack of good faith (*apistis*).

[140] Pl. *Rep*. 422a.

[141] Pl. *Rep*. 422e–423b. In general: Fuks 1977; 1979. See also pp. 125–6.

[142] Arist. *Pol*. 1265b12–14, *Rhet*. 1391a16–19.

[143] Isoc. 14.46, 7.44–5. See also 8.129–31.

[144] See also Arist. *NE* 1116a13–14: here Aristotle links poverty with fear, arguing that a courageous man does not seek death to escape from poverty. This draws on the Periklean notion of civic virtue.

from the position of Lysias who, in his *epitaphios*, links freedom and bravery (*arete*) with poverty and exile as key factors in the Athenian victory at Salamis; these virtues are then diametrically opposed to slavery, shame, and wealth.[145] Lysias often uses the idea of shameful or criminal poverty-escapes, not to deride the poor as such but—like Perikles—to encourage them to action.[146] The defendant in Lysias 27, Epikrates, is a wealthy man, who has enriched himself further through (it is alleged) corruption.[147] The jury are encouraged to overcome the shame inflicted on them by his actions and collectively convict him.[148] Likewise Ergokles, the Corinthian War general who was impeached in the Assembly for embezzlement.[149] Given that he was a *strategos* with an (alleged) fortune of 30 talents by the time of his conviction, it is clear he was not a regular *penes*. It therefore required the courage of the jury acting collectively to convict him. This narrative, which links criminality with poverty-escape, should be seen as much as a political weapon with which to attack (often wealthy) opponents as it is a way for the poor to acquiesce in their moral inferiority or to unleash the politics of envy.[150] As a fragment of a Menandrian play which has survived in the form of a proverb states: 'farms that give poor returns make people brave.'[151]

In a number of instances poverty is presented as life-without-burden, that is, it is contrasted with wealth to point out the responsibilities and difficulties of being rich. When Xenophon's Charmides, for example, was wealthy he was subject to political duties, personal theft, and blackmail. Now he is poor he sleeps well and pays no taxes. According to Charmides, a prosperous life was marked by instability and excessive responsibility, whereas poverty was not only freedom from these things, but also a high-minded pursuit in itself.[152]

145 Lys. 2.33. On *andreia* and *arete* see Balot 2004: 407–8. On courage actively promoting well-being see Balot 2014: 309–12.

146 Regardless of whether the depiction in Aristophanes' *Wasps* of juries consisting of old and poor men queuing up for their subsistence is accepted, juries must have been composed of large numbers of *penetes*. The system simply could not have functioned without them. See Markle 1985.

147 Lys. 27.9. On Epikrates see *APF*: 181.

148 Lys. 27.2, 16.

149 Lys. 28.2.

150 *Pace* Rosivach 1991: 191. Other examples involve sykophants (Lys. 25.26, Isoc. 8.124), political figures performing controversial tasks (Lys. 30.27, Dem. 23.209), or *rhetores* in general (Dem. 24.124).

151 Menander, *The Cousins*, F 63.

152 Xen. *Symp*. 4.29–32. *Penia* allows Charmides μέγα φρονεῖν: Xen. *Symp*. 4.29. For poverty as a philosophical pursuit in general see Desmond 2006.

Xenophon here subverts the ideas that linked poverty with instability and instead connects it to wealth. Similarly, Isokrates contrasts the lives of 'those who have means' with those who do not, judging the former to be 'more burdensome'.[153] Sokrates points out to Kritoboulos the great number of expectations placed on him because of his wealth—he needs to perform expensive sacrifices, entertain people lavishly, and pay liturgies frequently.[154] That he is considered to be 'rather poor' by Sokrates as a result of this, as well as an object of pity, implies that these expectations are a burden which not being rich removes.[155] That is, Sokrates' remarks here inhabit precisely the same intellectual space as the argument in the *Symposium*.

This is a discourse which on the surface appears to be sympathetic: Charmides voluntarily gives up his riches, Sokrates (supposedly a *penes* himself) demonstrates to Kritoboulos that it is possible to live the good life without being rich. But in fact it presents poverty as the Other, abstracting it from the people for whom this was the (real, not chosen) experience of life. Charmides' role reversal from rich to poor flips the experience of poverty to that of the rich man: he is hounded, beset by instability and fear, and his freedom of movement curtailed. It should hardly need stating that paying liturgies, though no doubt resented by some, is distinctly different from the day-to-day struggle of providing enough food to eat. Nor does Antisthenes' response really address the difficulties of life without wealth. He plays up the importance of frugality and links prudence with honesty, but still characterizes the poor as thieves, burglars, and kidnappers who are beset by want.[156] Poverty for Antisthenes is noble: it is connected to self-control and acceptance of one's lot in life. This might seem sympathetic on one level, but philosophical praise of poverty like this can also be seen as a justification to persuade others not to share in the rewards of wealth. Telling those without assets not to covet them is the politics of privilege.

In fact, the poverty described by these authors is not the experience of poverty per se, but poverty as a philosophical construct. It is a metaphor for constraint, a lack of freedom, or restrained appetites,

[153] Isoc. 8.128. [154] Xen. *Oik.* 2.5–8.

[155] Xen. *Symp.* 4.36, 42. See also Xen. *Oik.* 2.2: *σὺ . . . πάνυ μοι δοκεῖς πένεσθαι*, 2.4: *ἐμὲ δὲ οἰκτίρεις ἐπὶ τῇ πενίᾳ*; On the obligations of wealth see Roubineau 2010.

[156] He does, however, acknowledge the importance of thinking of poverty in relative, rather than absolute terms, i.e. he places *behaviour* rather than *resources* centre-stage, but this relativity is bound up in ideas about virtue as opposed to concern for the poor.

and it takes its shape by being contrasted with luxury, softness, or uncontrolled gain. Poverty might have been seen as a noble 'lifestyle choice' by some, but philosophers' adoption of an impoverished lifestyle is problematic for understanding the lives of the (actually) poor. Sokrates, for example, though eschewing the trappings of wealth, nevertheless maintained the lifestyle of a member of the elite. His social circle (or at least that constructed by his admirers after his death) consisted of wealthy, well-educated men, he was a regular participant in *symposia*, had enough resources to serve as a hoplite, yet he is remembered biographically for being dishevelled and refusing to enter into economic transactions.[157] Given that Xenophon felt it necessary to refute charges that Sokrates used Homer to chastise the demos and the *penetes*, it is likely that his behaviour could be interpreted, at least by some, as doing precisely this.[158] Diogenes, famous for his destitute-like lifestyle in Athens, was from a politically influential elite family in Sinope.[159] Their poverty was ascetic.[160] Other philosophers behaved in a similar fashion: the Pythagoreans stereotypically refused to eat beans (an important source of protein for many people in the ancient world), not because they could not afford to, but because they chose not to; the Cynics chose to forgo worldly possessions.[161] But not everyone had a choice about whether to live a life of poverty, and not everyone was socially connected enough to get away with this life of 'virtue'.

QUESTIONING POVERTY: WHO DESERVES TO BE RICH?

The relationship between wealth, poverty, and virtue was a major theme of public discourse in classical Athens. Not only was it debated

[157] See Pébarthe 2014, who presents cogent *philosophical* reasons for the portrayal of Sokrates as poor (and therefore calls into question the reality of his poverty). On the other hand, Sobak 2015 argues that Sokrates was 'craftsmen-obsessed' (p. 678), i.e. deeply entrenched in the world of the *penetes*.

[158] Xen. *Mem*. 1.2.58–9.

[159] On Diogenes and his father Hikesias in Sinope see Desmond 2006: 7.

[160] There is a parallel between the biographical tradition surrounding Sokrates with that of Homer. See Graziosi 2002.

[161] See also the monasticism of late antiquity, whereby monks swapped the 'risks of common poverty' for a kind of 'regulated poverty': Patlagean 1997: 20.

by philosophers, it was dramatized on the stage and utilized in the lawcourts. As we have seen already, discourses on poverty were shaped by these questions. Euripides, in particular of the tragic poets, was concerned with the disconnect between wealth and nobility, and many of his characters explore situations in which the rich and well-born have been reduced to poverty (the 'hero in rags' motif).[162] In *Elektra*, Elektra is depicted as a self-pitying avenger, whereas her nameless husband, ostensibly a poor farmer (though one with a distinguished ancestry and oxen), is shown not only as the most noble of all the characters in the play, but the one who introduces the theme of nobility and virtue for Orestes to take up subsequently.[163] It is the farmer who stands up for the ideals of *xenia*, offering hospitality to the strangers (who turn out to be Orestes and Pylades) even when Elektra—still in the dark about their true identity—berates him for this. He is pious and honourable, refusing to consummate their marriage, and shows good political judgement in not recognizing Aigisthos' authority in Argos. As such he is the defender of aristocratic virtue—he is even described as *aristos*—whereas Orestes is lacking in it.[164]

Elektra frequently laments her condition (and that of Orestes), but every time she does so she emphasizes her high status: it is not poverty per se which she has difficulty dealing with, but *her* poverty; she shows no concern whatsoever for the poverty of her husband.[165]

[162] See Mastronarde 2010: 50; Roselli 2005. This was not confined to Euripides, but Euripides uses it frequently.

[163] The section of Orestes' speech which is sometimes thought to be an interpolation (ll. 368–72) raises the question whether virtue corresponds with wealth. Here, it is noted that the son of a noble (*gennaios*) father can be a nobody, whereas the children of the bad (*ek kakon tekna*) can be—paradoxically—good (*chresta*). The following lines (371–2) contrast the rich and the poor in a double sense: on the one hand the rich are associated with *phronema* (mind, spirit, pride) and the poor with *soma* (body), but this is quickly subverted. The *phronema* of the rich suffers through famine (*limos*), whereas the *gnome* (judgement, intelligence) of the poor is great. Euripides (or his interpolator) is implying that it is the rich who are lacking and the poor who are virtuous. On the inserted lines see Distilo 2012: 162–5.

[164] The farmer as *aristos*: Eur. *El.* 382. For Orestes as cautious, passive and deceptive see Mastronarde 2010: 287–8.

[165] The external markers of poverty which so distress Elektra in herself—the clothes, cleanliness of hair, ability to attend festivals, and so on—are never commented upon in connection with the farmer. Elektra's conception of poverty is entirely self-centred. See Eur. *El.* 54–63, 114–24, 175–89, 198–212 (and compare with the following note).

In this sense, these characters profess a similar idea to that of Xenophon: poverty is fine for the poor, but is problematic when suffered by the rich. However, this disguises a more complex series of ideas. When juxtaposed against the farmer's apparent virtue, poverty is articulated rather differently. Euripides acknowledges the social isolation of poverty: Elektra is cast out from her home, she undertakes manual labour such as fetching water or working at the loom, has filthy hair and tattered clothes, but he also emphasizes that virtue (albeit aristocratic virtue) is attainable *despite* these characteristics.[166] Elektra's isolation is self-inflicted—she has slaves who can help her, and her husband has urged her to stop her toil—whereas the farmer's labour is imposed: he has to work the fields.[167] The farmer's perspective collapses the hierarchies that Elektra and Orestes are so desperate to maintain, and although deferential to the social order, it places emphasis on equality between rich and poor.[168] The farmer's namelessness, then, is not merely a tragic convention but points perhaps to the nameless face of poverty, disarticulating the dehumanizing rhetoric of poverty from those who experienced it. He is rewarded by the gods with 'great wealth'.[169]

The placing of the rich and well-born in situations of poverty is common in Euripidean drama, a feature which was also parodied by Aristophanes.[170] Menelaos in *Helen* is also a mighty king reduced through shipwreck to penury, and is also less than happy about it, and Telephos is disguised as a beggar in the fragmentary play of that name. Like Elektra, Menelaos' condition is even more pitiable because of his high status, his aristocratic character juxtaposed against the appearance of poverty.[171] But it is an appearance, and appearances can be deceptive, a point made clear throughout the play with the phantom-spouse plot device.[172] Although Menelaos has no food when he arrives in Egypt, has rags for clothing, and is forced to beg at the palace, this is not a permanent state for him, and it is clear that

[166] Electra's labours: Eur. *El.* 307–8; hair and clothes: Eur. *El.* 182–3, 304–6.

[167] Eur. *El.* 64–6, 140–2.

[168] Eur. *El.* 426–31.

[169] Eur. *El.* 1286–7.

[170] See Roselli 2005: 19–23. He concludes that parody is 'evidence for the expectation that the audience would *appreciate* Euripides' kings-in-rags' (p. 23, original emphasis). Coin-Longeray 2014a: 61–2 discusses the Homeric resonances of the trope.

[171] Eur. *Hel.* 510–4.

[172] Aristophanes satirizes this aspect of Euripidean plays: Ar. *Ach.* 440–4.

these external markers are deceptive in themselves. Helen's fearful reaction to Menelaos re-creates on the stage many of the negative ideas about poverty discussed in this chapter already. She thinks he is savage, a violent criminal from whom she needs the protection of the gods, and a thief.[173] She is horrified at his begging, not because she is sympathetic to his hunger, but because it brings shame on her.[174] However, it is not virtue that changes Menelaos' fortune but his and Helen's deception.[175] In the *Orestes*, Menelaos' and Helen's prosperity is contrasted with the torments and misery of Orestes and Elektra, underscoring the idea that deception is a means (for the rich?) to evade the misfortune of *penia*.[176]

Comic drama also deals frequently with the question of who deserves to be rich. This is the central question of Aristophanes' *Wealth*, a reversal-of-fortune fantasy in which blind Ploutos, the god of wealth, is given his sight back in order to reward financially those who were morally good. The play derives humour from the observation that 'many people are wealthy despite being scoundrels, while a good many worthy people fare badly and go hungry'.[177] There are fragments of other comic plays too which seem to deal with similar themes. Kratinos' *Ploutoi*, for example, appears to be concerned with the unjust possession of wealth: a surviving fragment seems to put on trial one of its characters, Hagnon, the wealthy son of Nikias.[178] Pherekrates' play *Agathoi* (the Good Men) is cited by the *Suda* as 'The Good Men or the Money Vanishes', which has led some to speculate that it concerns a similar reversal of fortune. Snippets of other comedies suggest that this was a not unusual topic.[179]

[173] Eur. *Hel.* 544–55. Telephos reflects additional negative thoughts: his expectation is that the leaders of the Greeks he is addressing will resent him for daring to speak (F 703; see also F 712a).

[174] Eur. *Hel.* 790–1.

[175] On deception see Mastronarde 2010: 73–4, 302–3. For Mastronarde, Menelaus is a 'deficient hero' (p. 302).

[176] Eur. *Or.* 449–55.

[177] Ar. *Plut.* 501–4.

[178] Kratinos F171, ll. 57–76. See esp. l. 68: 'this man has not gained his wealth justly here and so <he should be punished>.' For discussion of the fragment and reconstruction of the political background of the play see Bakola 2010: 209–20. Pl. *Laws* 631c associates 'keen-sighted' (ὀξὺ βλέπων) wealth with wisdom, and Theophrastos (commenting on this passage) laments wealth-acquisition among the *kakoi*: Fortenbaugh et al. 1992: no. 507 (see also Fortenbaugh 2011: 481–4). Both Aristotle and Theophrastos wrote (no longer surviving) treatises *On Wealth*.

[179] Krates F 48, Eupolis *Demes* F 126, Diphilos F 104.

The fragmentary plays build a wider context in which to read the more complete comedy by Aristophanes. Classicists have claimed that the plot of *Wealth* reflects a sense that poverty was rampant in late fifth- and early fourth-century Athens as a result of the Peloponnesian War, or that it is a general call for the redistribution of wealth.[180] But it reveals nothing about the *depth* of poverty: simply placing Poverty on stage does not necessarily depict the lives of the poor in a realistic or sympathetic light; it was a trope of comic drama to lampoon wealthy men by styling them as *penetes*, after all.[181] Chremylos is hardly an admirable character (he is selfish and greedy), as is Philokleon in *Wasps*. In fact, the ludicrous nature of the proceedings after Ploutos regains his sight, and the ultimate failure of the scheme, serve to reinforce the idea that the poor do not deserve wealth—only the wealthy do. As Sommerstein himself admits, 'Aristophanes . . . instinctively speaks the language and thinks the thoughts of the well-to-do'.[182]

Moreover, the scheme put forward by Chremylos and Karion is not born from any political ideology or any serious attempt to think through the idea of wealth redistribution.[183] It is not a blueprint for action, but reveals instead a conception of wealth and poverty based on moral judgements: the good should be rich instead of the wicked, and the usual suspects are reeled out to demonstrate who or what is wicked (sykophants, sexually aggressive old women, and so on). The play is not concerned with the redistribution of wealth in anything

[180] Sommerstein 1984; Olson 1990; Lévy 1997.

[181] See p. 33, n. 12. Roselli 2005: 32, 38, n. 157 views these not as attacks against these men with the aim to keep them down, but reflections of their popularity and therefore success. Be that as it may, it nevertheless reveals how the rhetoric of poverty could be used as a weapon.

[182] Sommerstein 1984: 314. Sommerstein goes on to argue that there is a shift in Aristophanes' thinking connected to his admiration for the 'Attic peasantry . . . [who were] being crushed' after the end of the Peloponnesian War (p. 333). See, however, Rosenbloom 2004a and 2004b, who argues that the comic ridicule of personalities like Hyperbolos is part of a culture war between aristocratic and democratic values in the late fifth century. If he is right it would be difficult to see Aristophanes as the social reformer implied by Sommerstein.

[183] Zelnick-Abramovitz 2002 argues that the play is framed around debates of the late fifth century and the themes of Old Comedy. Through its reconstruction (and parody) of a Golden Age, it is much more backward-looking than a close comment on contemporary economic relations. The dual dates of performance (408 and 388) also make reading the economic or social context of the play, in anything but the most general terms, very difficult to sustain, *pace* Sommerstein 1984; 2001: 4; Olson 1990.

but a comically inspired moralistic sense. By exaggerating the effects of newly found wealth on Athenian society (if everyone was wealthy, no one would work), it strongly reinforces the status quo.[184] As such, it does not differ significantly from the notion articulated by Antisthenes that the poor should put up and shut up. Aristophanes, despite claiming that he 'is the [comic poet] who has compelled his rivals no longer to scoff at rags or to war with lice', often pokes fun at the poor.[185]

POVERTY DISCOURSES IN ATHENS

The poor are hardly invisible in the literature of late fifth- and fourth-century Athens, but until recently they have tended to be viewed in a fairly reductionist manner.[186] It is clear, however, that there were many complex and sometimes competing ideas about poverty and the poor, and by examining these multiple discourses we can begin to unpick the complex narratives which shape poverty in the ancient world. Poverty was seen as something to fear, but it also provoked courage; it was a civic duty to try to escape it, but the acquisition of wealth was looked upon with deep suspicion. The poor were deficient and never satisfied, but they possessed qualities of thrift, moderation, and stability which were held up for admiration. That is, we can see in these differing narratives how poverty was contested.

It has been noted by other historians that the language of poverty was used to construct a moral universe which shaped the behaviour of both the rich and the poor.[187] Frequently we see this discourse

[184] In a similar way Timokles' description of the emotional relief of a tragic audience at seeing a poor (or mad, blind, lame, and so on) character on stage in his *Women at the Dionysia* reveals little about the actual response of an audience to their own misfortune (F 6: 'For someone who's poor, once he's learned that Telephos was a greater beggar than himself can then endure his own poverty more easily'). As Rosen 2012 shows, this is a parody of tragic didactic pretensions similar to that of Aristophanes' *Frogs*, and should not be taken as a straight statement of fact: 'the exempla are meant to come across as comically banal, if not downright ludicrous' (p. 182).

[185] Ar. *Pax* 739–40. See also Sommerstein 2005: 167.

[186] The collection of papers in Galbois and Rougier-Blanc 2014c is an important breakthrough in this regard. See also Roubineau 2010; 2012; 2013.

[187] Dover 1974; Ste. Croix 1981: 123–5; Rosivach 1991; Coin-Longeray 2014b.

centring not on the economic condition of a person but on their relative position within society, in a way which constructs and maintains social distance. With the exception of how poverty affects political decision-making, when the poor appear in literary texts the effects of their poverty is rarely of interest to the authors. These texts are not directly concerned with the day-to-day struggles of (for example) maintaining a family life or providing security for them, but in virtue and justice. Instead, poverty is used as an ideological vehicle to explore aspects of elite and/or civic life. Poverty is bearable under the right conditions, but the 'right' conditions are morally constituted through citizenship, masculinity, and being well-born. It is a condition to be borne temporarily or as part of a philosophical lifestyle, and in this sense the actual experience of poverty is marginalized by these discourses. This means that using the comic presentations of Aristophanes or the complaints of the Old Oligarch about the moral virtues of the poor as a starting-point for understanding the experience of poverty is deeply problematic.

The social construction of poverty in Athens frequently juxtaposed poverty with wealth, and when we follow this lead, poverty is framed in terms of absences or deviation from a normative—though not normal—lifestyle. This shapes our own assumptions about what poverty ought to be like or how the poor should behave, whilst at the same time silencing their voices.[188] Such an approach, however, does not fully recognize the complex and contested nature of these discourses and therefore downplays the multidimensionality of poverty. It might even be argued that viewing poverty in this way does a disservice to those who experienced *penia* and their ability to make use of the social and economic resources available to them, because it implies that poverty is a result of their own bad choices rather than being shaped by various structural factors or social processes.

Ideas about the behaviour, characteristics, or attitudes of the poor, as well as how poverty is conceptualized, are fundamentally moral and political judgements.[189] This is most clearly demonstrated in Athens by the lack of acknowledgement of anything other than the poverty of (usually male) citizens. The contours of poverty in Athens

[188] Sommerstein 1984: 333, for example, views (the later) Aristophanes as 'a spokesman of the barefoot', without regard for whether 'the barefoot' desired, needed, or responded to his representation.

[189] du Toit 2009: 228–30.

are very much shaped by contemporary cultural, ideological, and political concepts such as ideas about moderation, democratic egalitarianism, or freedom and slavery. That Isokrates or Xenophon perceived that poverty was some kind of problem is indeed critical for evaluating a poverty discourse.[190] But these authors define poverty in specific ways which are rooted in elite concerns, and if these ideas are decontextualized they have limited traction for investigating the complex condition of poverty in Athens. Aristophanes' *Wealth*, for example, might suggest in general terms how the poor could have been viewed, but it gives little indication as to whether poverty was a common state, and is hardly a political rallying-call for the redistribution of wealth: as Chremylos admits, everyone wants to be richer, no matter what his resources. Examining poverty through these representations alone will always be limited for certain types of questions. These discourses, therefore, though fundamental to an understanding of how poverty was perceived within certain circles, do little to highlight what poverty was actually like for those who experienced it. In order to investigate this, we have to rethink our approach.

190 Isoc. 7.32–5, 52–5, 83; Xen. *Por.* 1.1.

3

Poverty and the Distribution of Income and Wealth

Was Athens a place where poverty was rampant, or a place where most people were not poor? Judging by the discourses of poverty we encounter in the literary sources, we might expect the former to be closer to reality; certainly the impression we get from the previous chapter is that the Athenians spoke, wrote, thought, and laughed about poverty fairly frequently, and for a number of purposes. This appears to imply that it was a familiar experience for many, shaping elite and popular culture alike. However, this picture contrasts somewhat with recent research that has shown Athens to be an affluent and comparatively egalitarian city where standards of living and wages were high.[1] Indeed, Athens scores highly on all comparative measures of success.[2]

This chapter explores these two contrasting pictures of Athenian society and asks how poverty and inequality should be evaluated outside of those ancient discourses discussed in Chapter 2. In doing so, it asks four main questions. What proportion of the Athenian population was poor? How deep was their poverty? How big was the gap between rich and poor? And did this gap change over time? The aim here is twofold. First it is necessary to juxtapose the picture we get of poverty through ideological categories with methodologies that draw upon sociological ones. Second, it is important to focalize conclusions about affluence and inequality from the position of the worst-off in society, however these groups are defined. Doing so contextualizes our assessment of life in Athens, but it also highlights

[1] Ober 2010; 2015; Scheidel 2010; Kron 2011. [2] Ober 2008.

some methodological difficulties with developing tools to measure poverty and inequality in the ancient world.

Recent research has outlined some of the different ways in which wealth, poverty, and inequality in the ancient world might be estimated, arguing that cities like Athens underwent sustained economic growth from the eighth century to the fourth, and that as a result large numbers of Athenians lived above subsistence levels.[3] How should we assess poverty in Athens if this picture is correct? This chapter begins by examining the wealth and income distribution models that spring from this line of thinking in order to see what poverty looks like, even if we assume relatively low levels of economic inequality within Athens.

THE RICH

Paradoxically, in order to understand poverty in Athens it is necessary also to assess wealth. I will start this chapter, therefore, by briefly exploring the distribution of wealth within the wealthy elite, predominantly because our evidence is weighted towards this group. Being wealthy in Athens was defined, in part, by financial contributions to the polis.[4] These richest citizens paid liturgies (voluntary contributions for public projects) and, it is likely—albeit controversial—that a broader group of men were also liable for *eisphorai* (war taxes).[5] Liturgists can rightly be considered an economic elite. As such they formed a very small proportion of the total population: around 4–5% of citizen men and less than 1% of the Athenian population as a whole.[6]

It is clear that performing liturgies was not only a financial responsibility, but also constituted an important part of the social identity of those who paid these contributions. These men regularly outline (and

[3] Morris 2004; 2005; Ober 2010; 2015; Lagia 2015a; 2015b; Bresson 2015.

[4] See e.g. Arist. *Pol.* 1291a33–4.

[5] Davies 1981 calls these groups the 'liturgical class' and 'leisure class' respectively, but there is debate about how much they overlap. It is certain, however, that *eisphorai* were only raised from those with relative wealth: Ste. Croix 1953: 32–3. Liddel 2007: 264–79 provides a good recent overview of the different financial obligations on the wealthy, but see also nn. 9–17 here on specific controversies.

[6] Assuming a fourth-century citizen population of 30,000 and total population of 250,000.

perhaps overstate) their spending in the lawcourts in order to be seen as favourable to the community at large, although some historians have argued that significant numbers of the wealthy deliberately hid their wealth in order to avoid paying.[7] Be that as it may, more is known about this group than any other part of Athenian society, due in large part to the survival of evidence; indeed they are over-represented in our sources in general.[8] However, it is rare that we have anything approaching complete property records even for this section of society, and the evidence that does survives is often rather partial, deriving, for example, from opponents attacked in court for their extravagance or meanness, or property-owners deliberately obfuscating their wealth.

Whilst it is uncontroversial that liturgists formed an economic elite, there are various debates surrounding the size of this body, their relative wealth, and the extent to which the group of liturgists and *eisphora*-payers overlapped.[9] Paying *eisphorai* was not considered a liturgy in the same sense that a trierarchy or festival liturgy was, and it is possible that payment sometimes fell on those outside the core body of liturgists; as Liddel notes, this must have varied depending on the amount which needed to be raised.[10] But even if we assume that this is not the case and that *eisphora*-payers and liturgists were essentially drawn from a smaller and richer group whose wealth was in excess of 3–4 talents, there are still grounds for arguing that those men who fall just short of this, that is, those with wealth of over a talent, could also be considered 'wealthy'. Narrowly defined, these men are not part of the economic elite because they did not serve the

[7] See Lys. 21.1–5, Dem. 21.154–72 for pride in liturgies. See Christ 1990; Gabrielsen 1994: 53–60 on the question of avoidance.

[8] See the catalogue of Davies 1971.

[9] Davies 1981: 19–20, 34 estimates the number of liturgists to be between 200 and 400 (except between 357 and 340, where he accepts the figure of 1,200), but see Rhodes 1982; Gabrielsen 1994 for a higher estimate (1,200–1,500). Ruschenbusch 1978 (and in his series of subsequent articles) and MacDowell 1986 argue that the liturgists and *eisphora*-payers were one and the same group (i.e. the 1,200 richest Athenians) with a minimum wealth of 3–4 talents whereas Davies, Rhodes, and Gabrielsen argue that there were larger numbers of potential *eisphora*-payers (i.e. a group of 2,000 or more) with a lower level of wealth (Davies suggests 1 talent, whereas Ste. Croix 1953: 33; Jones 1957: 28–9 suggest 2,500 dr. and a potential pool of 6,000 payers, but the evidence for this is problematic). See also van Wees 2011: 111–12. The parameters of this debate are summarized in Table 3.1.

[10] Liddel 2007: 274–6.

polis with their wealth, but in a broader sense they were—they were propertied and had considerable leisure.[11]

These controversies of definition aside, there are some observations we can make. Although in the process of being updated, what is clear from Davies' catalogue is that there was not a static group of propertied families in Athens. This group changed chronologically, compositionally, and socio-politically during the classical period. That is, their number grew in size over time (partly because the levels at which one might be expected to pay decreased as the burden was shared amongst a larger group of people), the families who were liable did not, as far as we can tell, always remain the same, and the relationship between this group and the rest of Athenian society changed over the course of the fifth and fourth centuries, for example, in their relative contributions to politics.[12] The organization of public spending during the late fifth and fourth centuries is complex. However, we can deduce from the legislative changes, particularly those in the mid-fourth century, that there was a strong political commitment to this system of public finance, which placed voluntary financial obligations towards the polis on its wealthiest citizens, and that there were anxieties about the ability of the rich to pay their share. The system of public finance as a whole is commonly interpreted as a way Athenians mediated inequalities of wealth and the political egalitarianism of the civic body.[13]

Davies estimated that personal property worth around 4 talents ensured a citizen was unlikely to escape liturgical service during the fourth century, and that between 200 and 400 men had wealth above this level.[14] That is, this was the core group of trierarchs and other liturgists who formed the basis of the 'liturgical class'. However, this estimate assumes that each man was actively contributing to the city every year without exception which is something we know not to be the case.[15] Taking account of exemptions, more like 1,200–1,500 liturgists were needed each year (during the fourth century) in order for the system to function, with many more *eisphora* payers in addition.[16]

[11] Ste. Croix 1981: 114–20.

[12] Davies 1981; Taylor 2007a; Kaiser 2007.

[13] Ober 1989; Liddel 2007: 280–2.

[14] Davies 1971: xxiv; 1981: 34 (with comments of Gabrielsen 1994: 45–53, who argues for a broader range).

[15] Dem. 20.8; *Ath. Pol.* 56.3.

[16] See Rhodes 1982: 11; Gabrielsen 1994: 176–80, 189–90. Gabrielsen argues that Davies' 4 talent threshold for liturgy-bearing properties is questionable and that some

Of these 1,200–1,500, 300 served in a year as *proeispherontes*, advancing payments to the city and reclaiming the balance from the members of their symmory. It is reasonable to assume that there was some turnover in this group too, and this therefore suggests that at least 500–600 estates were worth considerably more than 4 talents, perhaps averaging at more like 8 talents.[17]

My aim here is not to go into depth about the workings of the system of public finance, but to point to some patterns of wealth distribution among those who we can plausibly suggest owned properties worth 1 talent or more (and therefore whom we have grounds to call 'wealthy' in the broadest terms).[18] Given the numerous controversies surrounding aspects of liturgies and *eisphorai*, the intention is not to get drawn into the debates about how those systems functioned, but to present different scenarios for comparison (see Table 3.1 for a summary of the various positions).[19] Of course, all estimates of the wealth of Athenians based on how the public finance system operated should bear in mind that these calculations rest on self-assessment of property that was made available for fiscal purposes. These assessments, no doubt, underestimated the wealth of many.

One aspect that is clear from looking at the distribution of wealth within this group is that the very richest owned properties were

properties which supported liturgical spending were almost certainly worth less, whereas MacDowell 1986 and Ruschenbusch 1978 argue for a 3–4 talent minimum range but that *eisphora* payers did not exceed 1,200 in number.

[17] See Osborne 1992: 24; Gabrielsen 1994: 180. An estate worth 8 talents would support a trierarchy from the interest alone, assuming a 6% rate of return (Scheidel and Friesen 2009: 75) and no losses (though this assumption might be overly generous). See Davies 1981: 24 for the cost of a trierarchy at approximately 3,000 dr. Demosthenes' reforms of 340 assume that this group is considerably wealthier than the 'average' liturgist and that the burden of payments should fall on them: Dem. 18.102–8.

[18] One talent is an essentially arbitrary threshold, of course, but one that is used by many historians (see Table 3.1). On the most optimistic scenarios, no more than 10% of the citizen population would have had estates this large. This represents about 1% of the total population.

[19] See also, for example, the wealth-distribution tables of van Wees 2011: 112. These are nuanced here in the upper ranges to explore patterns of wealth distribution among the elite. Table 3.1 presents the outer ranges of plausibility; modifying the figures in response to the various debates about the working of the system—i.e. the discussions about the number of liturgists and *eisphora*-payers and their relative wealth (see n. 9)—changes the outcomes (though not significantly and always within these parameters). The model of e.g. Kron 2011 falls within these parameters.

considerably larger than most—which is obvious when we juxtapose the estate of, for example, Pasion, to the properties of those whose wealth was more in the region of 1–3 talents.[20] Indeed, those whose wealth did qualify them for regular liturgical service (on Davies' assessment, those with 4+ talents) had estates that were also rather small in comparison to those with the largest fortunes: men like Onetor, who allegedly had property worth 'more than 30 talents', or Demosthenes, with an estate of at least 14 talents.[21] Pasion himself had property worth 20 talents in land and houses and another 20 talents in loans, in addition to the shield factory, and Euthykrates allegedly had property worth 60 talents.[22] Together the fortunes of these four men outstripped the public revenues of Athens in the 350s.[23] We have no idea how many Athenians had properties on this scale; here I assume they constituted around 1% of the *eisphora*-paying group at any one time (Table 3.1).[24]

If we average the wealth of this subsection of elite citizens—the richest 1% of the 1%—based on the properties of these four men, we come to an estimated figure of 36 talents. In reality this probably underestimates their wealth, perhaps seriously so (and is considerably less, of course, than the 60 talents associated with Euthykrates). Even so it is between six and fifteen times larger than the mean and between twelve and thirty-six times larger than the fortunes of the least well-off within this elite group, which has a within-group Gini index of between 0.39 and 0.54, depending on the model followed (Tables 3.1, 3.2).[25] This calls to mind the complaints of Demosthenes

[20] The annual income of Pasion's property (worth at least 40 talents: see n. 22) would be approximately 2.4 talents: i.e. the capital of these estates.

[21] Onetor: Dem. 30.10. *APF*: 423. On Demosthenes' estate see *APF*: 127–35 (14 talents is considered by Davies to be a conservative estimate).

[22] Pasion's property: [Dem.] 36.5, 20, 36, 41 with *APF*: 431–5. Little is known about Euthykrates, but it is thought possible that mining interests were responsible for a large part of his wealth: Hyp. 4.34 with *APF*: 192. The wealth of some men in the fifth century is reported to be even larger: Nikias' estate was reportedly 'not less than a hundred talents', Ischomachos' more than 70 talents, Kallias' over 200 talents (Lys. 19.46–8), Oionias' estate (on Euboia) fetched almost 82 talents in auction (*IG* I^3 422, ll. 375–8), the speaker of Lys. 26 claims his estate was worth 80 talents before the years of war took their toll (Lys. 26.22). See further pp. 100–1.

[23] Dem. 10.37 estimates public revenues as 'not exceeding' 130 talents. The combined fortune of these men is at least 144 talents.

[24] This is consistent with Kron 2011.

[25] The total wealth of this group was estimated in antiquity to be around 6,000 talents (Dem. 14.19; Polyb. 2.62.7–8: 5,750 talents), though this no doubt

Table 3.1. Parameters of wealth in Athens

Average wealth (T)	No. of citizens (min.)	Bibliography	No. of citizens (max.)	Bibliography
1+	1,200	Davies 1981: 34–5 (1,200–2000) Osborne 1992: 23 (1,200+) Kron 2011: 129 (1,200 total) van Wees 2011: Table 1 (2,000 total)	3,000	Rhodes 1982: 11 ('a somewhat larger' group than the 1,200 liturgists) Hansen 1990: 353 (3,000–3,500) van Wees 2011: Table 2
3–4			900*	Gabrielsen 1994: 180 (1,200–1,500 liturgists, 600 of whom are *proeispherontes* and additional numbers of *eisphora*-payers) MacDowell 1986: 444 (1,200 liturgists/*eisphora* payers with a minimum of 3-4T)
4–8	300	Davies 1981: 24, 34 (200–400 with wealth above 4T) Osborne 1992: 24 (500 with average wealth of 8T) Kron 2011: 131 (300 with average wealth of 9T)	600	Wallace 1989: 479–80 (1,200 liturgists and some turnover in the Three Hundred *proeispherontes*)
36+	20+	See p. 74	50?+	See p. 74
Total number of citizens	1,520	Christ 2007: 63 (1,500 total)	4,550 (1,550)**	van Wees 2011: Table 2
Total wealth of group (T)	4,420		12,500 (9,500)**	

Notes: * i.e. the 1,500 max. for Gabrielsen's liturgical class, minus his suggested 600 *proeispherontes*.
** If the 1,200–1,500 liturgists only are included. For debate about the overlap between the liturgists and *eisphora*-payers, see Ruschenbusch 1978; Rhodes 1982; MacDowell 1986.

Table 3.2. Within-group inequality of the *eisphora*-paying elite

	Number of potential *eisphora*-payers		
	1,200	1,500–2,000	4,550
Wealth minimum (T)	3	1	1
Mean wealth (T)	5–6	2–3	2–3
Mean wealth as multiple of wealth minimum	1.9	2.4–2.9	2.75
Gini index	0.39	0.51–0.54	0.51

that liturgies always fell on 'poor' men; that is, these inequities within the elite did have political consequences.[26] In contrast to the very richest, Demosthenes is probably correct: far more men seem to have had assets closer to the threshold than far above it (or claimed as such). The picture is supported by the relatively high turnover of wealthy families over generations. Few trierarchs, for example, appear to be able to sustain multiple liturgies in their families for more than two or three generations.[27] Whether this suggests that wealthy families learned to hide their wealth to avoid paying liturgies or spent down their assets on them (that is, redistributed their wealth to pay for public goods) is a matter of debate.

underestimates the total amount of their wealth, given that this is the property declared available for fiscal purposes. Three thousand would be a large, though not implausible, estimate of the size of the potential *eisphora* pool (Jones 1957: 28–9 suggests 6,000), but note that this refers to the number of Athenians who potentially had properties over a talent (or, in Jones' case 2,500 dr.) rather than how many were needed for the symmories to function in any given year—which is essentially the root of Davies' lower figure and drawn from our knowledge about the reorganization of 357 (Periander's reforms). These reforms extended the system of organization devised in 378/7 for the *eisphora* (i.e. the symmories) to the navy and created a panel of 1,200 who were henceforth liable for naval liturgies. Demosthenes in 354/3 argued the pool of 1,200 was too small for this purpose and the Athenians needed 2,000 men to ensure the 1,200 places were filled, but his proposal was never adopted (Dem. 14.16–17). His reform of 340, however, shifted the burden away from the 1,200 and more onto the Three Hundred *proeispherontes* (Dem. 18.102–8). Davies' estimates of the size of the group of liturgists as a whole (200–400) is surely too small (see p. 71, n. 9), but 500–600 *proeispherontes* with properties in the region of 8 talents fits with the evidence (see also Osborne 1992: 24, Gabrielsen 1994: 180, Kron 2011: 131). For extended discussion of the pros and cons of using the Gini index, see pp. 86–90.

[26] Dem. 18.108. On Demosthenes' reforms of 340 see Gabrielsen 1994: 209–12.

[27] Kaiser 2007.

HOW MANY PEOPLE IN ATHENS WERE POOR?

Understanding the distribution of wealth within the richest group of citizens alone is difficult because of the various controversies surrounding the evidence that survives. However, placed in the context of the rest of Athenian society, the wealth of this group—whether we define them in relatively broad or narrow terms—was pretty extensive, and they constituted a relatively small part of the citizen body (and an even smaller part of the total population). Is it possible to assess the distribution of wealth within the rest of the Athenian population? There are two key difficulties: first, even though our knowledge of the wealth of liturgists and *eisphora*-payers is limited, in contrast to the property portfolios of those who were not part of this group, the evidence we have is full and detailed. Second, as we have seen in the previous chapter, the literary sources tend to conceptualize the rich and poor in a more or less binary fashion, but these categories are contested and are based more on ideological than economic criteria. This means it makes no sense sociologically to categorize liturgists and/or *eisphora*-payers as 'rich' and all non-payers as 'poor'. Who, then, should we include in a count of the 'poor'?

Previous approaches have suggested some answers by focusing on subsistence minima, for example, the number of calories needed for survival.[28] I will discuss the advantages and disadvantages of these in more detail in a later chapter; here it is necessary to note that such approaches necessarily draw a very low poverty line (survival or starvation), are more variable than might often seem to be the case, and provide no reliable way of quantifying those (such as slaves) who we might suspect had poor access to food.[29] But if Athens was a city in which (at least some) wages were relatively high and nutrition relatively good, then bare subsistence, conceptualized in calorific terms, might not be the most appropriate measure; as Ober and Scheidel point out, pay in the region of 1 drachma per day would be enough to have a decent 'middling' life.[30]

[28] Foxhall and Forbes 1982; Gallant 1991.

[29] See pp. 122–6 for further discussion.

[30] Ober 2010; Scheidel 2010. 'Middling' here indicates 'above subsistence', but not wealthy. This is obviously a broad (and potentially varied) group (and therefore up for debate who it includes and how we should analyse it), but makes the point that subsistence living should not necessarily be the basic assumption for large parts of ancient populations.

In addition, it is difficult to measure the poverty of women, children, metics, and slaves—that is, the more than 80% of the population who were not male citizens—in anything other than the most general sense, not only because the data do not survive to quantify their access to economic resources in the same ways as for (some) citizen men, but also because their ownership or control of assets was legally distinct. One solution is to count women and children as part of households, but models which do this tend to assume regular-sized households of 2 adults and 2.5 children, which necessarily simplifies a complex social picture.[31] Whether this is an acceptable trade-off depends on the questions one wishes to ask and the level of detail in which one is interested. In some cases it is necessary—factoring in non-citizens to economic models of Athens is fundamental if we want to understand the economy at large—but at other times it obscures important social and economic patterns. So, for example, comparison of wealth across households tells us nothing about the distribution of wealth *within* households, yet this is arguably more critical for assessing the poverty of women, children, and slaves, and therefore the 'overall' poverty within an ancient society. In sum, models such as these assume an equal distribution of wealth or income within the household, but there are strong reasons to believe that this might not have been the case.[32] Here we can see clearly how consideration of income and wealth dynamics at the micro-level problematizes the conclusions drawn through study of macro-level changes across the Greek world.

Likewise, in models which attempt to account for the whole Athenian population it is difficult to quantify the poverty of slaves (if this is, indeed, the most appropriate way of conceptualizing the economic position of an unfree group of people). On the one hand, slaves had few or no economic resources aside from their own exploited labour, so we might consider the majority (or indeed, all) of them to be 'poor', but this glosses over differences in the types of activities slaves performed, their relative levels of freedom, or the financial success of a few (not to mention other more important inequalities).[33] Qualitative methodologies are likely to be more useful

[31] Ober 2010. [32] See pp. 128–33.

[33] Ober 2010 suggests that as many as 10% of slaves in Athens could earn enough to live a 'middling' lifestyle. See p. 23 on slavery as a category of 'dependent poor'.

here for picking up on the details (as will be argued in Chapter 6). It is clear from this discussion, and that in Chapter 2, that the 'poor' were not a homogeneous social group.[34]

This is not to argue that quantitative modelling does not have a place in the study of the ancient world: it certainly does. It offers a different perspective on the societies we are familiar with through their literature and material remains, and allows comparison across time and historical context. It is an essential part of the ancient historian's toolkit. Indeed, drawing on the models of Ober (2010) and Kron (2011), it is possible to develop further their parameters for 'wealth' and 'poverty' in Athens. Ober and Kron both seek to argue that Athens had a relatively egalitarian distribution of income or wealth, and so their models assume a large 'middle', but where Ober focuses on income, Kron concentrates on wealth (for the difference in these two concepts see discussion on pp. 84–5). Regardless of whether their interpretations are accepted (either in part or in entirety), however, placing a spotlight on those parts of Athenian society which were not affluent or were considerably poorer than others is necessary for drawing conclusions about equality and inequality within Athenian society as a whole. Doing so allows us to better understand what poverty might have looked like, even if we assume Athens was a fairly affluent or relatively egalitarian society. These two models are therefore used as starting-points for assessing poverty and wealth here.

In some sense, using these models is a pragmatic decision based on available published research.[35] The aim here is to test the calculations suggested by other historians (that is, to replicate their findings), and to see what poverty looks like in Athens based on their assumptions and within the constraints of their models. Of course these assumptions can be changed, and others might indeed modify various aspects of Ober's or Kron's models based on different assumptions, but for our purposes this does not matter because these models simply provide a vehicle to think with (that is, to explore what poverty looked like within the societies Ober and Kron build). What is noteworthy here, however, is that both historians argue that Athens

[34] See also Galbois and Rougier-Blanc 2014a: 18 for a similar conclusion.

[35] This research is ongoing and seeks to develop more sophisticated models of wealth and income distribution, but does not significantly change the picture here. I thank Josiah Ober for giving me access to some of his unpublished work.

was comparatively egalitarian in the distribution of both income and wealth (though there will, of course, be different patterns here too) and that large numbers of people were living above subsistence. For further discussion of the detail of these models, and what we would have to change to alter the picture given here, see Appendix 1.

Poverty in Athens According to the Distribution Models of Ober and Kron

According to Ober's 2010 model, lightly modified in 2015 (Table 3.3), median annual income was in the region of 450 drachmas per year (or a maximum of 1.5 drachmas per day, assuming 300 days per year are available for work).[36] Is this too high? Probably not significantly, since it correlates well with what we know about wages in the later fourth century at least: this was the pay for attendance at the *kyria ekklesia* in the 320s, and certain groups of craftsmen working at Eleusis (and not just those with high levels of skill) in 329/8 were also paid this rate.[37] It was clearly possible to earn this, if not every day, then on some days for some activities. This makes it a reasonable median. Within Ober's model, approximately half of Athenian citizens—and two-thirds of the total population of Athens—in the late fourth century lived below this median income (between 44% and 55% of citizens, and between 60% and 71% of the total population: Tables 3.4, 3.5). In comparison, using Kron's model of wealth distribution, 77% (just under 24,000) of Athenian citizens owned less than the median wealth of 2,650 drachmas (Table 3.5).

However, given that Ober and Kron both argue that large numbers of people in the ancient world were living at levels substantially above bare subsistence, the fact that more than half of the population fell below the median of income or wealth is less relevant than calculating

[36] On average there seems to have been a festival every 7–10 days or so, but 300 days availability for work might be an overestimate: Scheidel and Friesen 2009: 72 estimate between 225 and 250 working days for the Romans. Lowering this figure lowers the median and reduces the financial rewards of wage labour in particular—indeed this instability of income is likely to have been a feature of poverty. However, no or low income on one day might be cancelled out by higher wages on another, so the effect on the model overall is minimal. For further discussion see Appendix 1 (pp. 249–50).

[37] *Ath. Pol.* 42.2; *IG* II^2 1672 (carpenters, masons, hired labourers).

Table 3.3. The distribution of income in Athens in the late fourth century

Level		Drachmas per household		Population		Z
		Per day	Annually	Optimistic	Pessimistic	(Median)
Subsistence	1	0.3	90	32,917	44,783	-0.12
	2	0.5	150	32,917	44,783	-0.10
	3	0.75	225	32,917	44,783	-0.07
Middling	4	1	300	46,292	33,375	-0.05
	5	1.5	450	46,292	33,375	0.00
	6	2	600	46,292	33,375	0.05
Elite	7	8	2,400	900	900	0.64
	8	16	4,800	900	900	1.43
	9	32	9,600	900	900	3.01
Total				240,327	237,174	

Source: Ober 2010 (modified).

Table 3.4. The population of Athens living below the median income (450 dr.)

	Optimistic		Pessimistic	
	Number	%	Number	%
Citizen population	13,167	44	16,500	55
Total population	145,043	60	167,724	71

Source: Ober 2010.

Table 3.5. Athenian citizens living below, and significantly below, median income/wealth

	Below median		At or below half of median	
	Number	%	Number	%
Income	13,167–16,500	44–55	5,000–10,000	17–33
Wealth	23,770	77	16,950	55

Note: Median (income): 450 dr.; (wealth): 2,650 dr.

Sources: Ober 2010, Kron 2011.

(i) the proportion of the population who lived at or below half of median income or wealth, and (ii) how far short their incomes/wealth were in comparison to the rest of Athenian society. What do their models suggest about these questions?

On Ober's model, between 41% and 57% of the total population of Athens lived at or below half of median income (225 drachmas, or 4½ obols per day: Table 3.6). This can be disaggregated into citizen and non-citizen groups: between 17% and 33% of male citizens lived below this threshold compared with between 45% and 60% of non-citizens (Table 3.6).[38] We might tentatively think of this threshold as a 'poverty line'; effectively, what we are doing here is counting the proportion of Athenians whose income falls under a certain level. Before we evaluate the pros and cons of this approach on a theoretical level (there are specific reasons why we should be cautious: see pp. 85–6), we can ask whether it makes sense in the context of the ancient evidence. This is, of course, fragmentary, but enough evidence on rates of pay survive to suggest that 1 drachma per day was a common, though not universal, rate.[39] That our half-median line is drawn below this is noteworthy—those who regularly earn 1 drachma per day would not be counted as 'poor' on this measure. On the other hand, those (such as jurors) who earned 3 obols per day certainly would (if, that is, this was their sole income). That this level of income was associated with 'the poor' receives support from the literature. Aside from Aristophanes, who parodies jurors as being old and poor, Xenophon assumes that half a drachma per day could be distributed to citizens as part of his scheme to alleviate the 'poverty of the masses'; presumably, then, 3 obols was considered to be a welcome amount for a significant section of the demos.[40] Indeed, within Ober's model, 3 obols per day (155 drachmas per year) is the mean income of those who fall below the half-median line. We are within the range of plausibility here.

On the other hand, this also implies that regular labour would indeed be enough to raise a person from bare subsistence, should work be available.[41] There is nothing to suggest that this was not the

[38] Arguably Ober—following Davies 1981 (see p. 71, n. 9)—underestimates the number of citizens in his elite group. Because my aim in this section is to investigate what poverty looks like within the constraints of his model, I do not amend this here (this is not the case with Tables 3.12 and 3.13 with accompanying Figs. 3.4 and 3.5, where changes are made, for reasons discussed in Appendix 1). In fact, increasing the number of citizen elite makes very little difference to the poverty statistics discussed here: the differences are shown, however, in Table 3.14, for reference.

[39] Loomis 1998: 232–9.

[40] Xen. *Por.* 1.1, 4.14–17.

[41] See also Ober 2010. Milanovic 2006: 468 suggests that average incomes in pre-industrial societies might be considered 'a bit more than twice the subsistence minimum'. That the Athenian median is more likely four times this is noteworthy.

Table 3.6. The population of Athens living at or below half of the median income

	Optimistic		Pessimistic	
	Number	%	Number	%
Male citizens	5,000	17	10,000	33
Non-citizens	93,751	45	124,349	60
Total population	98,751	41	134,346	57

Note: Half median income: 225 dr.

Source: Ober 2010.

case: Athenians complain about being forced to work for others in a slavish manner, not the lack of opportunity for work. Wages were available from a variety of state-run projects (political pay, building projects, theatre attendance, and so on), markets in Athens and the Piraeus appear to have been busy, there were a large number of workshops (mostly, though not always, employing family members and slaves) with high specialization of activities, pay for military service was regularly available, and there also seems to have been a casual labour exchange.[42]

In contrast, around 55% of citizens on Kron's model lived at or below half of median wealth (1,325 drachmas; see Table 3.5). That there are greater numbers of citizens living at half of median wealth than half of median income is entirely expected: income is the flow of resources derived from (a) capital wealth (so, returns on investments, produce from the land, payments of loans, profits made from sales of goods or services, and so on), or (b) from labour (that is, wages), whereas wealth is net worth.[43] Income derived from labour does not rely on capital wealth, except inasmuch as those wages might be saved for future spending. Income derived from wealth requires wealth to begin with: land or other property must be inherited or otherwise obtained, loans have to be offered in order to be paid back, goods have

In fact, Ober 2010 and Scheidel 2010 prefer 'wheat wages', i.e. a multiple of the basic cost of wheat, to smooth out differences over time in the purchasing power of any specific income.

[42] On the latter see Fuks 1951.

[43] Keister 2000. Of course, income can be saved to produce wealth, and wealth used to produce income.

to be produced before they are sold. For these reasons, wealth is usually distributed more unequally.

Wealth and Income

It is worth pausing at this point to distinguish further between wealth and income, because they provide for different needs. Whilst the line between wealth and income is sometime difficult to draw in the ancient world, and there is of course some overlap, teasing out the differences is useful because it places greater emphasis on diversified agricultural strategies as well as the non-agricultural economy in which wage-earning and commercial activities played a larger part. Wealth brings financial security, it can be used to create more wealth through investment or inheritance, and it is a source of social status (see, for example, the importance of land for citizen ideologies). Income provides for daily needs; it can be spent on the consumption of goods or services (which, of course, can in themselves make a claim to social status and also be converted into wealth), but it is more sensitive to micro-decisions within family units (whether to let a field grow fallow, when to marry, whether to borrow or lend money, whether to work that day, and so on).[44] In Athens, we can estimate income derived from capital to account for something in the range of 33–44% of the total income of citizens, rising if we assume that those who were poorer saw less of a return. That is, unsurprisingly, those with assets were in a significantly more secure position than those without.[45]

Income derived from wage labour provides economic resources but also will often be more insecure than that derived from capital: physical incapacitation from illness or accident prevents the sale of labour and the accumulation of resources. Wealth and income are often, but not necessarily, correlated with one another: it is possible to have a large house or plot of land which generates little income on

[44] Keister 2000: 6; Keister and Moller 2000: 64–5. Foxhall 2007: 43–4 argues that diversification in the property of wealthy shows how their estates were geared for production of income as much as preservation of wealth.

[45] Piketty 2014: 50–2. The wealth-income ratio (β) is derived by dividing total wealth by total income. Income from capital (α) is derived by multiplying the rate of return (r) on capital by β. In Athens: total wealth (Kron): 15,719 T; maximum total citizen income (Ober): 2,847 T ($\beta = 5.5$) with a rate of return of 6–8%.

which to live. It is equally possible to have a large income and spend it all. But in general we should start from the assumption that those with larger assets also had larger incomes. Those with larger farms or bigger workshops, for example, would have been able to derive disproportionately larger incomes from them than those with smaller holdings, and this is a way in which poverty can be reproduced.

This also means that inequalities in wealth and income might be different and that they might increase or decrease at different rates, though this is difficult to detect in the source material.[46] Research into economic strategies of poorer groups in developing countries today shows that they frequently rely more on their incomes than their assets, meagre as they are, as they are likely to need to spend greater proportions of their financial resources on their daily consumption needs and have less opportunity to save or store their income. In times of hardship poorer groups typically reduce consumption to preserve the small amount of assets that they have, whereas those with stored wealth are often able to use these resources to preserve their levels of consumption.[47]

Evaluating Headcount Measures of Poverty

Asking how many Athenians lived at or below half of the median income or wealth is a moderately useful but fairly crude way of measuring poverty. In effect, it draws a 'poverty line' and counts the number of people who fell below it at a specific (abstracted) point in time. Whilst headcount measures such as these provide a simple tool to assess how many Athenians might be considered poor at any one time, it is necessarily a binary calculation which makes a judgement about whether a person or a group is 'poor' or not, whilst ignoring how poor they actually are.[48] In this sense it is (arguably) little different from the Athenian elite position that defines poverty as the absence of wealth without regard for the massive range of economic-statuses that this likely encompasses, although the bar is, of course, drawn at a different place. Regardless of whether drawing a

[46] See Brandolini and Smeeding 2009.

[47] Barrett, Carter, and Little 2006. Compare the stories of Aristarchos and Euxitheos discussed in Chapter 4 (pp. 118–21).

[48] Sen 1973: 168–70; Brady 2009: 40–1. For alternative measures see the remainder of this chapter with Appendix 2.

'poverty line' is a good way of understanding poverty at all (critics argue that it is not), small differences in the numbers of people assumed to be at or around the half-median income line will have a disproportionate effect on the outcome.[49] These issues might be considered particularly problematic for the ancient world, given the gaps in the evidence.

Additionally, this measure cannot tell us anything about the depth of poverty nor about how it was experienced, yet these are crucial aspects of understanding the role or impact of poverty on a society. In Athens, too, it is also difficult to factor in women, children, metics, and slaves into poverty headcounts in anything other than the most impressionistic way because we have little demographic or economic information about these groups. Whilst half of median income/wealth is a standard measurement of poverty in the social sciences—and has the benefit of being sensitive to change (that is, it measures relative rather than absolute poverty)—it is also essentially a rather arbitrary line: why should 50% of the median be any better an indicator than, say, 60% or 40%?[50] In addition, the median (and therefore the half-median) is sensitive in the first place to the assumptions that are built into the model. Arguably, what we gain in developing a simple range of figures, we lose in complexity.

CONTEXTUALIZING POVERTY: INEQUALITY INDICATORS

The Gini index provides one way in which to contextualize such data, as it provides a simple measure of inequality within a given population. As such, it has been used to provide an indication of whether Athens was a society in which wealth or income was comparatively equally or unequally distributed. The calculations of Athenian land distribution by Foxhall and Osborne, and reinterpreted by Morris, suggest that—in the context of the wider ancient Mediterranean world—there was a relatively egalitarian distribution of wealth in Athens because the Gini index for both distributions were low.[51]

[49] For a critique of poverty-line approaches in general see pp. 124–6.
[50] Atkinson 1987. On absolute and relative poverty see pp. 17–19.
[51] Foxhall 1992; Osborne 1992; Morris 2000.

Table 3.7. The Gini index compared

Publication	Date	Size of citizen population	Richest *x*% own *y*% of *z*	Gini index
van Wees (2001)	Fifth century	40,000–60,000	3.3–5% own 25% of land	0.61
Foxhall (1992)	Fourth century	22,000	9% own 33% of land	0.39
Osborne (1992)	Fourth century	27,000	7% own 30% of land	0.48*
van Wees (2011)	322	30,000	4–7% own 27–43% of land	0.59–0.63
Kron (2011)	Mid–late fourth century	31,000	1% own 31% of wealth 10% own 60% of wealth	0.71
Ober (2010, 2015)**	Late fourth century	29,900	1% own 16–18% of income 23–9% own 49–51% of income	0.33–0.41

Notes: * Morris notes the Gini score here is 0.38, though my calculations of the same data suggest this is an error. However, his conclusions do not change with the adjustment. ** Citizen population disaggregated from total population.

This is supported by other evidence which implies that the Attic properties of the rich (even those like Euthykrates) were not of the same magnitude of those of (for example) the Roman elites.

Other historians have since developed models which show different ranges (Table 3.7). At least some of the variation is simply due to the emphasis of each author on income or wealth, but the interpretation of the figures is also varied. Kron, for example, argues that a Gini coefficient of 0.71 provides ‘an extremely important corrective to the common assumption that Athenian political democracy co-existed with a basically aristocratic and inegalitarian social structure’, which seems to imply a certain degree of egalitarianism, whereas van Wees interprets his data (with a lower Gini score) as signifying ‘a highly unequal distribution of wealth’.[52] Can they both be right?

In a sense they can: this is because inequality is, at least partially, subjective. Van Wees’ position is based upon looking at the distribution of resources amongst the richest 4–7% of citizens, so it is

[52] Kron 2011: 134; van Wees 2011: 111. Van Wees 2001; 2011 does not calculate the Gini coefficient, but he publishes enough data for this to be done, and these are the figures inserted in Table 3.7.

not a great surprise that viewing wealth through this lens magnifies inequality.[53] Kron (like Morris) compares Athens to a variety of other societies (in his case, from fifteenth-century Tuscany to late twentieth-century North America) and interprets Athens as being less unequal than a number of these.[54] The Gini index gives an indication of relative equality or inequality on a scale of 0 to 1, but what it cannot do on its own is reveal exactly how wealth or income is configured within this distribution, and therefore societies with very different structures of wealth might have superficially similar scores.[55] So Kron's comparison of late fourth-century Athens with 1950s America might appear to suggest similar levels of inequality (Gini scores of 0.708 and 0.710 respectively), but the difference in scale, economic complexity, industrialization, or levels of consumption of the two places make such comparisons very difficult to use on anything but the most impressionistic level.

Gini coefficients are necessarily reductive. Lower scores tend to reflect societies with larger middles, whereas higher scores reflect those where wealth or income is more polarized (so in this sense it is no surprise that Ober's model has a low score: he assumes a large middle). On the other hand, lower scores can also be a feature of having fewer income or wealth categories to begin with.[56] They are also not easily decomposable, that is, the total Gini calculated for the whole of a society is not equal to the Gini scores of the subgroups which make up that society.[57] This means that comparing models of inequality based on the citizen population and those based on the wider population are problematic (hence disaggregating Ober's data in Table 3.7).

A recent development uses the divergence of actual Gini scores from the maximum feasible Gini score to assess the degree of elite extraction from the economy (that is, to ask whether the elite could

[53] The same is also true of Foxhall 1992 and Osborne 1992.

[54] Kron 2011: 134, Table 1.

[55] As we will see below for Athens and Rome: see Table 3.10 and discussion on pp. 93–4.

[56] This explains why Foxhall and Osborne's scores (which measure land—therefore wealth) are so low. If we modify (e.g.) Foxhall's model simply by creating more categories and distributing the population evenly in them, we raise the Gini score. See further Sen 1973: 32–4; Coulter 1989: 55. This does not inspire confidence in the robustness of the figure. Incidentally, Ober's new income distribution model (as yet unpublished) addresses some of these concerns.

[57] On the advantages and disadvantages of decomposability see Sen 1973: 180–7.

Table 3.8. Income inequality and the elite

	Gini index		Maximum feasible ('inequality frontier')	Actual Gini as % of the maximum feasible
	Min.	Max.		
Athens	0.40	0.45	0.89	45–50
Rome	0.42	0.44	0.42–0.57	80

Sources: Ober 2010, 2015; Scheidel and Friesen 2009.

have captured more of the economic surplus than they actually did). This is a technique devised by Milanovic in order to calculate what he terms the 'inequality frontier', or the maximum amount of inequality possible in a given population if the elite extract the maximum surplus after basic subsistence needs are met.[58] Calculating this for Athens reveals a large difference between the actual and maximum feasible range (Table 3.8). The maximum Gini score feasible (0.89) is well above the actual ranges estimated by Ober (0.40–0.45) and considerably less than that estimated in the Roman Empire.[59] This means that the richest 1% could have extracted approximately twice as much from the rest of the population than they actually did. No doubt of little comfort to those living close to subsistence, but income inequality in Athens could have been much greater than it actually was.

The Gini index provides a useful tool to assess inequality in Athens, but inevitably it compresses a multidimensional and complex reality into a single figure which is affected by a variety of viewpoints and subjectivities. Indeed, Foxhall disputes Morris's use of the Gini coefficient for comparing Athens with other ancient societies.[60] This, she argues, is a meaningless measure because inequalities of wealth were only too evident within the confines of Athenian society. If we focus on the headcount measures above, this is certainly true: on the most optimistic projections, one in six Athenian citizens lived in poverty,

[58] Milanovic 2006; Milanovic, Lindert, and Williamson 2011.

[59] Scheidel and Friesen 2009: 87, n. 88.

[60] Foxhall 2007: 31–2. Other comparanda from the ancient world include Egypt: Karanis: 0.64 (*c*.308/9 CE), Antinoopolis: 0.63 (*c*.350 CE), and Aphrodito: 0.62 (*c*.525/6 CE): Bagnall 1992: 137; Morris 2000: 141. Byzantium (*c*.1000 CE): 0.42–0.43: Milanovic 2006.

and maybe (that is, more pessimistically) as many as one in three. Considerably more non-citizens did so. However, measurements like the Gini coefficient are designed to abstract complexity, not to disguise but to reveal further lines of enquiry. Inequality is, at least in part, a matter of perception: Morris and Foxhall (as well as van Wees and Kron) are asking different questions. The upshot is that different measures of (both) poverty and inequality need to be combined in order to see if they tell the same or a different story (as well as viewed in conjunction with other evidence) and to interrogate where these converge and where they depart from one another.

HOW POOR WERE THE POOR IN ATHENS?

In addition to a headcount measurement or the Gini coefficient, other measurements can be used to shine a light onto different aspects of poverty and inequality. It may have been the case that the Athenian elite did not extract as much as they could have, but they did have much greater economic resources compared to everyone else. Figure 3.1 shows this relationship by standardizing income by the median (that is, it shows how many standard deviations from the median each income group lies: for data see Table 3.3).[61] This highlights the considerable difference between Ober's elite (levels 7–9) and the non-elite groups (levels 1–6). However, we might also estimate from this graph that the depth of income poverty in Athens was not particularly great (at least on Ober's model, which is, of course, fairly optimistic): the groups which fall below the median (levels 1–4) do not fall massively below it. I will investigate this further presently.

Likewise, comparison of the gap between the top 15–20% and the bottom 15–20% highlights significant differences between the two groups. On Ober's model (Table 3.3), the average income of the top 15–20% is forty-eight times the size of the bottom 15–20%.[62]

[61] Standardizing by the mean shows an even greater divergence.

[62] Average income of the top 15–20%: 4,350 dr.; average income of the bottom 15–20%: 90–100 dr. This probably underestimates the top of the distribution and might even overestimate the bottom. (Note that there is some elasticity in these figures based on the 15–20% ranges used; this range is shaped by how Ober and Kron construct their models).

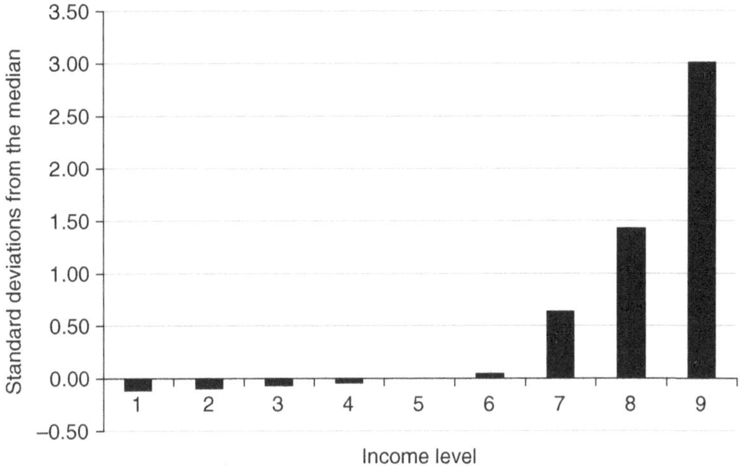

Figure 3.1. Income distribution in late fourth-century Athens (Ober's model) standardized by the median (Z)

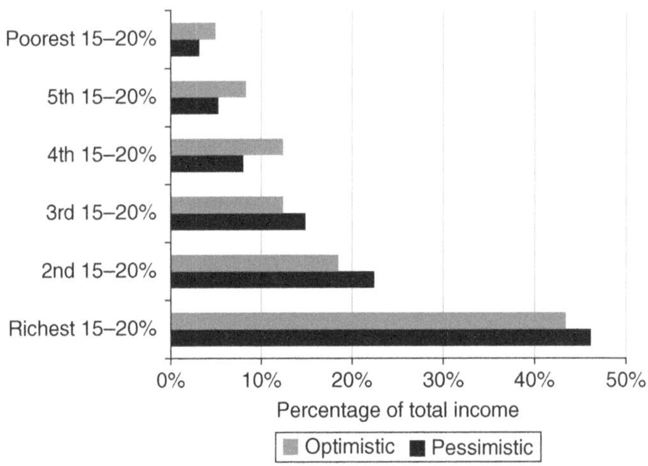

Figure 3.2. Income distribution in late fourth-century Athens (Ober's model) by proportion of population

The top 15–20% have incomes which account for 43–46% of the total, fourteen times the bottom, who cumulatively have only 3–5% (Fig. 3.2). On Kron's model the top 20% of citizens own 74% of Athenian wealth, whereas the bottom 20% own less than 1% of Athenian wealth (Fig. 3.3). Wealth in Athens was considerably less

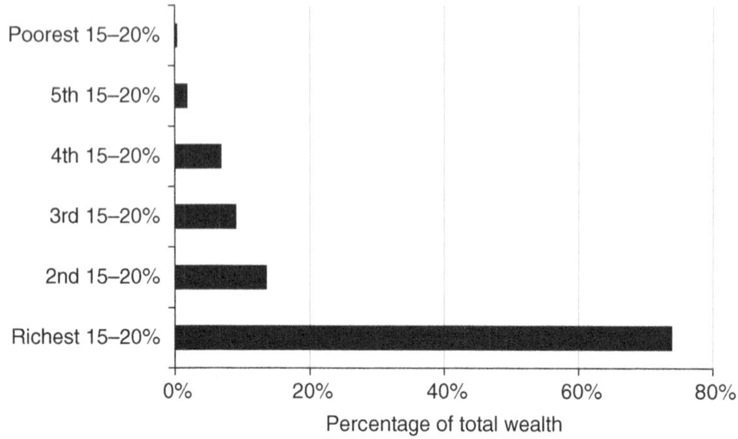

Figure 3.3. Wealth distribution in late fourth-century Athens (Kron's model) by proportion of population

equally distributed than income. Seen through this lens, economic egalitarianism looks rather far off.

If the threshold at which an Athenian became liable for liturgies is taken to be 3–4 talents, it would take the average Athenian living at the median income at least forty years to accumulate enough property to be considered of the liturgical class. It would take the average 'poor' Athenian (that is, those falling below our hypothetical poverty line) over 116 years, spending nothing at all.[63] However, if the wealth of Athens was divided equally between citizen men (on Kron's model), each would have had an estate worth approximately 3,043 drachmas. Compared with the median of 2,650, this is a gap of 393 drachmas, only about three and a half years' income of those with the lowest income and less than a year for those earning a middling wage (though this assumes again, of course, the impossible scenario that nothing at all is spent on daily living expenses). This suggests that (despite the outliers of Euthykrates et al.) the Athenian citizen elite were not massively rich, which is a conclusion which fits with dominant ideas about moderation and excessive wealth (and the discussion above).[64]

[63] 'Poor' here is defined as the mean income of those living at or below half of the median: 155 dr. (or about half a drachma per day). See p. 82.

[64] See pp. 88–9.

Table 3.9. The poverty gap

	P_1	Average shortfall per household (dr./year)
Income	0.311	140
Wealth	0.647	1,714

Sources: Ober 2010; Kron 2011.

However, the wealth of Athens was never distributed equally between citizens, and to present the data in this way glosses over the economic inequalities that were present in Athenian society. These can be better assessed by measuring the depth of poverty. This can be done by using an income-gap measurement (sometimes called a poverty-gap measurement) which calculates the average distance between the incomes of the poor (that is, those living at or below half of the median) and the median income, and so provides an assessment of this group's shortfall from the 'poverty line'.[65] In Athens this group lacked on average (on Ober's model) about 140 drachmas per year, which is approximately half a drachma per day, depending of course on how many days are worked (Table 3.9). This would have provided enough to feed a citizen and his family.[66] The wealth gap is considerably larger, as is expected: at 1,714 drachmas per year it is approximately the cost of a house (if the properties of Kiron are anything like representative), just above the cost of a sick horse, or approximately the same as a herd of goats and a mule.[67]

If the Athenians wanted to close this income gap, they would have needed to redistribute between approximately 2,300 and 3,200 talents each year directly to the poor.[68] If they were to restrict this just to

[65] See Appendix 2 and Sen 1973: 168–70.

[66] Cost of wheat: 5–6 dr. per *medimnos* (*IG* II^2 1672, ll. 282–8). Daily ration per person (generous): one *choinix* (1/48 of a *medimnos*): Foxhall and Forbes 1982: 55–7. Three obols would therefore buy 4–5 *choinikes*. Ar. *Eccl.* 547–8 (*c*.390) implies that a *hekteus* of wheat (8 *choinikes*) cost the day's pay of the Assembly (3 obols). Ar. *Pax* 253, on the other hand, jokes about expensive honey costing 4 obols. See also the calculations of Markle 1985: 280.

[67] House (Is. 8.35): Kiron owned two houses in the city, one let to a tenant and worth 2,000 dr., the other—his residence—worth 1,300 dr. The mean is 1,650. This correlates well with other data on house prices: see Nevett 2000: 341 with fig. 5. Horse (Lys. 8.10): 1,200 dr. pledged as part of a debt (the horse then died). Goats (Is. 6.33): herd of goats sold by Euktemon for 1,300 dr. with a mule worth 550 dr.

[68] Population at or below half of median: between 98,751 and 134,349 x 140 dr = 2,304 to 3,135 talents. This accounts for 15–23% of the total income of all those in Athens on Ober's model.

Table 3.10. Income inequality: Athens and Rome compared

	Optimistic		Pessimistic	
	Athens	Rome	Athens	Rome
Headcount (P_0) %	41	91	57	94
Poverty gap index (P_1)	0.311	0.625		
Poverty severity index (P_2)	0.097	0.391		
Poverty intensity (P_i)	0.128	0.566	0.176	0.584
Gini index (G)	0.40	0.42	0.45	0.44
Ordinal index (P_s)	0.184	0.242	0.253	0.250
Proportion of total income needed to close poverty gap (%)	15	27	23	43

Sources: Scheidel and Friesen 2009; Ober 2010.

citizens they would need between only 117 and 233 talents per year (5–10% of total citizen income). Bearing in mind that the Athenians spent between 77 and 87 talents on liturgies annually, these figures appear strikingly low,[69] but they are particularly noteworthy when compared with Rome. Using Scheidel and Friesen's model of income distribution for comparison in the Roman Empire, the requisite Roman figure is between 27% and 43% of total income that would need to be redistributed for the Roman poor to close their income gap.[70] In addition, a considerably larger proportion of the Roman population in the second century CE lived at or below half of the median income (on Scheidel and Friesen's models) than in Athens—between 91% and 94% of the population—and the intensity of poverty in Roman society was also significantly stronger (Table 3.10).[71] Ober comes to a similar conclusion by comparing wages in the two societies.[72]

[69] Gabrielsen 1994: 216.

[70] Scheidel and Friesen 2009 model the Roman Empire of the mid-second century CE (obviously a much larger geographical area). They conclude (pp. 62–3): 'that the top 1.5 per cent of households controlled about one-fifth of total income; that economically "middling" non-élite groups accounted for a modest share of the population (around 10 per cent)... and that the vast majority of the population lived close to subsistence but cumulatively generated more than half of the overall output.'

[71] If the Roman median is calculated as 2,948 kg wheat, half of the median (z) = 1,474. This draws z at approximately the same level as in Athens, i.e. between 1.7 and 3.3 times subsistence. In Athens z is 2.5 times subsistence. For explanation of these poverty measures see Appendix 2.

[72] Ober 2015: 94–8.

Poverty intensity is a measure which combines headcount and depth data, thereby providing a different measure for comparison.[73] This is necessary in this case because the Gini indexes of Athens and Rome are similar, but this disguises two very different structures of income distribution (as we might guess by glancing at the headcount measures: see Table 3.10). Because the intensity calculation combines information about both the quantity of poverty and its depth, it provides a relatively simple way of assessing what this difference looked like: we can conclude that, on these models, poverty in the Roman Empire was about four times greater than in Athens. The poverty severity index (P_2) and the ordinal measure (P_s) develop this further by weighting the poorest so their contribution to the index is stronger.[74] Again, both of these metrics show poverty to have been considerably worse in Rome than even the most pessimistic assessments of Athens.

Whilst this comparison disguises a number of important observations about ancient economies (notably, non-elite income stratification, discussion of which is a major strength of Scheidel and Friesen's article), it does demonstrate that the texture of poverty and inequality in Athens was of a different order to that in the Roman Empire. What is clear from these calculations is that there was considerably greater poverty in mid-second-century Roman society than in Athens in terms of the proportion of society deemed to be poor and in terms of the depth of their poverty.[75] In addition, the Roman elite were much more 'effective' at extracting economic surplus than the Athenian elite (compare the percentage of actual versus potential inequality in Table 3.8). Simply put, Athens does better on all measurements.

[73] Intensity (P_i) is the product of the headcount and income gap. See Appendix 2 for further details.

[74] See Appendix 2 for discussion of these metrics.

[75] The difference might be overplayed: Ober's model does not explicitly distinguish between subsistence and below subsistence, whereas Scheidel and Friesen assume that between 10% and 22% of the Roman population fell into this category. This brings the ordinal measures more into line (at least for the pessimistic Athenian projection), because the weighting of the poorest of the poor plays a considerably large role. On the other hand, Ober's lowest subsistence category assumes under 2 obols per day—which if not below subsistence would be pretty close to it—and includes 14–19% of the population, so perhaps the differences are not so great after all. Appendix 1 discusses various details of Ober's model in more depth. In comparison, however, skeletal material from classical Athens shows a better-nourished population than that at Roman Velia in southern Italy. Which supports the conclusions here: see Lagia 2015a: 137–8.

All of these measurements of wealth and poverty have advantages and disadvantages. This is not only because of the assumptions lying behind the historical data that are put in to the calculations (the gaps in the data—these can be controlled for), but also because they seek to investigate different aspects of poverty or inequality. Headcount measurements are simple to read and relatively easy to calculate, but they do not distinguish between those who are very poor and those who are moderately poor, so tell us nothing about the depth of poverty. Income-gap tests provide further information about how relatively disadvantaged the poor are in income or wealth terms, but do not reveal anything about how many people fell into this category. The Gini coefficient can give a simple measure of inequality, but does not tell us what that inequality looked like. All of these measures are static and—as they stand—do not tell us anything about change over time. Nor do they reveal how poverty was experienced, constructed, nor how it was conceived. As will be argued in the subsequent chapters, understanding poverty (however defined) requires not only examination of economic measures such as these, or investigation of the discourses of poverty, but also requires an assessment of what Athenians were able to do or to be with the resources they had available.

DID THE GAP BETWEEN THE RICH AND THE POOR CHANGE?

Is it possible to uncover changes in the distribution of wealth or income over time? Given the developments in the Athenian economy over the course of the sixth to third centuries and the changes in Athenian politics—the development of democracy, the acquisition and loss of empire, the Macedonian occupation—this seems plausible. The years of the Peloponnesian War and its aftermath provide a case study here, not only because they detail how Athenians suffered hardship as a result of the loss of life, land, and property, but also because they allow us to examine the effects of the demographic changes which occurred during this period. Although difficult to quantify in detail, this investigation implies that the distribution of wealth and income changed as a result of the disruption of the final years of the fifth century and the early part of the fourth. In effect, the gap between rich and poor (both broadly defined) may have been reduced. What is the evidence for such a claim?

It is well known that in the early years of the Peloponnesian War Perikles encouraged the Athenians to move from Attica into the safety of the Long Walls. The influx of immigrants resulted in overcrowding within the city and created the conditions for the quick spread of disease.[76] Thucydides vividly describes the effects of the plague on Athenian life during this period, and in doing so states that the indiscriminate loss of life led to changes of individual fortune, and that this sudden inheritance of wealth created social tensions:

> Athens owed to the plague the beginnings of a state of unprecedented lawlessness. Seeing how quick and abrupt were the changes of fortune which came to the rich who suddenly died and to those who had previously been penniless but now inherited their wealth, people began openly to venture on acts of self-indulgence which before then they used to keep dark. Thus they resolved to spend their money quickly and to spend it on pleasure, since money and life alike seemed equally ephemeral.
>
> Thuc. 2.53.1–2 (trans. Warner)

Thucydides interprets this change moralistically: sudden prosperity causes vice. Nonetheless, his depiction implies a state of social unrest, but this unrest was not configured by starvation and disaster; rather, it involved some people suddenly becoming wealthy because more of their relatives had died than usual and they had inherited property unexpectedly. These people did not know how to behave appropriately and used their new-found resources badly. His description tells us that the poor ('those who previously had nothing') suddenly became rich as a result of the social disruption caused by the plague. In describing the circumstances in this way he provides a valuable insight into how the Athenians viewed the acquisition of wealth: it was morally problematic, but in order for it to be perceived as so, it must have been widespread enough to be visible—at least to men of the elite like Thucydides.

[76] Sallares 1991: 244–62 discusses the identification of the disease and its possible demographic outcomes. Recent discoveries of a late fifth-century mass burial in the Kerameikos allow for DNA analysis of dental pulp, which suggests typhoid fever: Parlama and Stampolidis 2000: 271–3; Papagrigorakis et al. 2006 although this is disputed by Shapiro, Rambaut, and Gilbert 2006. Of course, these people might have died from a disease different from that to which Thucydides refers.

Thucydides' observations imply that the disruption caused by the plague resulted in the poor becoming enriched, and there is other evidence to support this claim. The accuser of Epikrates, brought to trial for embezzlement some time during the Corinthian War, echoes Thucydides' view of the instability of wealth when he complains that it is 'those who previously . . . were not able even to maintain themselves' who now have the trappings of wealth'.[77] He demonstrates that it was not just Thucydides who perceived the poor to be getting richer: this was not simply the maverick view of one individual with an axe to grind. Indeed, the rebuilding of the Kerameikos bathhouse after the restoration of democracy in 403 perhaps also points to the same process. The new building had a larger cistern capacity, which not only reflected the latest developments in hydraulic engineering, but was also designed to serve a greater number of clients. The bathhouse which stood there before had been destroyed during the turmoil at the end of the fifth century and the area used for the burial of the Spartan allies of the oligarchs.[78] We might therefore see the rebuilding of the bathhouse as a symbol of democratic pride in restoration, a reclaiming of the space from the oligarchic faction, and a resurgent demos, but given the enlargement it also implies that greater numbers of Athenians were expected to frequent this facility. Perhaps this indicates too an increase in their income or wealth: the Old Oligarch complains, after all, about the use of bathing facilities in the late fifth century by 'the demos . . . [and] the *ochlos*'.[79]

Furthermore, there are examples where we can reasonably say that specific families appear to have improved their lot during this time.

[77] Lys. 27.10: 'We have reached the point where those who previously, in peacetime, were not able even to maintain themselves, are now contributing to your *eisphorai* and serving as *choregoi* and living in large houses.'

[78] Stroszeck 2014.

[79] [Xen.] *Ath. Pol.* 2.10. Although there is no evidence to suggest how much bathhouses charged to visit, Trümper 2013: 40 views bathing as 'symboliz[ing] a certain affluent, refined urban culture and lifestyle'. There could be other explanations for the expected increase in number of clients: the growth in city residents as a result of the war might have made it more popular (though like all Athenian bathhouses, it does, of course, lie outside the walls), but large numbers of these 'extra' residents would have returned to their demes by the time of the rebuild, so perhaps this is not a complete explanation. On the increasing participation of non-elites in gymnasia and athletic activities see Fisher 1998.

Timomachos of Acharnai, *strategos* in 367/6 and 361/0 and married to the daughter of the wealthy Kallistratos of Aphidna, was probably the son or grandson of a carpenter working on the Erechtheion in 409/8.[80] Likewise, Iasos of Kollytos, *choregos* in 387/6, was probably related to (or perhaps the same man as) the Iasos of Kollytos named as a sculptor on the same building project in 408/7.[81] Not all families would have risen from daily-paid craftsman to liturgist, but the fact that we can point to some that probably did supports the argument that this forms a pattern.

The idea that the rich were getting poorer is also prominent in the late- and post-Peloponnesian War world. The resounding complaint about the political events of the late fifth century was that they were a drain on the resources of the rich: expenditure on warfare was high and resented (at least in 412–411), and when Athenian overseas influence was curtailed after 404 the wealth of the wealthy was also put at risk. In the *dokimasia* case enacted against the archon Euandros in 382, the unnamed speaker—a wealthy man—notes the reduction of fortune of his family over the previous generation:

> He [Thrasyboulos] cannot even claim that we obtained our property in wartime and spent nothing on the city. Quite the reverse, our household was worth 80 talents in peacetime, and it was all spent during the war for the purpose of preserving the city.
>
> Lysias 26.22 (trans. Todd)

In giving the reasons for his comparative impoverishment, he emphasizes his own impeccably upstanding civic-minded motives (giving money to the city), in contrast to his opponent's (Thrasyboulos) methods of self-enrichment (bribery, treason, sykophancy), but it is the fact that he highlights the changes in fortune of his own family which is important here.[82] Rather than assuming that this is simply rhetorical exaggeration—a way to ingratiate himself with the jury—we should be prepared to ask whether, for example, familial impoverishment did occur, perhaps as a result of warfare and liturgical

[80] Xen. *Hell.* 7.1.4, Dem. 19.180, *IG* I^3 475, l. 245. On his subsequent impeachment see Hansen 1975, nos. 91 and 92. See *APF*: 280.

[81] *IG* I^3 476, ll. 178–9; *APF*: 242. See also Fisher 2001: 193. Iasos' remuneration (80 dr.) was one of the largest recorded, whereas Timomachos' carpentry earned him a more regular 17 dr. See further Feyel 2006: 408 with fig. 21.

[82] The speaker is a supporter of Leodamas, the first archon selected in this year, who was ousted at his own *dokimasia*. Euandros, the replacement, seems to have won the case, passed the *dokimasia*, and served as archon for 382/1. For discussion see Todd 1993: 285–9.

(over-)spending, but maybe also as a result of other factors. Isokrates complains, too, that his family lost their wealth during this period: 'When I was a child,' he says, 'having wealth was thought to make one so secure and dignified that nearly everyone claimed to have more money than they really had, for they wanted the prestige of wealth. But now [354/3], one must carefully prepare a defence against being rich as if it were one of the worst crimes, if one wants to remain secure.'[83] Isokrates credits this change to sykophants, the high costs of liturgies ruining the wealthy, and the general (as he sees it) decline in public life. His experiences, however, fit into a broader pattern.

Other evidence also points toward the depreciation of the property of the wealthy during this period. Lysias 19.45 (dated to *c.*387) lists a group of men whose assets were not as great as expected on their deaths: Ischomachos' property decreased in value from 70 talents to 20, Kallias of Alopeke had only 2 talents after his family had become wealthy through ownership of mining-slaves, and it is claimed that the property of Aristophanes was not worth as much as expected on confiscation in the 390s.[84] These cases are, of course, not unproblematic. It suits the context of the speech to exaggerate the scope of impoverishment: the speaker is trying to show that his family did not loot the property of his executed relative Aristophanes before it was confiscated by the polis. But suggesting a decline in wealth for some of the richest in Athens during this period is not preposterous and fits with other evidence: some were outwardly hostile to continued funding of the war for precisely this reason, others would have lost resources at home or abroad as a result of Athens' defeat and loss of empire.[85] Slaves freed, for example, after Arginousai, would have ended one source of income (hiring slaves out to the fleet) and potentially ended another if, as Hunt suggests, men like Kallias had lost the slaves they had used predominantly in the mines.[86] Others

[83] Isoc. 15.159–60 with 161 on Isokrates' family (mis)fortunes; also Isoc. 8.124–5. See Too 2008: 172–4.

[84] There seems to have been a certain degree of anxiety amongst the demos during this period that the properties of wealthy men had not yielded as much as expected: see Todd 2000: 201–2.

[85] See the vast overseas properties confiscated from those convicted of the Herms and Mysteries affair, 415: *IG* I^3 422–30; Pritchett 1953; 1956; Amyx and Pritchett 1958. This was curtailed in 377 by the founding of the Second Athenian League (*IG* II^2 43). See further Bresson 2015: 216–17.

[86] Hunt 2001: 372. On the desertion of over 20,000 slaves during the Dekeleian War see Thuc. 7.27 and pp. 183–4.

would have had their business interest curtailed, directly or indirectly, by Athens' loss of navy in 403.[87] Others would have had property confiscated during the political upheavals of the late fifth century.[88] It is perfectly reasonable to suggest that some wealthy citizens did see a reduction in their assets during the last decades of the fifth or first decades of the fourth century, for whatever reason.

Impoverishment is, of course, relative. These men did not become destitute nor even, in any reasonable sense, 'poor', but it is entirely possible that significant numbers of them had their resources reduced and therefore became much more aware of the possibilities of not being wealthy or not being as wealthy as their fathers or grandfathers had been. This no doubt played into the perceptions among the elite that wealth was unstable, moderation in spending was a good thing, and that to fall into poverty was something to fear.[89] The isolated misfortunes of the families who complain about their own declining wealth appear to be touching on an underlying trend, then: warfare, disease, and *stasis* affected the deep pockets of the wealthy, but we should question whether they were as catastrophic for those who were poorer to begin with.[90]

CHANGING PATTERNS OF POVERTY AND INEQUALITY

When we think about wealth and poverty in Athens it is easy to be blindsided by the rhetoric (and experiences) of the wealthy, because they dominate the source material. However, the complaints of impoverishment that we find are highly likely to represent anxiety amongst the elite provoked by what they perceived as changing structures of wealth. Although it is possible to point towards examples of individuals or families who became richer or poorer during this

[87] On the navy as a protectionist force for Athenian trade interests by the late fourth century and probably earlier, see Gabrielsen 2015.

[88] Lysias F 7 (*Against Hippotherses*). This is a case which is concerned with the retrieval of property confiscated by the Thirty. Presumably the rich were much more affected by the loss of property in this way than the poor.

[89] See pp. 55–7.

[90] For recent arguments that link war and disaster with a reduction of inequality see Piketty 2014; Morris 2014.

period, it is questionable whether individual examples reveal anything more than individual circumstances; that is, it is easy to either view the experiences of the wealthy families mentioned above as typical or to dismiss them as atypical. But this does not get us very far. The problem is that conceptualizing social mobility (upward or downward) on an individual level runs the risk of divorcing it from its social context and all too easily ascribes social processes to the presence or absence of 'individual pluck or luck'.[91] Instead we need to think about the social structures which shaped poverty and wealth more broadly. Primary here—not least because we have evidence for it—is demographic change.

The current consensus amongst historians is that the late fifth century saw significant demographic change within Athens. How this affected Athenian society can be debated—the degree of demographic decline is disputed (and precision is impossible)—but the best estimates suggest that by the end of the fifth century the population of Attica had been considerably reduced from a peak in the first half of the fifth century.[92] According to Akrigg, the last decades of the fifth century saw considerable losses amongst the population of Attica. At the outbreak of war the total population of Athens was in all probability in the region of 300,000 (the largest it would be until the nineteenth century), and Attica was densely settled.[93] By the beginning of the fourth century, however, this population had considerably diminished, principally through war and disease, but also through emigration. If this degree of demographic change is accepted (and even if it was smaller by half), it is inconceivable that the reduction in population would not have been felt in at least some aspects of Athenian life. There are two important ways in which this may have affected the structure of wealth: (i) in terms of inheritance of

[91] Tilly 2007: 47.

[92] The order of magnitude of population decline is disputed, but that there was some kind of downward change is generally agreed. See e.g. Hansen 1985; Strauss 1986: 70–86; Akrigg 2007. For a critique of historical demography in the ancient world, and particularly the methodologies applied by Greek historians, see Akrigg 2011.

[93] Akrigg 2007: 37. This fits in with Hansen's estimates of the total population of the Greek world during this period: Hansen 2006. Akrigg suggests that the citizen population may have been reduced by as much as one-third to one-half. The total population is likely to have fallen to approximately 250,000.

property, and (ii) in terms of changes within social relationships which give people access to resources.

As Thucydides indicates, the plague resulted in normal patterns of inheritance being disrupted, and this had a significant effect on the distribution of resources. Although we cannot be certain, a plausible scenario is this: in a large population (like that in the fifth century) there may have been comparatively more competition for, and therefore scarcity of, resources, whereas a reduced population would have reduced this pressure (particularly on availability of land and therefore agricultural produce), made labour more scarce (and hence raised wages, paid in cash or kind for those who needed to supplement their agricultural production, or those who had no land at all), and improved economic living standards.[94] Overseas property ownership and imported grain would have expanded the resources of the Athenians, but the benefits were not equally distributed throughout society, and the disruption caused by the events at the end of the Peloponnesian War would have only exacerbated the reliance on land in Attica, at least for the short term.[95]

If this scenario only approximates the situation in Athens, the impact of demographic change would have been significant. Ober's model, based in the late fourth century, can be adjusted to reflect this change (Tables 3.11 and 3.12).[96] One effect of assuming a large mid-fifth-century population which declines in the fourth century is that the percentage of the population of Athens who had incomes at or below half of the median also falls, and although this has to acknowledge the caveats of using headcount measures of poverty discussed above, it nevertheless points to a situation in which there was a significant decline in poverty. If we focus on the citizen population—the group for whom we have data that we can be the most confident about—we can see these trends starkly: not only did the proportion of citizen poor in post-war

[94] See Akrigg 2007. If considered on the micro-level, this in itself would have promoted a range of strategies to enable an *oikos* to consistently support itself: not least selling one's own labour (see Gallant 1991: 139). Akrigg suggests that one possible effect of a large fifth-century population is that it may have stimulated local markets and polarized the distribution of wealth: the more people there are, the more plentiful the labour supply and workers get paid less. See Akrigg 2007: 39–40.

[95] Overseas property ownership and the wealthy: Moreno 2007: 213–14; grain trade: Stroud 1998; Moreno 2007; Oliver 2007.

[96] Note, however, that his 'citizen elite' category (Table 3.12) is expanded to take into account Gabrielsen's emendation of Davies' 200–400 liturgists. For the rationale behind this, see p. 71, n. 9, p. 251.

Table 3.11. Changes in income distribution in the Athenian population

	Mid-fifth century				Later Peloponnesian War and aftermath				Late fourth century (pre-322)			
	Optimistic		Pessimistic		Optimistic		Pessimistic		Optimistic		Pessimistic	
	Number	%	Number	%	Number	%	Number	%	Number	%	Number	%
Subsistence	129,907	46	196,287	70	97,197	40	128,286	54	98,751	41	134,349	57
Middling	148,241	53	81,889	29	140,418	59	107,493	45	138,876	58	100,125	42
Elite	3,600	1	3,600	1	2,700	1	2,700	1	2,700	1	2,700	1
Total	281,748		281,776		240,315		238,479		240,327		237,174	

Table 3.12. Changes in income distribution in the citizen population

	Mid-fifth century				Later Peloponnesian War and aftermath				Late fourth century (pre-322)			
	Optimistic		Pessimistic		Optimistic		Pessimistic		Optimistic		Pessimistic	
	Number	%	Number	%	Number	%	Number	%	Number	%	Number	%
Subsistence	14,000	23	42,000	69	3,775	12	9,025	29	5,000	16	10,000	32
Middling	45,000	73	17,000	28	25,725	84	20,475	67	24,500	80	19,500	63
Elite	2,500	4	2,000	3	1,200	4	1,200	4	1,200	4	1,500	5
Total	61,500		61,000		30,700		30,700		30,700		31,000	

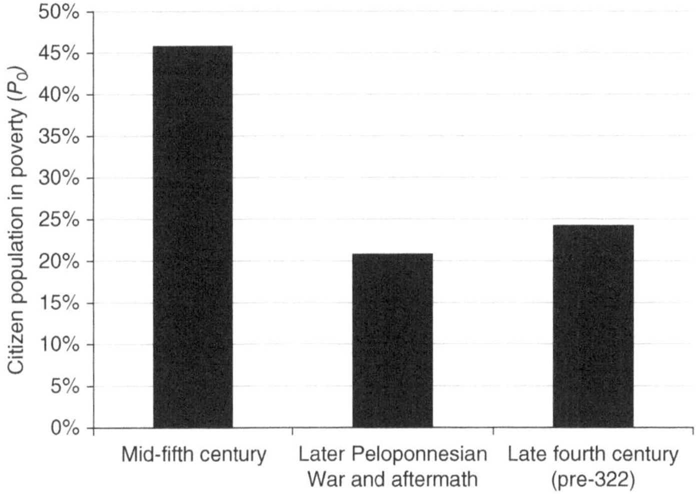

Figure 3.4. Citizen poverty in the fifth and fourth centuries (average of optimistic and pessimistic models)

Athens decline, but there was also a decrease in the intensity of their poverty (Table 3.13, Fig. 3.4).[97]

The question then is, what is the evidence for demographic change? Without detailed census figures (which were not kept by any Greek city), the evidence for a decline in the population of Athens in the late fifth century is indirect, but it is persuasive. Comparison of army strength from the outbreak of the Peloponnesian War and the Corinthian War suggests that the Athenians could not muster as many citizens to fight during the first half of the fourth century as in the 430s.[98] Epidemic disease, as described by Thucydides, implies mortality was higher than otherwise would have been the case (which, when combined with death in battle, is likely to have added up to significant numbers). Some of the political innovations of the fourth century (Assembly pay, reorganization of liturgical spending) similarly point to—though of course do not establish on their own—a smaller citizen population. In comparison, in the mid-fifth century

[97] See Appendix 2 for further discussion of the assumptions which feed these models. Note too that Fig. 3.4 shows the average of the optimistic and pessimistic models.

[98] Hansen 1985: 36–43; Strauss 1986: 78–80.

Table 3.13. Changes in citizen poverty and inequality

	Mid-fifth century		Later Peloponnesian War and aftermath		Late fourth century (pre-322)		Late fourth century (post-322)*	
	Optimistic	Pessimistic	Optimistic	Pessimistic	Optimistic	Pessimistic	Optimistic	Pessimistic
Headcount in % (P_0)	23	69	12	29	16	32	25	70
Poverty intensity (P_i)	0.071	0.214	0.038	0.091	0.051	0.100	0.300	0.300
Gini index (G)	0.44	0.54	0.37	0.45	0.38	0.48	0.59	0.63
Theil's T	0.55	0.87	0.37	0.47	0.39	0.51	0.47	0.56

Note: * See the caveats discussed in Appendix 2 (pp. 257–8).

the Athenians considered it necessary to tighten up the basis for claiming citizenship rights, the Old Oligarch noted the large presence of non-Athenians in Athens during the 440s/30s, and the enactment of Perikles' citizenship law in 451/0 suggests that the Athenians were more conscious of the non-Athenian population in their midst during this period.[99]

In sum, the size of the population (citizen and non-citizen) in the mid-fifth century does seem to have been large and appears to have been smaller by the mid-fourth century. But the size of the population is not the only—or arguably the most important—question to ask about the demography of Athens.[100] Demographic change is important not only because it tells us about the size of populations, but because of the effect of population structure on the ways in which social relationships are both configured and used. Changes in population size are important insofar as they affect the structure of that population; for example, the ratio of men to women, citizen to non-citizen, old to young or rich to poor.[101]

It is, of course, the impact of demographic change on the structure of inequality which is of primary interest here, and the first thing to consider is whether increased mortality, such as that which is suggested to have occurred during the late fifth century, affected the wealthy and the poor in different ways. Although it is possible that poorer groups might have been more susceptible to overcrowding within the city, or might have been particularly affected by war casualties through service in the fleet, it has been considered unlikely that they suffered mortality at a greater rate than the wealthy.[102] Thucydides explicitly says that the plague affected the weak and

[99] On the demographic background to Perikles' citizenship law see Patterson 1981.

[100] See Akrigg 2011: 57–9.

[101] Holleran and Pudsey 2011: 5–7 and chapters in that volume.

[102] Comparative evidence shows that elites, when they spend significant amounts of time in urban environments, lose their 'wealth advantage' when it comes to evading mortality. Roman imperial elites, Scheidel 1999 argues, could not expect to live significantly longer than the general population, and the same can be said for English peers in the sixteenth to eighteenth centuries. See Scheidel 1999: 280; Livi-Bacci 1991: 64; Johansson 1994: 114, who suggests that the rural poor may even outlive the urban elite in many societies. Kron 2012 argues that the infrastructure of ancient cities (notably, access to water) would have improved standards of living across the board, and standards of living in Athens, as we have noted, are thought to have been relatively high.

strong alike (himself and Perikles included), and hoplite losses were also heavy, which suggests that the effects were felt throughout Athenian society.[103] Additionally, many non-citizens rowed in the fleet, making them just as liable to be killed in war as citizens.[104] Increased mortality, therefore, does not seem to have been felt more strongly by one social group than another, but the *impact* of this increased mortality was.

As mentioned already, it is important to note that demographic change affects society not simply in terms of numbers (how many people died), but in terms of social structures (how were these affected by, and how did they respond to, increased mortality?). This can be seen in changes in the creation, maintenance, and instrumental use of social networks. Ober has shown the importance of the political institutions of the democracy in developing these networks for citizens.[105] His main aim is to suggest that the social networks fostered by (for example) the deme allowed the accumulation and aggregation of knowledge, which then provided a basis for informed political decision-making, but the extent to which this institutional setting encouraged the expansion of social ties, especially for non-elite citizens, which could then be exploited in business, marriage, or wealth creation, is clear from his model.[106] Any form of demographic change on the scale of that suggested for Athens would have affected these networks in a variety of ways, destroying links between people without regard to their social standing, and creating new links between others, but even a reduction of population to a much lesser degree would have effected change. Indeed, Thucydides notes the decimation of kinship groups in this context: inheritance came to those who did not expect it.

If Ober is correct in arguing that the political institutions of the democracy served to foster the creation of new networks (which were particularly useful for non-elites to gain access to power and resources), we might see that these themselves counteracted at least some of the negative social effects of increased mortality towards the end of the fifth century and into the fourth. What is important to note here is that, crucially, it is likely that this process favoured those traditionally outside the wealthy elite. Since the wealthy and socially

[103] Thuc. 2.52.2, 2.13.6; Xen. *Hell.* 4.2.17.

[104] Xen. *Hell.* 1.6.24; Diod. 13.97.1.

[105] Ober 2008: 142–55.

[106] Ober 2008: 147.

prominent did not need to rely on political institutions (particularly those for which service was limited to one year) to create their networks—they relied to a much greater extent on traditional networks of kin, symposium, and gymnasium groups for their access to wealth and power—they benefited less from the stability which these institutions provided. The networks favoured by the wealthy, therefore, were precisely those *least* able to respond quickly to demographic change, and so it is likely that the long-term *effects* of such change were felt particularly by this group. As noted by Davies, a number of the great aristocratic families of the fifth century were no longer prominent in the fourth.[107] Conversely, those who were less reliant on the power structures provided by these avenues were comparatively able to gain. The upshot is that not only did the demographic changes of the late fifth century have an impact on the distribution of property in the short-to-medium term, it is likely that they also affected the social networks which allowed citizens to gain access to resources over longer periods of time. What is also clear from this is that the institutions of the democracy helped to maintain the poorer members of society not simply with regards to political pay.

Population decline does not always bring benefits for survivors, and the effect of demographic change on the social structure need not, of course, follow the pattern suggested above.[108] But even if the degree of decline is not large as that suggested by Hansen or Akrigg, it is clear that any change would have had a wider effect than hitherto suspected, because the political culture of Athens fostered the institutions which enabled poorer citizens to build and rebuild networks to their advantage, and this was crucial for maintaining access to resources.[109] The upshot is that in late fifth- and early fourth-century Athens, those outside the wealthy elite had considerable 'bargaining power'; that is, they had access to knowledge and information which

[107] Davies 1981: 84–7, 116–17. Indeed, aristocratic groups or influence are hard to find at all.

[108] See e.g. the situation at the end of the second century CE: Jongman 2007; 2012 argues that late antiquity was characterized by the richer getting richer at the expense of the poor, and the Antonine plague was a result, rather than a cause, of already declining standards of living prompted by climate changes. It is possible, for example, that the size of the fifth-century Athenian population is overestimated (resulting in a much less stark decline), but all the evidence we have suggests that this is not the case. For discussion see Morley 2011.

[109] On social networks providing access to resources see Granovetter 1973; 1983, with Chapter 5 here. In a very different ancient Greek context: Taylor 2011c.

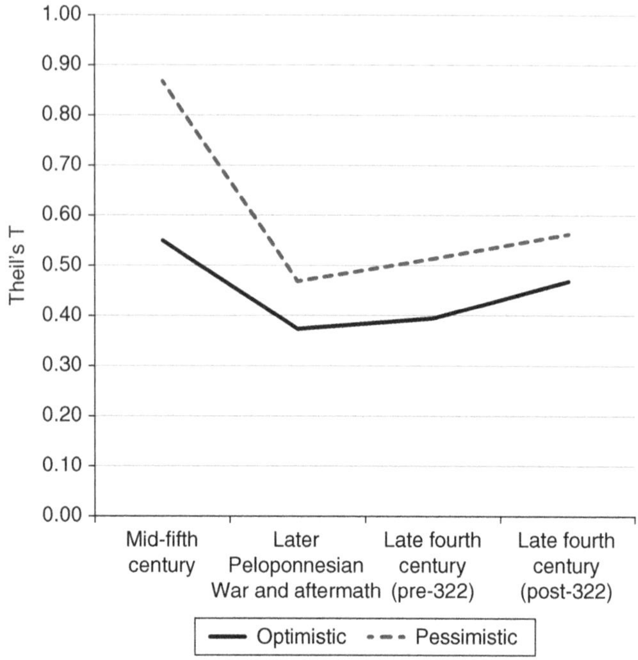

Figure 3.5. Citizen inequality in the fifth and fourth centuries

could be used in a variety of ways, high levels of political autonomy and self-determination (at least for citizens), and family structures which were maintained despite the exiles of 404 and the civil war which followed.[110] The allocation of political pay to the Assembly gave poorer citizens immediate access to financial resources, thereby lifting them from bare subsistence levels and reinforcing the positive aspects of democratic participation on Athenian society at large. At the same time, the resources of the wealthy were under strain. This implies that the gap between rich and poor was narrowing—at least for a short period of time.[111]

[110] Access to knowledge/information: Ober 2008; restoration of democracy and subsequent amnesty: Loraux 2002; Wolpert 2002; political autonomy/self-determination: Thuc. 2.34–46; maintenance of family structures during periods of stress: Xen. *Mem.* 2.7.1–14.

[111] There is evidence to suggest that after *c.*350 this changed: see discussion in Chapter 5.

Figure 3.5 provides a schematized view of what this change might have looked like. Drawn from the data in Tables 3.12 and 3.13 (Ober's model is supplemented by van Wees 2011 for the post-322 period), it graphs the decrease in citizen inequality measured by Theil's T from the mid-fifth to the late fourth century. Like the Gini index, this measures inequality on a scale of 0 to 1, where 0 is equality and 1 is inequality.[112] Even on the most optimistic scenario, there is a small-to-moderate decrease in inequality from the mid-fifth century to the fourth century before inequality rises again throughout the course of the fourth century. A more pessimistic (realistic?) interpretation is that citizen income inequality did indeed fall considerably during this period before growing again throughout the fourth century. Inequality between citizens in Athens was therefore at its lowest in the late fifth and early fourth centuries.

POVERTY AND INEQUALITY IN ATHENS

Measuring poverty and inequality reframes the discourses of poverty that we see in the literary evidence. Although all measurement tools (like all historical methodologies) have their advantages and disadvantages, together they point to a consistent picture of poverty and inequality in Athens: that even if Athens was an affluent society, a significant proportion of the citizen population was relatively poor compared with their fellow citizens in both income and wealth terms, that an even bigger proportion of the non-citizen population was, but that these figures are dwarfed by those from the second-century CE Roman Empire. There are strong indications that there were far fewer poor in Athens than in Rome, and that Roman poverty was considerably more intense than that in Athens.

Viewing these models side by side with the evidence discussed in Chapter 2 forms an important backdrop to the Athenian elite's discomfort with poverty and praise of moderation that is evident in the literature of the late fifth and fourth centuries. The greater sensitivity of authors to the existence of *penia* and the problems of excessive wealth might not have arisen as a result of considerable poverty

[112] For discussion of the statistic and assumptions that feed the graph see Appendix 2.

Table 3.14. Summary of late fourth-century Athenian income and wealth distribution

	Income		Wealth
	Total population*	Citizen population*	Citizen population
Mean (dr.)	2,068	2,068	20,680
Median (dr.)	450	450	2,650
Standard deviation	3,040	3,040	68,661
Coefficient of variation	1.47	1.47	3.00
Gini	0.40–0.45 *(0.39–0.47)*	0.33–0.41 *(0.38–0.48)*	0.71
Headcount (P_0), %	41–57 *(41–56)*	17–33 *(16–32)*	55
Poverty gap (P_1)	0.311	0.311	0.647
Poverty severity (P_2)	0.097	0.097	0.418
Poverty intensity (P_i)	0.128–0.176 *(0.127–0.174)*	0.052–0.104 *(0.051–0.100)*	0.354
Ordinal (P_s)	0.184–0.253 *(0.183–0.250)*	0.075–0.149 *(0.073–0.144)*	0.010
'Poverty line' (z), dr.	225	225	1,325
Mean income of poor (dr.)	155	155	468

Note: * Figures in italicized brackets show changes that occur if Ober's 'elite' category is increased from 400 citizen men to 1,200–1,500: see Appendix 1.

Sources: Ober 2010; Kron 2011.

amongst the population of Attica, but was instead a reaction against the changing texture of inequality within the community as a whole (Table 3.14 summarizes the Athenian data). That is, such discourses point towards a noticeable change in the distribution of wealth or income in Athens, rather than being a result of large and constant numbers of very poor people. Despite the economic turmoil of the Peloponnesian War and its aftermath, not all Athenians were impoverished during these years, nor was the city destroyed. Economic inequality appears to have been greater in the mid-fifth century and the late fourth century (especially after the end of democracy) than it was during the period of greatest democratic activity (late fifth to mid–late fourth centuries). Things began to change around *c.*350, however, as Chapter 5 will discuss in greater depth.

The discussion here emphasizes the importance of viewing poverty and inequality as dynamic and subject to change over time, but it cannot answer questions about how poverty was experienced, and here we need to turn back to the qualitative evidence. Necessarily, the emphasis in this chapter has been on the material side of poverty, but as I have already argued, this is only one part of what it means to be poor. Tracing through the ramifications of these models can only go so far in answering that question, even when we focalize them from the point of view of those who were towards the bottom of the wealth or income distribution. The following chapters, therefore, look more closely at the diversity of poverty experiences, emphasizing in contrast the non-material aspects of poverty. Doing so allows us to raise questions about the structures, processes, and institutions which shaped the picture of Athenian society suggested here—the tangible resources such as political pay as well as those less tangible resources that are provided through various social networks. It also allows us to consider the agency of those who were categorized as poor to negotiate their own well-being in a variety of ways. The remainder of this book, therefore, will view poverty in terms of social relations and consider in greater depth the multiple experiences of *penia*.

4

Experiencing *Penia*

The Dynamics of Poverty

Whilst previous chapters have examined the discourses of poverty and the problems related to its measurement, this chapter explores the temporalities of poverty experiences and their diversity. I will argue here, and in the remainder of this book, that poverty needs to be understood not just in terms of a set of discourses which presents *plousios* and *penia* as contrasting conditions (contested though these positions are), or as a state that someone is in or not in as a result of the presence or absence of wealth or income, but rather as a sociological set of relationships within a temporal and dynamic framework. Aspects of poverty, whether material or non-material, are subject to change over time and over circumstance. They are also shaped by the very discourses through which they are brought to light. By recognizing the ideas about poverty that circulated in Athens in the classical period and reading these within a dynamic framework, it is possible to distinguish more clearly between different types and different experiences of poverty. As is clear from the previous chapters, poverty is not a monolithic condition nor an unchanging category. We should therefore expect to discern different experiences of, as well as different views about, poverty within the source material.

This chapter will therefore consider poverty as multidimensional and dynamic. It does so by isolating three principal ways in which poverty can be examined: in terms of duration, in terms of depth, and in terms of differential experiences. Together, these case studies frame poverty not as a discourse (though it draws on these), nor as a material condition (though it involves this too), but as the outcome of a complex and socially embedded set of processes.[1] The material discussed here is therefore deliberately varied, chosen because it highlights the diversity of *penia* as a lived experience.

In what follows, I use the term 'duration' to refer to the length of time households spent in hardship (as defined by those households themselves) and consider the temporality of these spells (that is, whether they were long or short). Viewing poverty in this way places emphasis on its conjunctural nature, whereby it is experienced as a result of a crisis or series of crises.[2] This provides insight into the types of precipitating events that led to hardship which are attested in the source material, and outlines how the Athenians responded to them—or, at least, presented themselves as responding to them. 'Depth', on the other hand, differentiates between poverty which is transitory and that which is chronic; that is, instead of time being the key variable it is the persistence of poverty that is under investigation. There is, of course, a relationship between duration and depth: those for whom poverty is persistent are poorer for longer periods of time. By drawing on the discussion of the narratives surrounding *ptocheia* outlined in Chapter 2, and contrasting these with subsistence approaches to understanding poverty, I argue, however, for the reframing of chronic poverty in terms of social recategorization rather than viewed solely in terms of economic deficiency.

Finally, because experiences of poverty in Athens varied according to civic status, age, and gender, the final part of this chapter will examine poverty through a gendered lens. By doing so this chapter deliberately views poverty within the context of social relations in order to act as a counterweight to the discourse which constructs poverty as a stable, or bounded, economic condition only worth discussing when it affected male citizens.[3] Because the processes of production and survival of source material mirror and reinforce the structures of power which frequently work to silence various groups within Athenian society, it is necessary to decouple the idea of 'poverty' from that of 'lack of wealth' (or indeed, 'moral deficiency') and instead emphasize its multidimensionality. Seeing how poverty affected women differently from men—and the means by which

[1] Green and Hulme 2005; Green 2009; Chicone 2011b.

[2] On conjunctural poverty see Garnsey 1998: 226–7; Morley 2006: 28–9; Allen and Sitzler 2009: 26–7; Galbois and Rougier-Blanc 2014a: 18–19.

[3] Richard 2011; Spencer-Wood 2011.

women could foster their own responses to it—provides an important corollary to this discourse. Here we will draw on debates within the field of feminist economics in order to reframe some of the ideas about poverty highlighted in Chapter 2.

TEMPORALITIES: THE DURATION OF POVERTY

The discussion begins with an exploration of the temporality of poverty in order to place an emphasis on the processes through which poverty occurred. Central to the discussion here, because of its conjunctural nature, is the concept of transitory poverty. This is poverty experienced for a relatively short period of time, often as a result of events which are predictable: the birth of a child, for example, the death or incapacitation of a member of the household, or the marriage of a son or daughter.[4] Events such as these potentially result in hardship for the household as a whole and may require adaptation (borrowing, selling property, finding new opportunities for labour, reducing consumption, and so on) as well as new strategies to ward against future crises.[5] Previous research suggests that peasant households in the ancient Greek world—employing strategies such as these—were fairly resilient against food shortages; if this is the case then we should be thinking more in terms of transitory than chronic, or persistent, poverty, at least for citizen families who owned land.[6] However, households with fewer resources to begin with, those who were landless or with weak social networks to draw upon in times of difficulty, or those which experienced a series of crises over time, must have been disproportionately affected by isolated events such as these and therefore more likely to experience longer spells of poverty.

Poverty, viewed in these terms, is dynamic, and it is this dynamism which allows different types of poverty experiences to be identified. By looking at the circumstances in which Athenians claim that they have

[4] Barrett, Carter, and Little 2006: 168–9. Not all causes of transitory poverty are internal to the household. External factors such as food shortages, drought, war, and so on, can also be precipitating factors, but the distinction here is between events that are recoverable from and those which might be seen in terms of structural constraints (on these see Chapter 5).

[5] See Gallant 1991. Foxhall 2007 discusses the temporalities of strategies of wealthier households.

[6] Gallant 1991.

fallen into poverty, or otherwise suffered hardship, we can elaborate on the observation in Chapter 2 that poverty was considered to be something to fear. There it was argued that sentiments of this kind are always presented through the eyes of the relatively prosperous, and the examples discussed here reinforce that notion. This type of poverty is nearly always presented as being relatively short-term and as having solutions. These experiences of poverty—the types of events that the Athenians singled out as precipitating hardship and which are described as pushing the otherwise non-poor into more difficult circumstances—can, then, be juxtaposed with the discussion in Chapter 5 which focuses on how poverty was structurally reproduced (that is, experiences of poverty that are longer-term and intergenerational). Taken together, both of these discussions provide insight into the multiple processes which gave rise to poverty.

Transitory Poverty

What kinds of events are associated with periods of hardship? The literary sources provide a number of examples, but these also problematize poverty in ways which we have noted already. For example, Xenophon tells the story of Aristarchos in the *Memorabilia*, whose house in the Piraeus was filled with his female relatives after the revolution of the Thirty.[7] Fourteen members of the family lived together at this time, 'without counting the slaves', and Aristarchos describes the pressures which this placed on the family as a whole.[8] The episode is well known: Sokrates offers Aristarchos advice to ease his *aporia*, he swallows his pride, borrows money, puts his household to work making clothes, and everyone, eventually, is happy.[9] As I have noted elsewhere, this episode is useful for thinking about the

[7] Xen. *Mem.* 2.7.1–14. [8] Xen. *Mem.* 2.7.2.

[9] On the episode see Gray 1998: 12–13, 136–7. The question of whether this has historical value is a difficult one, bound up in Xenophon's representation of Sokrates within the *Memorabilia* and in other writings. For the sake of argument, it is assumed here that he presents situations which were readily recognizable for a fourth-century audience, regardless of whether the details of the specific encounters are literary constructions or whether this is a romanticized portrayal of the past. One does not need to accept that Aristarchos had this conversation with Sokrates to recognize that these were the types of concerns which did pervade Athenian society during this period. Arguably, literary elements in the work (the motif of usefulness, juxtaposition of new and old, helping impoverished friends) reflect Athenian social concerns in the fourth century.

importance of kinship networks in poverty alleviation.[10] Going to live with their wealthy relative was a crucial strategy for the sisters, nieces, and cousins of Aristarchos when faced with crisis, and the decision to manufacture clothes ensured that the misfortune was temporary. Aristarchos, after all, had access to considerable resources before 404: he owned land, he rented out a house, he owned enough movable property that he could envision selling it in hard times, and he was able to borrow money.[11]

Aristarchos attributes his current hardship to the *stasis* of 404 and the social obligations he had for his female relatives.[12] He complains that their living conditions were now overcrowded and that food was short: 'it's hard', he says to Sokrates, 'to watch your relatives perish (*apollumenous*), but impossible to feed (*trephein*) so many in times like these.'[13] The family was certainly worse off than before, and no doubt suffering real hardship, but they were not so impoverished that they could not alleviate their situation. Even after their misfortune they were not the poorest of the poor: the women could rely on Aristarchos' hospitality, and he was sufficiently well connected to find someone to lend to him even in the dire circumstances of 404/3.[14] There is no suggestion that the slaves be sold to raise capital or to ease pressure on resources; on the contrary, they are assumed to be part of the household.[15]

Euxitheos, the speaker of Demosthenes 57, also describes the hardship his family went through as a result of war. His father, Thoukritos, was away fighting with Thrasyboulos during the latter part of the Peloponnesian War, taken prisoner, sold into slavery in Leukas, ransomed, and eventually made his way back to Athens after a period of some years.[16] Euxitheos uses his absence as a justification

[10] Taylor 2016. Also on this episode see the comments of Gallant 1991: 154; Millett 1991: 73–4; Cahill 2005: 60.

[11] Xen. *Mem*. 2.7.2.

[12] See also *Ath. Pol*. 56.6 (legal protection for elderly parents), Lys. 3.6 (brother takes in sister after death of husband).

[13] Xen. *Mem*. 2.7.2.

[14] Xen. *Mem*. 2.7.12.

[15] But see Garnsey 1988: 34 for the idea that slaves were 'unsaleable in famine conditions': it is possible that they would receive no buyers. Regardless, it is telling that Aristarchos does not even bring this up when discussing his possibilities (Xen. *Mem*. 2.7.2).

[16] Dem. 57.18–19, 42. This, according to Euxitheos, was a long enough period of time to be used as an explanation of his father's foreign accent. Lacey 1980: 59 suggests 10–15 years.

for Nikarete's activities as a wet-nurse and ribbon-seller in the agora, activities thought of as servile and/or foreign.[17] He says that this was a not-infrequent recourse for citizen women in times of hardship. Whether this was true or not we do not know, but the effect was to normalize this activity; Euxitheos thinks, at least, that he can rely on the sympathy of the jury here. And crucially, he argues that strategies like this were successful: 'many who were poor then [that is, in previous years when the city suffered misfortune] are now rich.'[18] I will return presently to the complex web of dependency relations between wet-nurses and their employers and what this means for an understanding of gendered aspects of poverty.[19] Here it is important to note that the example of Euxitheos' family reveals multiple events which are associated with a slide into poverty: war, enslavement, and absence of a family member on the one hand, perhaps also the death or illness of a mother on the other.

What is notable about these examples is that not only do they provide information about the types of events which caused hardship for families, but they are framed to highlight that the protagonists are not at fault; they are the sufferers of misfortune rather than poor estate-managers. They also provide evidence for the strategies used to ameliorate the situations described: Euxitheos' mother takes on paid work, Aristarchos provides for a wider group of relatives that he would have ordinarily. No doubt this is due to the nature of the source material in which these examples are preserved—these are families which experienced relative prosperity at some point in their lives—but as far as we can tell, strategies such as these were successful: Aristarchos is portrayed as the bringer of happiness to his family, Euxitheos believes his opponent will attack him for being wealthy.[20] Citizens who have experienced episodes of hardship, or who present themselves as doing so, are not uncommon.[21] There were undoubtedly many more examples which do not survive in the historical record.

There are numerous other types of events that might have pushed families into temporary crisis, such as the birth of a child if resources were scarce, the inability to pay back debts, or untimely disease or death, but it is clear that when events like these are mentioned they

[17] Dem. 57.35, 41 with discussion on pp. 135–6. [18] Dem. 57.45.
[19] See pp. 135–40. [20] Dem. 57.52–3.
[21] On the claims of poverty as argument in lawcourt speeches see Cecchet 2013. See also Chapter 2.

mostly refer to those who had some kind of resources to start with.[22] This is significant in itself: on the one hand it provides a useful catalogue of the types of events which were perceived to be potentially catastrophic and highlights the fluidity of wealth—important observations in themselves—but these are responses filtered through the experiences of male citizens whose strategies for survival and/or prosperity were ultimately successful. As Foxhall has shown, wealthier households were likely to develop strategies of diversification, owning different types of property and having multiple, different income streams.[23] Poorer households would be more vulnerable to the types of events outlined here because they would have had fewer assets to draw on. More important for these groups would have been seasonal variations in work, either through political pay (military service, jury work, and so on), building projects, or agricultural labour, which undoubtedly would have affected the ability to buffer life-cycle events such as the birth of a child or the death of an adult, or sudden and unforeseen expenses such as ransoms.

Additionally, and perhaps more importantly, it highlights how relations of power dominate not only the discourses of poverty but also the historical processes that preserve those statements for historians to uncover. The most direct evidence we have for the types of household events which potentially led to spells of 'poverty' are strongly rooted within the experiences and lifestyles of relatively prosperous male citizens. Although women are crucial parts of these narratives, their experiences of poverty are filtered through the world of their male relatives. I will return to discuss this point presently, but the conclusion I wish to draw now is that the most socially isolated—the poorest—are rendered powerless by these processes.[24]

THE DEPTH OF POVERTY

Thinking about the temporality of poverty is useful for distinguishing the processes through which different groups of Athenians became or

[22] Roubineau 2014 investigates the abandonment of children as a possible response to poverty, arguing that it was not perceived solely as a practice of the poor but as an economically rational act by those of all levels of wealth (i.e. it forms a part of good estate management).

[23] Foxhall 2007.

[24] Green 2007; Richard 2011.

remained poor (I will return to this question in Chapter 5), but the metaphor of 'depth' can also be a useful conceptual tool. This not only recognizes the diversity of poverty experiences (for example, the difference between transitory and persistent poverty), but also highlights its relational nature.[25] Deprivation occurs, after all, in degrees, encompassing the needs of basic subsistence as well as social isolation or exclusion, and it is shaped by the discourses used to construct or describe the poor. In Chapter 3 I suggested that one way to think about the depth of poverty was through poverty-intensity measurements. Here I want to outline how different conceptualizations of deprivation challenge the way we think about this question. I will start by considering the value and problems of subsistence approaches, before reimagining chronic poverty (destitution) not from a financial or temporal point of view, but as social reordering.

Ancient sources—particularly comic drama—frequently portray the population of Athens as hungry. Fantasies of food are commonplace on the comic stage, implying that not having enough to eat was a common part of life, and food shortages have been suggested to have occurred at various points throughout the classical period.[26] Access to food, and food stability, are clearly an important part of poverty discourses, and it appears to make sense to ask, then, whether those living in Athens had their food needs met. A number of historians have pursued the question of subsistence, attempting to outline the basic minimum needed to survive by identifying the calorific requirements required to avoid starvation.[27] Calorific needs for adults have been estimated, which range from less than 2,000 to over 3,000 calories per day, and depend on different factors such as age, gender, and levels of activity.[28] This has led to some fairly pessimistic conclusions: despite arguing for the resilience of peasant households, Gallant, for example, describes life in the ancient world

[25] Green and Hulme 2005: 873–6; Richard 2011: 175–6.

[26] Hunger or poor-quality food: Ar. *Plut.* 253, 283, Autokrates F 3, Kratinos F 47, 346, 349, Eupolis F 16, 77, 275, 347, Pherekrates F 14, 61, 172. Fantasies of abundance: Ar. *Plut.* 802–22, Kratinos F 149, 150, 154, 155, Pherekrates F 113. On food shortages see p. 18, n. 50.

[27] Foxhall and Forbes 1982; Garnsey 1988 (and for Rome: Garnsey 1998: 226–52); Gallant 1991. For a critique see Galbois and Rougier-Blanc 2014a: 18–19.

[28] See Foxhall and Forbes 1982: 47–50; Gallant 1991: 62–75 for discussion of the variability of calorific requirements and the difficulties of assessing this in an ancient context.

as 'highly precarious . . . With alarming regularity [ancient Greek peasants] would have found themselves running short of food in the face of climatically induced shortfalls in production.'[29] However, recent analysis of skeletal material suggests nutrition in Athens was comparatively good for a pre-modern society.[30] Vitamin-deficient diseases, such as anaemia, did affect the Athenian population, but they are at their lowest during the classical period.[31] This suggests that these approaches need to be balanced by asking other questions too.

This is not to claim that no one ever went hungry in Athens, but the food shortages we can detect, for example those of the 330s, are most commonly considered to have been short-term supply problems, from which it is thought the population (as a whole) ultimately—and quickly—recovered.[32] And whilst this overrides different individual or household responses to such shortfalls which undoubtedly would have occurred, it does imply that the hardship experienced as a result of a reduced grain supply was, for large numbers of people, transitory rather than persistent. This picture seems to fit with the food fantasies of comic drama: this also seems to imply that such hardships were familiar enough to Athenian society, although we cannot, of course, uncover the degree to which some groups were affected more than others. However, it is problematic to place the comic evidence centre-stage, since almost all of the fragments which survive—and which produce such a vivid picture of the desirability of certain types of food items—are preserved in Athenaios' *Deipnosophistai*, a text which is situated at an unfeasibly large symposium where guests quote passages of Greek literature in order to display their cultural knowledge of food. Whilst by no means intending to underplay the appearance of food-related discourse in these texts, it is likely that they overemphasize the centrality of food fantasy to comic drama, and this limits the ability of historians to extrapolate meaningful information about the centrality of these ideas to an Athenian reality of poverty.

In comparison, Ober's approach to subsistence (see his model discussed in Chapter 3) is not so much focused on deriving the

[29] Gallant 1991: 110. However, see Hodkinson 2000: 390–1 for a critique of Gallant's methodology which results in an 'over-estimation of the peasant household's subsistence difficulties'.

[30] Lagia 2015a; 2015b with discussion on pp. 17–18.

[31] Lagia 2014: 106 with figs. 6 and 7.

[32] Garnsey 1988; Moreno 2007: 310–11. See further pp. 182–3.

minimum food intake needed for survival, as in identifying a subsistence range in income terms (from less than 2 to approximately 4½ obols per household per day).[33] These ranges are subject to scrutiny, of course, but they probably capture an important aspect of the lives of the poor—that is, that income and consumption were variable, both within the groups that can be categorized as poor and within households themselves on a day-to-day or longer-term basis.

Subsistence measures can be an important tool because they encourage examination of the 'very basics' needed to survive. However, to conceptualize poverty solely in terms of subsistence ignores significant aspects of what it means to be poor, and is, therefore, more problematic than at first appears.[34] Approaches which focus exclusively on subsistence—those, for example, which attempt to establish calorific minima—are, in effect, attempting to draw a kind of 'poverty line' below which survival is difficult, unpleasant, or impossible. But, as discussed in the previous chapter, poverty lines in themselves reveal nothing about the duration, depth, or experience of poverty, and gloss over the structural relationships which keep the poor poor.[35] Identifying a subsistence range allows emphasis to be placed elsewhere, but nevertheless, both approaches imply that—with certain behaviours—households will be able to cross a threshold into not being poor. These, however, rarely distinguish what 'not being poor' might look like or how those behaviours are socially and culturally constructed.[36] They also assume that subsistence is a static rather than dynamic state of being, whereas research shows that even the most chronic forms of poverty changes over time, as spells of even the most severe hardship can be compensated for with relative success.[37]

[33] Ober 2010: 121–2. Ober models between 5,000 and 10,000 citizen men (equating to between 22,500 and 35,000 people if their families are included) in his subsistence range, with a minimum of around 100 dr. income per year. Including metics and slaves brings the total to between approximately 98,500 and 135,000 people, i.e. 41–57% of a population of 250,000. This sounds like a lot, but if this is our definition of poverty Athens has fewer poor than many modern democratic states, according to World Bank Development Reports: see Krishna 2008: 2 (69% of the population of Mozambique, for example, live in poverty). Those living at subsistence are outnumbered by those living above it by a minimum of 2:1 and as much as 5:1, according to Ober.

[34] See also Galbois and Rougier-Blanc 2014a: 18–20.

[35] Carter and Barrett 2006; Lister 2004: 41–3.

[36] See e.g. the discourse on good estate management (p. 47).

[37] Addison, Hulme, and Kanbur 2009a. Ober's subsistence ranges, therefore, might go some way to reflect this.

These approaches also implicitly assume the extremely unlikely scenario that households stop production or refuse to engage in any further labour as soon as they have (for example) enough to eat, rather than developing strategies to accumulate further.[38] The poverty threshold might be crossed, but how and for what purpose?

If poverty is viewed in subsistence terms alone, chronic or persistent poverty is reduced to a state of not having enough to eat or not having an income which reaches a defined level. That the calorific requirements and income levels are—to a large degree—rather arbitrary (and imposed by historians—that is, outsiders) is less problematic than the fact that this approach misses the social context through which poverty derives meaning. Instead of thinking about the depth of poverty in terms of subsistence alone, then (a question I will return to in Chapter 6 from a different angle), I want here to consider how social relations shape chronic poverty, and in particular, destitution. We have seen in Chapter 2 how *ptocheia* is socially constructed to be an emotional intensifier, and that *ptochoi* are depicted as dishonourable outsiders. In being portrayed so they are distinct from *penetes* in their social isolation, providing a touchstone from which *penia* can be defined and distanced.[39] As Roubineau argues, *ptochoi* were considered lazy and useless in contrast to the work and activity that is associated with *penetes*, an observation which exemplifies this distinction.[40] As discussed in Chapter 2, the term *ptochos* is never used to describe real beggars: in tragedy they are always aristocrats in disguise, whereas in oratory the term is used to articulate problematic social mobility.[41] They are never depicted in visual culture outside of a mythic context, and even this is not common.[42] Aside from Plato's

[38] See Foxhall 2007: 38–42. Indeed, Gallant 1991 himself discusses many of these accumulation strategies.

[39] Roubineau 2013: 17–18, 21; Coin-Longeray 2014a: 57–61.

[40] Roubineau 2013: 36.

[41] This can be used (i) as an insult, e.g. Dem. 18.131; (ii) as an example of political instability or the embezzlement of politicians, e.g. Dem. 3.29, 8.66, 10.68, 23.209, 62.53, Lys. 30.27; and/or (iii) as an example of an absolute fall from a previous social position, e.g. Lys. 32.10 (and discussion here). See further Roubineau 2013: 21–3; Galbois and Rougier-Blanc 2014b: 43 and compare with the Roman and late antique sources where 'real' beggars are depicted: see Parkin 2006.

[42] Odysseus disguised as a beggar appears occasionally, but is not as common as scenes of Odysseus as a young, heroic man. Geras appears with Herakles in a few scenes (though of the six examples in the Beazley archive none were found in Athens, which suggests this is not a scene popular for the Athenian market). See further

desire to expel *ptochoi* from his ideal polis, they were not outlawed or prevented from congregating in certain parts of the city: no actual surviving law mentions them.[43] *Ptochoi*, therefore, are not only voiceless but actively deprived of any kind of voice.[44]

These depictions of *ptochoi* as wanderers or exiles, dressed in rags and lacking nourishment, serve to cast them as socially isolated rather than living below a 'poverty line'.[45] That is, *ptocheia* is a social status, created by the reordering of entitlements, rather than an economic condition characterized by lacking wealth. *Ptochoi* are, after all, and as we have seen, outsiders without polis or *oikos*. The same is true of *parasitoi* (men who sponge dinners without invitation or reciprocation, depicted particularly in the fragments of fourth-century comedy that survive in Athenaios' work). Depicted as insatiable yet idle, as lacking autonomy and moderation, they are recast as anti-social figures: servile and degraded. But as recent studies have shown, they are equally likely to be depicted as gluttons interested only in luxury eating than as men driven to extremes because of poverty or a need for food.[46] That is, they become socially recast as a result of the community's judgement of their behaviour, defined not against the wealthy elite but the ordinary citizen.

This shift of emphasis is important because it highlights that poverty is a product of social relations, which shapes—and is shaped by—the discourses of poverty discussed in Chapter 2 as much as it is a question of having enough to eat. Sometimes these discourses are very distinctly controlled by men of wealth for their own ends, but in other cases there are more complex mechanisms at play. When wealthy men claim in court that their families are, or will be, reduced to

Villanueva-Puig 2013: 100–6 and Jacquet-Rimassa 2014: 185–8, who discuss the meagre evidence.

[43] Pl. *Laws* 936c. This is in contrast to the diversity of anti-vagrancy laws in Europe and the USA: see e.g. Kusmer 2001; Beier 2008, or indeed anti-begging laws in late antiquity: see Patlagean 1997: 20. Rougier-Blanc 2014: 111–12 associates *ptochoi* with *xenoi*, as both are defined by their wanderings (at least in the Homeric poems), arguing that the responses to them, and the liminal spaces they occupied within the city, were similar.

[44] See Harriss-White 2005: 882, who argues that destitution is not just the state of having nothing, it is also being nothing.

[45] Roubineau 2013: 36 sees this in terms of social death which provides an interesting analogy with slavery (Patterson 1982). See also Corner 2013b: 227, who argues that *ptocheia* is 'a contingent circumstance that may befall any man', i.e. it is configured in terms of (lost) autonomy.

[46] Corner 2013a; 2013b.

ptocheia, this is a rhetorical ploy which draws on the emotionality of *ptocheia* to build a narrative of social worth. For example, the speaker of Lysias 32, a speech which deals with the mismanagement of an estate after the death of an extremely wealthy father, presents his case in terms of moral justice. He is speaking on behalf of his brother-in-law, a young man who has recently come of age to discover that his uncle (who is also his grandfather and the guardian of the estate) has squandered his inheritance. The speaker puts into the mouth of the young man's mother a condemnatory speech in which she criticizes the behaviour of the uncle, who is also her own father, a man named Diogeiton.[47] Here she juxtaposes the behaviour of Diogeiton towards her own sons (his grandsons) with that towards her younger half-siblings. They are being brought up in affluence, whereas her children have been thrown out of their house and disgraced as *ptochoi* rather than treated as the *plousioi* they are. Her sons are described as if they are destitute: they are 'wearing only threadbare garments, without shoes, without attendants, without bedding, without clothing, without the household furniture their father left them, and without the sums on deposit which he placed in . . . [Diogeiton's] hands'.[48] The argument here is not that there is no money left—the daughter is careful to acknowledge that Diogeiton is absolutely right to bring up his own children in prosperity (καὶ ταῦτα μὲν καλῶς ποιεῖς), but that her children do not deserve to be treated differently from his. They do not deserve to be poor, they do not deserve to be socially isolated from the rest of the family (or from society at large). It is a question of social worth, whereby the sons have been recategorized as non-deserving members of the family, a status the mother actively resists.

Inheritance disputes like this one—commissioned by men of considerable property—attempt to gain control of a changing social order within the family by asserting their claim over patrimony and seizing control over this process of recategorization. Where the speaker of Lysias 32 argues that the sons of Diodotos do not deserve to be treated as poor, Aristodemos' son (the speaker of [Demosthenes] 44) constructs a case which claims that his side of the family deserve the four-generations-old estate of Archiades (his grandfather's uncle) because they are poor. He demonizes the behaviour of Leochares and emphasizes his own father's poverty and powerlessness. His family are poor,

[47] Lys. 32.15–17. [48] Lys. 32.16.

but deserving; Leochares' is neither poor nor deserving. In a similar fashion Apollodoros goes out of his way to emphasize the servility of his stepfather, and former slave of his father, Phormion, whilst highlighting the *endeia* (need) of his own (citizen) daughters. The purpose is to paint Phormion as undeserving of Pasion's fortune and himself as deserving.

This rhetoric of social worth linked to claims of poverty and (imagined, or perhaps, feared) destitution by men who were wealthy works partly because it is designed to appeal to the jurors' sense of pity or outrage. But it also demonstrates how crucial it is to conceptualize poverty in terms of social relations, and that these are a matter of concern for the whole community. When wealthy litigants make these claims they are attempting to use the broader community (the jury) to recategorize the social position of their opponents and place them outside the normative social relations of the family. They are able to do this because poverty for them—whether articulated in terms of *penia* or (the more emotionally fraught) *ptocheia*—was a conceptual tool which enabled them to actively define and redefine (their own and other people's) entitlements.[49] That it is directed in these instances towards their relatively wealthy relatives merely serves to emphasize that poverty is not solely an economic condition but a social status—like slavery—which is created through relations of power. Although our evidence only permits examples that are very firmly rooted within the world of the *plousioi*, they do show how these processes of social reordering might work in practice throughout Athenian society in general. As Corner states with regard to the parasite, 'it is not poverty and dependence that make him useless, but rather uselessness that makes him poor and dependent'.[50] Destitution, therefore, is more than the space between poverty and death.[51] It is the most chronic form of disempowerment.

POVERTY EXPERIENCES: GENDERED POVERTY

This chapter began with the anecdote of Aristarchos and his female relatives. They were advised by Sokrates, so Xenophon tells the story,

[49] See Green 2009. [50] Corner 2013a: 55.

[51] See e.g. Morley 2006: 29, who draws a distinction between poverty and destitution, arguing that the latter is a state which is definitionally temporary: 'most of [those in destitution] would quickly recover or perish.'

to use their skills to make clothes for sale. After some persuasion, Aristarchos agrees, and whilst the women appear to have been unused to such work, they nonetheless gained reward from their labour.[52] By the end of the anecdote Aristarchos is himself cast in the role of dependant, not the women, a role-reversal much like that of Charmides discussed in Chapter 2.[53] He has to reassert his masculinity by becoming a guard-dog, not merely to protect but in order to have a role within his family at all.[54] This episode not only, therefore, provides an insight into the strategies of families to ameliorate their hardship, but also demonstrates the importance of viewing poverty through a gendered lens. Since men and women in Athenian society had distinct ideologically defined roles, the distribution of resources—and the mechanisms by which these allowed both men and women to function—are likely to have been different.[55] Men and women did not necessarily have access to the same resources, did not necessarily use them in the same way, nor imbue them with the same meanings. In sum, poverty is highly likely to have affected women and men differently in the ancient world, because poverty is structured in a gendered way.[56]

The reason for investigating the gendered nature of poverty is not to argue that women were disproportionately poorer than men, although it is probably true that the opportunities for personal financial enrichment were fewer for women: the most profitable activities outside the household (tax-farming, banking, land ownership) seem to have been exclusive to men.[57] Nor is it to point out that women could, and did, control property of various kinds from land, to loans, to slaves, as well as moveable goods like furniture and clothes.[58] One difficulty with this approach is that it is not personal property but the *oikos* which is the best unit of analysis here.[59] Resources were tied to the *oikos* as a whole, and so the lines between 'men's property' and

[52] Xen. *Mem.* 2.7.12. [53] See pp. 58–9. [54] Xen. *Mem.* 2.7.13–14.

[55] As noted by e.g. Johnstone 2003: 271: 'women acted in relationship to property under very different conditions than men', with further bibliography in following notes.

[56] Daly 1992; Jackson 1998; Razavi 1999; Nussbaum 2000b; Molyneux 2002.

[57] See further Ste. Croix 1970; Cohen 1992; Burford 1993; Stroud 1998.

[58] Land: *Agora XIX*: P5, ll. 62–70. Loans: Dem. 41.8; *SEG* 42.149. Clothing: the Brauron dedications (*IG* II^2 1514–30) include Amorgan linen (or possibly silk), purple (*halourgos*) clothes, gold-plated decorative items or clothes decorated with gold, clothes such as the *cheirodotos* or *kandys* which were associated with Persia, and ritual cloaks (*chlainis*). See Foxhall 1989; Harris 1992; D. Cohen 1998; Cleland 2005.

[59] Foxhall 2007. On the socialization of women within the *oikos* see Foxhall 2003.

Table 4.1. Age at death of fourth-century skeletal material (Kerameikos)

Age	Male	Female	Unclassifiable	Total
Under 20	0	3	9	12
20–9	4	9	1	14
30–9	6	11	0	17
40+	14	6	0	20
Unknown	3	13	23	39
Total	27	42	33	102

Note: The data are drawn from the Corner Terrace, the *peribolos* of Demetria and Pamphile, and the *peribolos* of the Messenians only. A number of skeletons have been destroyed since discovery (particularly those excavated in the early twentieth century). Bisel's tables are therefore expanded upon with the aid of Kovacsovics's catalogue, but the age and sex identifications here may be less reliable. The outlined trend is still visible, however, from Bisel's study alone.

Sources: Bisel 1990: 152, 158, with Kovacsovics 1990.

'women's property' are inevitably blurred: this, at least, is the implication of, for example, the inheritance dispute discussed in Isaios 3, which, although taken through the lawcourts and fought out through two male family members, appears to have had two women and their households at its centre.[60]

Instead, it is important to ask whether men and women had equal access to, or control of, the resources of the *oikos*, and it is clear that these were divided along gendered lines.[61] Analysis of the fourth-century skeletons from the Kerameikos shows that although there are more female burials within the sample as a whole, men are better represented in the older age groups, which perhaps suggests that access to nutrition may have been gendered (Table 4.1 and Fig. 4.1).[62] Women in this sample appear to have lower levels of magnesium and zinc in their diets, which indicates less consumption of protein (especially red meat) than men, although levels for both genders are not low by pre-modern standards, and women were not, as far as we can tell, protein deficient.[63] This is a snapshot, of course, of a particular site at a specific time, but the

[60] Pyrrhos' property, which had been claimed by Phile and the sister of Pyrrhos, is the underlying issue here, although the speech itself is a charge against Nikodemos of bearing false witness. Phile and Pyrrhos' sister are represented by their *kyrioi* in court.

[61] Xen. *Oik.* 7.35–7.

[62] For discussion of recent palaeodemography techniques see Buikstra and Lagia 2009.

[63] Bisel 1990: 155–7, table 3. Lagia 2014: 108; 2015b: 163. Foxhall and Forbes 1982 assume that women were less well nourished than men; this seems to confirm their suspicions.

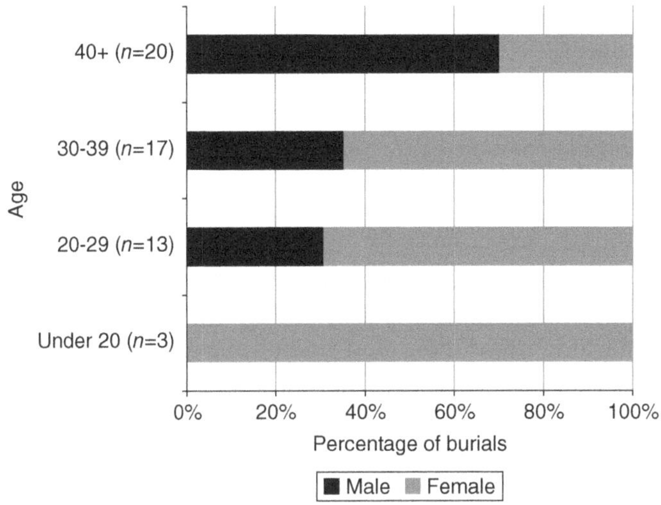

Figure 4.1. Gender and age of fourth-century skeletal material (Kerameikos)

Note: Determining the sex of pre-pubescent sub-adult populations is more difficult, since the skeletons have not matured; for new developments in bioarchaeology using odontometric methods see Viciano et al. 2011. These have not been used on the Kerameikos material, not least because most sub-adults in this cemetery were given cremation burials (see Lagia 2007b). All of the skeletons for which sex has been determined here are post-pubescent.

Sources: Bisel 1990: 152, 158, with Kovacsovics 1990.

conclusions are replicated in other Attic cemeteries, as the recent studies by Lagia show.[64] Furthermore, the skeletons of women found in the Kerameikos, and in the cemetery at Plateia Kotzia, show a higher prevalence of osteological stress-markers, which indicates anaemia, particularly in childhood.[65] The difference in mean $\delta^{15}N$ values (an indicator of nutrition) is starker for earth pit graves than for tile or cist graves, as well as for those buried in *periboloi*.[66] This probably indicates that poorer women were more likely to be even less well nourished than their wealthier counterparts.

It is also probable that the types of work women did within the household did not generate a great deal of income for it. With perhaps the exception of textile production (although this was also typically for family use rather than for profit), food preparation, fetching water,

[64] Lagia 2015a: 133–4. [65] Lagia 2014: 104–7.
[66] Lagia 2015a: 134 with fig. 8.9 on p. 136.

household chores, and childcare were time-consuming, and the burden of these activities fell on women and (female) slaves.[67] The recent excavation of agricultural tools in graves of women in Attica attests to women's involvement in food production, but the burial of these tools, and the emotional relationships they imply and status claims they indicate, also demonstrate that it is not simply the economic output of the *oikos* which is important here.[68] In fact, it is the investment of time—of women's time—in these day-to-day activities which must have had a significant effect on the household as a whole.[69] It is the quality of the food, the fineness of the clothes, the production of children which provided the most visible symbols of the living standards of the *oikos*, and the time needed to devote to such tasks was unending. The economic and social impact of women's work was, therefore, on the *oikos* as a whole rather than for women individually. Women's activities—and their relationships—within the household were therefore vital for the poverty (or wealth) of the *oikos*.[70]

It was not just that access to resources were gendered, but women and men were highly likely to have experienced wealth and poverty in different ways: inheritance provides a good example.[71] Not only did men and women typically inherit different types of property (men inherited land, whereas women inherited movable goods as part of their dowry), they did so at different stages in their lives (men inherited on the death of their fathers, women, at a much younger age, on marriage).[72] Inheriting land, perhaps especially if this came unexpectedly, was most likely extremely welcome, since this would have increased both the assets and the income of the *oikos*. But such an inheritance might be rather disruptive on a woman's life, for example if her husband suddenly became the closest male relative to an *epikleros* and took the opportunity to remarry in order to have access to a new estate. The mother of Euxitheos, the speaker of

[67] Textile production is, however, wealth-generating even if the surplus is not sold for income. Tsakirgis 2016 argues that textile production for market was likely a strategy of wealthier families who could produce a surplus. The investment in looms and other equipment would have meant poorer women were less likely to be weaving at home or with other women, and more likely to be selling offcuts in the market (Dem. 57.35), as Lin Foxhall (pers. comm.) argues.

[68] Kakavogianni and Galiatsatou 2009: 406–7; Kakavogianni 2000: 133–4.

[69] Daly 1992: 7; Lister 2004: 59.

[70] Molyneux 2002; Lister 2004: 60.

[71] Jackson 1998: 74; Razavi 1999: 410, 429.

[72] Foxhall 1989; 2003.

Demosthenes 57, was in exactly this situation. Nikarete was divorced by Protomachos—a *penes*—who took the opportunity to inherit a larger estate by marrying an *epikleros*.[73] Not only this, Isaios 3.64 appears to claim that women who were already married could be divorced and remarried on becoming *epikleroi*.[74] Inheriting land, therefore, had the potential to impact men's and women's lives very differently, and this affected the lived experience of wealth and poverty in highly gendered ways.

EXPERIENCING POVERTY IN GENDERED TERMS

How, then, did gender affect the experience of poverty in the ancient world? This can be seen through an examination of the ambiguities surrounding women's labour in Athens, with particular reference to wet-nursing and midwifery as case studies. The investigation of these ambiguities, as configured in sources such as forensic oratory, can be juxtaposed with other, mostly material evidence in order to throw into sharper relief not only the constraints which were felt differently by men and women, but also the different expectations placed on slave and free women. That is, they highlight the possibilities and limitations of what women were able to do or to be, rather than simply pointing out that they lacked income or freedom.[75] Examination of wet-nursing and midwifery also provide a glimpse into this crucial part of the fabric of Athenian society, and a critical aspect of ancient economies, yet one usually hidden from view.

Attitudes towards labour in Athens are complex; the dominant discourse is one of elite disdain for banausic irrespectability and profit-making, where issues of citizenship, status, and freedom are paramount.[76] But these attitudes are ambiguous and disputed.[77] Practising a *techne*, Cuomo argues, is linked with social mobility

[73] Dem. 57.41. Protomachos subsequently arranged Nikarete's marriage to Euxitheos' father (Dem. 57.41), but it is by no means clear that this happened in all cases.

[74] The speaker is, however, using this to discredit Phile's claim on the estate (the argument is that because this did not happen to her, she is not the legitimate daughter of Pyrrhos). That litigants sometimes misrepresented the law is demonstrated by Lys. 1.

[75] See Nussbaum 2003.

[76] Arist. *Pol.* 1278a8, 1337b4–23, Xen. *Oik.* 4.2–3. See Balme 1984; von Reden 1992.

[77] See Chapter 6 for further discussion.

and affluence, not with marginalization and abject poverty.[78] However, ambiguities surrounding attitudes towards labour were not just affected by concerns about status and citizenship, they were gendered too, in that there appears to be differences in the ways in which men's and women's work were viewed. Although all forms of labour were to some extent considered servile by certain portions of Athenian society, the types of work which women did (or more precisely, appear to have done exclusively), such as nursing, selling certain types of goods in market, textile manufacture, or childcare, is work which is also strongly associated with slaves.[79] The servile connotations of working for others are, of course, present for men too: Eutheros, returning from a cleruchy overseas, needs to be encouraged by Sokrates to become a farm overseer.[80] But the problem for Eutheros here is not the activity—running a farm is a perfectly acceptable occupation—but the relationship of dependence he puts himself in by performing this act for others. This is not quite the same for women: for them the problem appears to be the activity *as well as* the relationship of dependence. The result of this is that a discourse is perpetuated in which citizen women only work in times of hardship, and to do so symbolizes low status.[81] However, ideologies do not necessarily map onto reality with ease. Instead they show how discourses on gender shaped the ability of women to gain access to resources and demonized those who did so with accusations of servility or low status. These are, to be sure, ideologies of power which were very much rooted in citizen concerns and constrained the ability of both women and men to negotiate their own lives. But examining contexts in which women did work for others demonstrates ambiguities in these discourses, and perhaps even suggests that the disdain we find so frequently was actively resisted and contested: women's work was perhaps even reconfigured in some contexts as something to be valued.[82] This

[78] Cuomo 2007: 7–35. See also Pomeroy 1977: 62 for the positive effects of practising a *techne* for women. *IG* I^3 766 (*c*.500–480) seems to make this explicit: 'whoever has a *techne* has a better livelihood', [*hòs γὰρ*] *hέχει τέχνεν λôι*[*ο*]*ν' hέχ*[*ει βίοτον*].

[79] See e.g. Pl. *Laws* 805d–e for the association of working women with Thrace, an area from which many slaves were brought.

[80] Xen. *Mem*. 2.8.1–6.

[81] Dem. 57.42, 45, Xen. *Mem*. 2.7.2.

[82] On the range of women's work see Brock 1994: 336–7, 339; Hanson 1996. On agricultural work: Scheidel 1995; 1996. Karanika 2014 shows how women's work songs became embedded in literary texts, a process that supports the argument here.

provides, therefore, an insight into a different experience of *penia* than that which is found in the evidence discussed in Chapter 2.

Wet-nursing

Historians have juxtaposed the many grave markers which describe foreign or slave women as *titthai* with the accusation of Euboulides that his opponent's mother was as a wet-nurse, and (not unreasonably) viewed wet-nursing as a servile occupation only undertaken by citizen women in times of hardship.[83] Euxitheos even says as much:

> [Euboulides] has said this too about my mother [Nikarete], that she served as a wet-nurse (ἐτίτθευσεν). We, on our part, do not deny that this was the case in the time of the city's misfortune, when all people were badly off; but in what manner and for what reasons she became a nurse I will tell you plainly. And let no one of you, men of Athens, be prejudiced against us because of this; for you will find today many Athenian women who are serving as nurses (νῦν ἀστὰς γυναῖκας πολλὰς εὑρήσετε τιτθευούσας); I will mention them by name, if you wish . . . for the charges which my opponent makes regarding Kleinias and my mother's having served as nurse—all this too I will set forth to you clearly.
>
> Demosthenes 57.35, 41

The hardship explanation is one picked up frequently by historians, but hardship cuts both ways: wet-nurses are needed when babies are at risk of starvation through the death of the mother, or her inability or lack of desire to feed the child. The 'market' for wet-nurses, therefore, is shaped not only through women like Nikarete needing work, but also because of hardship within the child's family. In some cases wet-nurses might become available as a result of the death of the wet-nurse's own child. The decision to hire a wet-nurse, as well as to hire oneself out as one, therefore, is not necessarily a purely economic one. Indeed, it can be seen as a decision that is made to avert family

[83] The women are identified as foreign or slaves based on their ethnics (*IG* II^2 9112: Malicha from Kythera; *IG* II^2 9079: Phanion from Korinth) and/or the addition of the epithet *chreste* (*IG* II^2 11647; *IG* II^2 12387 (Fig. 6.2 here)): see Bäbler 1998: 37–40; Kosmopoulou 2001: 306–12, and in general: Bäbler 2005. *SEG* 12.209 suggests that *titthai* in Roman Athens could be held in high esteem (τίτθη [Ἰσι]ạ̀ṣ ἀρίστη{s} [Ε]ὐφήμου [γυ]νή) and Kennedy 2014: 134–6 disputes the assumption that *titthai* were typically slaves. On Dem. 57, see Brock 1994: 336–7; D. Cohen 1998: 58–61.

disaster, or as a result of family disaster. It is possible that wet-nurses were hired as a status symbol, but there is little evidence to suggest this was normally the case in Athens.[84]

Considering how Nikarete's (and other women's) lives may have been affected by wet-nursing shows how this activity allowed women to develop networks of relationships, primarily with other women, which they could mobilize (probably) on their own terms when necessary. By connecting women with households outside their own, these networks allowed women like Nikarete to ameliorate their immediate poverty, but also to negotiate their own social roles by challenging the discourse which devalued this activity. Wet-nursing, therefore, can be seen as an activity through which women (in Senian terms) expanded their capabilities.[85]

Given that Euboulides uses Nikarete's work as a smear to attack Euxitheos' citizenship status, it is revealing that Euxitheos does not deny the accusation outright. Presumably, in the case of the wet-nursing charge at least (though less so for the market-trading charge), this would have been quite easy to do, given that it must have occurred a substantial amount of time (that is, decades) before.[86] Since childcare was almost exclusively the duty of the mother (along with other female members of the household), and the arrangements not in the public realm, it is difficult to imagine how Euboulides obtained his knowledge about Nikarete's breast-feeding activities. In contrast to the market-trading charge, which would be much less easy to refute given the more public setting of the agora, wet-nursing must have been a much more private arrangement

[84] According to Plut. *Lyk.* 16, Alkibiades had a Lakedaimonian nurse, Amykla, but if having a wet-nurse was common amongst the wealthy, it was not much commented upon.

[85] Textile production can be seen in the same light, as the recent work of Lin Foxhall makes clear: weaving is a group activity which creates and maintains women's social networks.

[86] Biologically Nikarete must have begun wet-nursing when Euxitheos or one of his four siblings were infants (Dem. 57.28), and she and Thoukritos, Euxitheos' father, were presumably deceased by the mid-340s. Although we do not know whether Euxitheos was the oldest or youngest child (or somewhere in the middle), at the time of the speech he is a mature adult having already served as demarch for Halimous (Dem. 57.63) and phratriarch (Dem. 57.23), so it is quite likely that Nikarete's wet-nursing of Kleinias took place as much as thirty years before. It is likely, however, that their relationship continued for a considerable time: see following discussion.

between households and between the women of those households.[87] The question is, given that the details were unlikely to have been public knowledge, and given the length of time passed since Nikarete's employment must have occurred, if it was as shameful as Euboulides implies, why not simply deny it outright?

One possible answer to this, of course, is that Euxitheos' lack of denial touches on a counter-discourse to the one outlined above, one which emphasized value rather than disdain; this is certainly the impression gained from the funerary evidence, though as far as we can tell, this mostly commemorates non-citizen women.[88] Furthermore, terracotta figurines, although sometimes depicting nurses as old or grotesque, also show them in more idealized ways.[89] These show that wet-nurses were not always portrayed in terms of servility or Otherness, but were also valued for the work they did. This is reinforced by the role nurses have in literature: they appear as knowledgeable characters, close confidantes, and authority figures within the household.[90]

Presumably there was also a significant weight of opinion for whom citizen women working as wet-nurses was less shameful than Euboulides' accusation implies, otherwise it would have been hushed up or denied completely; Euxitheos thinks, at least, that he can rely on the sympathy of the jury.[91] Although the stigma of non-citizen birth or servitude was potent (for citizen women as well as men), the material evidence hints that there were some positive sides to wet-nursing, allowing women to construct or cement

[87] Dem. 57.34. Breast-feeding was not a common theme in Greek visual culture, but human milk was suggested as a treatment for various ailments in the Hippocratic corpus: Bonfante 1997; Laskaris 2008.

[88] See n. 83.

[89] Kosmopoulou 2001: 305, n. 244: 'the respect shown for nurses on gravestones of this period is paralleled by a change in their representation on contemporary terracotta statuettes, where they turn from ugly creatures with negative physiognomic traits into beautiful, lady-like figures.' See also Schulze 1988: 50–5; Pfisterer-Haas 1989: 40–2.

[90] See examples discussed by Golden 2011: 141–2.

[91] The 'my mother was so poor she had to work' line admittedly does plays into Euxitheos' general strategy to counter Euboulides' claim that he is not poor at all (Dem. 57.52), so should not necessarily be believed. It is possible, of course, that Euboulides is right: other branches of the family were certainly *euporoi*, there appears to be some land (even if this was inaccessible at certain points), and Euxitheos can afford the services of a prominent logographer, but his citizenship is on the line. See further *APF*: 93–5; Lacey 1980. However, the strategy could be pursued with equal success with the market-trading admission alone.

networks of relationships with other women and link into (probably) wealthier households.[92] It is likely that wet-nursing, far from providing the stigma of poverty and servitude, also provided women with access to other resources, expanded their capabilities, and gave them social value. If weaning did not take place until 2–4 years of age, these relationships were potentially longlasting.[93]

Indeed, the ways in which wet-nurses might be valued can be seen by considering their social relationships. As far as we can tell, childcare seems to have fallen almost exclusively to women, older children, and slaves, and although there is little direct evidence, it seems unlikely that men were involved in the decisions to employ or acquire nurses for their own children; these transactions were probably conducted between women and controlled by them.[94] Furthermore, there are no hints that these relationships were antagonistic.[95] *Titthai* seem to have been remembered with great affection and a special effort made to commemorate them in death: this is by far the largest attestation of a profession which appears in a funerary context, and in terms of iconographical representation, they are not depicted as slavish. Instead they appear seated, wearing a chiton and mantle, sometimes in scenes of *dexiosis*, which are all common representations of citizen women.[96] Indeed, Euxitheos' mother seems to have

[92] Men. *Sam.* 84–6 suggests that this was the case (*πρότερον δ' ἔγωγε πάντ' ἂν ὑπομεῖναι δοκῶ ἢ τοῦτο τίτθην ἐν συνοικίᾳ τινὶ ε . . .* [. . .]) but wet-nursing can also take place under other circumstances, as noted (e.g. when a child is orphaned or the mother otherwise unable to breast-feed). Scheidel 2010: 433–4 estimates that wet-nurses in Roman Egypt earned approximately one third of a male worker's annual pay; there is no evidence in Athens for their earnings.

[93] Kwok and Keenleyside 2015.

[94] Childcare: Golden 1990: 123, 128. Papyri letters from Egypt suggest that women did sometimes arrange these services (e.g. *BGU* IV 1058 = Rowlandson 1998: no. 213, 13 BCE), but many of these provide for slave children within the household rather than the women's own children (see also Bradley 1986). When men are involved in the transactions it appears that they are hiring out *their own slaves* as wet-nurses. See further Masciadri and Montevecchi 1984. The Hippocratic author of *De morbis* (4.55.1–2, 7.600L) is concerned with the quality of the nurse's milk and her subsequent ability to nourish the child, but this is the only mention of wet-nursing in the corpus: see further Hanson 1996: 169–70.

[95] *SEG* 57.296 is a curse tablet found in a grave in Myrrhinous which attacks a woman named Titthe, but there is no indication of what she (nor the five other people named here) did to acquire the wrath of the curser, whoever this may have been: see Anetakis et al. 2009: 201.

[96] For images and discussion see Kosmopoulou 2001: 287–90; Kennedy 2014: 133–6; also Fig. 6.2 here.

retained some sort of relationship with the family for whom she worked, since the name of the child (Kleinias, now presumably an adult) is remembered and mentioned in the speech.[97] The nurse in Menander's *Samia* is also portrayed as being emotionally attached to her former charge Moschion: she loves his child just as much as him.[98] Epitaphs of nurses often mention the children who were nursed.[99] Furthermore, literary representations of nurses often depict them as trustworthy, and there are a number of examples of adult men remaining attached to their nurses and supporting them in their old age.[100] The epitaph of Melitta, the daughter of Apollodoros, a metic awarded *isoteleia*, further emphasizes the longlasting emotional bonds between nurse and child and also emphasizes the social role that nurses could fulfil. Melitta here is not only loved but honoured for the role that she performed.[101]

This shows another side to wet-nursing than the servile discourse allows. Although the evidence is fragmentary, it is possible to detect a counter-discourse which emphasizes value and reflects the social and economic relationships between women (slave and free) which usually went under the radar of men. We can only scratch the surface of these networks, precisely because they were of little significance to Athenian men, who tended to ignore them or configure them as shameful or servile. But they were no doubt crucial to women, because they had the potential to expand their capabilities and develop higher functionings.[102] Nikarete's work, after all, enabled her *oikos* to survive when Euxitheos' father was away fighting.[103] Melitta

[97] Dem. 57.41, 44: the family even serve as witnesses for Euxitheos.

[98] Men. *Sam.* 245–8.

[99] *IG* II^2 9112: 'Here the earth holds the nurse of the children of Diogeiton from the Peloponnese. This most just woman, Malicha from Kythera.' See Kosmopoulou 2001: N4.

[100] [Dem.] 47.55–61. See also Eurykleia (the nurse of Odysseus): Karydas 1998; Golden 2011: 141. Further, Men. *Sam.* 236–48.

[101] *IG* II^2 7873: Above the relief: 'For [[Melitta]] the daughter of Apollodoros, *isoteles*.' On the relief: 'Melitta; Nurse.' Below the relief: 'Here under the earth lies Hippostrate's good nurse; and Hippostrate still longs for you. While you were alive, I loved you, nurse, and even now underneath the earth, I will honour you as long as I live. For I know that for you beneath the earth, if there is reward for the good, honours will be yours first, nurse, in the realm of Persephone and Pluto.' See also Kosmopoulou 2001: N7 (with *CAT* 1.969; *SEG* 29.220).

[102] On the impact of strong ties for women's social networks see Lowndes 2000; Molyneux 2002.

[103] Dem. 57.42.

evoked not only strong emotional bonds but also was honoured for her work. Women's networks, which often crossed boundaries of status, therefore were likely to have provided crucial mechanisms by which households made ends meet and perhaps also prospered.[104] With husbands at home, women were presumably less likely to exercise this function.

Viewed in this way, the relationships of dependence are complicated, and in some cases completely reversed. It is not only the wet-nurse who is dependent on the child's family for work, but the child's family is also dependent on the wet-nurse to avoid the death or malnutrition of their kin. For the hiring family, their intergenerational survival was potentially at stake, and with that the maintenance of their citizenship and prosperity (given that passing on inheritance was a key concern of the *oikos*). These networks of women, in this context, therefore might be seen as being crucial for the maintenance of the citizen body (in that they provide emergency resources for families in different kinds of need), but at the same time they enabled a whole different set of relationships to emerge which cut at the heart of male citizen domination. From a feminist economics perspective, therefore, they were crucial for shaping women's well-being.[105]

Midwifery

The evidence that survives for wet-nurses is strong, but it is not the only arena in which we can see these networks functioning. Examination of midwives and midwifery also demonstrates how women created networks of relationships with one another which could be mobilized for economic as well as social means, and at the same time contested the discourse which devalued their relationships and activities and instead emphasized their social value. Plato famously describes the idealized character and activities of midwives in a passage which also claims (without shame) that Sokrates' mother Phainarete worked as one.[106] Midwives (*maiai*) are, according to

[104] There is a longstanding association in the social sciences that women-headed households are disproportionately poor. This is debunked by Jackson 1998 and Razavi 1999. On these in Athens see pp. 146–7.

[105] Jackson 1998.

[106] Pl. *Tht.* 149a–151e. On the historicity of Phainarete as a midwife, and her 'astonishingly appropriate' name for the job, see the discussion of Burnyeat 1977;

Sokrates, supposed to be sensible and dignified, post-menopausal, but having had children already.[107] They should be able to reduce labour pains as well as procure abortions, and also be upstanding—but not meddlesome—matchmakers.[108] In addition, they need technical skill to cut the umbilical cord and ease pain.[109] There is no evidence that Sokrates perceived (or intended to portray) midwifery as servile, although it is clear that the skills of midwives do not compare to Sokrates' art in tending to the souls of young men.[110]

Whilst King has shown that we should not necessarily assume that all birth attendants were women, the presence of female helpers at births appears to have been commonplace.[111] Women assisting family, friends, and neighbours in labour are widely attested, and it is likely that this was a common duty which was carried out for friends and relatives.[112] Performing the function of a midwife might not, therefore, have been considered primarily as an economic transaction, but instead was intended to cement the social bonds between women; Elektra uses her lack of midwife to demonstrate the loneliness of her poverty.[113] These ties cut across status: slaves are depicted in funerary scenes of childbirth, assisting the mother, and in most cases they are physically the closest figures to them.[114] On the other hand, these social relationships might well have had an economic impact too: if the depiction of Praxagora in the *Ekklesiazousai* is anything to go by, it is possible that even such informal assistance was financially rewarded. Praxagora constructs a tale to explain why

Tomin 1987; Tarrant 1988. For the midwives in Greek epigraphy in general see Laes 2011.

[107] Pl. *Tht.* 149a, 150a: *γενναίας τε καὶ βλοσυρᾶς . . . σεμναὶ οὖσαι*, 149b: *αἵ ἤδη ἀδύνατοι τίκτειν*, 149b–c.

[108] Pl. *Tht.* 150d. [109] Pl. *Tht.* 149d.

[110] Pl. *Tht.* 150b. Sokrates was not, as Hanson 1996: 180 states, '*as expert* in the delivering of the souls of men *as his mother was* in delivering the bodies of women' (my italics); he was better: 'such are the things midwives do, but their deeds are lesser than mine (*τὸ μὲν τοίνυν τῶν μαιῶν τοσοῦτον, ἔλαττον δὲ τοῦ ἐμοῦ δράματος*)'. Midwifery is strongly associated with slaves and freedwomen in the Roman world: Laes 2011: 156.

[111] King 1998: 172–87.

[112] Hippoc. *Mul.* 1.21, 8.60.16–17L. See also Ar. *Eccl.* 528–49, *Thesm.* 502–16.

[113] Eur. *El.* 1128–33 (with discussion of this play on pp. 61–2).

[114] See e.g. NM 1077 (*CAT* 3.282), Louvre 3115 (*CAT* 3.375), NM 749 (*CAT* 4.480): the seated women are supported by a figure who is either short-haired or shorter in stature (or both). On death in childbirth scenes in general see Vedder 1988; Scholl 1996: 159–64.

she has been out of the house all night: she claims she was needed at the labour of a 'dear friend'.[115] Her husband, Blepyros, is annoyed, not that she has gone per se, but that she took his boots and cloak which meant that he could not go to the Assembly the following morning and pick up the 3-obol attendance fee. Praxagora responds that her assistance in the birth of a boy makes it all worthwhile.[116] The implication is that she can expect to be reimbursed (through payment or gifts) a sum greater than this. Assisting at births might well have been financially, as well as socially or emotionally, rewarding.

Other women were considered to possess expert knowledge about pregnancy and birth, and this expertise was highly valued. Judging from the Hippocratic corpus, these women were seen as healers (*asketrides*), and their knowledge relied on and developed by writers of gynaecological treatises.[117] Viewed as having medical skills, like doctors, they no doubt charged a fee.[118] Midwives like these are attested cutting the cord of the newborn, preparing medicines and chants, and were knowledgeable about the survival rates of close-to-term foetuses.[119] Women like Phanostrate, who is identified on her grave stele as a midwife and a doctor (*maia kai iatros*), were no doubt well educated in the techniques of successful childbirth.[120]

Found in Acharnai, and dating to the mid-fourth century, Phanostrate's stele shows her in a standard Athenian woman's pose (seated, in a *dexiosis* scene, dressed in a chiton), perhaps the daughter of a man from Melite (Fig. 4.2).[121] The seated woman is identified by an

[115] Ar. *Eccl.* 520. [116] Ar. *Eccl.* 548. [117] Hippoc. *De carnibus* 19.

[118] See Pl. *Rep.* 454d for female doctors (*ἰατρικὴν*): Pomeroy 1978.

[119] See Pl. *Tht.* 149c–e, Arist. *Hist. an.* 587a9, Hippoc. *Mul.* 1.68, *De carnibus* 19.3. On midwives possessing expert knowledge, even though 'midwifery did not appear as a well-defined medical profession in the fifth century', see Totelin 2009: 114, 119, 247. Also Demand 1994: 63–70. On *De carnibus* see Hanson 1996.

[120] *IG* II^2 6873: 'Phanostrate. Midwife and doctor, Phanostrate lies here. She caused pain to none and all lamented in her death.'

[121] Daux's reading of the first line above the relief (*Φανοσ[τράτη----] Μελ̣ι̣τ̣[έως]*) would show that she was a citizen as she proclaims she is the daughter of a man from Melite (Daux 1972: 550–4) *pace* Kosmopoulou 2001: 301, 306 who suggests she was a metic or freedwoman (if so, it is highly unlikely that she would claim her father was from a citizen from Melite). Clairmont 1970: 130–1 reads *Φανοσ[τράτη ----]| μα[ῖα]*, but Daux's restoration is accepted by *SEG* 33.214. Kennedy 2014: 141–2 suggests Melos or Miletos as the ethnic; the latter would place Phanostrate in the large group of (female) Milesians in Athens (suggested by Vestergaard 2000 for the later Hellenistic period at least).

Figure 4.2. Grave stele of Phanostrate, midwife and doctor (NM 993)

additional inscription as Phanostrate and the standing figure as Antiphile. The four children at their feet serve as testimonies to Phanostrate's role as midwife, highlighting the success of her activities. It is even possible that Phanostrate retained some kind of social bonds with the children she delivered or their mothers. Antiphile might be a sister or other relative, but it is also possible that she was a patient of Phanostrate.[122] If so, this would clearly indicate that women considered the relationships with their midwives important and their skills were recognized and valued.

Other grave stelai also commemorate women as midwives, although their attribution is even less certain because they lack inscriptions which explicitly name them as such and have therefore been misinterpreted as death in childbirth (as opposed to assistance in childbirth) scenes.[123] Malthake's stele, for example, falls into this category. The stele commemorates her as the daughter of Magadis, and although it is not stated in the inscription, it is possible that she is represented as a midwife here.[124] Not only is she standing by another woman reclining on a couch in a way reminiscent of other childbirth scenes, she is actively assisting her (and is therefore suggested by Demand to have been a midwife and commemorated as such). The epitaph describes her with what might well be a metronymic, not a patronymic.[125] It is possible that she is a metic: the name Magadis is considered, by Clairmont at least, to be 'of Eastern origin'.[126] However, with the exception of one epitaph from Sicily, the name Magadis is, in fact, only attested within Attica.[127] Indeed, the name Malthake is far more common in Attica than anywhere else in the Greek world: 94% of the attestations are from Attica.[128] Regardless of her status,

[122] This, at least, is the interpretation of Kosmopoulou 2001: 300.

[123] For a catalogue see Demand 1994: 127–34; 1995.

[124] *IG* II^2 12026: *Μαλθάκη ⋮ Μαγάδιδος χρηστή*. Demand 1994: 133; 1995: 288; Bäbler 1998: 90–1, Kat. 27. Stewart and Gray 2000: 261, n. 26 argue that because she is called *chreste*, 'the stele surely honors Malthake in her (unfulfilled) role as mother, not as a midwife'. They do not explain, however, how the fact of being a 'metic, freedwoman, or slave' provides effective contraception.

[125] The name Magadis is recorded in *LGPN* as either masculine or feminine.

[126] *CAT* 2.457. Clairmont links the name to the description of a *magadis* (a Lydian stringed instrument named after Magdis of Thrace) by Athenaios (634–7).

[127] No such name is attested in Thrace outside the story of Athenaios; see previous note. It is attested in Sicily: *ILipara* 225: *Μαγά̣διος* (*SEG* 45.1381, 36; third/second century). Compare, however, *IG* II^2 10559/60: *Ἀγάθων Μάγαδις*, *IG* III App. 16: *Ἀρμένιος [Ζώι]λος Μάγαδι[ς]*, *DT* 72: *καταδήω . . . Μάγα[δ]ιν*.

[128] There are thirty-three attestations of Malthake in *LGPN*; thirty-one of them are Attic.

however, the iconography of the stele emphasizes the close, tender relationship between the two women depicted, and this implies that Malthake was highly skilled in putting her patients at ease.[129] It seems that midwifery provided a means by which she could negotiate her own social value.

The identification of Phanostrate as *maia* and *iatros*, and the Hippocratic corpus which relies, in part, on women's knowledge and expertise about birth, suggest that midwifery and medicine could be economically profitable activities, but also show that they were firmly rooted within women's social relationships. No doubt the range of expertise was wide, and the regularity of women's employment or assistance at births varied according to circumstance, but it is likely that, like wet-nursing, midwifery was an arena in which women could increase their capabilities, gain social value, and cement social ties between themselves and other women.[130]

Emphasizing the positive impact of wet-nursing and midwifery on women's lives is not meant to override the clear gender disadvantages which constrained both men's and women's ability to function within the *oikos* or within Athenian society as a whole, or suggest that these were the only types of work women did—there is plenty of evidence for a wide range of occupations.[131] Nor is such a focus meant to paint a rosy picture of lives which were no doubt harsh (involving perhaps slavery, death of a child, economic deprivation, and so on). It is clear that there was some kind of social stigma attached to citizen women working as wet-nurses (though less so for women acting as birth attendants or midwives), and the structures of constraint which prevented (some) women developing the same capabilities as (some) men were massive and very real. But what was devalued in one context was clearly contested in another. Both wet-nursing and midwifery gave some kind of social value not just to slave and metic women (in that it made them integral members of households), but also to citizen women too. Focusing on poverty in this way therefore enables the work of women to be viewed not just as the activities of

[129] A similar scene appears on a stele from Alexandria: Vedder 1988: 163, pl. 23.2; Demand 1994: 125, no. 9.

[130] Tarrant 1988: 118–19 views the term *maia* as 'delightfully non-technical', which in some contexts it probably was, but this overlooks the undoubtedly expert knowledge of women like Phanostrate and Malthake and the contribution of such expertise to the Hippocratic authors of gynaecological treatises. See n. 119.

[131] Harris 2002a.

people in dire straits (economic deprivation, slavery, and so on), as victims of circumstance or poor household management, but instead allows these women, slaves, and non-citizens to be seen as active agents in their own lives, renegotiating their social relationships to their own advantage. Poverty in this sense is rehabilitated from its associations with deficiency, fear, and dissatisfaction.

It is a choice historians make to view all economic activity performed by women in the ancient world through the lens of servility, otherness, or indeed prostitution.[132] We do not have to follow this line. Instead, it is preferable to examine the contexts in which women's lives were precarious, the measures they took to negotiate this, and the constraints which prevented them from doing so. This allows us to reframe women's economy activities and consider elements of women's well-being outside of, or at least in dialogue with, the dominant discourses of citizen men. That women could gain prosperity through their own labour is highlighted by a number of dedications. Melinna, for example, explicitly speaks of having raised her children through her own *techne* and the work of her own hands in a dedication to Athena Ergane.[133] Earlier examples, dated to before the Persian Wars, suggest that such activities were more common than appears in our source record.[134]

Elsewhere we see glimpses of women-headed households (that is, those where metronymics were used instead of the more usual patronymic), which show women as economic actors.[135] A number of these households were non-Athenian, but not all.[136] In fact, in many

[132] On the scholarly overemphasis on prostitution see the important discussion of Kennedy 2014.

[133] *IG* II[2] 4334: 'Melinna, having raised her children with her hands and through the skills of her labours, and with righteous courage, set up this memorial to you, goddess Ergane, offering a share of the possessions she earned in honour of your favour (*charis*).' It is thought that Melinna was a weaver or potter, given the association of Athena Ergane with these activities. I thank Lene Rubinstein for discussing this stele with me.

[134] *IG* I[3] 546, 573, 700, 794.

[135] These are distinct from later Hellenistic funerary inscriptions that note women in their role as mothers but state also their relationships with other men, such as *IG* II[2] 5392. See Wilhelm 1978: 69 for examples.

[136] Some examples where families are likely to have been non-Athenian on the basis of their names: *IG* II[2] 11568: Hegeso daughter of Persis (Bäbler 1998: no. 48), *IG* II[2] 11566: daughter of (a different) Persis (Bäbler 1998: no. 47), *IG* II[2] 10892: Aspasia, daughter of Mania (Bäbler 1998: no. 72), *IG* II[2] 8917 (*SEG* 28.289): Zopyrion, son of Morphe. Incidentally, it is unlikely that those commemorated here were children at the time of their deaths. Malthake was certainly not if the midwife interpretation is

instances both mothers and daughters have names absolutely typical of citizen, such as Nikomache, Archestrate, and Phile, or Phano, Kallistion, and Aristarete.[137] It is possible that some of these families were citizens themselves, with absent husbands or fathers, as we saw in the case of Nikarete and Euxitheos.[138] On the other hand, if these are non-Athenian families this might provide evidence of naming practices being used as strategies of integration.[139] This in itself might well have enabled women to strengthen their social ties with other women, enabling them to alleviate their economic precariousness through their social relationships, and ameliorating their social exclusion.

THE DYNAMICS OF POVERTY: DISCOURSES OF SOCIAL WORTH AND LIVED EXPERIENCE

The aim of this chapter has been to confront the idea that poverty is dynamic and multidimensional, not only in terms of individual or household experiences of the duration or depth of poverty, but also in terms of how different social groups, particularly women, experienced and responded to their own economic deprivation and social exclusion. This dynamism places poverty and wealth much more on a continuum of social experience than the dichotomous rhetoric of labour and leisure would lead us to believe. Secondly, recognizing poverty dynamics emphasizes that poverty is embedded within—and produced by—a complex network of social relations and social values. These shape the experience of poverty in different ways, often reproducing relations of power, but also highlighting the multitude of strategies that those who are categorized as poor used to contest the

correct, and none of the stelai show iconography related to children. These are in all likelihood adult children using a metronymic.

[137] *IG* II^2 11793: Kallistion, daughter of Nikomache; *IG* II^2 12575: Rhysis or Physis, daughter of Archestrate; *IG* II^2 12138: Milakon, daughter of Phile; *IG* II^2 12876a: Phano, daughter of Oinanthia; *IG* II^2 10753: Aristarete, daughter of Myrrh. In addition there is *IG* II^2 10205: Oinanthe, daughter of Kallistrate of Salamis and *IG* II^2 11103: Demetrios, son of Theodote, who seems to have been adopted into Erxis of Halai's household (*CEG* 548, Tsagalis 2008: 145–7) or perhaps was the son of Erxis' first wife, Theodote, who predeceased the birth of his other children (Marchiandi 2011: 394–6).

[138] See also Ar. *Thesm.* 446–58.

[139] See also Vlassopoulos 2015.

discourses which devalued their lives. Viewing poverty as a dynamic process, therefore, helps to link poverty as a series of discourses with poverty as a lived experience.

It makes a difference to our understanding of Athenian society whether poverty was experienced as a long-term condition—a trap from which it was difficult to escape—or whether it was considered to be a short-term situation, feared by many because it was thought that *penia* would touch the lives of many. It is easy to get the impression from the material discussed in Chapter 2 that the latter was the case: the frequent jokes, for example, about the poor and their lifestyles on the stage suggests the bulk of the audience was familiar enough with what being poor was like to find comic relief at their portrayal in the theatre. However, this impression is built on a series of discourses which conceptualize poverty predominantly in terms of citizenship; that is, it systematically ignores the poverty experiences of non-citizens (women, non-Athenians, slaves). Chronic poverty is, by contrast, framed as being alien, as something citizens do not ordinarily suffer from: it is as a recategorization outside citizen-defined social norms that centre on the *oikos* and the polis.

Moreover, to frame the problem this way neglects to notice that those who were categorized as poor actively sought to redefine their own worlds. This chapter argues, however, that it is possible to fit these groups back into our understanding of poverty in the ancient world regardless of the fact that the social relationships which shaped poverty are precisely those which excluded women and non-Athenians from civic life. It does so by suggesting that poverty is not a condition experienced in isolation, nor was it experienced in the same way by all those living in Athens, but by recognizing how, for example, women developed social networks (and were constrained by them) through which they were able to negotiate their own well-being. This emphasis, therefore, not only recognizes the dynamism of poverty, but also its heterogeneity. These observations again caution against constructions of poverty which dichotomize the poor and the rich and imply that these categories were strongly bounded and unchanging. The reality was quite the opposite.

5

Experiencing *Penia*

The Reproduction of Poverty and the Consolidation of Wealth

The political institutions of Athens emphasized political equality among citizens whilst also redistributing wealth (to some extent) within the citizen body because the city extracted money predominantly from the wealthy through taxes, payments, and liturgies and provided a wide array of economic benefits to the demos as a whole. This not only enabled a broad level of political participation through pay for office and other activities, but probably contributed to the relatively high standards of living that have been argued for the classical period. With a couple of exceptions it was only the relatively well-off who paid taxes in Athens, that is, Athenian taxation was progressive (rather than regressive): the *eisphora* was levied only on those of relative wealth, sales taxes were paid by the buyers of land (usually those with land to start with), and harbour taxes and mining fees were paid by those economically active in the Piraeus and Laurion respectively.[1] In addition, liturgists made voluntary donations to provide public goods such as warships and festivals in exchange for honour.

Aside from providing an insight into Athenian fiscal organization, tax practices also demonstrate two concurrent social processes which shape Athenian inequalities and which underlie the investigations of this chapter. First they emphasize the ongoing importance of civic status. The highest honour a metic could receive, for example,

[1] On taxes see Fawcett 2016.

recategorized him as a citizen-for-tax-purposes (*isoteleia*). Under normal circumstances metics had to pay a poll tax (*metoikion*)—seemingly regardless of their own wealth or poverty—and they were required to contribute to *eisphorai* if their wealth permitted it.[2] In contrast, there were no poll or income taxes for citizens, but there is some evidence for a tax on prostitutes (*pornikon*), which probably was, in practice, an additional tax on non-citizens.[3] Civic entitlements therefore very much shaped access to resources in Athens, providing a buffer against hardship for some but structuring constraints on others. The first part of this chapter, therefore, will explore the institutions which acted, directly or indirectly, as poverty relief, and discuss those features which alleviated or reinforced economic hardship. Frequently we will see that civic status, rather than economic need, shaped such access.

Second, changes in the organization of public finance during the second half of the fourth century led to the increasing use of targeted donations (*epidoseis*). These allowed benefactors to pick and choose where their money went, allowing them more control over their public spending.[4] This symbolizes a change in the way private resources were used for public goods, and evidence suggests that frequently payments were financially (as well as socially or politically) rewarding for those who made them. Together with a series of other indicators, this points towards the consolidation of wealth during the second half of the fourth century in favour of the well-off and at the expense of the demos as a whole. This, I will argue, had significant ramifications on the poor and on poverty in Athens.

The present chapter, therefore, explores the factors that shaped the reproduction of poverty and the consolidation of wealth in democratic Athens. The discourses surrounding poverty conceptualize it in terms of behaviourial or moral categories, but the aim here is to interrogate instead the institutions which shaped these experiences and therefore provided the means through which aspects of poverty could have been alleviated as well as those that created constraints. By placing emphasis on the social processes which alleviated or reinforced poverty we can

[2] *Metoikion*: Xen. *Por*. 2.2. Whitehead 1977: 75–7.

[3] *Pornikon*: Aeschin. 1.119. Not all prostitutes were non-citizens of course, but those classed as *pornai* predominantly were. See Glazebrook 2011: 35.

[4] Gabrielsen 1994: 199–206 on naval *epidoseis*. Used increasingly commonly in the third century: Oliver 2007.

examine the structures which kept Athenians (and non-Athenians) poor or provided them with the means to live above subsistence.

POLITICAL PAY, POVERTY RELIEF, AND CIVIC UNITY

Aristotle thought that truly democratic cities ought to help those amongst their citizenry who were extremely poor (*lian aporon*).[5] He took it as a marker of good governance that surplus revenues should be distributed from the *euporoi* to the *aporoi*, and that this should be used for buying land, as capital for trade, or just given directly to the people. This, he argued, was a better system than the provision of political distributions—the proverbial water-jar with a hole in it, controlled by demagogues—because it was fairer to all, led to more lasting prosperity, and reduced the need for the *euporoi* to undergo expensive liturgies. Such a system might well have gone some way to alleviate poverty over the long term by providing assets to the poor which, with proper management, could be grown, preserved, and passed on as inheritance. However, Aristotle's scheme does not envision this. Rather than being based on a desire to move citizens out of poverty per se, it is instead designed to cut off the day-to-day income of those who relied on the distributions from the Assembly and lawcourts in order to convert these groups from hired labourers (bad citizens) into farmers or traders (good citizens).[6] Self-sufficiency is therefore at the heart of the plan; his aim is to 'improve' democratic regimes by modifying the economic activities of the demos. The best form of democracy for Aristotle, after all, was the agricultural sort, where the farmers stayed on their farms and minded their own business.[7]

Aristotle's scheme is less about poverty alleviation than about political recategorization. It removes from the citizen body the stigma of thetic or banausic labouring and places this back onto the slaves where (in Aristotle's view) it belongs. Xenophon, likewise, in his plan to relieve the 'poverty of the masses' similarly focuses his

[5] Arist. *Pol.* 1320a29–b4.
[6] Keyt 1999: 219–20.
[7] Arist. *Pol.* 1318b10–17.

attention on improving the citizen body.[8] He suggested that a 3-obol daily stipend (*trophe*), generated by publically owned slaves leased out to the mines, be distributed to all citizens. The aim of providing this stipend, however, is less to reduce the material poverty of the poor than to ensure civic harmony: Xenophon sees it primarily as a way to reduce the burdens on the rich, make the city more prosperous and secure whilst improving its reputation overseas, and to ensure that citizens are 'more obedient, better disciplined, and more efficient in war'.[9] That is, like Aristotle, he wants Athenians to be better citizens, not just better-off ones.

Distributing money directly to the demos was a central part of Xenophon's plan. Like Aristotle, self-sufficiency is also key here: the scheme is proposed as a way to enhance public revenues without recourse to imperialism—to improve the self-sufficiency of the polis; indeed, Xenophon talks extensively in the *Poroi* about ways in which Athens can generate revenue and be more productive.[10] He wants to provide the stipend so that citizens are able to devote themselves to citizen-worthy pursuits: managing slaves, training in the gymnasium, and being better soldiers.[11] Its provision is, therefore, envisioned as a way to strengthen their ability to perform their civic responsibilities.[12] For both Xenophon and Aristotle, then, poverty relief is firmly rooted in civic, rather than material, concerns.

Other, more extreme, measures also demonstrate the centrality of civic concerns in discussions of poverty. Isokrates' solution, for example, to the problem of poverty and the perceived deficiencies in the Athenian system of political pay was to encourage the poor to live elsewhere.[13] He suggests this as part of a panhellenic plan to settle Greeks in the Chersonese (with land provided by Philip) or in Asia

[8] Xen. *Por.* 1.1.

[9] Xen. *Por.* 4.51, 6.1. Note that these characteristics directly contrast with the material and moral qualities the poor were thought to lack: see pp. 45–6 and that Xenophon is arguing for a citizen body that is shaped by elite ideas of self-definition (see pp. 47–8) to avoid instability (see p. 57).

[10] Self-sufficiency: Xen. *Por.* 1.1, 4.17–18; productivity: 2.7, 3.3–5, 12–14, 4.1.

[11] Xen. *Por.* 4.22, 51–2.

[12] See Gauthier 2010: 130–2.

[13] His view was that demagogues and sykophants ('bad advisors') drew their power from those who were reliant on the incomes they obtained through the Assembly and the courts. The aim of these *rhetores*, therefore, was to keep the demos poor—to keep them dependent on this income—in order to maintain their own political stature: Isoc. 8.129–31. That is, ideas about self-sufficiency and dependency are central here too.

Minor (with land taken from the Persians).[14] It is not just the poor of Athens who would be eligible, but settlers comprising citizens from different poleis, including those who were serving as mercenary soldiers. For Isokrates the benefit was to provide land and resources for those who lacked them (see also the fifth-century Brea decree), but this is a solution to poverty which again relied on political re-categorization rather than addressing the socioeconomic needs of this group; here citizenship is effectively revoked from the poor who are encouraged to emigrate which leaves those remaining better able (in Isokrates' view) to run their cities effectively. Removing the poor from the city entirely was also the solution of the oligarchic regime in 322.[15]

None of these plans were put into practice, but they do reveal how these authors link political pay specifically with the poor. Regardless of the conclusions that they draw from this (that is, about how pay shapes politics, negatively in their view), we might therefore reasonably ask whether political pay acted as a form of poverty relief. However, although it is probably true to say that—in numbers alone—more poor(er) citizens would have been recipients than wealthy ones, and that pay enabled them to participate in democratic institutions, it is not the case that it aimed to alleviate poverty per se. In fact, the various different forms of civic and political distributions were shaped (just like the alternate schemes put forward by these authors) much more closely by ideas about civic unity than those about poverty relief.

This is not to argue that the poor did not benefit financially through the provision of political pay, but to stress that this was given to citizens—and citizens alone—regardless of wealth for duties performed. The depiction of Philokleon in Aristophanes' *Wasps* as an old, poor man living off jury pay has been influential in shaping the views of historians, but the wealthy Perikles was just as entitled to receive it as Philokleon's non-fictional counterpart.[16] These payments were targeted not according to need but according to citizenship status, and restricted to citizens in exchange for their labour fulfilling

[14] Isoc. 5.120–3, 8.22–4, 12.13–14.

[15] Diod. 18.18.4–5, Plut. *Phoc.* 28.7.

[16] Markle 1985; 1990; Todd 1990. Arist. *Pol.* 1320a26–7 suggests that the *euporoi* might not even take up their *dikastikon* all of the time, but it was nevertheless available for them. Isokrates makes a virtue out of not profiting from public office: Isoc. 7.24–5, 12.145.

political or military duties of different kinds. Payments for office-holding, to those attending festivals, and to the disabled were for citizen men only (or for the orphaned sons of citizen men). Likewise, distributions of grain and other monies were restricted to citizens, and whilst these payments might have recognized the catastrophic effects of poverty, they were very much restricted to specific groups defined ultimately by their civic status.[17] Xenophon's scheme is no different here.[18] After 336/5, hoplite armour was provided at public expense as part of the reorganization of ephebic training, but this was, again, restricted to citizen men. Provisions for providing dowries for poor *epikleroi* were limited to citizens, and indeed were framed so as to benefit the closest male relative rather than address the poverty of the woman herself.[19]

These measures were not motivated by an impulse to provide a route out of poverty but by a desire to cement a sense of civic identity. In doing so they effectively bypassed established patronage networks as a means for support.[20] Even though the cost of providing these payments rose over the course of the democratic period, which indicates a continual commitment to the practice of payment, it is clear that they were not intended to constitute a coherent social policy, did not aim to alter the social structure through the targeted relief of need, and were not instituted to overcome economic inequalities in any serious way.[21] Even the *diobelia*—a (probably temporary) 2-obol payment instituted by Kleophon after the restoration of

[17] Disabled: Lys. 24 (with comments on pp. 48–50). Festivals: *Ath. Pol.* 43.1. Orphans: *Ath. Pol.* 24.3. Distribution of grain: Plut. *Per.* 37.4, *IG* I^3 379. See Dillon 1995; Roubineau 2012.

[18] Gauthier 2010: 126–31.

[19] [Dem.] 43.54. See Roubineau 2012: 170–3, who argues that the law provides essentially a 'get-out clause' for the nearest male relative who did not wish to marry the thetic *epikleros*.

[20] Patronage: *Ath. Pol.* 27.3 with Millett 1989; Dillon 1995. Civic identity: Roubineau 2012.

[21] Increase in Assembly pay: *Ath. Pol.* 41.3; for *adynatoi*: Dillon 1995: 38. In general: Podes 1993: figure 2. Rosivach 2011 links the commitment to pay in the fourth century directly to the effects of the Peloponnesian War: citizens used to state pay for military and jury service now demanded it for other activities. It might be the case that the continued economic growth of the fourth century was, at least in part, related to the commitment the Athenians showed towards political pay and other civic distributions (because it kept the economy afloat).

democracy in 410—was not targeted at the poor as such.[22] Instead it provided money 'for the demos', that is, for all adult male citizens.[23] In addition, the descendants of honoured individuals such as Aristeides or Aristogeiton were also singled out to receive public assistance, and although these are ad hoc cases, they reinforce the idea that public distributions should be seen in terms of reciprocity for civic service rather than as targeted aid.[24] It was not until late antiquity that the poor as a group, citizen and non-citizen alike, were recognized as deserving of aid because of their poverty rather than because of their civic status.[25]

It is undeniable, however, that political pay would have helped poorer citizens make ends meet in the short term: there were many opportunities for office-holding, jury service, military service, or attending festivals. But these were not intended to be poverty relief. It seems unlikely that pay—with perhaps the exception of rowing in the fleet—would have provided a long-term route out of poverty, because service, and therefore pay, could not be relied upon at any given time: most offices were selected by lot, thereby introducing a degree of randomness into selection; they were held for limited periods of time; and many political duties probably did not require frequent attendance.[26] Although 3 obols as payment for serving on a jury was no doubt welcome and perhaps even raised citizens from bare subsistence to having a higher standard of living if they served often enough, the complexities of selection meant that one could not rely on being chosen and therefore could not depend on the stability of that income.[27] *Theorika* for festival attendance cannot have been

[22] Some historians assume it was, however (presumably because they follow the elite sources' conflation of *demos* and *penetes*, on which see Chapter 2, n. 8): Ste. Croix 1954: 35: 'apparently a form of poor relief'; Roselli 2005: 17: distributed to 'destitute citizens'. This may have been an effect of the law, but it provided aid for all. See following note.

[23] *Ath. Pol.* 28.3, *Etymologicum Magnum*, s.v. *diobelia*. See Rosivach 2011: 182, n. 22: 'I understand *ho dēmos* here as referring to all adult male citizens, or at least to all those who chose to present themselves.'

[24] Plut. *Arist.* 27.3–5: Demetrios of Phaleron allegedly persuaded the Athenians to give a 3-obol pension to some female descendants of Aristeides (but see *APF*: 51–2 for discussion of the questionable historicity of the tradition). On pay and distributions as reciprocity see Hands 1968; Liddel 2007: 169; Cecchet 2014.

[25] Brown 2002. [26] Podes 1995: 12–13.

[27] *Ath. Pol.* 27.3, 62.2.

handed out more than a few times a year, and then only to those attending the theatre.[28]

For office-holding, Pritchard has recently tabulated the time commitment required to fulfil these duties, concluding that the majority of offices required full-time work: 60% of positions, from the *strategos* to the *agoranomoi* to the *tamias* of the Boule, are likely to have needed a considerable amount of time.[29] This picture, it should be noted, is drawn from a tally of the many different types of boards. However, if we look at the number of positions available within these boards a different conclusion emerges. Of the 656 known offices which an Athenian could hold in any given year, two-thirds are actually half- or quarter-time (67%), with only a third requiring full-time commitment (Table 5.1). The vast majority of positions, then, would not have provided a full-time income; those that did include the elected offices, those which were prestigious, and those which the Old Oligarch complains that the poor never held.[30] Moreover, if we assume that most officials were paid an average of 1 drachma per day for their service, office-holders might expect to receive an annual income more in the range of 75–150 drachmas than the 300–350 drachmas that a full-time office might supply.[31] Citizens might be able to piece together different kinds of service year after year, but relying on this alone would likely have been fairly precarious.

The primary reason for political pay and other forms of civic distributions, therefore, was compensatory for time spent away from other duties, rather than purely redistributive. In this sense they are most unlike contemporary policies which are concerned (at least rhetorically) with alleviating poverty. Instead, the aim was to reinforce existing social relationships by preserving the polis and the rights of the citizens within it.[32] The primary function, then,

[28] Roselli 2009 argues that payments existed on an occasional basis in the fifth century. From the 350s on they were more regular and controlled by the theoric fund, see Cawkwell 1963. Hands 1968: 98–9 argues that it was distributed to all, rather than just given to the poor.

[29] Pritchard 2013: 10–12.

[30] [Xen.] *Ath. Pol.* 1.3.

[31] Average of pay of the positions mentioned by *Ath. Pol.* 42.3, 62.2 is just under 1 drachma per day. Hansen 2014: 416, n. 25 estimates 354 working days a year. Larger numbers of half- or quarter-time positions might indicate, however, an expectation that most office-holders had other duties (farming, workshops, other business interests, and so on) that they needed to perform.

[32] See also Roubineau 2012. This also served to highlight differences between citizens and non-citizens: see, in the context of the *theorikon*, Wilson 1997: 100.

Table 5.1. Time commitments of democratic office-holders

	Type of office			
	Full time	Half time	Quarter time	Total
Number of boards	41	14	13	68
%	60	21	19	100
Number of positions available	219	123	314	656
%	33	19	48	100

Source: Pritchard 2013: Table 1.

was to reinforce a sense of civic unity rather than to lift Athenians out of poverty.

The relationship between pay, poverty, and civic unity can also be traced in the public funding debates of the 340s. These dealt with raising revenue and its expenditure, and led to reforms in liturgical service.[33] Demosthenes, speaking in the *Fourth Philippic* (dated to 341), places the theoric fund at the centre of the debate, and presents himself, Solon-like, as mediator between the two sides: the *euporoi* and the *aporoi*.[34] He portrays the *euporoi* as critical of the fund, perhaps to the point of wishing to remove it altogether, whereas the *aporoi* overestimate its importance and behave irresponsibly.[35] Although he acknowledges the material effects that the fund has—it provides for those in need—he frames this in the idea of collective fortune (*tyche*) and the need for collective action: the city as a whole has increased its revenues, all should share in this, because all should prepare for war. The presence of poor citizens is acknowledged as a cause for distress within the polis, and providing for them is (as for Aristotle) a matter of justice. But Demosthenes' family metaphor at this point in the speech is revealing. Here he compares the treatment of the poor to the duty of providing for elderly parents.[36] However, it

[33] Gabrielsen 1994: 207–13.

[34] Dem. 10.35–45. See also Dem. 3.10–18, 30–6, 13.1–2. The traditional view that Demosthenes was hostile to the fund has been disputed by Harris 1996. See further Hadjú 2002: 284–332.

[35] Dem. 10.36. Note that he only uses the term *ptochos* once in this speech (10.68) when talking about the disgraceful actions of those who have rapidly become rich through siding with Philip (see p. 159). He never refers to the poor as *penetes* here. On Demosthenes in the Solon role see Harris 1996: 135.

[36] Dem. 10.40–3: 'In my opinion it is only proper that we take on and willingly discharge for our parents a debt of gratitude, which is doubly required, both by nature

is not the *aporoi* who in this metaphor are the parents to whom care is due, it is the citizen body as a whole (*koinous . . . tous goneas sumpantas*).[37] This is less, then, a call for aid to be given to the poor out of concern for their poverty, than part of a strategy which emphasizes togetherness in the face of hostility to Philip.

Providing for the poor is for Demosthenes a pragmatic decision to foster unity.[38] He argues that helping to provide the necessities of life is to the advantage of the *euporoi* and not to do so risks *stasis*, but he also tells the *aporoi* not to confiscate the property of the wealthy. He frequently refers to the poor as being in need, but also portrays them as dissatisfied too, constantly conniving to take property from the *euporoi*. In this sense, then, their depiction here, despite Demosthenes' efforts at mediation, is very much in line with the discourses outlined in Chapter 2. Eight years earlier, in the *Third Olynthiac*, he claimed to have 'brought order' to the organization of the fund, by establishing 'a uniform system of pay and of service, whether in the field or in the lawcourts or wherever each man finds a task suited to his own age and to the needs of the occasion'.[39] Here he demonstrates the basic premise of all forms of political pay—it was conceptualized as payment in return for service—and he is critical of those who do not provide such service. It is the active, not the idle, who deserve pay; that is, it is civic action, not poverty, that is at the heart of the distributions. Those who are not active citizens are associated with servile dependency, docility, and moral decline.[40] Idleness is anti-social and by definition uncitizen-like, and non-citizens do not deserve pay.[41] In this way Demosthenes pushes this group, that is, those who do nothing (or, perhaps rather, those who are perceived by the *euporoi* as doing nothing) in return for their pay, to the peripheries of civic society. They are no longer behaving as good citizens.

If we follow Harris, then the controversy surrounding the fund does not appear to be in its existence but in its management.[42] This is certainly the case in the *Fourth Philippic*, and arguably so too in the other speeches in which Demosthenes talks about the theoric fund.

and by law. Just as each one of us has a parent, so we should think of all the citizens as the collective parents of the whole city. Far from depriving them of whatever the city gives them, we should consider, if they receive nothing, what other sources we can use to ensure that they have whatever they need,' (trans. Trevett).

[37] Dem. 10.41. [38] See also Xen. *Por.* 6.1–3. [39] Dem. 3.35.
[40] Dem. 3.29, 31. [41] See also Isoc. 7.44–5, 8.75–6. [42] See n. 35.

It is not the fund itself which is the problem, Demosthenes argues, but the talk surrounding it: that is, the unfair criticisms, or exaggerated importance, of its role.[43] Demosthenes' solution, therefore, is rhetorical as much as practical: civic unity is better than civic discord. This is underscored by his frequent use of the word *koina* (and its cognates) throughout this section of the speech, highlighting the togetherness for which he is arguing. This is a call-to-arms for the Athenians to unite against Philip and actively (rather than reactively) prepare for war.

Payments to the demos certainly shaped equality and inequality in Athens, but political pay and other civic distributions were more concerned with political rather than economic equality. They were conceived in terms of reciprocity rather than as social aid to the poor.[44] This is not to suggest that they could never be a significant resource for poorer Athenians: direct payments in cash are often thought by modern poverty researchers to be a beneficial method of reaching those in need, because it allows them to spend that money on the things most helpful to them, and Demosthenes' cautious moderation when talking about the theoric fund, stylized though this may be, suggests such payments were highly valued.[45] However, what is important to stress here is that these entitlements are shaped by the presence or absence of citizenship—indeed, in both Aristotle's and Demosthenes' view the presence or absence of *good* citizenship—and therefore served to mark these statuses. It is possible that dependants of citizens (wives, children, slaves, and so on) could indirectly benefit by their husbands or masters receiving payments, but with the possible exception of Aristeides' descendants (the historicity of which is doubted), they did not receive them in themselves and they were

[43] Dem. 10.36.

[44] Theophrastus, in his characterization of the *agroikos*, assumes that hired agricultural labourers (*misthotai*) not only do not attend the Assembly, but have no real right to be there (and therefore claim its pay): *Char.* 4.6. See also literature cited on p. 154, n. 17.

[45] The efficacy of direct payments is related to ideas about the role of markets in reducing poverty: the rationale rests on the theory that the poor are excluded from markets and cash transfers not only allow them to be integrated into the broader economy but also invest in human capital (e.g. children's schooling, healthcare). See Fiszbein and Schady 2009. That these payments need not be envisaged in neo-liberal terms see Ferguson 2010, but there is no hint in Xenophon's *Poroi* that he envisages his stipend in this way: here, it frees up citizens to be better soldiers. He does not imagine that they will spend more.

vulnerable to intra-household decision-making.[46] Political pay and other civic distributions may have added to the family income, but they also served to reproduce poverty amongst those who were not entitled to them as well as among those who did not regularly serve the city.

LOCAL INSTITUTIONS AND SOCIAL NETWORKS

Civic status, therefore, shaped the experience of poverty through the institutions of the polis, but we can also examine how other institutions performed a similar role. Here I will investigate, first, the role of local political structures, primarily in the demes, in responding to the needs of their members, before examining how social networks more broadly shaped access to resources. Given that the demes provided opportunities for Athenians to be politically active within their local communities, promoted political participation and local autonomy, and had various religious duties which brought demesmen and their families together, it is reasonable to ask whether these institutions were organized in a way which alleviated hardship amongst their members. As reasonably small hereditary groups, demes were, at least in theory, not only in a good position to know whether their members required assistance, but also had the political power and resources to provide this. However, the evidence suggests that this picture is questionable at best.

After discussion of the role of the demes, I will then consider the role that social networks played in providing assistance for various groups among the poor, investigating voluntary associations, structures of credit, and the distribution of sacrificial meat. It is clear, for example, that some voluntary associations provided resources to their members, but it is also necessary to ask: what were the limits of this assistance? There is no evidence that associations acted like charities, targeting relief to those in need, nor did they seem to help those who were not in the group. In this sense, then, they act much like civic institutions, providing resources for members but having little concern for non-members. However, because there is abundant evidence

[46] See Chapter 4, pp. 128–33.

that such associations were common, diverse (they incorporated a broad range of people: women, non-citizens, and slaves, as well as citizen men), and firmly embedded in Athenian society, we can also use them as a case study for investigating the relationship between social capital and poverty alleviation and reproduction. To what extent did the patterning of social networks play a role in buffering poverty? To what extent did they reproduce relations of power, creating additional structures of constraint which were difficult to break? These are the questions I will investigate in this section.

Poverty-Alleviation Structures in the Deme?

Given that demes were hereditary groups of families centred on a specific locality with civic and religious responsibilities, one might expect that they were fairly tight-knit communities which may have had knowledge about general patterns of hardship among their members—this is, for example, the idea that Euxitheos taps into when explaining his family's situation.[47] It is reasonable to assume, for example, that the median deme had something in the region of 180 adult male members, which suggests a total population of just under 1,100.[48] However, some demes were much larger (the largest deme, Acharnai, probably had a fourth-century membership in the region of just over 1,300 men; including women, children, and slaves suggests a population approaching 8,000), and patterns of migration and mobility meant that not all demesmen lived in their deme.[49] The *diapsephismos* of 346 suggests that there was anxiety about membership and that part of this anxiety was that non-citizens were passing themselves off as demesmen, thereby gaining access to resources they were not ordinarily entitled to: citizenship status, the ability to own land and/or marry a citizen, political participation, access to justice, and so on.[50] This reinforces the idea that civic status was central to the provision of resources.

47 Dem. 57. On demes as 'face-to-face' societies see Osborne 1985.

48 This assumes a fourth-century population of 30,000 divided evenly according to bouleutic quota between the demes, and that every demesmen has (on average) a wife, two children, and two slaves: a hypothetical but plausible reconstruction. On the relationship between bouleutic quota and deme population see Taylor 2007a: 76–7, n. 10.

49 Osborne 1991; Taylor 2011b.

50 See Dem. 57, Is. 12; on the alleged lax registration habits of Sounion and Potamos see Anaxandrides, *Anchises* F 4, Harp. s.v. Potamos with Whitehead 1986: 259, n. 15, 342.

Were there mechanisms in the demes (or other local groups) which can be seen in terms of poverty alleviation, even if only indirectly? The epigraphic record suggests that one of the primary activities of the deme was to perform sacrifices at the appropriate time. Sacrificial calendars marked in detail what offering was required, to which deity, and when, highlighting the central role of religious practice to the community.[51] Like other groups, such as phratries and *gene*, demes maintained sanctuaries and shrines, and appointed priests to serve the community of worshippers.

If we look across the variety of religious groups in Athens, it is clear that priesthoods were held by a diverse group of people, and whilst some were undoubtedly prestigious and drawn from members of the wealthiest families, not all were dominated by the wealthy elite.[52] Being able to demonstrate appropriate lineage to serve as a priest appears to have been more important than wealth in gaining a position—at least such is the argument of Euxitheos in Demosthenes 57, who uses his deme priesthood, despite his emphasis on his family's own poverty, as a measure of his citizen ancestry.[53] Appointment by lot appears to have been the norm for *gene*, which would have ensured that they were drawn from a broad portion of the *gennetai* rather than just certain families.[54] The vast majority of priests whose names survive were not otherwise prominent men or women.

This raises the possibility of whether serving as a priest provided a kind of indirect 'support mechanism', particularly at the local level where communities were relatively small and the number of priests relatively high. The changing meaning of the term 'parasite', which developed from designating a religious official whose duties allowed him to eat with the priests, in the archaic period, to a dinner-chaser in the fourth century, implies this is not impossible (although it also indicates that certain types of consumption were not tolerated).[55]

[51] Parker 2005: 64–6.

[52] The priestess of Athena Polias was probably drawn from members of the Eteoboutadai (see Connelly 2007: 59–64), whereas Demosthenes lampoons Aeschines' mother for being a priestess of a *thiasos*: Dem. 18.130, 284.

[53] Dem. 57.46–8. See also the outrage that the jury is meant to feel at Phano's alleged deception of her husband, the archon basileus: [Dem.] 59.73.

[54] Blok and Lambert 2009, who also discuss the deme priesthood of Euxitheos on pp. 100–1.

[55] Corner 2013a, 2013b.

The primary reward of being a priest was, for sure, religious in nature, but priests also received perquisites: generally the choicest cuts of meat, sometimes other animal products such as skins (presumably to dispose of at their will, which includes selling at profit), as well as money for their services.[56] An inscription from Aixone details these transactions within that deme.[57] Here, numerous local religious officials (priestesses as well as priests) are recorded receiving the distribution of skins and meat from the sacrifice, as well as a 5-drachma fee. These payments appear generous, and as such it is tempting to view priestly service here not just in terms of the religious needs of the community but in its broader economic function in providing for members of the local community. However, it is likely that the payments occurred irregularly, perhaps even annually, which would then suggest that any such support was more infrequent than frequent. This in turn suggests that opportunities to use priestly service as a means of economic support were limited.

In general, the epigraphic evidence from demes shows that networks of local elites were prominent in many communities, receiving honours and performing benefactions.[58] Collectively, demes (as well as phratries and *gene*) sought to raise income for their communal purpose, but frequently these reflected the patterns we have seen already within the civic body: that is, the aim was to reinforce community status rather than alleviate the economic hardship of members.[59] It seems reasonable, for example, to expect that those with small or no landholdings would have been able to rent land or other property from the demes in order to maintain, at the very least, a subsistence lifestyle. Non-citizens were prevented from landownership after all, and as many as 5,000 citizens were supposedly without land in 403, which suggests, in broad terms at least, a need.[60]

[56] Lambert 2002a; Tsoukala 2009.

[57] *SEG* 54.214. See Parker 2010. Parker discusses whether this is a deme or a *genos* document, coming down on the side of the deme. If so, this would mean that there are five attested priests and seven attested priestesses in Aixone and presumably more (*SEG* 54.214 is broken at the top).

[58] See e.g. the epigraphic record of Aixone where, from a small corpus of inscriptions, two families (that of Auteas and that of Chremes) dominate activity: cf. *IG* II^2 2492 with *SEG* 36.186 and *IG* II^2 1199 with *IG* II^2 1200.

[59] Dem. 57.58 hints at some of the tensions that could occur within demes, particularly surrounding the *diapsephismos* of 346: Euxitheos accuses Halimous of expelling elderly poor men from the deme.

[60] Dion. Hal. *Hypothesis* to Lys. 32.

These people had to live somewhere and support themselves somehow, but the system of deme land rental does not appear to be designed to provide resources for this group of people.

Aside from maintaining the religious traditions of the community, a key part of the activity of demes and other groups was to lease out property; mostly (though perhaps not always) this was to members of their own community.[61] Such leases provided opportunities to acquire access to mineral and water resources as well as agricultural and pasture land and other properties such as houses, but in most cases these were not designed to give poor men things that they did not have.[62] On the contrary, prosopographical examination of the surviving leases suggest that land-leasing—across all corporate bodies—was not taken up by those who were poor but predominantly by men who were demonstrably wealthy, well connected, and keen to show their *philotimia*.[63] As Papazarkadas shows, those who leased land did so for a variety of reasons: some plots were close to properties they already owned, others leased land to further their businesses, some had family or cultic ties which provided connections to the land or the community. Rarely were these men poor. Indeed, often leases were more like quasi-liturgies providing opportunity for religious patronage, family profit, and social esteem rather than providing relief for the landless or those who had little.[64] They required guarantors who were solvent, or sureties to be paid, and probably terms were settled at public auction.[65] That some renters sometimes defaulted is also likely, because it seems that demes did indeed acquire property this way.[66] All of these factors would have weighted this activity towards the more affluent. Leasing, therefore, far from being a

[61] Papazarkadas 2011: 152–3. *IG* II^2 2496 records land owned by the Kytherioi in the Piraeus rented by an Acharnian. It is likely that examples like this disguise links between men through matrilineal marriage or adoption, however.

[62] Osborne 1988: 291.

[63] See Papazarkadas 2011: 299–325 for a valuable and nuanced re-evaluation of Shipton 2000.

[64] Osborne 1988: 288–9; Papazarkadas 2011: 150–5. Note the prevalence of father–son pairs in Papazarkadas' discussion: generations of family involvement suggest special interests. See also Andreyev 1974: 44.

[65] Auction was the primary means by which confiscated land was sold off: *Agora XIX*: p. 58. Papazarkadas 2011: 55–6 discusses the alternatives, concluding 'that auctions constituted . . . normal practice' for other bodies as well. Competitive bidding would favour those with the greatest levels of disposable resources. On solvent (*axiochreous*) guarantors at Eleusis see *IEleusis* 85.

[66] Papazarkadas 2011: 131–2.

way for landless or poor Athenians to gain access to land, should in fact be seen as a way in which poverty was reproduced.

A possible exception is a lease from the Piraeus dated to 322/1.[67] This lease distinguishes between rentals below 10 drachmas and those above; the former, according to the recent reinterpretation by Papazarkadas, refers to pasture lands, while the latter to arable. This inscription, he argues, formed part of a direct response to the political situation of 322 from the democratic heartland of the Piraeus, which was considerably affected by the mass disenfranchisements, abolition of state pay, and resulting increased numbers of impoverished residents.[68] Both citizens and metics—anyone with no or little land—would have been provided by the deme with the opportunity to bid for pasture land if they could find a guarantor, whilst those who could provide sureties in the form of land were able to rent the more expensive agricultural plots.[69] This latter group faced additional restrictions on what they could and could not do with the plots, following normal practice within the corpus of leases, but the deme encouraged renters by offering (essentially) tax breaks.[70]

However, given that it is only the relatively wealthy who paid contributions such as the *eisphora* mentioned here, this measure should be seen as directly appealing to them. The more profitable and more productive plots, therefore, seemed to have been rented to the same group of people as the other leases, and although the financial requirements for leasing pasture land were lower, renters were still required to provide guarantors (so needed to be sufficiently well connected to know men of property willing and able to help); returns on these plots were presumably, as a result, lower.[71] This lease, too, therefore reproduces the structures of wealth and poverty rather than breaking them apart.

There is some evidence that demes used the terms of their leases to buffer certain types of economic shocks. The Prasiai lease, dated to

[67] *IG* II^2 2498.

[68] Papazarkadas 2011: 121–2. Disenfranchisement: Diod. 18.18.4.

[69] Securities of real property: Harris 1993: 86. This is standard practice.

[70] *IG* II^2 2498, ll. 6–9.

[71] However, see Hodkinson 1992, who makes a strong case for pastoralism as a key part of wealthy farmers' market-oriented production. In these terms, then, one would not expect much difference in those who leased pastoral and agricultural land.

the second half of the fourth century, includes a clause in which the deme assumes some liability in case of war damage to the crops.[72] Similar measures are included in leases from Aixone, Teithras, and the Dyaleis phratry in Myrrhinous.[73] But if these were measures to safeguard renters, they only did so in exceptional circumstances: they only provided assistance to those who took up the leases, and as we have seen, these were not typically the poor. In fact, most historians have seen these clauses as being much like those which provide tax relief: they are designed to encourage renters—predominantly wealthier members within the designated community—to take up the leases by allowing the community as a whole to take on some of the risk.[74]

SOCIAL NETWORKS: MAINTENANCE OF THE POOR OR MAINTENANCE OF POVERTY?

Civic status was therefore an important factor in shaping access to resources in Athens, and political pay alleviated forms of economic hardship, but its primary aim was to maintain civic bonds rather than provide a welfare system as such. Even within relatively small citizen-only groups such as demes and phratries, it is clear, particularly with regard to land-leasing, that social relations shaped access to resources to a large extent. Finding guarantors necessitated gaining assurances from those who had surpluses. This suggests that the patterning of social networks is a factor which deserves further scrutiny, not least because these cut across civic status and so potentially provide an insight into the strategies of those who were not citizens as well as those who were. Here we can examine three areas: the role of voluntary associations in providing access to resources, differential structures of credit, and the distribution of sacrificial meat at festivals.

[72] *SEG* 51.153.

[73] *IG* II^2 2492, *SEG* 24.151, *IG* II^2 1241. See Papazarkadas 2011: 122–3; Oliver 2007: 157–8.

[74] Whitehead 1986: 156.

Voluntary Associations

Recent research has placed renewed attention on the diversity of voluntary associations in the ancient Greek world. In Athens these formed a central part of society, providing a forum for commensality and often cutting across divisions of status: some associations allowed both men and women, slave and free, citizen and non-citizen to join.[75] Being a member of an association brought various benefits: aside from sociability and participation in cult, some explicitly state that they will provide various kinds of assistance to their members. Others were formed to 'aim at some particular advantage', be that profit, the provision of credit to their members, companionship, or celebration of festivals.[76]

Although associations aided their members by providing assistance, and although some groups certainly engaged in moneylending, this assistance was not always specifically financial.[77] It is stretching the evidence too far to say that associations routinely aimed to help their members in economic hardship. First of all, each group was different. Some groups were exclusive and for elite citizens only, such as the *synomosiai* of 412/11 that 'existed for the management of lawsuits and elections', or the *hetaireiai* involved in establishing the Thirty, and there is no evidence at all to suggest groups like these were concerned with helping non-members.[78] Others, such as the *thiasotai* of Bendis, charged a fee to join, although where evidence survives as to the sum it is low; some others required moderate leisure to participate; others lent money at interest, presumably for the benefit of the group as a whole.[79] Providing help with burials is attested, but not until the third century,[80] and this need not be a financial

[75] Arnaoutoglou 2003; Gabrielsen 2007; Vlassopoulos 2007a; Gottesman 2014.

[76] Arist. *NE* 1160a14–30.

[77] See e.g. *IG* II^2 1275 (*c*.325–275), which provides help to members who are wronged: 'if someone is wronged, they and all the friends shall come to his assistance (*ἄν τις ἀδικῆται, βοηθεῖν καὶ αὐτοὺς καὶ τοὺς φίλους ἅπαντας*).' On the credit activities of *eranistai* see discussion that follows.

[78] Thuc. 8.54.4, *Ath. Pol.* 34.3.

[79] Fees: *IG* II^2 1361 (330–324/3; 2 dr.), *IG* II^2 1298 (248/7; unknown fee), *IG* II^2 1291 (mid-third century; unknown fee). Time: *IG* II^2 1263 (300/299) has an *agora kyria* (implying fairly regular meetings). Lending money at interest: see discussion by Thomsen 2014: 173–4.

[80] *IG* II^2 10248 (third century?), *IG* II^2 1277 (278/7), *IG* II^2 1278 (272/1; though note *taphikon* is restored here), *IG* II^2 1323 (194/3). Kloppenborg and Ascough 2011: 98 assume that *IG* II^2 1278 is predominantly a metic association (on the grounds that

obligation as much as a religious one.[81] Indeed, it is possible that such support was conceived not as a means of assisting those who would otherwise have gone without any proper burial, but rather in addition to that already provided by the family or the deceased themselves.[82] In this sense, the *taphikon* becomes a means by which to promote family or cultic honour rather than a form of poverty relief.

Aside from those who are honoured as benefactors, it is difficult to draw conclusions about the financial status of association members without heavy speculation, but it is possible to examine the structural effect that such groups had on Athens as a whole. The frequency with which they appear in the historical record and their diversity of membership suggests that Athenian society was densely populated with such groups; many more would have likely existed which did not leave a trace of their activities. This implies that we should supplement an analysis that focuses on the characteristics of each association (important though this is) by thinking about them structurally in terms of social networks and their role in fostering social capital.[83]

Social capital can be thought of as a resource embedded in social networks which can be utilized to some end, good or bad. It can provide access to resources (social, political, economic) and create and uphold shared norms and values, but it can also produce conflict, inequality, and exclusion. That is, groups such as voluntary associations, as well as providing resources for their members (and therefore expanding the circle of contacts that a person in difficulty can call on), can reproduce or reinforce existing inequalities and relations of power.[84] Gottesman provides a nice example of this in his discussion of the late third-century honorific decree of the Sarapiastai. Here a woman, Nikippe, clearly has a position of authority within the *eranos* (she has the title *proeranistria*), but the text of the inscription reveals

it helped pay for burials and citizens would have had families to do so for them), but it might be the case that *koina* like this stepped into the gap that political pay and/or deme governance filled for citizens in the fourth century. If van Wees 2011 is correct in identifying 'metics' post-322 as including disenfranchised citizens, then both positions could be reconciled. Based on onomastic criteria it seems likely that *IG* II^2 1277 includes metics or slaves. *IG* II^2 10248 is a grave-marker set up by *eranistai* for Artemidoros of Seleucia.

[81] *IG* II^2 1275 is concerned with ensuring attendance at funerals rather than helping with the costs of them. See Kloppenborg and Ascough 2011: 52–8.

[82] Kloppenborg and Ascough 2011: 8.

[83] See e.g. Taylor 2015.

[84] See Bourdieu 1984; Portes 1998; Putnam 2000.

her deficit of honours in comparison to the male *tamias*, *grammateus*, and *epimeletes* who are honoured effusively here.[85] Whilst Nikippe has a role in the association—possibly one connected to her financial support of the group—it is one that appears to be constrained by her gender.[86]

As a concept, social capital is useful because it forces us to consider the role that different kind of networks play, the contexts in which we find them (or, perhaps, the contexts in which they survive), the different types of value they bring, and the exclusions they promote.[87] Not all social networks work in the same way at all times: they are not fixed entities, but can be thought of in terms of processes through which interpersonal relations are defined and redefined, through which meanings are constructed and challenged, and status is negotiated.[88] The rich tapestry of voluntary associations in Athens, then, can be assessed both in terms of their direct impact (for example, on their relationship to polis institutions or their religious practices) and in a broader, more indirect way. Associations fostered strong ties between members: they came together socially and took part in cult activity. This is, of course, an association's principal function. The relationships formed in these associations do not appear to have been explicitly conceived in terms of patronage: although they sometimes appoint officials and provide honours, these groups do not appear to be especially hierarchical.[89] Although voluntary, there is no evidence that they demanded services or political support in return for membership, and—as far as we can tell—they did not seek to create asymmetrical relationships between their members; instead they

[85] *IG* II^2 1292. See Gottesman 2014: 53.

[86] On her possible financial role as benefactor see Arnaoutoglou 1994b: 109.

[87] There are two main criticisms with social capital as an idea: (i) the intangibility of defining a 'resource embedded within social networks' on a theoretical level, and (ii) the application of the idea in practice. Many different disciplines have developed their own versions of social capital and adapted the idea for their own use, which has led to some rather large (and mutually incompatible) claims, i.e. critics argue that it can easily become an explanatory factor for almost anything and therefore loses its heuristic value. See esp. Gaggio 2004; Fine 2010 for discussions, but also feminist critiques, which are of particular importance for the ancient world because of their emphasis on relations of power: Kovaleinen 2004; O'Neill and Gidengil 2006.

[88] Gaggio 2004; 2007; Carnevali 2011.

[89] Benefactors are sometimes styled as euergetists, e.g. *IG* II^2 1252 (late fourth century), *IG* II^2 1271 (299/8), but these mimic the language of honorific polis decrees (whereby the demos is certainly viewed in terms of equality).

framed their activities within a legalistic and honorific framework.[90] They were venues of sociability and commensality, intrinsically valuable in themselves.

Aside from bonding members together, each member of an association was linked to others within Athens (and beyond) through friends of friends, acquaintances of acquaintances, relatives of relatives, and so on. These weak ties (or bridging social capital) have been shown to be instrumental in providing access to resources otherwise unavailable, and are a way through which people can (though do not necessarily) accrue a variety of benefits.[91] These are different types of social relationships where connections are indirect, but which link families, associations, or other groups together. Whilst we only have snapshots of certain parts of this process—and these in themselves are highly selective—we can piece together such evidence to say, at the very least, that Athens was a densely networked society, and use this as a basis for exploring inequality.[92] Strong ties tend to act as a safetynet: Athenians call on their friends, families, and neighbours for help, but weak ties (for example, the indirect connections made through a *thiasos*, through service on the Boule, or through business deals to others within Athens) can allow people to flourish.[93]

In a densely networked associative society which is rich in weak ties there are many opportunities to gain access to resources otherwise unavailable. These resources might be social (new friends), political (greater influence), or economic (increased business opportunities). The simple act of belonging to a group is a critical way in which poor people become part of a community and develop social capital. We have seen this already in Chapter 4 in relation to women, and Chapter 6 investigates this further, exploring the advantages that it might bring.[94] Here, however, I want to focus on the constraints. If we assume that Athens was a society such as that described, those with fewer social networks to begin with are placed at a distinct disadvantage and become, as a result, increasingly vulnerable. Research among the poorest groups in contemporary societies shows that they frequently lack social capital and have fewer social networks. The social

[90] Arnaoutoglou 1994a, *pace* Gallant 1991.
[91] Granovetter 1973.
[92] Participation in voluntary associations is also related to robust democratic institutions: Putnam 1993; 2000. In Athens: Ober 2008; Gottesman 2014: 63–76.
[93] For further examples and discussion see Chapter 6, pp. 219–33.
[94] See also Stewart 2005.

networks which are less 'productive' are more dependent on networks bound with strong ties which are subject to fracture, and are frequently constrained by tightly proscribed social norms which promote or discourage certain behaviours.[95] In Athens, debt-bondage might be thought of in these terms.

Enslavement for debt was prohibited by Solon, but debt-bondage is clearly present in a play of Menander's, and historians assume that this reflects an under-documented part of Athenian life.[96] It most likely formed a strategy of last resort for people who needed help but had nothing but their labour with which to pay back, and despite the lack of direct evidence for this type of credit, such arrangements might well have occurred more frequently than attested, both during and after the end of the democratic period.[97] In *Heros*, the plot centres around a freedman shepherd, Tibeios, who has borrowed 200 drachmas (in two separate instalments) and then died. His son Gorgias then borrows more money for his father's funeral before going to work with his sister, Plangon, for their creditor and his wife. Despite the fragmentary text (the full plot is known only in outline), this is clearly an arrangement which is stigmatized. Social norms, therefore, discourage this kind of action, but Gorgias and Plangon have limited social capital to draw on (they cannot get the money from elsewhere and do not have the resources to work independently whilst paying back the debt) and so have to rely on this type of arrangement.

Aside from the fact that debt-bondage shows up rarely (and controversially) in the source material, which reflects the sense that it is a source of shame, this stigma is configured in the play through the status of the men who are sexually interested in Plangon. Daos, a household slave, in love with the young woman, is arranged as a husband for Plangon, but he loses his bride to Pheidias, a citizen, once it is revealed that Plangon is really the daughter of her mistress Myrrhine and therefore a citizen herself. When she is the daughter of a freedman she is in service (*diakonei*) and fair game for the attentions of a slave; when her 'true' identity is revealed she becomes

95 Cleaver 2005; Thorp, Stewart, and Heyer 2005.

96 Men. *Her.* 27–39. See Harris 2002b for other possible examples. Across the Greek world: Ste. Croix 1981: 136–7, 162–5 (on p. 287 Ste. Croix implies that debt bondage and enslavement for debt are particularly associated with the exploitation of the poor in oligarchic regimes).

97 See Millett 1991: 77–8.

a wife. Although not enough of the play survives to know what, if anything, happened to the debt at the end of the plot, the likelihood is that Pheidias was a rich man, and the assumption is therefore that it is paid off. Plangon and Gorgias have to renegotiate their place in society after the death of Tibeios, and this gets renegotiated once more when their true parentage comes to light. Their social capital is enhanced through their new-found circumstances.

Structures of Credit

Access to credit, that is, access to additional resources, was therefore shaped by social networks. Whether money was needed to pay for life-events such as dowries or funerals (as with Plangon and Gorgias), to tide a family over after a bad harvest, to use for business expenses, or to pay for manumission, the availability of credit demonstrated who belonged to the community and who did not. Credit was available from a wide variety of sources: groups such as demes, phratries, or voluntary associations, as well as from individual citizens with surpluses. In fact, lending and borrowing are so frequently mentioned that it is clear that credit was not just available for the wealthy but was widespread and pervasive throughout society. Slaves, for example, frequently used credit to pay for their manumission through *koina eraniston*, and a woman is mentioned as a loan-collector for a group of *eranistai* on a *horos* inscription.[98] These examples show that debt is not necessarily a bad thing—it can provide resources to significantly improve the quality of life—but what is important here, of course, is the ability to pay back loans. Although debt was a significant political issue across the Greek world, leading to many calls for its abolition (and resulting *stasis*), there was no serious call to do so in fourth-century Athens.[99]

However, despite the fact that credit was seemingly pervasive, the evidence is nonetheless weighted to the practices of, if not wealthy, then wealthier citizens, or at least those who owned land. This is demonstrated particularly by the *horoi* inscriptions, which delineated the boundaries of an encumbered property and in doing so provide

[98] *SEG* 42.149: Harris 1992.

[99] Ste. Croix 1981: 162–3, 215; Fuks 1974. Compare, of course, the situation that led to the reforms of Solon.

information about the credit-raising activities of landowners.[100] Whilst many of these are for relatively small sums (Harris reports from an updated catalogue that the median loan is 750 drachmas), some land was nevertheless required in order to pledge as security.[101] Those without land, of course, were not able to provide security on it, reducing their options for borrowing considerably.

Whether this was a problem or not depends on what other types of property could be used as security, and we should not necessarily assume that the landless were always poorer than landowners. However, with the exception of an Aristophanic joke, whenever such pledges are mentioned they are also items of often considerable value.[102] Both gift-giving and *eranoi* loans potentially filled a gap here, as did debt-bondage (although loans provided by *eranistai* are frequently secured on land, and legal mechanisms existed in order to deal with disputes arising from them).[103] For the borrower, *eranoi* loans provided credit and were usually collected from multiple *philoi* until the required sum was furnished.[104] Given that Neaira was able to secure her freedom this way, it is clear that such lending was widely available and not restricted to citizens.[105] However, borrowers would still need to be sufficiently well connected—have lots of strong ties through whatever social networks were at their disposal—to be able to find willing creditors (Neiara, for example, calls on her wealthy clients for help). Those whose networks were limited were at a disadvantage here too.

The provision of loans is presented in the lawcourts as being a normal part of life for citizens who had surpluses, a way to help one's

[100] Finley 1985. On the function of such loans compare Millett 1991: 59: 'only exceptionally, if ever, did a borrower take out a loan with the intention of increasing his wealth', with Foxhall 2007: 48–50, who discusses why categorizing borrowing as 'productive' or 'non-productive' is problematic. See further Bresson 2015: 280.

[101] Harris 2013: 136. Is 750 dr. a relatively small sum? On Ober's model (see Chapter 3), this accounts for a minimum of two years' income whilst spending nothing for a citizen whose earnings were a drachma per day.

[102] Dem. 27.9–11: slaves; Dem. 33.6: ship; Dem. 35.21–2: cargo of wine; Dem. 41.11: *phiale*, jewellery, textiles; [Dem.] 49.50: copper; [Dem.] 53.9: gold crown. Lys. 8.10: horse. The humour of Ar. *Eccl.* 746–55 surely derives from the mundanity of the objects pledged. See further Millett 1991: 77.

[103] *Ath. Pol.* 52.2.

[104] Thomsen 2014: 156–7 points out that the interest-free status of these loans is actually an assumption based on the fact that lenders were *philoi*. Cohen 1992: 207–15 is entirely sceptical of their interest-free nature.

[105] [Dem.] 59.30–2.

friends and neighbours. Indeed, lending may have been a way not just for the relatively wealthy to aid members of their community, but for less wealthy groups to negotiate risk against future hardship by calling in debts.[106] Parkin argues that in the Roman world non-elite groups probably provided most help for the destitute, but that this is precisely the day-to-day giving that rarely shows up in the evidence, and the same might be true of Athens.[107] Frequently, Athenians advertise their help to others or are vaunted by their fellow citizens for doing so, not only through the provision of loans, but by providing food, armour, paying ransoms, providing money for dowries, or paying for funerals.[108] Caring for one's fellow citizens was, therefore, a way to demonstrate civic-mindedness and good character in a public setting, and there were strong social (and in some cases legal) pressures to provide for certain groups of poor, such as elderly parents or freed household slaves.[109] Priests of the Bouzygai *genos* annually cursed those who did not provide basic assistance to those in need, suggesting that community action or cooperation was a key part of dealing with the very poor (although the 'poor' here are conceptualized not as members of one's own community but travellers seeking assistance).[110]

However, these good deeds are presented exclusively from the point of view of the 'giver' rather than the 'receiver' of the help.[111] Reciprocity required repayment, something that might have been difficult or impossible for some, and placed the receiving party in a relationship of dependence on the gift-giver.[112] Theophrastos mocks

[106] The wealthy and prominent are not disproportionately represented among *eranistai*. See Arnaoutoglou 2003: 80, albeit with Gabrielsen 2015: 197–8 for the exceptions.

[107] Parkin 2006: 69.

[108] Food: *Ath. Pol.* 27.3, Andoc. 1.147, Theophr. *Char.* 23.5. Armour: Lys. 16.14. Ransoms and dowries: Dem. 18.268–9, Lys. 19.59. Funerals: Lys. 19.59 (but see also [Dem.] 40.52 for *borrowing* money for funerals). See also Men. *Sam.* 15–16 (or perhaps even [Dem.] 45.75) for the general expectation that wealthy citizens help out those in need.

[109] *Ath. Pol.* 55.3, 56.6, [Dem.] 53.29, 59.22.

[110] Diphilos F 62. See Parker 2005: 282 *pace* Christ 2010: 264. By the Roman period this list explicitly included giving money or food to a beggar: see Parkin 2006: 66.

[111] Perhaps Arist. *NE* 1155a12–13 is an exception ('in poverty or any other misfortune men think friends are their only resource'), but this comes as an aside to discussion of the necessity of friends to rich and powerful (as means for them to show their beneficence), and is nevertheless focalized through the benefactors.

[112] Millett 1991: 31–4.

the *mikrologos* (penny-pincher) for forbidding his wife to lend household goods, and other literary sources suggest frequent borrowing between neighbours, but the social norms which made this common also placed pressure on the borrower to repay, and for the poorest this might have been burdensome.[113] Receiving assistance such as this was also dependent on strong social ties between parties.[114] Aside from comic parodies of mundane neighbourly assistance, however, most examples are for one-off expensive items which probably indicate the sorts of difficulties which pushed poorer households to the limit, but do not say much about the day-to-day difficulties. Not being able to provide a dowry for a daughter, not being able to ransom a relative kidnapped overseas, or not being able to pay for a funeral might well have been the result of shortage, but also must have been the cause of considerable shame, and although juries are clearly meant to view these benefactors in a good light, never are the recipients of such largesse specifically named unless they are being shamed, in turn, themselves.[115] Those in need are, in effect, effeminized by their silence; like respectable women, their names are withheld from public discourse.[116] The good deeds of the wealthy towards their fellow citizens, therefore, served to highlight the gaps between the haves and have-nots as much as close them.

The wide availability of credit and the culture of reciprocity in Athens likely aided the poor in one sense, because it allowed them to gain access to additional resources. It may have even enabled some to live above subsistence, if only temporarily, but it also demonstrates the structures of power within Athenian society. Those who were the most lacking in the types of social networks which allowed for such borrowing would have been the least able to draw on the help of others, but conversely, they were the most vulnerable to stigmatized institutions like debt-bondage. When Theophrastos disparages moneylenders who charge excessively high interest rates, he emphasizes the shamelessness of breaking the social bonds between peers, even if those peers are the low-status *agoraioi* who run market

[113] Theophr. *Char.* 10.13, Lys. 1.14.

[114] See e.g. Arist. *NE* 1160a3–9: 'it is more shocking to defraud a *hetairos* of money than a *polites*; or to refuse to help a brother than a stranger.'

[115] See [Dem.] 53.6–12: the intention here is precisely to shame Nikostratos. Arist. *Rhet.* 1385a25–6 links acts of charity to a discussion of shame.

[116] See Thuc. 2.45.2; Schaps 1977. On the effeminization of poverty see p. 54.

stalls.[117] This underlines the fact that social relations are at the heart of lending, and that lacking these is likely to have been detrimental to the availability of credit.

Thomsen's recent study has done much to clarify some of the most difficult points relating to *eranoi* loans and groups of *eranistai*, thereby illuminating further the structural constraints on poorer groups within Athens. There he argues that as well as loans provided by *philoi* (and therefore centred on the social networks of the borrower), other *eranoi* loans could be contracted through a 'loan organizer' (*plerotes eranou*).[118] These loans, therefore, were less 'friendly', in that rather than being drawn from multiple contacts of the borrower, they were arranged by a single organizer and, as such, were unlikely to have been interest-free. Such loans, then, were less reliant on the borrower's social capital; they appear, on the contrary, to have expanded the group of creditors to those whose social networks were lacking, for example slaves.[119] Loans such as these provided access to credit for those who lacked multiple contacts, but as Thomsen points out, the terms (interest-bearing, repayable in regular instalments) imply a social distance between the borrower and the lender.

We should not necessarily assume that the poorest were the most heavily indebted, however.[120] Millett connects Theophrastos' character with the *obolostates* (small-sum, short-term lenders), emphasizing that the people who relied on such lenders were likely those with few assets, or few other options to gain credit, to begin with.[121] Such loans typically ameliorate the short-term needs of the income poor, but they are frequently exploitative, charging exorbitant rates, and therefore serve only to increase financial difficulties over the long term. Resorting to these forms of credit, like debt-bondage, might, then, have been a necessary strategy for certain groups among the poor to survive, but short-term lending is frequently seriously unfavourable

[117] Theoph. *Char.* 6.9. This example comes in a series of behaviours which illustrate shamelessness (*aponoia*). Millett 1991: 187 characterizes him as a 'hustler' rather than a man made rich through lending, which is surely correct.

[118] Thomsen 2014: 159–61.

[119] Hyp. 3.9–11. Midas is portrayed here as obtaining vast sums of money this way (5 talents).

[120] Comparative evidence from early modern Europe suggests that the very poorest have fewer debts than those who were even slightly better off (and better connected). See Ogilvie, Küpker, and Maegraith 2012: 150; Fontaine 2014: 25. See also Millett 1991: 74–6.

[121] Millett 1991: 179–88.

or even disastrous. It does little to ameliorate poverty in any significant way in the short term, and exacerbates it in the long term.

If debts were not repaid it seems that they continued into the next generation, and there is no evidence in Athens that outstanding debts were forgiven on the death of either a creditor or a debtor.[122] The fictional family of Tibeios discussed earlier provide a good example of the impact of the former. Debt, therefore, not only had the power to impoverish the original debtor but could do so inter-generationally. This process can be best traced, however, among wealthy families who incurred debts to the state as part of their service to the polis or through the fines that were levied on them.[123] These could survive over generations, trapping families in cycles of indebtedness created by their fathers and grandfathers. Pamphilos of Keiriadai, for example, was a wealthy hipparch who provided his daughter, Plangon, with a substantial dowry before he was prosecuted for embezzlement and his property confiscated by 388.[124] The fine appears not to have been paid off forty years later (and long after his own death), leaving his three sons responsible for it. Whilst they managed to retain their citizenship, the family was to some extent tarnished and his descendants appear to have fallen out of the liturgical class as a result. The sons of other debtors feared disenfranchisement, and their daughters became unmarriable.[125]

Through state debtors it is possible to see different relations of power, this time with the demos exerting authority over the behaviour of elite families. Demosthenes notes the case of Pyrrhos, a member of the Eteoboutadai *genos*, who was sentenced to death for sitting on a jury whilst being a debtor to the state.[126] Pyrrhos' motives are not painted here as *hybris* (he acts as a foil in this regard to Meidias), but simply that he needed the income, with the implication that he had become impoverished and desperate. Not all public debtors faired so badly, however: Agyrrhios spent some years in prison for his debts, but when he was released he was quickly able to recover his position and became the figure behind a highly profitable new tax-farming scheme.[127]

[122] See e.g. the will of Demosthenes' father, who had nearly 3 talents in outstanding loans at his death.

[123] Hunter 2000: 29–30.

[124] [Dem.] 40.22–3. See *APF*: 365–6.

[125] [Dem.] 58.1–2, 59.8.

[126] Dem. 21.182.

[127] Stroud 1998: 24.

Sacrifice and the Provision of Food

Although structures of credit provided access to resources whilst also reproducing poverty, it is possible that other mechanisms, such as the provision of sacrificial meat, provided more direct relief. The Old Oligarch accuses the *penetes* of gaining the benefits of regular sacrifices without having the financial outlay for them, and in doing so he demonstrates anxieties about community belonging.[128] His complaints demonstrate a tension between those who paid for sacrifices and those who took part in them, and this is something we can investigate further.

Although sacrifices were religious in nature, and should be seen primarily in this light, it is easy to see how regular distributions of food (protein-rich meat) would have provided an important source of nutrients for the Athenian population.[129] The epigraphic record demonstrates how central these distributions were to Athenian religious practice, and great lengths were gone to in providing highly detailed accounts of sacrificial expenditure.[130] On the one hand it is tempting to view sacrifice in terms of hardship alleviation: public distributions of meat were fairly regular and distributed equally to all those who took part in the sacrifice (that is, they are not 'means-tested' as such).[131] From the hellenistic period on, such distributions formed a central part of a wealthy citizen's benefaction to the city, or subsections of it. Although the evidence is weighted towards the sacrifices in which male citizens partook (that is, the evidence is derived from decrees of the polis or its subgroups acting in an official capacity), women were not as matter of course excluded, and in some cases metics and slaves also shared in the distribution.[132] It is not unreasonable to suggest that these distributions served a poverty-amelioration function, in that they provided food, and some

[128] [Xen.] *Ath. Pol.* 2.9

[129] See discussion of the skeletal material on pp. 17–18.

[130] Rosivach 1994; Lambert 2002a.

[131] Rosivach 1994: 66 calculates meat distribution from the various groups to have occurred 40–45 times throughout the year, approximately once every eight or nine days. Of course not all citizens participated in every sacrifice, and not all sacrifices could have fed all those in the group, as Rosivach acknowledges.

[132] Women: *Agora XVI*: 161 (early third century): distribution of sacrificial meat to men and women of the *orgeones* of Echelos and the Heroines, half-shares for their sons and daughters, and one female attendant (ἀκόλουθος). Metics: *IG* I^3 244 (deme decree from Skambonidai), see Humphreys 2004.

of those sharing in the conviviality may have been in need of it. It may have been possible to avoid starving to death in Athens at least partly as a result of public sacrifices, but it should also be emphasized that sacrifice is never conceptualized in these terms by the Athenians, and frequently the amount of meat received would have been small.[133]

However, although it is possible that distributions of meat provided resources for poorer Athenians, sacrifices—like political pay—were also used to mark status distinctions.[134] Partaking in the sacrificial meat was restricted to the member of the group for whom the sacrifice was performed (the polis, the deme, the *genos*, the participants in the festival, and so on), and this was frequently delineated through civic status. Even though distributions of meat sometimes explicitly included metics and woman, and may in some instances be interpreted as an inclusive measure incorporating non-Athenians into the religious life of the community, more often they served to exclude non-members, and never do they explicitly *include* the hungry. Sanctuaries could serve as points of asylum for runaway slaves whose survival was precarious, but frequently tales of sanctuary asylum result in starvation or other humanitarian crimes. The Theseion seems to have been a place of such sanctuary in Athens, whereby slaves could request resale to a new master.[135] However, desperate runaways certainly could not count on being fed in this way, though presumably enough did find new masters for it to become a stock joke. Other Athenian sanctuaries actively took measures to keep out those in most need.[136] If these measures are seen in terms of poverty alleviation, then, they must be understood as ways in which the Athenians protected and reinforced their own power over others.

The differential structures of credit available in Athens, and the social networks people belonged to, were as instrumental in both alleviating and reproducing poverty as political pay. Social networks were protective, in that they buffered the effects of food shortages,

[133] Parker 2005: 66.

[134] See Tsoukala 2009 for the development of choice-cut imagery to symbolize not just sacrificial contexts but honorific ones too.

[135] See Christensen 1984; Gottesman 2014: 160–79.

[136] *IG* I^3 45 provides for the construction of a wall around the Akropolis to keep out runaway slaves (*drapetes*) and thieves (*lopodutes*); Andoc. 1.116 notes supplication at the City Eleusinion was banned during the Mysteries. Other poleis specifically outlawed the feeding of slaves at their sanctuaries: *IG* V, 1 1390 (Andania), *SEG* 27.545 (Samos). See further Chaniotis 1996.

temporary hardship, death in the family or war, and even old age, but they could be equally destructive in that those they excluded were placed far outside the realms of assistance. Whilst Athenian citizens had—in the context of ancient societies at least—numerous advantages (there was a strong commitment, political and religious, to the types of behaviours which potentially provided material resources), the social relationships, institutions, and forms of democratic politics which provided a relatively good standard of living for citizens structurally reproduced the poverty of large numbers of non-citizens.

Citizens could buffer, or perhaps even enhance, their incomes through the activities of simply being a citizen, but this created and reproduced social divisions. The associational phenomenon was widespread in Athens, and belonging to such a group was part of everyday life for many, which did directly or indirectly provide access to resources. However, as much as *koinoniai* were diverse, and as much as political institutions assisted citizens, the very poorest were constrained in multiple ways. With fewer social networks to start with, the poorest needed to draw on these more often and risk depleting the resources (or goodwill) of friends, family, or neighbours. With fewer assets, and reliant on their own labour, they no doubt had less time to devote to cultivating new social relationships or participating in collective institutions; that is, their agency was further constrained (see, for example, the social recategorization of *ptochoi* discussed in Chapter 4). We do not know how many in Athens fell into this category (Chapter 3 suggests relatively few, but we could be more pessimistic); our sources are simply silent on the matter. What we can say, however, is that social networks, like political pay and other civic distributions, might have served to alleviate hardship and expand capabilities for some, but they likely reinforced such hardship for others.

THE CONSOLIDATION OF WEALTH IN THE LATE FOURTH CENTURY

Poverty was also reproduced through the economic structures of Athenian society which enabled the wealthy to consolidate resources. This is particularly clear in the late fourth century, when a number of economic changes can be identified. In many different spheres, however, a case can be made for a broad portion of Athenian society doing well during this period, at least before the Lamian War: the post-Chaironeia recovery appears to have been strong, political pay was maintained, the developments in the theoric fund arguably redistributed wealth to poorer citizens. Building projects provided work as well as new facilities, strong links with the Hellespont ensured the grain supply, legal innovations made commercial disputes easier to resolve, and the demos were politically strong.[137] However, in many of these developments we can also see the wealthy getting wealthier. In fact, re-evaluation of Athens in the second half of the fourth century over the past decades strongly indicates a process of wealth-consolidation in a number of arenas, for example, mining, public finance, landownership, and the grain trade.[138]

To return first to land-leasing. As was clear in the previous discussion, the wealthy and well-connected are disproportionately prominent in this activity. Although there are examples of leases earlier, the majority of the surviving evidence comes from the second half of the fourth century. Papazarkadas connects this with the post-Social War financial reforms which, taken in their totality, suggest not so much a return to Periklean 'good [financial] sense', as previous generations of scholars have interpreted them, but a series of measures which ensured the most prosperous were well provided for.[139] Whilst the leasing of property was a generator of income for the corporate body concerned, leases were tightly regulated to ensure prompt payment of rent and appropriate use of the land, and lessors had the ability to seize assets if renters defaulted. In addition, the predominance of family ties and connections to religious officials (that is, those in locally prominent positions) among those who took up leases suggest a degree of protectionism within groups.[140] Few metics were involved in leasing, despite the fact that metics could not own land; of the four that are, one was *isoteles*.[141] These institutional arrangements, as we have seen earlier, in the main bypassed the poor.

A similar pattern can be seen in the sales of public land during the late 340s and 320s. The prominence of wealthy citizens as buyers here

137 Cawkwell 1963; Cohen 1974; Hintzen-Bohlen 1997; Moreno 2007; Burke 2010.

138 See e.g. Lambert 1997; Oliver 2007; Papazarkadas 2011; Bresson 2015.

139 Cf. Cawkwell 1963: 50 with Papazarkadas 2011: 238–43, 322–3.

140 Osborne 1988: 291; Papazarkadas 2011: 319–23.

141 Papazarkadas 2011: 323–5. All of the metics are recorded on *Agora XIX*: L6 (based on prosopographical indicators, it is possible that two of these were freed slaves or their descendants).

suggests this was not a scheme designed to provide resources to poorer citizens who lacked land, but effectively functioned as a kind of privatization programme selling off communal assets to predominantly wealthier citizens. Even though some of this property appears to have been marginal land (both in terms of being outside the core properties held by the group and with regard to its agricultural use), and might have been taken up as a quasi-liturgy, nevertheless it was disproportionately wealthier citizens who took advantage.[142] Doing so ensured their wealth, enabled them to diversify their investments, and allowed their local standing to grow at the expense of the economic resources of the group as a whole. One outcome of the sales was that it shifted social relations between landowners and land-users. As Lambert points out, negotiating, for example, the use of a threshing floor on what was once a communal plot of land but was now owned by a local individual, who was more likely than not to be wealthy, would probably have changed more than the local balance of wealth.[143] Here we can see very clearly shifting power relations too.

In the 330s and 320s, broad patterns of participation aside, elites appear increasingly prominently in public life, the epigraphic record emphasizing their visibility in politics and in their role in public finance through the provision of honours and rewards.[144] The political activities of the wealthy went hand in hand with their economic pursuits: this is particularly clear in the grain trade, and Gabrielsen's examination of the networks surrounding Demades, for example, shows the intersection of private and public interests in maintaining the grain supply.[145] Demades' activities in the Assembly deal with various naval matters, from repaying trierarchic debts to making voluntary contributions to the Grain Fund, but they also materially aided the business interests of his peers who were prominent in anti-piracy expeditions and other naval activities in the Hellespont and Black Sea. We might seek to explain the coalescence of political and economic activity in terms of expertise: the men best placed to advise

[142] Lambert 1997: 236–8, 244–8, 288–9. A disproportionate number also have family or political ties with Lykourgos and Xenokles of Sphettos, the men thought to be behind the programme.

[143] *IG* II^2 1594, (F7a), ll. 17–22: Lambert 1997: 208–9, 291.

[144] Faraguna 1992; Liddel 2007: 94–102, 249–50. On the 'new emphasis' on *epidosis* see Lambert 1997: 282–3, with the late fourth- and third-century changes analysed in detail by Oliver 2007: 196–200.

[145] Gabrielsen 2015; also Moreno 2007.

the demos on matters of the grain supply, the argument would go, were those with naval experience in these areas. Such an explanation emphasizes the performance of civic duty among the elite, who ensured the availability of grain back home whilst performing the duties of their trierarchies.

However, these close collaborations also used public resources (triremes, political institutions) for the pursuit of private business interests in ways which cemented solidarity within these networks, reduced the risks of the grain trade for individual investors, and financially enriched those involved.[146] These were effectively monopolistic cabals which controlled the Athenian grain trade, rather than 'lone operators', and they shaped the grain policies of Athens to benefit themselves. Supplying grain was a public good, but the grain shortages of the 330s and 320s suggest that the mechanisms for supply worked better for the rich than for those who depended on grain back in Attica.[147] As Gabrielsen observes, the commanders of the Athenian fleet, especially from the 350s on, are not just 'brothers in arms' but also 'brothers in private enrichment'.[148]

A similar process can be seen in the mining industry, where changing patterns of economic exploitation can be detected. Here too, investments appear to have enabled the wealthy to consolidate their resources. These changes become particularly evident when we outline the development of the mining industry over the course of the fourth century as a whole.

After being effectively shut down during the Dekeleian War, production in the Laurion mines resumed during the late 370s or early 360s, and during the second half of the fourth century the industry was at its height.[149] When Xenophon tells us about mine operations

[146] See e.g. Demades, whose claims of impoverishment at birth are juxtaposed with his wealth in later life (although Davies puts this down to his political gifts and subsequent receipt of bribes). See *APF*: 99–101.

[147] Garnsey 1988: 157–62 estimates at least five grain shortage crises between 338/7 and 323/2. We are less well informed about such frequent shortages at other points in Athenian history.

[148] Gabrielsen 2015: 204. This occurs at the same time as syntrierarchies were becoming more common, or at least more visible (350s onwards): see Gabrielsen 1994: 175.

[149] The mines were—according to Xenophon—at the peak of their production in the fifth century (Xen. *Por.* 4.3–4). Both Conophagos 1980 and Kalcyk 1982 follow Xenophon, but Lauffer 1979 argues that the fourth century was the heaviest production period, and this is the current orthodoxy. It is certainly the period with the heaviest involvement of the polis in the running of the mines (Hopper 1953) and a

in the fifth century he mentions three wealthy men, Nikias, Hipponikos, and Philemonides, who each owned large numbers of mining slaves: between them they owned almost 2,000. If Lauffer's estimates of slave numbers are anything like correct (that there were between 10,000 and 20,000 slaves working in the industry during the fifth century), this means that between 10% and 20% of the workforce of the region was owned by these three men.[150] This is a massive proportion. In contrast, Xenophon implies that no one individual owned quite so many by the time he wrote the *Poroi* (355/4).[151] By the mid-fourth century, then, it seems that a small number of very wealthy individuals did not dominate production in the same way.

The Peloponnesian War appears to have had a significant effect on the Laurion region and silver production. Not only did the mines, if not cease, then massively reduce production, but large numbers of slaves deserted, taking their skills with them.[152] If a small number of men owned this much of the productive capital of the industry, even if the workforce accounts for a fraction of this, their fortunes cannot but have been seriously affected by a shutdown which lasted for more or less a generation. This must have affected the model of wealth distribution outlined in Chapter 3.

After the mines reopened we can detect patterns of investment through the epigraphic record. Bissa's study shows that the wealthy were prominent in landownership and other processing activities (owning a workshop or smeltery), but less prominent, though still present, in ore-extraction activities.[153] The former required higher levels of capital, long-term investment over an undefined time period, and provided an income without necessitating day-to-day

period of considerable technological innovation; see van Liefferinge 2013: 112–13 on water management.

[150] Lauffer 1979: 140–70. There are other estimates too, based on number of people needed for the annual production of 20 tonnes of silver (Conophagos 1980: 341), the number of workers needed in each mineshaft (Kalcyk 1982: 159–65), and the number of people required to run a washery (Jones 2007: 278). Xenophon envisages a state-owned slave workforce of 10,000 to 'generate an income of 100 talents' (Xen. *Por.* 4.22–3). If the slaves of Nikias et al. earned (a low) one-quarter of a drachma per day, they would generate 25 talents of income for these three men alone.

[151] Xen. *Por.* 4.14–15, 28–9. See further Gauthier 1976: 137–44; 2010.

[152] Thuc. 7.27.3–5: desertion of more than 20,000 slaves, 'the majority of [whom] were *cheirotechnai*'. See Rihll 2010: 211–16 for the loss of collective knowledge this represents.

[153] Bissa 2008.

involvement, whereas the latter was higher-risk but required less capital up-front. These 'prospectors' could make a great deal if they struck a seam, but risked losing their investment if not.[154] Even here, however, some up-front investment was required: leases needed to be paid (although initial fees were low: 20 drachmas), tools purchased or otherwise acquired, expertise and/or labour sought, not to mention the day-to-day expenses required to feed and house however many workers each 'prospector' required.[155] Moderate, but not large, surpluses would be necessary here.

The involvement of wealthier investors in processing activities is important for two reasons. First, these are more stable investments over the long term, providing regular income, whereas extraction relied on the finding of a seam and was more risky. Second, similar networks of elite cooperation appear in the mining industry as appear in the grain trade, and these can be detected in the processing industries in particular. Both of these patterns would have allowed the wealthy to consolidate their resources over time, and whilst we cannot say that this trend led to a situation like at the end of the fifth century, where a very few wealthy men controlled extremely large resources, the direction of travel is certainly towards this. One demesmen of Sounion was able to accumulate enough to donate a plot of land for a new deme agora, a unique benefaction for the classical period.[156]

Networks of cooperation can be seen in the ore-processing workshops of the Soureza valley, for example, the site known as the Asklepiakon (Fig. 5.1). Here, excavators have found a number of closely connected workshops dated to the second half of the fourth century.[157] That these workshops were involved in some kind of mutual cooperation is shown by two main features: first, they are built close together, with workshops 2 and 3 linked by an enclosure

[154] Davis 2014: 269–71 argues that profit margins would have been low even if a seam was struck.

[155] Rihll 2010: 208. Acton 2014: 119–22 argues that smaller teams were just as effective as larger ones here, whereas larger groups and economies of scale are found more commonly in the ore-processing industry.

[156] *IG* II^2 1180: Leukios' dedication is undated, but from some point in the mid-fourth century; his known activities stretch from owning property in 367/6 to paying a liturgy in *c*.330. My guess (and it is admittedly no more than that) is that the benefaction occurred more towards 330 than 367, but see Stanton 1996: 351 for arguments for earlier.

[157] Conophagos 1980; Tsaimou 1979.

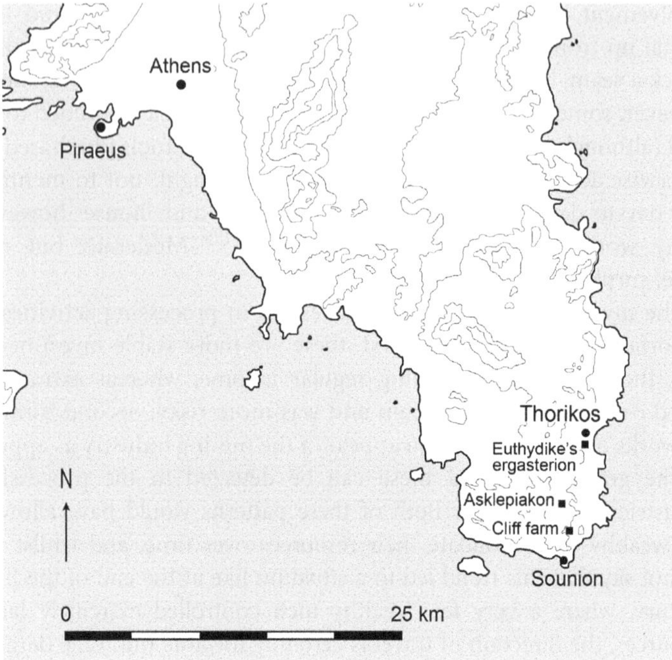

Figure 5.1. Map of southern Attica

wall, suggesting some degree of deliberate planning.[158] Second, they have a shared water-management system, with large cisterns which collected rain-water run-off from the hills, gullies which supplied it to the cisterns and then to each of the workshops, and considerable investment in water-loss reduction with heavy use of waterproof plaster.[159] These were technological innovations which ensured that water was available year-round at this site, water that was crucial for the ore-processing activities. This is not a pattern which is replicated across the Laurion region. In contrast, water management at Thorikos does not show such central planning or sophisticated design, suggesting that they are more 'ad hoc' installations which grew up with less cooperation between owners.[160]

158 Jones 2007: 273.
159 van Liefferinge 2013; van Liefferinge et al. 2014: 280.
160 van Liefferinge 2013; van Liefferinge et al. 2014.

The owner of workshop 3 was Simos of Paiania, who used this property as collateral for a number of loans from groups of *eranistai*, one headed by Neoptolemos of Melite and another headed by Epiteles of Kerameis.[161] At least one of these loans was substantial (1 talent); in total they amounted to over 7,500 drachmas. Neoptolemos, as has been observed elsewhere, was an associate of Meidias and then Lykourgos, and one of the men who paid off the debts of trierarchs in Demades' grain-fund scheme mentioned earlier.[162] Simos' son, Diodoros, was a trierarch himself in 334/3 and a syntrierarch twice in the 320s, and although there is no evidence of his involvement in the grain trade this family clearly falls within the same nexus of 'common financial interests' among those who were, and who are highlighted by Gabrielsen.[163] Here we see cooperation on two levels: between investors to provide common resources for the processing of ore, and between *eranistai* to provide credit. It is possible, then, that Neoptolemos and Simos were part of the same cult association.

Further possible examples of wealth consolidation can be suggested for other properties: an *ergasterion* complex a short distance outside the main settlement at Thorikos, and the property known as the Cliff farm (Fig. 5.1). The former, dating to the late classical period, consisted of a domestic area as well as washeries used for the processing of silver ore (Fig. 5.2).[164] There was considerable investment in this property, which suggests the owners were (at least moderately) well off: an andron, marble thresholds, a paved (rather than beaten-earth) courtyard, and the use of waterproof plaster were found here. An inscription records the boundaries of the property and reveals, in addition, the presence of a garden and slaves, and that the property belonged to Euthydike, an *epikleros*.[165]

The neighbouring complex, located 200 m to the south, also included an *ergasterion* with washeries, as well as a large rectangular courtyard, and at least ten (poorly preserved) rooms (Fig. 5.3).[166] *Horos Philok*[*ratous*] was inscribed on the southern boundary of the property (*SEG* 48.166), a name which is also found inside Euthydike's property, inscribed twice on the paved slabs in the courtyard (*SEG*

[161] *SEG* 32.236. [162] Millett 1991: 159, 222; Gabrielsen 2015.

[163] Gabrielsen 2015: 201–2. Other members of the same network (Blepaios) also lent money for mining ([Dem.] 40.52).

[164] Mexa plot: Oikonomakou 1997: 87–8; 1998: 83–4; Jones 2007: 269–71.

[165] *SEG* 50.187. [166] Kavodokano: Salliora-Oikonomakou 1996: 133–9.

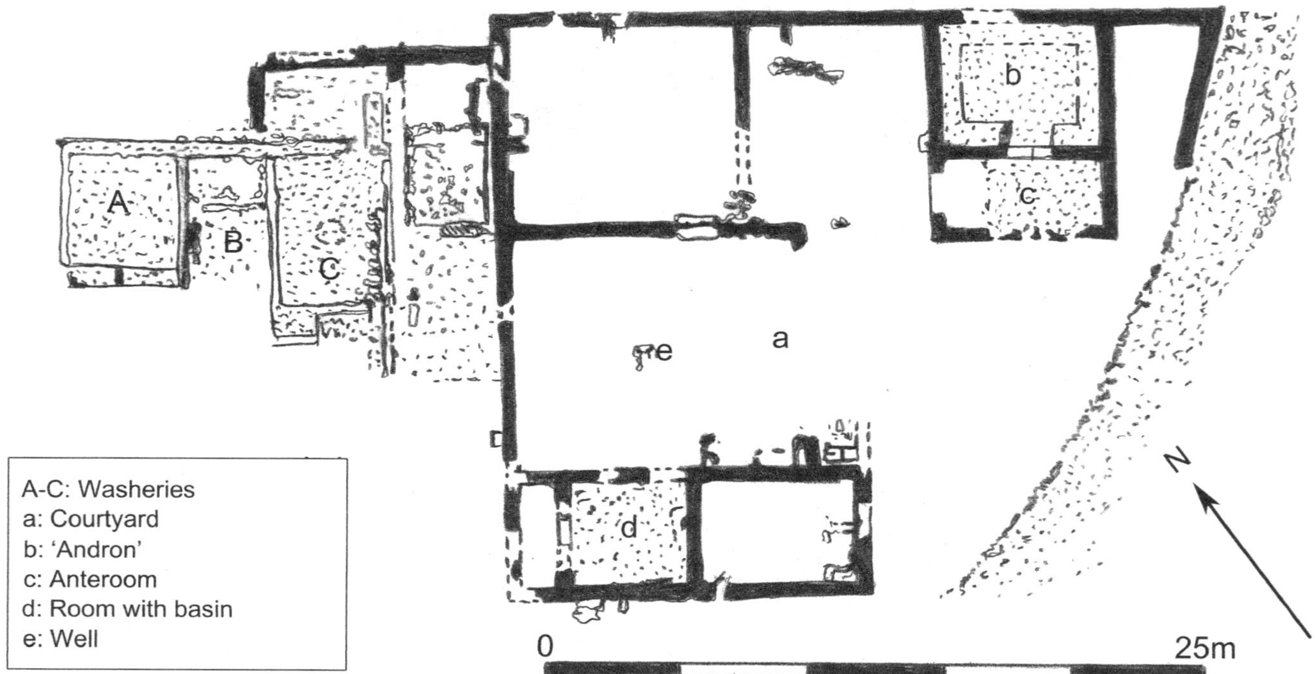

Figure 5.2. Euthydike's *ergasterion* (Mexa plot)

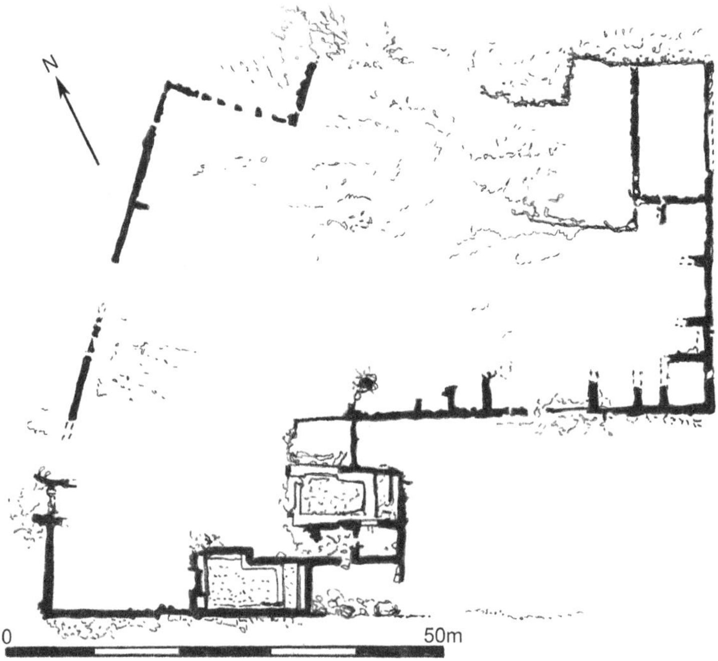

Figure 5.3. Kavodokano *ergasterion*

52.244, 247) as well as on a beehive sherd found inside the building (*SEG* 44.240). The discovery of the name Philokrates at both properties suggests that they were owned, at some point, by the same person or family, but the layout of the complexes, and the duplication of facilities within them, imply that this was not always the case.

Both properties must have been independently constructed, given that they both have washing platforms which are set apart from other parts of the building and both have areas for residential use: in Euthydike's property the washing platforms are separated from the courtyard and the residential area by a door; in Philokrates' they are at the southernmost part of the complex (not enough of the building survives to be able to tell whether a similar arrangement occurred here, but it is clear that they are situated in a separate part of the building). The similarity in layout suggests that the properties were originally independent entities, but the presence of Philokrates' name in both suggests that they were owned, or used, by the same family at some point in time; that is, one property was taken over by the owner of the other, and the ore-processing business expanded.[167] If Philokrates was indeed the husband or *kyrios* of Euthydike, as suggested by Oikonomakou, he may have acquired her workshop through marriage and then expanded to the neighbouring property, or owned the neighbouring property and then acquired her workshop (we do not have enough information to decide between the two possibilities).[168] However, it was important to Philokrates to visibly demarcate his property and indicate his ownership, whether in the form of a boundary inscription, a beehive, or by inscribing his name on the floor of the courtyard of Euthydike's house. This appears to be a successful expansion of property ownership during the late fourth century.

A second possible example comes from the Cliff farm, where an inscription records some kind of land transaction between Timesios and Aristomenes.[169] Although the inscription is fragmentary (and restored), one interpretation is that it documents the process of the loss of land through the non-repayment of debt from one landowner to another.[170] However, there are no similar epigraphic examples of such a transaction, and Langdon and Watrous' textual parallel refers to the transferal of ownership of a slave rather than land.[171] Another suggestion is that this records a loan, but the language that survives is different from that used on other *horoi*.[172] If the first interpretation is correct, then this shows the acquisition of wealth of a prominent local

[167] As far as we can tell, this is an expansion rather than a move to a different location: the archaeological material suggests the properties were in use concurrently. Both complexes have pottery dating to the late classical period, and both have similar-style washeries (Type I). Philokrates is, of course, a common name, and more than one man named Philokrates is mentioned on the *poletai* lists.

[168] Salliora-Oikonomakou 1996: 137 differentiates the use of the two properties according to status: Philokrates' property was where the slave workers lived, whereas Euthydike's property was the residence of the owners of the workshops. This is indeed possible, but strict separation of slave and free is difficult to demonstrate elsewhere within Laurion (see Jones 2007). Additionally, although poorly preserved, it is clear that there was considerable investment in the Kavodokano property (the so-called 'workers' quarters'): a marble threshold, a plaster-floored room, and olive presses have been found here too.

[169] *SEG* 26.227: [*Τι*]*μησίωι* [*τô*] *Ἀντιπάτρο* [*Ἀρισ*]*τομένης* [----] *πρὸς τὸν πύργ*[*ο*]*ν* [----]*μησεν*. *SEG* accepts Langdon and Watrous' restoration: see n. 172 for other possibilities. On the Cliff farm: see Young 1956: 124–6; Goette 2000: 81–2.

[170] Langdon and Watrous 1977: 166–8: 'To [Ti]mesios son of Antipatros, [Aris]tomenes [made over in settlement land?] in the direction of the tower.'

[171] [Dem.] 53.20.

[172] Vanhove 1994: 'For Timesios son of Antipatros, [Aris]tomenes accepted, after valuation, a mortgage on the [ground] for the construction of the tower.'

man at the expense of his indebted neighbour.[173] If the second is correct and the inscription records a loan transaction for the construction of a tower, this shows investment in the property in a way which is designed to protect its resources and exert control over the landscape: towers are common features of the mining region and surrounding demes, keeping property safe but also watching over those who worked there.[174]

Other archaeological evidence points towards the ownership of larger properties during the late fourth century, indicating that it was not just in the mining region where wealth was being consolidated.[175] Recent archaeological work has uncovered a number of late classical country estates in Attica; many of these are large and show high levels of investment. Those dating to the late fourth or early third century have been excavated at Kato Souli (Trikorythos), Agios Andreas-Zouberi (either Phegaia or Probalinthos), Merenda (Myrrhinous), possibly Merkati Thorikou (Thorikos, though the date is uncertain), as well as elsewhere.[176] The property at Kato Souli covered 690 m^2, had an olive press and stone grinders, numerous lead weights and clamps, nails and coins (some found in a hoard), and loom-weights, attesting to diverse economic activity.[177] That at Agios Andreas-Zouberi was at least 458 m^2 and had marble column bases and plaques added to the original limestone structure (though perhaps this phase occurred later in the hellenistic period).[178] The property at Merkati Thorikou was at least 832 m^2, also had marble thresholds, and had a wine press close by.[179]

173 A Timesios is listed as the owner of other property in the area (*Agora XIX* P5, l. 57). Goette 2000: 85 (followed by Stroud in *SEG* 46.282) argues that both properties were owned by the same family (that of Timesios). Another possible link is *SEG* 54.337: *Παμφ[ίλη] Θοραιέ[ως θυγάτηρ] Τιμησ[ίου ---- γυνή]*. See Salliora-Oikonomakou 2004: 84, no. 48 for the restoration which makes Timesios the husband of Pamphile of Thorai, though Bergemann 1997: 208 and Stroud in *SEG* 54 are more cautious (Pamph- could be part of the father's name, for example).

174 Morris and Papadopoulos 2005; Oliver 2007: 106.

175 von Reden 2007: 400–1.

176 Keratea: Oikonomakou 2001a: 357–9; Agios Asomatoi (road between Brauron and Erchia): Steinhauer 1994: 181–2; Kiteza Kalyviou (Thorai?): Oikonomakou 1993 (with dotal *horos SEG* 44.82).

177 Oikonomakou 2004: 164–72. *Horoi* attest to the property being used as collateral for loans: *SEG* 54.253–4.

178 Oikonomakou 2001b: 386–7.

179 Oikonomakou 2001a: 366 with figs. 72 and 73. The property is not dated by the excavators, but since production in the mines drastically reduced during the third century, it is likely it dates before this.

The north-west farmhouse at Merenda consists of at least fifteen rooms built around a central court with a compound covering an area of 1,372 m^2 and incorporating a small square structure which has been interpreted as a shrine or a tower.[180] All of these structures are considerably larger than the contemporary Vari house (241 m^2) and the probably slightly earlier Dema house (355 m^2), which are more representative of the median and mean for this period.[181]

Other houses of similar date show increased attention paid to construction and display. The West farmhouse at Merenda, in use from *c.*300 into the second century, and which lies on the road between Myrrhinous and Angele, has carefully built thick masonry walls of ~0.5–0.7m width.[182] The fourth-century house at Kalyvia Thorikou (Thorai?) contained a Panathenaic amphora, a prestigious item demonstrating the status of the owner.[183] Although there are a couple of earlier examples, *andrones* appear regularly in residential buildings (as opposed to public buildings or buildings with a cultic function) from the second half of the fourth century on.[184] Pebble mosaic floors begin to appear in the last quarter of the fifth century,

[180] Kakavogianni 2001: 322; Sklavos et al. 2009: 79–83.

[181] Jones, Graham, and Sackett 1973: 421; Jones, Sackett, and Graham 1962. According to Morris 2005: 110, table 5.1 the median for Greek houses between 400 and 300 is 240 m^2 and the mean is 325 m^2.

[182] Sklavos et al. 2009: 83–6.

[183] Tsaravopoulos 2001: 371 (Kiteza site).

[184] *Andrones* in houses have been identified in the Central House on the north-east slopes of the Areopagus (late fourth century: Shear 1973: 152–3; Jones 1975: 84–6); the House of the Greek Mosaic (late fourth/early third century: Jones 1975: 77–80; Thompson and Wycherley 1977: 181–2); houses at odos Virginia Benaki 13, (second half of the fourth century: Alexandri 1968: 43); odos Bourbaches 3 (end of the fourth century: Alexandri 1969: 28, fig. 4); odos Amphiktyon 17 (hellenistic: Alexandri 1967: 51, fig. 12); odos Keratsinios (hellenistic: Alexandri 1967: 88, fig. 41). In Attica: (a) Piraeus: Drakoulianou plot (late fourth–third century: *AR* 2002–3: 9; Petritaki 1997: 78–80); Fragkiadon 50/Lekka (hellenistic: von Eickstedt 1991: 1.151, fig. 49); Karaoli, Demetriou, Theatrou junction (late fourth century: von Eickstedt 1991: 1.40, fig. 47); odos Maurokordatou (classical–hellenistic: *AR* 2000–1: 13); (b) Southern Attica: Soureza Compound 3 (second half of the fourth century: Tsaimou 1979); Mexa plot, Neo Thorikou ('fourth century': Salliora-Oikonomakou 1996: 163–6; possibly Thorikos House 1, room C (identified as an andron by the excavators on the basis of red plaster found on the walls and dated to the third quarter of the fifth century; however, note that room E was originally thought to be the andron based on its square shape, and red plaster was also found in room H. See Mussche 1998: 46–50 and Mussche 1974: 49). The *andron* and mosaic floor in the recently discovered House Θ appear to be late fifth century, however: see Eleutheratou 2001: 148.

but become more popular in the late fourth.[185] Expenditure on funerary commemoration became more elaborate towards the end of the fourth century, before Demetrios of Phaleron's sumptuary reforms curbed what was seen as a growing excess.[186] Although on their own none of these things conclusively demonstrate that the wealthy were becoming wealthier, they do suggest that the consumption patterns of the elite were changing and that it became increasingly important to materially display wealth in a variety of different ways. Together with the evidence of leases, land sales, and grain-trade and mining activity, they point to a consolidation of wealth among the elite.

CONSOLIDATING WEALTH, REPRODUCING POVERTY

The patterns of economic change we see during the final decades of the fourth century strongly indicate that wealth was increasingly becoming concentrated into fewer hands.[187] We are best-informed about Athenian systems of credit in the second half of the fourth century too, but widespread access to credit did not prevent the consolidation of wealth during this time—it may have served to provide small resources to those who were not well off, but it fundamentally was used by the rich to diversify, spread risk, and to profit. As mining activity declined during the third century, the position of the farms which supplied the workers with food, charcoal, and other resources must have become more precarious. Archaeologically this can be detected in the decline of Atene, a deme which appears to have served the needs of mine-workers during the fourth century but

[185] In general see Westgate 1998. For examples of pebble mosaics from the Piraeus dating from the second half of the fourth century: *AR* 2002–3: 9; Petritaki 1997: 77–80 (Karantza and Drakoulianou plots). The mosaic at 9 odos Menandros is dated stylistically to the last third of the fourth century by Salzmann 1982: 30–1, 87, no. 21 (refuting Walter-Karydi 1994: 22–4: 'early fourth century' and Graham 1974: 53 with n. 11: 'mid-fourth century'). Morgan 2010: 51 even calls into question the identification of this building as a private residence, as very little survives outside of the mosaic itself. More securely identifiable as a residential building is the late fourth/early third century House of the Greek Mosaic: Jones 1975: 77–80; Thompson and Wycherley 1977: 181–2.

[186] Scholl 1994.

[187] See also Bresson 2015: 149–52, 199–203.

shrinks during the third. This suggests a significant contraction of a previously extensively exploited landscape; the implication is that a number of farms appear to have gone out of business.[188] The grain trade may have made rich men out of Demades and his friends, but as Bresson has argued, the farms that were least profitable (that is, the farms of the poor) were those that were most vulnerable to the kind of economic downturn which hit Athens after the Macedonian invasion.[189] In the political sphere too, Athens became increasingly reliant on its wealthier citizens as the fourth century drew to an end.

This culminated in the disenfranchisement and exile of thousands of poorer citizens in 322, when a 2,000-drachma property qualification was imposed, controlling access to citizenship.[190] Many seem to have left Athens at this time, encouraged to go to Thrace, not all of whom returned a few years later when Kassander overthrew Antipater's regime. In comparison, the rule of Demetrios of Phaleron was, at least according to the recent re-evaluation by van Wees, much less restrictive, re-enfranchising large numbers of citizens with properties worth less than 2,000 drachma but who could serve as hoplites with state support. However, those who were still excluded were reclassified as metics.[191]

Even before these events, however, many of the institutions, networks, and structures that provided resources did so not with the direct intention to alleviate poverty but with other motivations in mind. The provision of political pay, with its focus on civic unity, was designed to foster political rather than economic equality, demes and phratries provided resources in ways which favoured those with resources to begin with, voluntary associations provided assistance only to members, and mostly this was not financial. Social networks and social capital shaped access to credit as well as providing less tangible resources, but these too favoured certain groups. Certainly these factors would have allowed a broad range of citizens to live above subsistence, or at any rate avoid or ameliorate exploitation by the wealthy,[192] but they also reproduced the poverty of those outside these groups.

[188] Lohmann 1992; 1993. [189] Bresson 2015: 202.
[190] Diod. 18.18.4–5, Plut. *Phoc.* 28.7. See van Wees 2011: 108–9.
[191] van Wees 2011: 105–7. [192] Ste. Croix 1981: 287.

6

Appearing without Shame

Well-Being, Capabilities, and Standards of Living

As we have seen so far, expanding our conception of poverty—from a state which is defined by lack of possessions to consider also non-material aspects of life and the social relationships they create, define, and reproduce—is fruitful. This allows us to recognize the structures of constraint placed upon those who were categorized as poor, and how poverty was reproduced, but also how the *penetes* defined their own contribution to society and spoke for themselves, contesting and reshaping the discourses of poverty. This is visible in a number of settings: from the women using their social networks to create communities of value, to the recasting of *ptochoi* and *parasitoi* as outsiders different from the *penetes*, to the state provision of basic monetary resources to defined groups of citizens.

The present chapter explores this question in greater depth, examining how different groups of *penetes* negotiated their place in Athenian society. It does this by revisiting the standards-of-living debate but through the lens of well-being. The focus here is on *penetes* like Atotas, Mannes, and Potamon, whom we know only through their funerary stelai; these inscriptions display pride in work and accompanying skills, often making great claims about the deceased. Atotas, for example, had no rival in *techne*, Mannes was the best woodcutter, Potamon the best *auletes*.[1] This agonistic language demonstrates the value placed on these activities not only by those who performed them, but also by those

[1] *IG* I^3 1361, *IG* II^2 8883, 10051. A fragment of a fourth-century comic play seems to replicate this pride (Philemon F 178): 'a man who's become poor cannot live his life securely if he hasn't learned a trade (*techne*). If one of us comes to rest in the haven of a trade, he's cast and fastened his anchor for security's sake. But if he's uneducated

who would view these monuments. They demonstrate a satisfaction with labour (and therefore being *penes* in terms of lacking leisure or of 'keeping at one's work') which elite discourses do not, or cannot, appreciate.[2]

Rather than reproducing the stereotypes about the poor that exist within the literary sources—that the poor are deficient, needy, and dissatisfied—and rather than assuming that poverty is defined primarily by a lack of wealth or income, this chapter instead explicitly draws on Sen's capability approach to examine the strategies used by the *penetes* to claim a place within Athenian society—to resist the processes of social exclusion. It will begin by reviewing previously used measures of living standards such as nutrition and consumption. Given that these show that (for many) living standards were relatively high in Athens, this suggests that poverty should be viewed as much in terms of 'living without shame' than as an absolute form of deprivation. Material evidence, such as grave stelai and votive dedications, are used here to assess self-fashioning among the *penetes*—that is, what 'living without shame' might mean in practice—and how this changes over time. Representational practices and consumption choices provide, then, a way to think about modes of expression among (some of) those who are categorized as poor; frequently these show values at odds with those discourses highlighted in Chapter 2.

As a result, the second part of this chapter focuses more explicitly on well-being and how it is related to poverty. Given that poverty is more than a question of material deprivation, recasting the standards-of-living debate in terms of well-being provides a mechanism through which to approach the lives of the *penetes* and other groups that are categorized as poor and assess how they viewed their own social roles. Doing so emphasizes, in particular, non-material aspects of *penia* and how those who were categorized as poor negotiated their own well-being through a variety of practices. It

(*apaideutos*), he shares the wind as he is borne along, he has no salvation from poverty in old age.' On this evidence see pp. 206–7.

[2] Ar. *Plut.* 553: *τοῖς ἔργοις προσέχοντα*. Johnstone 2010: 159–62 details the difference between 'work' (*ἔργον, ἐργάζεσθαι*) and 'toil' (*πόνος, πονεῖν*) to describe differently socially embedded acts of labour: the poor and slaves 'worked', whereas the elite 'toiled'. Cf. *IG* II^2 1261, three honorific decrees from 302/1–300/299 that praise Stephanos the breastplate-maker (*thorakopoios*), son of Mylothros ('the miller') for his contribution to the running of an association of Aphrodite and Adonis.

deliberately places emphasis on the agency of these groups to function in society and, in some cases at least, to resist their social exclusion.

BEING POOR: SUBSISTENCE AND CONSUMPTION

In Chapter 4 I reviewed some difficulties with approaches to poverty that focus exclusively on establishing subsistence minima, arguing instead that the most chronic forms of poverty can be better seen in terms of social recategorization. I want here to return to the idea of subsistence in order to highlight some further issues which are particularly important for the capabilities approach I will pursue in this chapter, before turning to different measures of living standards. As I argued in Chapter 4, defining subsistence without contextualization in a broader range of capabilities and functionings is problematic because it implies that subsistence is an end in itself, rather than a means to an end. This ignores the multitude of other factors that, aside from basic nutrition, shape poverty (for example, gender, ill-health, age, and so on), yet these affect whether a person has enough to eat.[3] In addition, this implies that subsistence is the 'aim' of all economic transactions, something that the evidence does not bear out.[4]

In addition, subsistence approaches implicitly try to universalize poverty experiences through reducing them to arguments about basic food needs, which may be useful in comparative perspective, but in doing so gloss over culturally relevant questions of value.[5] Ideas about value are directly relevant, however, to an understanding of poverty because they shape decisions concerning resource distribution (both within the polis or within the home), but our knowledge of these is derived primarily from the same group of texts which were discussed in Chapter 2, and, as we have seen, these are largely shaped by the concerns of those who were relatively wealthy and/or elite. We are,

[3] Sen 1991: 41.

[4] See pp. 122–5. That this is also not true of the archaic period, see van Wees 2009.

[5] Green 2007: 28.

perhaps without realizing it, back in the realm of moral and political judgement.[6]

The recent osteological research on the Athenian skeletal material suggests, however, that the classical Athenian diet was not lacking in nutrients, but instead consisted of a relatively high level of animal protein (meat and/or dairy) supplemented by marine resources, vegetables, and fruits.[7] There are long-term changes over time, and Athens fits into a wider pattern repeated across the Greek world, but the Athenian data typically show high nutritional values.[8] Moreover, both Athenian men and women were on average slightly taller than the Greek mean, which probably indicates better nutrition throughout the life-course and particularly in childhood.[9]

I mentioned in Chapter 4 that although incidents of anaemia and vitamin-deficient disease are present in the Athenian data, they increase over time from the classical to the Roman periods, particularly among the adult male population, which suggests an overall decline of health during this time.[10] There are those who suffered from malnutrition within the Athenian sample—an infant and a young adult male, both buried in the cemetery at Plateia Kotzia—but both of these are post-classical.[11] No skeleton from the classical sample has less than double the δ^{15}N value of these malnourished

[6] In the UK, for example, subsistence frameworks can be traced back to nineteenth-century responses to the 1834 Poor Law (which set up the workhouses and aimed to provide the bare minimum for the destitute in exchange for their labour). Defining subsistence (the 'poverty line') within this context, therefore, became very important and politically charged, ultimately leading to narratives about the 'deserving' and 'undeserving' poor. See further Scott 1994: 3–16. For a critique of the use of poverty-line measurements in contemporary American policy see Brady 2009: 23–9. On the 'slipperiness of hunger as a category' see Vernon 2007 (quote from p. 8).

[7] Lagia 2015a; 2015b. See also the large quantities of animal bone from the agora, which suggests the regular consumption of meat: MacKinnon 2014.

[8] For other ancient comparanda see Lagia 2015a: 135–8. It is particularly noteworthy in this context that the mean scores in classical Athens are similar to 'high status groups' within the Roman cemetery at Velia in southern Italy. Long-term panhellenic trends: Morris 2004; 2005.

[9] von Reden 2007: 388–90 with table 14.1. See also Kron 2005, who compares classical and hellenistic average height with that of Greek army conscripts in 1935. The former, he finds, were taller. Significantly taller heights might also indicate higher life-expectancies amongst populations. In general: Stekel 2005: 230–2.

[10] Lagia 2014; 2015a; 2015b.

[11] Lagia 2015a: 129 with table 8.1 on p. 124: infant (Plateia Kotzia 55): hellenistic; young adult male (Plateia Kotzia 63A): Imperial Roman. On the cemetery see Zachariadou and Kyriakou 1988.

people—even those from Laurion (Thorikos), which are the remains of people probably associated with mining in some capacity (and possibly slaves).[12] If the evidence therefore suggests that nutrition was relatively good at Athens, and not just among those who were buried in the prominent cemetery which was the Kerameikos, it indicates that subsistence and starvation are not the best measures by which to assess poverty—at least not on their own.

This thinking is reflected in recent investigations of living standards. Rather than asking questions about the bare minimum needed for survival, focus has fallen on indicators of human flourishing. In the Greek world these have typically been consumption measures (such as nutrition and housing), but income measures have also been used, particularly by Roman historians (and, of course, by Ober).[13] By using living standards as a proxy to understand economic performance and growth, these studies have argued that the Greek world was a much more prosperous place with higher standards of living than previously expected. There still remains a question, however, about how to assess poverty within the context of such studies; the housing evidence shows some of the difficulties.

Aside from the nutritional evidence, housing size has also been used as an indicator of long-term improvements in living standards. Morris has shown that the median size of houses increased across the Greek world from the eighth to the fourth century, a pattern again replicated in Attica.[14] Although over the long term it is probably correct to see a correlation between the size of a house and the wealth of the inhabitants, within any specific time or place poorer people might not have always lived in noticeably smaller houses. It is highly likely that their houses would be more densely occupied, however, if they had regular shelter at all.[15] The association of *synoikiai* in

[12] Lagia 2015a: 124 with table 8.1; Salliora-Oikonomakou 1985. In fact, two of Lagia's outliers—those who have higher levels of protein in their diet than the rest of the sample—come from the Laurion graves; see fig. 8.1 and pp. 124–5.

[13] Income: Rathbone 2009; Scheidel 2009, 2010; Scheidel and Friesen 2009; Ober 2010. Consumption: Morris 2005; 2004; von Reden 2007; R. Allen 2009. Scheidel's 2010 comparative analysis of wages in a variety of ancient and pre-modern economies uses a mixture of the two by converting wages into wheat-equivalent. This connects basic consumption with relative incomes.

[14] Morris 2004; 2005 see also Ober 2008: 22.

[15] On the poor who were homeless or who lived in precarious or changing places, see Rougier-Blanc 2014 for an attempt to locate these groups within the source material.

oratory with the seedier side of Athenian life from which wealthier Athenians made money implies that this might indeed be the case. The perception one gets from this evidence is that high-density dwellings were occupied by low-status, foreign, or disreputable people: people such as Alke, the manager of Euktemon's *synoikiai* in the Piraeus and the Kerameikos which functioned as a brothel and a bar respectively. Alke is cast here as a cunning temptress, enticing Euktemon with sex, drink, and drugs, and persuading him to introduce her (their?) son to the deme.[16] The fact that only citizens could own real property also may have reinforced the impression that the inhabitants of *synoikiai* were different in some way, though of course their economic resources would have varied.

The number of residents in a house is probably a better guide to the living conditions of its occupants than the size of the dwelling or the type of decoration, but unfortunately such information does not readily survive. We often assume, perhaps wrongly, that excavated houses were occupied by a single, though perhaps extended, family, and that they remained so occupied for the entirety of their use. Patterns of inheritance, however, might mean that houses were divided up into smaller and smaller sections, and sometimes these might not be archaeologically detectable, at least in a clear way (the use of curtains or other dividers is plausible).

Thucydides writes poignantly about the social problems which occurred (at least in part) as a result of migration to Athens during the 430s, and although these were unusually strained times, it gives us an idea of some of the difficulties which could occur through overcrowding in the city.[17] In circumstances like these, houses were much more likely to be densely occupied, even if only on a temporary basis. Aristarchos' house, for example, was likely to have been approaching (modern definitions of) 'overcrowded' when his female relatives and their slaves came to stay in the turmoil of 404.[18] Placing this family into the archaeological remains of a standard Piraeus house (for example, that excavated at Salaminomachon/Flessa) suggests that

[16] Is. 6.19–22. See also Timarchos' association with dodgy types in *synoikiai*: Aeschin. 1.43 (Timarchos lunching with foreigners), 1.123–5 (acting as a prostitute), and Chrysis' assumption that a wet-nurse might be found in one: Men. *Sam.* 84–6. Rougier-Blanc 2014: 133 is, however, sceptical about the poverty of those living in *synoikiai*.

[17] Thuc. 2.52.

[18] Xen. *Mem.* 2.7.1–12. Further discussion of this passage on pp. 118–19.

with eighteen people a house this size would be 'overcrowded'.[19] In Aristarchos' anecdote his household is at least sixteen people strong, and quite probably larger still.[20]

The house at Salaminomachon/Flessa is late fourth century in date, and median house sizes had increased since the dramatic date of Xenophon's tale. It is close in size to the median fourth-century house (240 m^2), but the fifth-century median is 106 m^2, so it might make more sense to place Aristarchos' *oikos* into a house more like this.[21] In a building this size, ten inhabitants would be considered 'overcrowded' (again according to modern definitions). Aristarchos considered himself a member of the elite: he owned land, as well as a house in Athens which was rented out, and his relatives were not used to working, so, despite his misfortune, he was clearly not poor (and so we might prefer to paint him into a house larger than the median).[22] But if Aristarchos with all his wealth was living in conditions that approximated these (however temporarily), we might expect much worse for others. Furthermore, it would not be out of the realms of plausibility that households approached ten people in size: extended families, slaves, former slaves, and elderly relatives are frequently mentioned as living together, and the smaller one's house, the worse this overcrowding would be. Overcrowding, therefore, might have been a much greater feature of Athenian life than we can readily detect. At the very least, Aristarchos' story demonstrates that the number of people who lived in a house, temporarily or permanently, was intricately linked with the well-being of the inhabitants (even for the relatively wealthy) as much as the size or decoration of the building itself.

These approaches to living standards, therefore, provide a baseline for understanding *penia*. But subsistence measures are limited in scope because they ignore the social context in which deprivation occurs, and comparative approaches necessarily have to flatten differences

[19] 'Overcrowded' is defined here according to the English housing and homelessness charity Shelter, as more than two people sleeping in a space approximately 10.2 m^2. Certainly an anachronistic measure, but nonetheless useful as a basic guide. On the archaeological remains at Salaminomachon/Flessa, which was approximately 228 m^2, see von Eickstedt 1991: 1.129 (figs. 43, 45). I assume, for the sake of calculation (perhaps wrongly), that the courtyard (approx. 37 m^2) was not used for sleeping all year round.

[20] He mentions fourteen family members, plus slaves (plural).

[21] Morris 2005: 110.

[22] Xen. *Mem.* 2.7.7–12.

and nuances within Athenian society in order to comment on a broader picture. The focus on economic performance has been fundamental in recontextualizing the Athenian material, but although economic growth can reveal many things, it fails to tell us much about social relations, the distribution of entitlements, or those who are poor or deprived within an affluent society.[23] Certainly, lacking material resources such as food or shelter is an important part of what it means to be poor, but conceptualizing poverty *only* in these terms is reductive.[24] In addition, it is too narrow a framework, because it ignores the symbolic and contextual meanings of those goods and behaviours which are deemed to be essential for 'appearing without shame', and overlooks the wider social and cultural context in which those behaviours are performed and which gives them meaning.[25] What is more, it also neglects to recognize how social norms and legal rules create, reproduce, or perhaps alleviate poverty, nor does it acknowledge gendered aspects of poverty, as we have seen in Chapter 4. Subsistence approaches to poverty, therefore, ignore a person's capabilities and actual functionings within society.

BEING POOR: APPEARING WITHOUT SHAME

If we accept recent arguments that Athenians had relatively high standards of living during the classical period, 'appearing without shame' should form a central part of understanding the experience of poverty. Indeed, one of the most useful contributions of the recent emphasis on living standards and economic growth is that it distinguishes between subsistence and 'respectability'.[26] 'Respectability' might be conceptualized in income terms (as with Scheidel), but it also includes the ability to have a family and form social bonds, or to

[23] See, in a different context, Nussbaum 2003.

[24] See also Green and Hulme 2005: 869, who argue that focusing on the link between poverty and food shortages (and therefore malnutrition) overemphasizes a biological picture of poverty as opposed to a human one.

[25] The idea of appearing without shame goes back to Adam Smith, but is developed by Sen 1987. See also Alkire 2005.

[26] See R. Allen 2009 and Scheidel 2010, who develop 'respectability' and 'bare bones' consumption baskets to assess living standards in Rome and beyond. See also Ober's division between the 'subsistence' and 'middling' populations.

have access to food, to keep healthy and strong enough to perform whatever physical tasks are necessary (from working in the fields to walking to a neighbour's house to taking part in athletic activities).[27] Morris's focus on consumption patterns, then, might be expanded to provide information not only about people's financial resources (what they can afford to buy), or their food intake, but also to investigate what they value, how they perceive their role within a community, their social networks, and their well-being. Consumption patterns are useful here because they reflect and reinforce social inequalities, but they also provide information on how different social groups represented their own role in society.[28] That is, they provide a good resource for thinking about questions of 'respectability'.

In addition, therefore, to examining nutrition and housing as indicators of living standards, we might consider funerary commemoration and dedicatory practice as forms of consumption that have a bearing on this question. Although these are 'occasional purchases'—and therefore more likely to have been items for which people save—they are widespread and allow assessment of change over time. Most important here, though, is that through the epigraphic and iconographical language of this material they also demonstrate the values deemed to be important to those commemorating or dedicating, providing a way to assess what living without shame meant for different groups of people living in Athens. Moreover, I want to argue here that, at least in some cases, (some of) those who were defined by the Athenian elite as being poor were instrumental in driving changes in consumption themselves, rather than emulating the practices of the wealthy elite.

First of all, the chronological and survival patterns of this material should be noted. Funerary commemoration of individuals became commonplace from the last quarter of the fifth century onwards (family grave-plots became more widespread in cemeteries and across the Attic countryside), accompanied by other changes in ritual that signified a dynamic negotiation of cultic, familial, and representational

[27] Fisher 1998.

[28] Bourdieu 1984 is the classic study of the symbolic value of consumption. He argues that consumption patterns reflect class distinctions which are maintained and subverted through ideas of good taste. See also Duplouy 2006, who argues that elites in the archaic period were constantly working to maintain their status through an active strategy of self-promotion as a way of avoiding shame.

relationships.[29] At approximately the same time in sanctuaries a greater number of votive reliefs were dedicated, growing throughout the fourth century, and terracotta figurines, although not uncommon throughout the archaic and classical periods, changed in form, perhaps function, and certainly popularity.[30] Commonly used as votive items, and sometimes placed in graves, changes in techniques of production (specifically, the use of moulds) meant that figurines could be effectively mass-produced.[31] A fairly limited range of scenes (mainly seated women) gave way to a wider selection of more naturalistic figures, with emphasis on caricatured features.[32] This was not simply a 'revolutionary technical innovation', but one which also symbolizes a change in the way people were being represented and emphasizes a change in their consumption choices.[33] Terracotta figurines are, of course, not only found in Athens—a great number were produced in Boiotia (and other places across the Greek world too)—and they became increasingly popular towards the end of the fourth century and into the hellenistic period.[34] What is important here, however, is that not only do these represent changes in patterns of production but they also highlight how Athenians were consuming certain goods differently. This might be linked to the changes in income and wealth distribution suggested in Chapter 3.[35]

Funerary commemoration in particular is thought to have been a way in which people could claim membership within a community (citizenship, ethnicity, locality, and so on), which means that the erection of these monuments, although certainly not universal, is likely to have

[29] See principally Morris 1992; Humphreys 1993; Marchiandi 2011. For the importance of being able to locate your family tombs, see *Ath. Pol.* 55.3; that this was a vital element of citizen identity, see Meyer 1993; Closterman 2007. On changes in depositional and disposal practices see Morris 1992: 128–55; Lagia 2007a.

[30] Votives: Robertson 1975: 373; Comella 2002. Terracottas: Higgens 1967; Burn and Higgins 2001: 20–8. Fewer terracottas are found in sanctuary contexts after the mid-fifth century, which might indicate patterns of survival but also perhaps reflects a change in practice. Additionally, the dedication of pottery votives (miniature cups) in the Agora begins in the mid-fourth century. See Rotroff 1997.

[31] Production techniques: Thompson 1966; Jeammet 2010: 62. Examples at Brauron: Mitsopoulos-Leon 2009; Kerameikos: Vierneisel-Schlörb 1997.

[32] So-called 'theatre' figures (which are thought to represent comic characters) were popular and were exported around the Greek world: Webster 1969; Vierneisel-Schlörb 1997: 90–6; Becq 2010.

[33] For discussion of the technology of mould-made terracottas see Jeammet 2010: 62.

[34] See esp. Besques 1954.

[35] See pp. 96–111.

been maximized. The question of cost is, of course, important here: commemoration, depending on the size of the monument and its location, *could* be very expensive, but it need not be, and it is likely that there were numerous sculptors selling grave monuments derived from pattern-books.[36] But the 'cost question' can also be misleading. Given that large numbers of people were commemorated with simple monuments within family *periboloi*, there is not a direct correlation between the wealth of the deceased and the 'wealth' (or rather, perceived wealth) of the funerary marker or dedication.[37] Instead it is the representational choices within the corpus of these monuments that reveal differences in ideas about status and attitudes towards consumption; that is, these are public statements of social inclusion.[38]

As a general rule, funerary monuments tend to be larger and more elaborate towards the end of the fourth century than at the beginning, but the popularization of funerary commemoration seems to have been kick-started by non-Athenians rather than by Athenians themselves.[39] The earliest group of stelai, which date from just before the 430s, commemorate a large number of foreigners, and their monuments are more elaborate than those thought to belong to citizens of this period.[40] By comparison, monuments set up by Athenians are more restrained in terms of size and ornament (considerably so when compared with those of the archaic period). But within a couple of decades Athenians were commemorating themselves in much greater numbers, developing 'non-Athenian' architectural and iconographical motifs such as *naiskoi* (architectural frames) or large human figures to express very Athenian civic values.[41]

[36] Bergemann 1997: 132–5 estimates the cost of building a large *peribolos* (like that of Hierokles in Rhamnous) at something like half a talent, but presumably this cost varied depending on where the *peribolos* was located, and other factors. Literary sources also give a guide to what was possible (or at least plausible) to spend at the upper end of the spectrum: Lys. 32.21: 5,000 dr., [Dem.] 45.79: 2 talents.

[37] Nielsen et al. 1989; Oliver 2000. The debate, as outlined by Oliver, demonstrates that binary categorizations of 'wealthy' and 'poor' are not particularly useful (see also Chapter 2).

[38] Meyer 1993 discusses the importance of funerary commemoration for citizens, but non-citizens also used grave markers to negotiate their own status within the wider civic community, as the examples in this chapter demonstrate.

[39] Large (1.5 m high/with life-size figures) funerary monuments vastly increase in number after *c*.330: Bergemann 1997: 124. See also Scholl 1994. This coincides with the changes in wealth distribution outlined in Chapter 5; see pp. 180–93.

[40] Stears 2000: 51.

[41] Hagemajer Allen 2003. On early stelai see Stears 2000.

The reasons for this change are well rehearsed: increased mortality due to war and disease, new representations of family relationships and the individual, or a focus on the 'private' rather than the 'public' have all been suggested as being contributing factors.[42] Close analysis of the material shows that certain types of scenes became increasingly common, most notably those showing family groups, athletes, soldiers, and the sitting-woman-with-slave motif.[43] This is particularly true of the more elaborate (that is, highly decorated, presumably made-to-order, and therefore probably more expensive) monuments. However, side by side with this development appears a different mode of representation. Less elaborate grave markers (that is, those with less technically accomplished or smaller sculpture, or ones which are suggested to have been derived from pattern-books) do not emulate these scenes: motifs displaying women with servants and athletic or military scenes were never popular here. In fact there is a different language of representation: banquet scenes, women in childbirth, and scenes with priests and other religious officials are common.[44]

At the same time, increasing numbers of funerary stelai and dedications fashion those who commissioned the monuments in terms of their work, contesting the discourses that devalued labour. Some examples have already been noted at the beginning of this chapter.[45] Others demonstrate how the deceased viewed their role in Athenian society: as fighters, as carers of children, as producers of the Panathenaic prize *amphorai*.[46] It is possible, of course, that monuments like these reflect not the social concerns of the person they commemorate but that of their owner or master, and therefore reflect not pride in work but patronizing elite attitudes towards it. Approximately one-third of thirty-nine examples that survive might plausibly fall into this

[42] Morris 1992; Humphreys 1993.

[43] See Bergemann 1997: 128. Seated women are also commonly represented in terracotta figurines of the period, see Higgens 1967: 74.

[44] Described by Scholl 1996: 164 as 'alternative iconographical form of expression', one which is 'exceptionally dramatic and realistic'. Demand 1995 makes a strong case for viewing some of the 'death in childbirth' scenes as memorials for birth attendants: see Chapter 4, p. 144.

[45] That this is an Athenian phenomenon (at least in the epigrams) see Tsagalis 2008: 208.

[46] Manes died in war (*IG* I^3 1361), Malicha (and countless other women) looked after the children of other families (*IG* II^2 9112), Bakchios, or his sons, produced the Panathenaic prize *amphorai* (*IG* II^2 6320); on this workshop see Papagrigorakis et al. 2006.

category; that is, using the name of the person dedicated as an indicator (for example, Thraix), or perhaps even the use of the attribute *chrestos/-e*, it is possible to suggest some kind of servile origin.[47] However, another third of the sample use their city ethnic, so should more likely be considered as freemen and women or freedmen and women (for example, Atotas or Mannes noted on p. 195, or *IG* II[2] 7873, which records Melitta, the daughter of a metic awarded *isoteleia*).[48] For the other third, Bakchios (*IG* II[2] 6320) is certainly a citizen—he mentions his demotic—but there is no indication in the text for the others about the legal status of the person commemorated; most have names, however, which are also attested for citizens.[49] We cannot, therefore, assume that funerary inscriptions that mention professions were always for slaves or the sentiments therein controlled by masters. Instead, they seem to speak to a different phenomenon: the articulation of a counter-discourse which reflects the attitudes of working people (the *penetes*), regardless of civic status.[50]

Relief votives also show imagery which speaks to similar concerns.[51] This was no new trend: it had been a pattern since the late sixth century, if the dedications on the Akropolis from potters, washerwomen, fullers, tanners, bread-sellers, and so on are anything to go by. For a century at least, those who derived their income from labour self-consciously fashioned their piety as being connected to their work.[52] From the late fifth century, dedications begin to represent

[47] e.g. *IG* II[2] 11689: Thraix, the slipper-maker (*persikopoios*); *IG* II[2] 12387: Paideusis *titthe chreste* (see Fig. 6.2).

[48] See Chapter 4, p. 139.

[49] e.g. *IG* II[2] 10843 (Artemisia the wet-nurse), *IG* II[2] 11681 (Thrasippos the baker), *IG* II[2] 11202 (Dion the digger), and so on.

[50] Another possible objection is that this evidence represents owners of workshops rather than workers within them (the 'Kleon as a tanner' objection: see p. 33), but this neglects to explain the large numbers of metic and slaves commemorated, the self-presentation of labour in votive dedications (Figs. 1.1, 6.1), and the lack of positive evidence outside of the fact of dedication/commemoration for any of these people being wealthy. Although the line between owner of a workshop and worker within it was for the most part blurred, it seems preferable to assume that these people are workers of some description.

[51] Comella 2002: 8–9.

[52] Potters: *IG* I[3] 620, 628, 633, 824. Washerwomen: *IG* I[3] 794 (perhaps related to *IG* I[3] 573 and 700: the same name, Smikythe, is recorded on all three inscriptions). Fullers: *IG* I[3] 554, 616, 905. Tanners: *IG* I[3] 646. Bread-sellers: *IG* I[3] 546. See also an architect (*tekton*): *IG* I[3] 606; kithara-player (*kitharoidos*): *IG* I[3] 666, 754; herald

their commissioners not as wealthy dedicants but as modest working people. For example, a carter appears on a dedication made to Asklepios, dated to the end of the fifth century or beginning of the fourth, dressed in a *pilos* and leading a wagon to approach Asklepios, Hygeia, and Epione (Fig. 6.1).[53] Although the iconography of 'dedicator approaching deity' is common on votive reliefs, it is noteworthy that the carter portrays himself here *as a carter* rather than as a more generic adorant. The scene is accompanied by a verse inscription (unfortunately fragmentary) which details why the dedication was made: it seems that the dedicator (whose name does not survive) was saved from war (or, depending on the restoration, falling rocks).[54] Another carter appears on a fragmentary relief, again for Asklepios, dated to *c.*410, as well as Dionysios, the cobbler who dedicates with his family to the hero Kallistephanos discussed in Chapter 1 (Fig. 1.1).[55] Although it is impossible to draw conclusions about the financial resources of carters and cobblers from this material (see p. 3), they are using their funerary commemorations and dedicatory activity to demonstrate their belonging to the community, and displaying a pride in work which contradicts the anti-banausic sentiments configured within elite ideologies. Being a *penes* was not a source of shame.

What is also noticeable about this material is that not only was the language of labour increasingly deployed, but it also seems that the representational differences between the more and less elaborate grave markers were driven by those outside the elite. This is because the scenes developed on less elaborate grave markers influenced those which were more expensive to produce, rather than the other way around.[56] Comparison of the most common motifs

(*keryx*): *IG* I^3 776; secretary (*grammateus*): *IG* I^3 841; ship-builder (?) (*naupegos*): *IG* I^3 589. See further Raubitschek 1949.

[53] *IG* II^2 4356/Acr. 1341. See Pipili 2000: 163–79 for discussion of the *pilos* as a rustic hat of 'lower-class countrymen'.

[54] *CEG* 764: [- ⏕ - ?Σπ]έṿδ̣[ω]ν ?Ἀνδ[- ⏕ - ⏑⏑ --] | [- ⏕]ωμ πετρῶν ἡγεμόνο[ς ⏑ ⏑ -] | [ἐκ πολέμο]ν σωθὲς δέ, Ἀσκληπιέ, το[⏑ ⏑ --] | [- ⏕]ν ἐς τέμενος, τῶι δίδο ϵ[ὐτυχίαν?]. Hansen suggests the dedicator's name could be Spendon, the son of And-, but only the epsilon is readable: see *CEG* 724. Güntner 1994: 39 suggests the rocks (*petron*) are what the dedicator has been saved from, but Hansen's restoration of *ek polemon* seems plausible enough.

[55] NM 1358 + Acr. 2966 (Comella 2002: Atene 98). On Dionysios, see pp. 1–3.

[56] 'Elaboration' is defined in terms of art-historical criteria: *naiskoi* have an architectural frame, *Bildfeldstelen* are usually flat reliefs confined within 'picture' frames within the stele. See Scholl 1996; Bergemann 1997.

Figure 6.1. Relief of the cart-driver, end of the fifth–beginning of the fourth century BCE (Acr. 1341)

(sitting women and mantle-wearing men, which are frequently found on both types of monument) suggest the opposite. If there was a top-down influence in how people chose to represent themselves in death, these scenes would be expected to be more common on the more elaborate markers, especially in the period between 430 and 390 when they were becoming popular. But the reverse is actually the case. A higher proportion of less elaborate monuments use this iconography, implying that the direction of influence is the other way around (Table 6.1). This is significant, because patterns of consumption, especially of 'luxury' or 'occasional' goods such as these, are often thought to change through top-down influence, with non-elites emulating the elites, but this does not appear to be the case here. Here we can see how (some of) the *penetes* portrayed themselves. This pattern also fits with Fisher's view of gymnastic activities not being a preserve of the elite during the classical period but being part of ordinary citizens' lives as well.[57]

Elaboration of sculptural elements on a funerary stele does not, of course, always correlate with economic resources, and the division between 'more elaborate' and 'less elaborate' is crude, but it does give an indication of how people wished to communicate their own position within society (or that of their family members) in a specific mode of representation. Depictions of jewellery, ornate furniture, slaves, and non-Greek (exotic) elements of decoration show that the display of economic resources was important in funerary commemoration.[58] Whilst we cannot assume that the least elaborate monuments were always erected by the least wealthy people, there is more likely to be a correlation with the most elaborate monuments and those who are most wealthy.[59] What Bergemann noted, then, as the 'astonishing stability' of themes found in funerary iconography represents not the emulation of the elite by the masses, but the flow of cultural practices from the masses to the elite.[60] Evidently consumption patterns, as reflected in what Hagemajer Allen describes as the 'new vocabulary of personal expression' provided by the funerary context, changed not because these 'trickled down' from the wealthy

[57] Fisher 1998. [58] Hagemajer Allen 2003: 225–9.

[59] This is not always the case, however: see Parker Pearson 1982; Tarlow 1999.

[60] Bergemann 1997: 127.

Table 6.1. Representation of popular scenes on grave stelai, *c.*430–390 (%)

	Sitting women	Mantel-wearing men
More elaborate (*naiskoi*)	30	25
Less elaborate (*Bildfeldstelen*)	40	40

Source: Bergemann 1997: 127–8.

elite to everyone else, but at least in the most popular scenes it was the other way around.[61]

Consumption patterns are important, because what people buy not only communicates ideas about the self to others but acts as a mechanism in which a person's place in society is created and reinforced. This is especially true of occasional purchases such as those discussed above. Increased production of funerary monuments, relief votives, and terracotta figurines should be seen as a response to the changing capabilities of people to fashion themselves in terms which previously would have been impossible. And whilst these might be seen as irregular acts of consumption because of their religious and/or occasional nature, the fact that they were so widespread throughout fourth-century Athenian society suggests that these activities permeated Athenian life. No doubt these were activities for which people saved, but this in itself indicates that significant numbers of people had the resources available to them to be able to accumulate enough to save in the first place. What these changes in consumption patterns show, therefore, is that the activities which were required to live without shame were configured differently from the end of the fifth century on, running broadly in parallel with the changes in wealth and income distribution suggested in Chapter 3.

BEING POOR: CAPABILITIES, WELL-BEING, AND QUALITY OF LIFE

Living without shame is a useful way to reframe discussions of *penia*, for two reasons. First, it unshackles the structuralist discourse which

[61] This might not be seen as too surprising given that many of the changes were driven by non-Athenian groups: Hagemajer Allen 2003: 229.

views *penia* as the opposite of *ploutos* and realigns it more closely to the voices of the *penetes* themselves who, as we have seen, actively contest these elitist ideas and actively change cultural practices.[62] Second, it goes further than subsistence approaches to delineate how poverty is shaped by social values and social relations, suggesting a dynamic process which fits more closely with the contemporary literature. It is legitimate to argue, however, that although examining consumption patterns as reflected in funerary commemoration and dedication provides a tool for understanding lifestyles outside of the richest, it does little to fill in the blanks for those who could not afford such monuments. This is undoubtedly true. We cannot tell from this material how the very poorest shaped their own world. However, it does broaden the base of evidence which we might consider, and it does provide a tool for outlining what 'living without shame' might look like in Athens in a way which is less filtered through the experiences of the wealthy elite.

Rather than viewing poverty in terms of economic measures alone, then, it is being unable to participate in society (capability deprivation) which is key to an understanding of *penia*. This allows us to shift the focus onto the lives of the *penetes* and their experience of the condition of poverty (however defined). One result of this is that it allows us to make adjustments for different social groups (for example, slaves, non-citizens, and women), rather than viewing poverty as a condition only worthy of comment when it involves (male) citizens or when it appears in public discourse. It also enables us to view the impact of poverty on households and within households, and to recognize the contributions of different social groups to Athenian society rather than viewing them as simply lacking various elite-defined characteristics (landed wealth, masculinity, freedom, citizenship, and so on). The result of this approach is that it reframes our conception of poverty from purely economic readings defined by the lack of possessions to contextualizing it as a part of the wider landscape of inequalities. As we have seen in previous chapters, poverty both creates and reflects social divisions in terms of how it is conceived, the measures that are taken to alleviate or ameliorate it, and the extent to which it is gendered.

[62] See also Sobak 2015, who expertly rehabilitates craftsmen as central to democratic life.

The rest of this chapter, therefore, foregrounds poverty as a product of a person's (or a group's) functionings by examining how the standards-of-living debate can be recast in terms of well-being. This allows emphasis to be placed upon the things in life which were valued (and to consider who they were valued by).[63] Thinking about standards of living from a capabilities perspective, therefore, takes into account not only subsistence costs (whether conceived as income or in terms of consumption) but also the context of social relationships, the extent to which people were involved in creating and sustaining communities, and whether they had access to resources or meaningful social contact. Whilst it is broadly true that the more resources one has the more one is able to consume, consumption patterns also symbolically reflect (and reproduce) social relationships, as we have seen already. The result is that there can be, but is not always, a direct correlation between income and consumption, or wealth and expenditure. What this indicates is that economic criteria on their own form only one part of an assessment of poverty: it is the social relationships surrounding these economic measurements which are important. In the ancient world, the processes surrounding manumission demonstrate this distinction nicely.

Recorded on the *phialai exeleutherikai* inscriptions of the late fourth century are manumitted slaves.[64] A number of them are shown to have bought their freedom by borrowing money from *koina eraniston*, groups of creditors often led by their masters.[65] For example, Bion, a jeweller living in Melite, borrowed from a *koinon eraniston* led by his owner Chairippos son of Chairedemos of Halai.[66] Bion would be required to pay back the loan, perhaps with interest, but if he 'lived apart' anyway he would have been subject to pay a proportion of his earnings to Chairedemos when he was enslaved (*apophora*).[67] This seems likely, since Bion and most of these slaves

[63] Sen 1987; 1991; Douglas and Ney 1998. Noted also by Jongman 2007: 615: 'standards of living do not simply depend on the performance of the economy at large, but also on the rules of entitlement to its benefits.'

[64] Meyer 2010 argues that these were metics being fined for non-payment of the *metoikion*. For a refutation see Vlassopoulos 2011b.

[65] See Zelnick-Abramowitz 2005: 220–2; Thomsen 2014.

[66] *SEG* 60.181, ll. 138–43.

[67] On the interest-bearing nature of some of these loans see Thomsen 2014: 161–2. We do not know in the case of manumitted slaves whether interest was charged; this was presumably in the control of the master.

are listed with their professions, often living in different demes than that in which their owners were registered. Until Bion paid off the loan he would have remained economically tied to Chairedemos, perhaps over a period of some years.[68] On a purely economic reading of living standards, one would argue that Bion's did not improve during this time—he could afford the same goods and services as before, and was still bound to his former owner—but in reality his quality of life did improve, because he now had the status of being free. His capabilities had expanded.

It is therefore important to consider what people like Bion were able to do or to be, that is, to develop a set of quality-of-life indictors which allow an analysis of the variety of life experience in the ancient world and encompass the differences between free and slave, citizen and non-citizen, or men and women.[69] Although income and consumption are, of course, important here (in that they provide specific measures within a multidimensional set of indicators), neither income nor consumption gets to the heart of Bion's experience of manumission. In sum, we need to contextualize the conclusions we can draw from studying subsistence alone.

There are, then, a number of different criteria which can be used to develop an assessment of well-being in Athens. These criteria might include access to land and/or economic resources (that is, wealth or income in the more traditional sense), involvement in local religious activity, political enfranchisement and participation, education, the ability to take advantage of business opportunities, and so on; what they show is how people used the resources they had available to them and how, as a result of this, they negotiated their place within a community. In Athens, some of these criteria were strictly laid out and exclusive: political decision-making and landownership were for citizens only unless specifically granted by the citizen body.[70] Others were attainable—at least in theory—by wider groups of people, and it

[68] Zelnick-Abramowitz 2005: 215–22.

[69] That these groups were intricately bound together in multiple overlapping networks, see Vlassopoulos 2007b; Gottesman 2014; Sobak 2015.

[70] Certain types of religious activity were reserved for citizens, e.g. sacrifices performed by the archon basileus and his wife: see [Dem.] 59.73 for the problems this causes the Athenians when they suspect a non-citizen has filled this role (but conversely also evidence for the fact that non-Athenians *could* perform this role without too much difficulty: it is only Apollodoros' feud with Stephanos that brings this accusation to the lawcourts). On *isoteleia* see Osborne 1981.

is through interrogating the capabilities and constraints placed on people here that we can evaluate well-being.

The usefulness of these criteria within Athenian society can be assessed by examining, for example, the family of Aeschines.[71] Though hardly the poorest of the poor, the family does not appear to have been especially wealthy in its own right, at least not after Aeschines' father, Atrometos, lost (some of?) his land during the Peloponnesian War.[72] Yet his mother was a priestess of a local cult (to which Aeschines also allegedly belonged), her brother a seer, and Aeschines makes much of his father's phratry affiliation, thereby reinforcing the family's religious involvement within the community.[73] Aeschines made a name for himself by speaking in the Assembly, but before he did so he, as well as his brother Aphobetos, served as *grammateis* and was therefore politically active.[74] The family once owned land, though presumably much of it was inaccessible during the Peloponnesian War, and Atrometos worked as a *grammatistes* for at least part of his life.[75] But it was this work which enabled him to gain access to other resources (pay), as well as educate his sons and set them up with good social contacts.[76] Aeschines' education was not confined to formal schooling, however. In his time as a *grammateus* he would have developed practical skills and knowledge of the workings of Athenian politics, whilst his spell as an actor would have trained him for public speaking as well as given him access to important cultural knowledge and political skills. We can see, therefore, in Aeschines' family how a number of these quality-of-life indicators might intersect (political involvement, education, access to land, social capital, and so on). On these measures one might suggest that Aeschines scores pretty highly.

In comparison with others in Athens, Aeschines was probably relatively well off in economic terms: he served as an ephebe before the polis began to subsidize this activity, which probably (though not necessarily) suggests access to some, not negligible, financial

[71] See E. M. Harris 1995: 21–33; Fisher 1998: 100–4. [72] Aeschin. 2.147.

[73] Dem. 18.259–60, Aeschin. 2.147, *SEG* 16.193. Of course, Demosthenes plays with this information to make it sound sinister, but scholarly opinion is simply that Glaukothea's cult is one of the many private religious associations which were present in Athens, and not at all unusual. For identification of the cult see E. M. Harris 1995: 25, with n. 24. On *SEG* 16.193: Papademitriou 1957. On phratries see Lambert 1998.

[74] Dem. 19.237. On the social demographics of *grammateis* see Taylor 2007b.

[75] Dem. 24.9. [76] See E. M. Harris 1995: 36–40.

resources.[77] Compared with Demosthenes he was relatively poor, of course (though who was not?), but compared with many others within Athens he was probably rather better off. However, comparing the wealth of these men like this tells us little on its own. The problem is that, except for the fact that Aeschines does not appear to have been a liturgist nor have come from a liturgical family, there is little that we can know about his wealth without controversy (unless some new evidence comes to light).[78] This means that presence or absence of wealth is a problematic measure of assessment, not least because much of what we know in this case is filtered through rhetorical attacks by opponents in court.

This is also true of the *penetes* as a whole. Given that we rarely have detailed data about the financial resources of this (large) group of people, we need to develop more sophisticated tools to assess the evidence that does survive and suggest plausible parameters of interpretation. The income- and wealth-distribution models of Chapter 3 provide one way of doing so which does focus on economic criteria, but these models should be read within the context of other (non-material) measures too. The discussion of consumption provides another way, but this is also limited by questions of a materialist nature. More importantly, however, is that framing the problem in this way is to miss the saliency of well-being as an analytical category, and to deflect the multidimensional experience of poverty into a dichotomy of having or lacking wealth. This—as argued in previous chapters—simply serves to reproduce the discourses of wealth and poverty of the Athenian elite whilst silencing the voices of the *penetes* themselves. Whilst economic resources are certainly an important aspect of poverty and form a necessary part of the equation for thinking about living standards, these need to be contextualized within a variety of other indicators. That we can isolate a number of these in Aeschines' biography demonstrates that these are criteria which we can parse in other contexts too, and therefore that they should be taken seriously within such an investigation rather than be dismissed out of hand as having

[77] Aeschin. 2.167. Harris uses the fact that Atrometos was a hoplite to suggest that he was not that poor, but hoplite armour could be subsidized by wealthier friends (Lys. 31.15) or handed down through the family. On the thetes-serving-as-hoplites debate see p. 14, n. 33.

[78] For discussion of Atrometos' wealth see E. M. Harris 1995: 21–6.

nothing to do with *penia*. We need not assume that Aeschines was the poorest of the poor in order to do so.

Well-being is obviously a subjective concept, and any abstracted measure of well-being masks individual perception and variation, not least because personal circumstances change throughout the life-course (see, for example, Atrometos' loss of land). But well-being is a useful concept for thinking about standards of living, because it allows us to shift the emphasis onto the experiences of the *penetes* themselves and highlight (or at least not deny) their agency in shaping their own social and political identities, as we can see by looking at the consumption patterns discussed in this chapter. This is particularly important in Athens, where much of our evidence for poverty, at least that which is derived from literary sources, is shaped by elite concerns (see Chapter 2). It also allows us to acknowledge the contexts in which low income or low wealth is absolutely fundamental to shaping a person's or a group's capabilities, but in addition to highlight those where it was less important.

Because there were high levels of political participation, governmental accountability, and relatively good economic performance in Athens we might expect that, broadly speaking, adult male Athenian citizens had a relatively good quality of life, at least in comparison with other groups of people in the ancient world.[79] The discussions of Chapters 3 and 5 bear this out. However, Chapter 5 also showed that poverty was more easily reproduced within the non-citizen population. It is worth seeing, then, how far we can assess the well-being of different groups of people within Athens. As was the case when discussing gendered poverty, the aim of such an investigation is not to deny that some groups in Athenian society were marginalized (even exploited) and deprived, nor to deny the unpleasantness of the personal or family circumstances of groups of people.[80] Instead,

[79] Frey and Stutzer 2000 find in a study of the Swiss cantons that 'strongly developed institutions of direct democracy... can be expected to raise citizens' subjective well-being' (pp. 920–1), and that 'causality runs unambiguously from direct democratic rights to satisfaction with life' (p. 927). For high levels of participation in Athens: Taylor 2007a; accountability: Roberts 1983; economic performance: Ober 2008.

[80] The use of the term 'marginalized' here refers to those outside of the 'citizen club'. Some might object to this terminology on the grounds of breadth, but citizenship not only shaped access to resources, it has also shaped historians' conceptualizations of ancient social and political relations. For discussion see Vlassopoulos 2007c.

its aim is to attempt to refocus attention on these groups in a positive way, and in a manner which has been defined (albeit sometimes in a highly restricted fashion) by they themselves. In effect, what we are doing here is considering (in Senian terms) their functionings, that is, what they were actually able to achieve with the resources they had available, whilst acknowledging that these were restricted in various complex ways. This approach does not simply attempt to describe those whose living standards might be considered low, or whose lives might be considered deprived in various ways, but seeks to assess how these groups viewed their own place within Athenian society, that is, how they contested the discourses that presented them as morally inferior.[81]

One advantage of investigating well-being is that we can use the evidence that survives to think across legal categories of status. Recent work has placed greater emphasis on the autonomy and agency of slaves, metics, and freedmen (and shows that there is considerable evidence for this), which provides a good starting-point for thinking about quality of life.[82] Certainly citizenship status would have shaped certain aspects of well-being (political activity, freedom, land-ownership, and so on—see Chapter 5), but in other contexts this played a much less important a role, and citizens and non-citizens demonstrably lived together, fought together, belonged to cult associations together, and worked together side by side.[83] Three factors have, therefore, been highlighted here for further investigation, chosen because they cut across legal status categories: affiliation, social connectivity, and the formation of relationships and emotional bonds. In these three areas evidence shows how Athenians and non-Athenians alike were able to use the limited resources they had available to shape their own well-being and therefore resist social exclusion.

[81] See pp. 19–22, with Lister 2004: 17 on the capability approach: 'Capability theorists focus on the positive—of the kind of life we want people to be able to achieve in order to "flourish"... —rather than the negative—of the lack of material resources that can prevent them from achieving it. In doing so, they integrate poverty into the wider concerns of the population as a whole and into a wider social scientific literature, rather than ghettoizing it in a separate box.'

[82] Taylor and Vlassopoulos 2015b. See esp. the comments of Davies 2015: 243–4.

[83] Randall 1953; Bäbler 2005; Feyel 2006. Bäbler (pp. 69–70) argues persuasively against the portrayal of slaves as Untermenschen.

Affiliation

Belonging to a social group and creating strong ties are important parts of well-being.[84] This allows people to construct their own identities, contributes to feelings of self-respect and self-worth, and provides access to material and social resources: that is, belonging to groups can expand individual capabilities, but it also provides a mechanism for shaping the well-being of the group as a whole within the context (or perhaps constraints) of the social structure.[85] This is particularly important in the ancient context, because it is debatable whether individualist approaches are useful or particularly relevant.[86] For Athenians and non-Athenians alike, affiliation was an important strategy for negotiating well-being and resisting patterns of social exclusion both within and outside of family units. There were many groups which facilitated this, from demes and phratries to networks of friends and voluntary religious associations, but I will focus here on three examples: the navy, the cult of Bendis, and the practice of dedicating joint votives. Together these show a variety of mechanisms through which citizens and non-citizens could create and maintain social ties and expand their capabilities in different ways.

First, the navy. In an important article, Strauss argues that rowing in the fleet served to expand the political consciousness of, and served as a political education for, those who took up oars.[87] These men were typically (though not exclusively) poorer Athenian citizens, whose service created a sense of group solidarity and ties of affiliation to their fellow rowers.[88] They received a stipend and fulfilled their civic duties in rowing, but in doing so formed important new communities and created new identities that had real political consequences. That these were strong emotional bonds too can be seen in the evocation of distress surrounding the events after the battle of Arginousai, where the Assembly was persuaded to execute the generals who failed to rescue the corpses of sailors who had drowned. Here, Xenophon portrays the generals as victims of the fickle demos, manipulated into a poor decision by Theramenes' tricks.[89] But it also shows the strength of bonds between the rowers and how this affiliation could

[84] Nussbaum 2003; Stewart 2005. [85] Jackson 2005.
[86] See discussion in Chapter 1, p. 20. [87] Strauss 1996.
[88] On slaves in the fleet see Gabrielsen 1994: 108–9; Hunt 1998.
[89] Xen. *Hell.* 1.6.19–7.35, Diod. 13.97.1–103.2.

ripple throughout Athenian society. In the words of Strauss, service in the navy 'taught poor men how to be free'.[90] It did so by expanding their capabilities and allowed them to develop their functionings.

A second example focuses on the cult of the Thracian goddess Bendis which was introduced into Athens during the late fifth century.[91] We know that both Thracians and Athenians participated in this cult: this is evident from Plato's description of Sokrates' visit to the Bendideia, which describes both groups taking part in the festival in separate processions.[92] Furthermore, Athenians are honoured in *IG* II^2 1255 (dated to 337/6) for their performance of various cultic activities, and a fourth-century dedication from Sounion by Daos confirms Thracian involvement.[93] It is likely that the cult of Bendis, therefore, provided a context for Thracians in Athens to develop religious associations of particular importance for their own Thracian identity.[94]

The epigraphic record reveals that the *orgeones* met on different days in the month (second: *IG* II^2 1324; eighth: *IG* II^2 1361), and this was interpreted in the early twentieth century as encapsulating ethnic divisions (one group for Athenians, one for Thracians). But this is merely a suggestion based on the two processions of Plato's *Republic*; there is no evidence within the inscriptions themselves to suggest the *orgeones* were divided in this way, and more recent models of Athenian religion emphasize integration more than separation.[95] It is no less likely that the *orgeones* included both Thracians and Athenians who were involved in cult activity side by side, which suggests that Thracians could develop close links with Athenians within a religious context cutting across literary configurations of them as a barbarian Other.[96]

[90] Strauss 1996: 320.

[91] *IG* I^3 136 (probably 413/2). See also *IG* I^3 383 (429/8): Bendis appears for the first time supported by public funds. See Planeaux 2000.

[92] Pl. *Rep.* 327a–328b. The third-century *IG* II^2 1283 also makes it clear that Thracians are involved: see further Parker 1996: 170–1.

[93] *SEG* 39.210: *λαμπάδι νικήσας Δᾶος Βενδίδι ἀνέθηκεν*. Daos is a characteristically Thracian name. Unfortunately we cannot (in most instances) tell onomastically whether any particular named individual recorded on the other inscriptions connected to the cult was Thracian or Athenian.

[94] See further Hunt 2015: 134–5.

[95] Wilhelm 1902, followed by Ferguson 1944: 98 and Simms 1988: 68, but not by Mikalson 1998: 140–1 or Arnaoutoglou 2003: 59–60.

[96] Pache 2001.

Even if this interpretation is incorrect, the cult nonetheless had a special status within Athens, encouraging a level of Thracian involvement within Athenian religious practice unparalleled by any other foreign group, and an Athenian acceptance of non-Athenian cults at a comparatively early date.[97] For the Thracians, this likely emphasized aspects of Thracian identity, the maintenance of cult practices in a foreign city, and affiliation with one another as well as the wider Athenian community.[98] The regulations state that a 2-drachma fee was to be paid by each member for the sacrifice; this was a low amount and presumably, therefore, did not price too many people out of participating.[99] In general, the cult actively encouraged as many *orgeones* as possible—as long as they could pay the fee.[100] It is possible that *enktesis* was granted in part because of the links between Athenian and Thracian elites, but it is unlikely that the cult excluded non-elite Thracians living in Athens, many of whom were slaves and freedmen.[101] Not only, therefore, does this cult demonstrate the adoption of non-Athenian religious practices into Athenian life, it also provided a forum in which citizens and non-citizens, rich and poor alike, could take part in cult activity side by side. This is a form of affiliation, therefore, that promotes the well-being of the participants.

Another important set of material for assessing affiliatory practices, particularly of non-citizens (for whom we have little other evidence), is joint dedications. These are the material remains of groups which formed for the purposes of cult activity, and, although in most cases we only have the snapshot evidence for a one-off dedication, sometimes we can suggest the possibility that they existed for longer than this. As I have argued elsewhere, the dedications of (probably slave) *eranistai* from Sounion appears to follow this pattern: five fourth-century inscriptions survive, recording the names of non-Athenian men who joined together to dedicate votives to (in all but one case)

[97] For political expediency as an explanation of the adoption of Bendis cult into Athens during the fifth century see Ferguson 1944: 87–8 and followed by Sears 2013: 153–4, but the cult could not have been sustained for well over a century unless people (Thracians and Athenians) participated in it. Other factors are discussed by Planeaux 2000: 179–82. In general: Garland 1992.

[98] Hunt 2015.

[99] *IG* II^2 1361, ll. 17–20. See also Jones 1999: 260–1.

[100] *IG* II^2 1361, ll. 20–5: *ἐξεῖναι [τῶι] βουλομένωι εἰσεν[έ]γκαντι [. . . δ]ραχμὰς μετεῖναι αὐτῶι τοῦ ἱεροῦ* (‘it is permitted for anyone who wishes to contribute *x* drachmas to become a member of the sanctuary’).

[101] Sears 2013: 155–6; Bäbler 1998: 183–98, with funerary evidence of Thracians in Athens at pp. 268–82.

unknown cults.[102] Since some names reoccur across these inscriptions, and at least some of these names are comparatively rare (Kadous, Tibeios), it is possible that the dedications refer to the same persons active in different contexts.[103] If this is the case, these inscriptions represent significant affiliations in the lives of the (probably slave) men recorded on them. Although of low status, the inscriptions demonstrate that, by joining together, the men had access to financial resources over a period of time (they were able to save enough to make a dedication), they were not ashamed of their group (they are keen to advertise the fact of their dedication through the writing of their personal names), they contributed positively to the local cultic economy, and engaged with and participated in a local community.[104]

Affiliation is 'empowering and enriching', providing access to resources—material and non-material—to those who lack them, and improving well-being.[105] I have argued elsewhere that forming groups like this, fleeting though they appear in the material record, served as a mechanism to expand the capabilities of those who belonged to them. They do this by providing a context to develop political knowledge, to retain and reinforce ethnic and other identities, to allow the development of relationships outside of the family unit, and to demonstrate collaborative and collective behaviour. That is, rowing in the fleet, taking part in the cult of Bendis, or dedicating a group votive are ways in which people in Athens who perhaps had limited economic resources could demonstrate their status as being

[102] On these inscriptions see further Taylor 2015: 46–9. They are *IG* II^2 2947, 2938, 2940, *SEG* 54.236, 54.388. Also Lauffer 1979: 187–95; Salliora-Oikonomakou 2004: 166–7, no. 87.

[103] The reoccurring names are Kallias, Sosias, Tibeios, and Kadous. Both Kallias and Sosias are very common. There are fourteen examples of Tibeios in *LGPN II* (including the two recorded on these inscriptions). Kadous is a more unusual name, however: only four examples of this name are recorded in antiquity, the two recorded on these inscriptions, plus *SEG* 17.118 (Bäbler 1998: no. 121: Thraitta Kadous, found in Markopoulo), *IG* II^2 10837 (Artimas Kadous, found in Athens); both gravestones commemorate women with their husbands/fathers. Perdrizet 1889: 85, n. 3 thinks Kadous is a Phrygian name (though note that all known examples of the name are in fact from Attica).

[104] See also Morris 2011: 184: 'if mine slaves bought cist burial with them from their homelands and maintained this custom as their death-rituals evolved in Attica, they may have retained control of important parts of their religious lives.'

[105] Stewart 2005: 185. Many groups formed amongst the poor can also be seen to 'improve their claim over resources' through affiliatory practices (p. 197).

part of a community rather than as being isolated from it. These activities form mechanisms to resist alienation and social exclusion.[106]

Social Connectivity

Affiliation is rooted in belonging to groups bound with strong ties, but social connectivity outside of these groups is also important, because it provided a broader social network crucial for the exploitation of weak ties and the development of social capital.[107] The many religious associations, particularly of the late fourth century, show how citizens and foreigners, slaves and free, moved in the same circles, and membership often cut across legal status lines.[108] This form of community connectedness would have been crucial to the well-being of non-elite groups within Athens, because it would have provided access to resources otherwise unobtainable for them. In Chapter 5 (pp. 166–77) I discussed the role of voluntary associations in terms of social networks and social capital, arguing that they could act as both a safety net for those in difficulty and as a mechanism which both constrained behaviour, but they also potentially allowed people to flourish.

One of the effects of the recent interest in network approaches in ancient history has been the emphasis on examining the diversity of interactions between people and how different types of evidence can be reframed with a focus on non-hierarchical, collaborative, and relational qualities.[109] Funerary commemoration, for example, aside from indicating the presence of family and/or friends to perform the funerary rituals after death and a desire to fashion oneself within a commemorative tradition, creates social links across time and space. The epitaph of Atotas, found in Laurion, demonstrates this well.[110] Atotas' ancestor Pylaimenes, real or fictitious, places him within a

[106] Taylor 2015: 48.

[107] On the importance of weak ties see Granovetter 1973; 1983.

[108] Gabrielsen 2007; Vlassopoulos 2007a; Taylor 2015.

[109] Taylor and Vlassopoulos 2015b; Sobak 2015.

[110] *IG* II^2 10051: 'Atotas the miner. A Paphlagonian from Pontos Euxine, the great-hearted Atotas who left his faraway land rests his body from the toils. In *techne* I have no rival. From the stock of Pylaimenes I descend, who from Achilles' hand died working.' See Bérard 1888. Both Hunt 2015: 136–40; Vlassopoulos 2015: 126 discuss this inscription further.

panhellenic poetic, even royal, tradition.[111] In mentioning this, Atotas appears to be consciously connecting himself with an epic past, demonstrating that he was an integral part of the Greek cultural experience despite his foreign status and banausic occupation. Indeed, this occupation was source of pride rather than shame (which might be underlined further by reference to heroic origins and, by an association with Hephaistos, the god of metalwork, emphasizing his banausic respectability).[112] By placing the emphasis on this, Atotas (or whoever erected his memorial) underlines that he was not a dispensable mining slave but a skilled craftsman, well regarded ('great-hearted'), rooted in social networks within Laurion as well as his Paphlagonian homeland.[113] It is the context of display which is important here—highlighting his Paphlagonian (or banausic, or epic) identity to an audience who would not acknowledge or appreciate this would be pointless—and the language in which Atotas (or perhaps his family) chose to honour him highlights how connected he was within a variety of social networks.

Other forms of commemoration reveal similar concerns. If we reconsider the 'washers' relief', a mid-fourth-century dedication to the Nymphs, in terms of social connectivity, it is possible to see how low-status people were situated within a variety of social contexts.[114] The dedication was made by a group which included metics and slaves, but Nymph-worship was not a 'foreign' cult activity;[115] it was an important part of religious life for Athenian citizens too,

[111] Pylaimenes as the leader of the Paphlagonians in Troy: Hom. *Il.* 2.851–5; 5.576; 13.658, see Raffeiner 1977: 14–16; Bäbler 1998: 94–7. For the suggestion that Atotas might be a descendant, if not of a king then of a real person named Pylaimenes, see Burford 1972: 177. On the creation of mythical genealogies, see Braund and Tsetskhladze 1989: 120.

[112] On the relationship between Hephaistos and technicians see Cuomo 2007: 38–40.

[113] Portraying Atotas as μεγάθυμος further links him with Achilles: it is the epithet used to describe him in Hom. *Il.* 20.498.

[114] *IG* II^2 2934: 'The washers dedicated this to the Nymphs and all the gods with a prayer: Zoagoras son of Zokypros, Zokypros son of Zoagoras, Thallos, Leuke. Sokrates son of Polykrates, Apollophanes son of Euporion, Sosistratos, Manes, Myrrine, Sosias, Sosigenes, Midas.' See Taylor 2015: 43–4.

[115] Zoagoras and Zokypros are Cypriot names, therefore these men are likely to be metics: see Masson 1961: 399. Thallos and Leuke were probably their slaves, given that they follow them on the inscription and have no patronymic. We cannot be so certain about the origins of Sokrates and Apollophanes (their names are too common), but it is possible that Apollophanes has Cycladic origins: the name of his father, Euporion, is not common (only twelve examples recorded in *LGPN*), with half of these from Delos

which places the washers in a cultic environment with citizens.[116] Additionally, they would have washed the clothes of citizens, as well as been acquainted with other citizens who formed a visible part of their industry.[117] It is inconceivable that this group was not socially connected to citizens of various statuses in a variety of ways. Given that Zokypros and Zoagoras were from Cyprus, it might also be suggested that they had connections within the relatively large Phoenician community within Athens.[118] Indeed, by the 330s and 320s the Athenians were actively encouraging Cypriot and Phoenician traders to come to Athens, perhaps placing Zokypros et al. in a pivotal position as long-term members of a Phoenician group within the city.[119]

The value of speculating about the social relationships of the washers is not simply to imagine them within an Athenian world, to create an unprovable fantasy narrative. Rather, it raises questions about the role of social networks within Athens, and how social connectivity is related to well-being, regardless of whether Zokypros

or Tenos during the hellenistic period. Sosistratos et al. are likely to be their slaves. On slave names see Vlassopoulos 2010; 2015.

[116] There are a number of sanctuaries to Pan and the Nymphs across Attica: at Vari, Parnes, the Ilissos valley, Phaleron, and Marathon, and also on the south slope of the Akropolis: see Brouskari 2002: 32–7. Further Travlos 1971: 361–4; Lupu 2001; Platonos-Giota 2004; Schörner and Goette 2004. Although we do not know the exact provenance of the washers' relief (and therefore cannot reconstruct the immediate community of worshippers, nor indeed say whether *individually* the washers had social contact with citizens), we can place the dedication in the wider world of Nymph worship and therefore within the *practice* of cult. Athenian citizens are securely attested as dedicants in the cult: see e.g. *IG* II^2 4886: -ippos of Phlya (Edwards 1985: no. 28); *IG* II^2 4548 (Xenokrateia); *IG* I^3 986 (Kephisodotos son of Demogenes of Boutadai).

[117] The distinction between washing and fulling appears to be slight: both seem to have required the collection and use of urine to clean the textiles, but Ar. *Plut.* 166 implies that washing was considered a worse job. The *gnapheos* cleans clothes, however, in Ar. *Vesp.* 1128. On fullers in the Assembly see Xen. *Mem.* 3.7.6 (see also Xen. *Ag.* 1.2c: camp-followers include fullers). In general see Bradley 2002: 21–2.

[118] It is common for migrants to cluster together on arrival in the host society: Cohen 1996; Loizos 2000, and this seems to be the case at least amongst the Plataians in Athens: Lys. 23.6. The bilingual Phoenician/Greek inscriptions (*IG* II^2 8388, 9031–6) suggest that Phoenicians retained various aspects of their own cultural norms (language, burial customs, and so on). See further Baslez and Briquel-Chatonnet 1991; Stager 2005; Xagorari-Gleißner 2009.

[119] *IG* II^2 360 records honours for Herakleides son of Charikleides of Salamis (dated 330/29–325/4); *IG* II^2 337 is a decree allowing the Kitians to found a temple of Aphrodite in the Piraeus (dated 333/2). See Parker 1996: 160, n. 29; Lambert 2002b: 76.

and Zoagoras actually developed networks with Athenians or Phoenicians. Groups like the washers both reinforce and challenge the structures of inequality within Athenian society: reinforce because they replicate status hierarchies between free and slave; challenge because they force us to recognize the consequences and value of belonging. Other groups show similar patterns: the Plataians meeting at the cheese stall, the Dekeleians at the barbershop (and workshops in general) demonstrate places for meeting, connecting, and generating social ties.[120] These frequently cut across social status, providing participants with access to those outside their immediate group. Certain individuals or groups would have acted as a 'bridge', that is, a link between different social circles.[121] It is through these bridging ties that members of one social circle or group gain access to additional resources.[122]

Being socially connected (or not), then, affects what one is able to do or to be, and provides (or constrains) access to material resources. Being part of a wide variety of social networks is an important indicator, therefore, of well-being.[123] Whilst we know nothing about the financial resources of these people, the fact that we can see indicators of well-being actively negotiated by different groups of *penetes* (citizen and non-citizen) in different contexts is revealing.

Relationships and Emotional Bonds

Forming social ties with others is important, but it is not only the number or strength of these which is key, but also the nature of the relationships which gives them value. Being able to form personal relationships and develop emotional bonds is another crucial indicator of well-being. Slaves, for example, have their capabilities to do this seriously curtailed; their enslavement cuts through their ability to form social relationships, keeping them socially isolated, but despite these constraints, numerous examples show that they did so all the

120 Lys. 23.2–3. See esp. Sobak 2015: 682–97.

121 Sobak sees Sokrates in these terms, because he connected elite citizens (in his well-known interactions) to craftsmen through visits to their workshops, but others would have also filled this kind of role: Sobak 2015: 697–703. On the importance of bridging ties for the spread of democratic knowledge see also Ober 2008.

122 Granovetter 1973.

123 Stewart 2005: 188; Thorp, Stewart, and Heyer 2005: 913.

same. Vlassopoulos argues that slavery should be seen not so much as a legal relationship of property as one of power and domination. This view, whilst not denying the asymmetrical relationship between master and slave, foregrounds the agency of slaves to shape aspects of this relationship and the institution of slavery itself.[124] That is, it regards slaves as having capabilities and functionings, even if these were restricted and controlled. Crucially, however, it recognizes that slaves themselves were not solely 'passive objects of exploitation'.[125]

With this in mind, we can turn to the collection of grave markers which attest to the bonds between slaves and their masters. These imply that slaves were an integral part of the *oikos* in an emotional as well as functional sense. Paideusis, for example, who is iconographically indistinguishable from an Athenian citizen woman, is shown seated, holding her mantle with an outstretched arm (Fig. 6.2).[126] This presents her as an active agent within the household, esteemed for her contribution to it as a wet-nurse and (presumably, given her name) as an educator of children. Whilst we should certainly recognize the ambiguities of these relationships, her commemoration emphasizes her value to the household, her name reinforces her role in life.

Here we should pause and consider the evidence through which slaves have been identified as such, especially the use of the term *chrestos*. When this appears on funerary inscriptions, historians usually suggest that it denotes servile status.[127] In many cases there are good grounds for this: the appearance of names common among slaves, such as Daos, Karion, or Syros, with this epithet suggests as much. Sometimes, too, city ethnics appear, therefore reinforcing the idea that the term is used primarily of non-Athenians.[128]

In this context the word *chrestos* is defined by Tod as 'goodness in action, goodness which finds an outlet in the service of those in the

[124] Vlassopoulos 2011a. [125] Vlassopoulos 2011a: 123.

[126] *IG* II^2 12387: *Παίδευσις. Τίτθη χρηστή* (Kosmopoulou 2001: N10). For other examples see Bäbler 1998; Kosmopoulou 2001. Are these markers bought from pattern books? This is possible. But it is nonetheless revealing that masters consider such stelai fitting for their slaves.

[127] Bäbler 1998: 65–6; Schumacher 2001: 240.

[128] See e.g. *IG* II^2 11041 (Daos), 11822 (Karion), 11861 (Syros). *IG* II^2 8554 records a city ethnic: *Ἄδα Ἡρακλεῶτις χρηστή*. However, of the sixty-six different names (used for eighty-three people) associated with the adjective *chrestos/-e* in the fourth century, just over half (53%) are also securely attested for Athenian citizens; twenty of these are used by women, fifteen by men.

Figure 6.2. The grave stele of Paideusis (NM 978)

home or the community, helpfulness'.[129] It is certainly used by and for citizens: until the end of the fifth century it was the political and social elites, high-status citizens who were usually well-born, rich, and prominent in a variety of aspects of public life, who were *chrestoi*.[130] This was also true in the fourth century: liturgists were *chrestoi* in terms of their contributions to the polis, as were the cavalry; however, we also see the term being applied to citizens of non-elite status in addition to its use by non-citizens in a funerary context.[131] Mantitheus' fellow demesmen were '*chrestous* . . . but lacking in resources', and his benefactions enabled them to perform their military service.[132] Polystratos was chosen by his tribe for office because he was *chrestos*.[133] Straton of Phaleron, the arbitrator whom Meidias attempted to bribe, is described by Demosthenes as poor, but 'all together *chrestos*'.[134] Being *chrestos* was therefore bound up with service to the polis, but it was also demonstrated by looking after family members, and in this context the use of the term to refer to slaves who worked within the *oikos* is unsurprising.[135] Women are described as *chreste* in their performance of wifely duties too.[136]

When men named Daos, Karion, or Syros or women named Paideusis use the term (or have it used of them), therefore, it is not just a designation of servile status but an articulation of their social worth. In the funerary context in particular, this social worth is predicated on the creation and maintenance of emotional bonds between master and slave. We do not need to sugar-coat these relationships—they were indeed asymmetrical—but equally they should also not be considered solely through the eyes of masters.[137] It has been noted that wet-nurses, in particular, frequently have the epithet used of them, and this attests to their strong social bonds within families for whom they worked.[138] Sometimes funerary commemoration of slaves is located in family *periboloi*, indicating the development (and display) of close ties

[129] Tod 1951: 186. [130] Contrasted with *poneroi*: Rosenbloom 2004a; 2004b.

[131] Cf. Is. 4.27, 7.37–42 with Dem. 21.83, Lys. 16.14.

[132] Lys. 16.14: μὲν χρηστοὺς ὄντας . . . δὲ ἀπορoῦντας.

[133] Lys. 20.2. That this office was membership of the ill-fated Four Hundred does not matter here; it is the reason for his selection which is important.

[134] Dem. 21.83. [135] Polis: Lys. 3.9, 14.4. Family: Dein. 2.8.

[136] *IG* II^2 7406, 12067, 12335. A Menandrian proverb notes 'a *chreste gune* is the rudder of the house' (Men. *Mon.* 155).

[137] See in a different context Baird 2015.

[138] *IG* II^2 9271, 11647, 12242, 12387, 12815, 12816, *SEG* 26.341, *Agora XVII*.1048. See pp. 135–40.

between the commemorated group, or at the very least a desire on behalf of masters to provide funerary rites for their slaves.[139]

For citizens the *oikos* was a central part of Athenian life and formed the focal point of social esteem: from the use of patronymics and demotics, to the maintenance of family tombs, to the provision of assistance to parents and elderly relatives, the *oikos* was the fundamental locus not only of subsistence but also of socialization and well-being. Social pressure not to sell the land of ancestors, for example, was one way in which families ensured they maintained their resources (both economic and in terms of social position), as were adoption and marriage.[140] These were ways in which wealth was passed down between generations of course, but they also sought to ensure not just survival but social standing and well-being.[141]

Not all slaves were able to form families of their own, nor were they able to maintain them, but some did: Philon and Rhodia in Thorikos were freed along with their daughter Kordype,[142] as were the family of Attas and Malthake, a pulse-seller and wool-worker in Keiradai, with their three children Plangon, Moschos, and Aristonike,[143] and Philotheros and Menestrate in Piraeus with their child Philokrates.[144]

[139] *IG* II^2 12696 (Marchiandi 2011: 326–7): Sphagis commemorated in the *peribolos* of Dionysios of Kollytos; *IG* II^2 12638 (Marchiandi 2011: 259–60): Sophon commemorated in the *peribolos* of Epainetos of Kephisia; *IG* II^2 10678, 8635, 12755 (Marchiandi 2011: 318–21): Anna, Dorkas, and Sophrone commemorated in the *peribolos* of the Messenians; *IG* II^2 12396, 11272 (Marchiandi 2011: 502–4): Pamphile, Epaphras, and Artimas in the *peribolos* of Agnochares of Paiania; *SEG* 30.288 (Marchiandi 2011: 512–13): Sangarios in a *peribolos* in Oe (see Kakavogianni and Galiatsatou 2009: 412–13).

[140] Adoption can be seen as a form of strengthening ties within the wider family: attested examples of *inter vivos* adoptions appear to involve more distant relatives (son of first wife, niece's son) than testamentary adoptions (nephew, half-brother, grandson). See Is. 2.5–10, 3.1, 10.5–6, 11.8, [Dem.] 44.17. Rubinstein 1993: cat. nos. 1, 3, 7, 16, 20, also Todd 1993: 221–5.

[141] See Foxhall 2007.

[142] *SEG* 60.181, ll. 464–75.

[143] *SEG* 60.181, ll. 112–22.

[144] *IG* II^2 1576B, ll. 57–63. Other possible slave families: *SEG* 60.181, ll. 489–96 (Herakleides and Thraitta, both market-traders in Melite); *SEG* 60.181, ll. 546–54 (Soterides, a donkey-driver with Sostrate, a child); *SEG* 60.181, ll. 93–6 ([-]rtinion, a muleteer in Piraeus (?) and Simon, a child); *SEG* 60.181, ll. 232–9 (Ariste with her two children Simalos and Nikariste); *SEG* 60.181, ll. 253–66 (a jeweller, two wool-workers, and a child in Melite); *SEG* 60.181, ll. 337–42 (Hediste in Skambonidai with an unnamed person (possibly a relative?), both owned by Misgolas son of Naukrates of Kollytos). See Rosivach 1989 for the identification of these *paidia* as slaves. Men. *Epit.* 378–80, 408 also has a comic representation of a slave family. Meyer's objection that slave families were not recognized, therefore these were not slave families, is not

These examples show that at least some slaves could have family lives. This is important, because family relationships are often explained in terms of citizenship and civic identity,[145] but even outside the citizen body there is an emphasis on ancestry and longevity, the key constituents in the presentation of the *oikos* to the outside world. Unsurprisingly, this is particularly clear for metics: on the epitaph of Sosinos, a metic from Gortyn, his children are directly mentioned as being responsible for the memorial of their father.[146] This emphasizes strong family relationships, the longevity of the *oikos*, and a desire to perform (and be seen to perform) the correct rituals upon death.[147] Like Atotas, Sosinos is a foreign worker, but the values attributed to him (*dikaiosyne*, *sophrosyne*, and *arete*) suggest he associated himself with, or wished to be perceived as part of, 'respectable' circles.[148] Indeed, these qualities also reflect back on the memorializing children themselves. It is impossible to tell from this monument the degree of Sosinos' financial resources, nor can we assess what he physically consumed, but we can make some claims about his personal relationships (and therefore his quality of life) from how he wished to be remembered in death.

Emotional bonds were not just confined to family relationships, of course. *Kalos*-names and other graffiti attest to (mostly male) emotions configured around sexual interaction (real or imagined); in some cases these express admiration, in others domination and humiliation.[149] Although it is impossible to say with certainty who

convincing: Meyer 2010: 24. As she points out in n. 55, there is indeed evidence that slave-dealers might respect the integrity of slave families: Hypereides, *Against Timandros*, for example, claims just this, rhetorical exaggeration or not. See Jones 2008 for restoration of this text and translation. In general: Golden 2011: 143–5.

[145] Leader 1997; Cox 1998; Patterson 1998.

[146] *SEG* 39.270 (*CEG* 96, *CAT* 1.202): 'Sosinos of Gortyn the copper-smelter. A memorial of *dikaiosyne*, *sophrosyne*, and *arete*, was set up by the children of Sosinos after he had perished.' See Scholl 1996: no. 464; Meyer 1989.

[147] For the importance of emphasizing longevity in epigrams see Tsagalis 2008: 183–98, 204–8.

[148] See also *IG* II^2 9112: 'Here the earth holds the nurse of the children of Diogeiton from the Peloponnese. This most just woman (δικαιοτάτην), Malicha from Kythera' (Kosmopoulou 2001: N4). Possibly also *IG* II^2 10593: 'having left many records of his *arete* and excelling in respect of his work (ἔργοις δὲ κρατή[σας]), here lies Athenokles, a virtuous man.' *Ergon* here, of course, may refer to 'the things Athenokles has done' rather than any work in the sense of labour. On this epitaph see Tsagalis 2008: 154.

[149] *IG* I^3 1405bis, *SEG* 54.82. See Langdon 1985; 2004; Taylor 2011a. Other examples: *SEG* 34.198 (Mussche et al. 1990: 184–6, no. 80); *SEG* 40.264 (Bain 1994);

inscribed any particular one of these texts or images, the fact that a number of them cluster in areas around quarries is suggestive.[150] Not only do they attest to emotional experiences between (probably) non-elite workers, they suggest a level of semiotic communication which might be interpreted as a form of literacy amongst these people.[151] As I have argued elsewhere, these seemingly idle scribbles demonstrate how people connected themselves with others over time and space, not only with the object of the writer's affections (or jokes), but with other people passing by at a later date and viewing a graffito with humour, appreciation, or disgust.[152] We do not need to know exactly who wrote these in order to see that they placed the writer within a context in which he was making claims about his own place within a community: his own quality of life.

The evidence discussed here, therefore, considers non-material aspects of living standards, arguing that we can assess well-being in terms of functionings and social relations. This shows how groups we would normally consider low-status, marginalized, or lacking in financial resources could use the resources they had available to function within society. Doing so broadens the standards-of-living debate from a concentration on establishing minimum (or optimal) levels for survival to consideration of what survival is for. By focusing on the functionings of people and groups, especially those outside of the body of male citizens, not only do we break away from the discourses of the Athenian elite and start from the assumption of agency and autonomy, constrained though this might be, but we see how well-being was defined and negotiated through a variety of mechanisms (belonging to a social group, developing emotional bonds, or being socially connected within their own communities). Adequate nutrition and/or income is part of this picture, of course, but if we ignore non-materialistic aspects of life it becomes impossible to assess what subsistence means in practice. This evidence, fragmentary though it is, shows

IG I^3 1402; *IG* I^3 1404 (Vanderpool 1962: 399, no. 1). Chaniotis 2011: 204–5 discusses the humiliatory power of this type of graffiti. On sexual relationships between masters and slaves in general (and their impact) see Golden 2011: 146–51.

[150] In Attica: Taylor 2011a. Thasos: Garlan and Masson 1982; Coulié 1998.

[151] *SEG* 55.84, 85 (Langdon 2005) record the graffiti of shepherds and goatherds on the Barako hill outside Vari. On semiotic communication see R. Harris 1995; 2000. In an ancient context: Webster 2008: 119–22; Baird and Taylor 2011: 9–11.

[152] Taylor 2011a.

how low-status groups in Athens, men and women who were considered by the discourses of the Athenian elite to be poor, servile, and Other, actually functioned in Athenian society and what they valued. It is by these criteria—these divergent strategies of recognition and claims of social inclusion—that we should judge poverty, not just by indicators of economic deprivation.

7

Poverty, Inequality, and Well-Being in Fourth-Century Athens

I have argued throughout this book that poverty in the ancient world needs to be conceptualized not just in terms of a lack of income or wealth, but in terms of non-material resources too and therefore considered hand in hand with the idea of well-being. That is, poverty should be understood not just as an absolute measure of subsistence and survival, but as the product of a series of interlocking processes which are shaped by multiple discourses, a diversity of experiences, and a variety of interactions between those who lived in Athens and the social worlds in which they operated. As is clear within poverty research in the social sciences, 'what constitutes poverty is neither obvious nor universal'.[1] Understanding poverty in Athens, therefore, involves situating analyses within the broader context of social relations, and recognizing that it is the social and political context that gives poverty meaning and shapes not only how it was talked about but also how it was experienced. Doing so provides a mechanism through which to consider not only the discourses surrounding poverty and the poor that developed primarily (though not exclusively) within elite circles, and so dominate our source material, but also to see how those discourses were contested and reshaped outside of those contexts.

Although aspects of poverty are frequently discussed within ancient literature, many of these debates are, in fact, rooted in elite concerns about moral behaviour and the responsibilities of wealth rather than the realities of poverty. As such they serve to construct and maintain a social distance between the rich and the poor, and in

[1] Green and Hulme 2005: 869.

doing so present a dichotomizing picture of Athenian society. That is, they systematically ignore the reality of poverty and construct a view of it which is at odds with lived experience. Viewed in isolation, therefore, such discussions present only a partial picture of Athenian poverty, and a misleading one at that. They present poverty and wealth as dichotomous, conflate poverty with the absence of leisure, and suggest that there were distinct differences between rich and poor. However, not only were these discourses actively contested by the *penetes* themselves, they are modified and remade to emphasize positive values rather than deficiencies, unity rather than difference. When juxtaposed with models pertaining to the distribution of wealth and income in Athens, the gap between rich and poor indeed seems rather smaller, and more dynamic, than we are led to believe by these narratives.

We can go further: examining the ways in which the *penetes* defined their own world provides a starting-point from which we can begin to piece together aspects of the diverse experiences of *penia*. That is, I have argued throughout this book that we can investigate not only the discourses which presented poverty in Athens in certain ways, but also the contexts in which people lived lives that were precarious, and the structures and institutions which shaped these. Doing so allows us to emphasize the agency of those who might be considered poor to ameliorate this precariousness in a multitude of ways, but also prompts us, as historians, to reflect on the categories that are used to talk about poverty.

This final chapter, then, seeks to bring together a number of threads which have run through this book by asking three questions. What do we gain by viewing poverty in the ancient world as multidimensional? How were poverty and well-being in Athens shaped by social relations? And what can we conclude about the nature of poverty and inequality within democratic Athens?

THE DIVERSITY AND MULTIDIMENSIONALITY OF POVERTY

Throughout this book I have emphasized that poverty is heterogeneous both in terms of the discourses that surround it and in how it is experienced. This is important for the following reasons. First of all it allows us to recognize the multidimensionality of poverty in terms of its causes and its impact, emphasizing that many different factors converge to shape these, rather than implying it is a singular entity unchanging over time. This encourages us to examine the complex interplay between different aspects of poverty—such as economic deprivation, social exclusion, and marginalization—and note that these are intertwined and are not necessarily static. A multidimensional view of poverty requires that we recognize not only the side of poverty that is characterized by the lack of wealth or the dearth of income, but that which is non-material and shaped by social relations.

Second, it is important to emphasize that experiences of poverty in the ancient world were diverse. This diversity can be explored in terms of temporality, that is, whether poverty is a short-term feature of life ultimately recoverable from, or whether it is shaped by inter-generational processes which are hard to break. A focus on temporality highlights distinctly different aspects of poverty, from conjunctural episodes to structural permanence, and therefore provides a framework for us to distinguish between the complaints we hear (from sometimes ultimately rather well-off families) in court from the more severely deprived and actively marginalized.

Alternatively, diversity can be investigated by examining how other factors (such as gender, civic status, or age) shape the experience of poverty and how these in turn intersect with different temporalities. Conceptualizing poverty in terms of capability deprivation is a useful tool here, because the capabilities approach provides a flexible mechanism to investigate these multiple experiences, highlighting where these are constrained as well as where they are less so. Thus we can see how women contested the discourses that devalued their labour and created social networks among themselves which were crucial support mechanisms in times of hardship, or how slaves and metics created family structures, cult groups, and local communities to resist the social exclusion that was created through their lack of citizenship or servility. This also turns poverty from being a condition conceptualized solely as lacking wealth or income to one where the social agency of those categorized as poor is recognized. The advantage of this is that it enables these groups to be viewed as active agents in their own lives, although operating within various (often severe) constraints, and not just placed in the silent spaces which cannot be filled with any other social actor. Neglecting this diversity, in contrast, simply serves to ignore the lived experience of large numbers of people living in Athens and homogenizes them into one single group.

Third, acknowledging heterogeneity provides a space to reflect on the categories used to describe poverty and the poor and how these are reinforced, modified, or contested.[2] This is particularly important given that the Athenian category of *penia* is so broad and strikingly different from modern conceptions of what constitutes poverty. Categorizing *ploutos* and *penia* as two more or less contrasting conditions defined ultimately through the presence or absence of leisure (albeit sometimes with various modifications) essentially means that 'poverty' is a state that encompasses almost everyone in Athens. It should, however, be uncontroversial to maintain that the notion of poverty that categorizes the destitute, the subsisting, and the comparatively well off together—and different to the *plousioi*—is a view that is shaped by the ideological concerns of the Athenian elite. Historians should not, however, become oblivious to the homogenizing nature of this (and other) poverty discourse(s), not least because they are actively contested by the *penetes* themselves. What is clear in the discussions throughout this book is that there is a difference between how the *plousioi* in Athens understood poverty and how the *penetes* did. The former considered poverty in terms of not being wealthy, and viewed it primarily in terms of material and moral deficiencies, of unfulfilled needs, of fears and dissatisfaction. However, there is a large body of evidence that shows alternative modes of thought amongst the *penetes* themselves—men and women, slave and free. There was much less of a scorn for labour than appears to have been the case among some sections of the elite, fears of poverty were countered with courage, and processes of social exclusion were actively resisted in multiple ways. The *penetes*, therefore, were not a monolithic group and had diverse experiences of *penia*.

The fact that the *penetes* (as defined by the Athenian elite) were a group of people with such different levels of income or wealth suggests that analysing poverty in terms of economic measures alone is not the best way to approach the topic in Athens. However, until very recently modern approaches to poverty have tended to view

[2] Green 2009; du Toit 2009; Chicone 2011b.

it primarily in terms of subsistence or survival. Not only does this prioritize a single aspect of deprivation and conceptualize poverty in absolute terms, but it also runs the risk of deflecting attention from the processes which gave rise to hardship (of various kinds), the strategies used by people to ameliorate it, and the institutions and structures that reproduced it. In this sense, debates about whether particular figures, such as Dionysios the cobbler, Euxitheos, the speaker of Demosthenes 57, or Aeschines the orator were *actually* poor—or not—are ultimately unproductive if their aim is simply to argue about the presence or absence of wealth within lives of which we have only a fleeting glimpse. As Euxitheos himself states when discussing the varying representations of his own family's economic position, 'which . . . [accusation: rich or poor] is one to believe?'[3] Such debates only serve to reveal the tensions between the different ways in which the category of 'poverty' is constructed—by speakers or their opponents in court, by the elite or the non-elite, by ancient authors or modern historians studying the ancient world. The difference between ancient conceptions of poverty and modern ones underscores the fact that the question of who is categorized as poor is a salient one.

Rather than viewing poverty in terms of lacking income or wealth, I have argued throughout this book that poverty in Athens is more profitably seen as a product of the interplay between (contested) discourses, social structures, and social relations which are, in turn, modified and reshaped by dynamic social forces.[4] Highlighting the diversity of poverty experiences therefore provides a way to parse out these complex dynamics and nuance our understanding of the lives and concerns of non-elite Athenians, as well as to see more clearly how poverty was socially constructed. Doing so turns Athens from a city which is comprised of a wealthy elite and a homogeneous mass of people defined by a lack of surplus to one where it is recognized that the discourses of poverty could be used to negotiate marginalization and articulate belonging for rich and poor alike, where standards of living were relatively high for large numbers of people—though not for all—and where poverty and wealth are viewed in terms of flexible and contested categories rather than as dichotomous states.

[3] Dem. 57.53. See discussion on pp. 119–20, 135–8.
[4] Richard 2011; du Toit 2009; Spencer-Wood 2011.

POVERTY, WELL-BEING, AND SOCIAL RELATIONS

Whilst there is clearly some kind of relationship between economic resources and the ability to function within a society (for example, if assets are severely lacking then many other capabilities are, as a consequence, constrained), poverty is about more than basic subsistence needs. Rather, it is situated within and is a product of social relations. Although it is not incorrect to suggest that poverty often has a material core, access to even the most basic of material resources, for example food, is also shaped by social values and norms. Moreover, the ability to earn a basic income was also shaped by factors such as civic status, gender, or age: citizens and slaves working side by side on state-funded building projects, or rowing together in the fleet, might well have received the same rate of pay, but it is unimaginable that masters did not take a portion of their slaves' earnings for themselves. Citizen men also had exclusive access to various types of political pay to supplement their incomes, greater recourse to land and to credit, more varied and more dense social networks within which to accrue social capital, and access to empowering political institutions. Viewed in this way, poverty is a more complex phenomenon than a simple lack of wealth. It is, in contrast, the consequence of institutionalized social relations (formal rules as well as informal social attitudes) that allow some groups to have access to resources and constrain others from attaining them.

Foregrounding the role of social relations is important, because doing so emphasizes the social contexts through which poverty derives its meaning. The discourses that distinguish *penia* from *ptocheia*, for example, are primarily articulated in terms of social exclusion rather than material deprivation, and therefore place *ptocheia* outside of normative social relations rather than as a state of extreme economic deprivation. As such they conjure a series of powerful emotional resonances that could be drawn upon in different circumstances. Our source material shows in particular when relatively wealthy families exploit these in court (to articulate claims to inheritance at times of family insecurity) or when playwrights place *ptochoi* on the stage as aristocrats in disguise. In doing so, they reveal that these discourses were a powerful tool to gain control of changing social orders, but they also act as a way of distancing *penia* from *ptocheia* and therefore mark the *penetes* as different from the *ptochoi*. This process actively denies a voice to those who actually were *ptochoi*, removes from them their autonomy, and casts them as anti-social. Associations of *ptocheia* with itinerancy further underscore such attitudes. Whilst *ptocheia* no doubt encapsulated material disadvantage in terms of economic deprivation, it is better understood in the context of negotiating social worth—a context that is shaped by relations of power not unlike Aristotle's desire to disenfranchise hired labourers.

Viewing poverty not just as a material condition but as a social relationship emphasizes, then, the capacity to function within Athenian society. It highlights that poverty is not simply an individual characteristic which arises as a result of the behaviour of the poor, or their moral capacity, but the product of a series of social and economic processes that give rise to vulnerability, hardship, isolation, or disempowerment, and often reproduces relations of power in doing so. Political pay, for example, provided citizens with financial resources, but this was not targeted aid for the poor, despite the characterizations of Aristophanes. Like other bodies that provided assistance to their members, pay was not provided primarily with a view to relieve economic hardship, but instead aimed to reinforce existing social relationships, foster civic unity, or honour the group in question. Belonging to such groups was, therefore, absolutely necessary to function in Athenian society; not belonging to them served as a symbol of, and actively reinforced, social exclusion.

Considering aspects of social exclusion and questions of well-being, therefore, are critical for exploring Athenian *penia*. Doing so more directly encourages the examination of non-material aspects of poverty, foregrounds the agency of those groups who experienced *penia*, and, because of the nature of well-being as a concept, is implicitly dynamic. Focusing on the strategies used to negotiate well-being by those who are categorized as poor, as well as their social networks, therefore, underlines not only where relations of power converge with material and social conditions, but also provides a glimpse into where they are resisted. We can say very little about the financial resources of most citizen men, and even less of women, non-citizens, or slaves, but by thinking in terms of well-being and capacities to function within society we can tentatively indicate contexts in, and methods through which, these groups actively resist their own social exclusion.[5]

In addition, the structures and institutions that allowed the accumulation of wealth (as well as those which prevented it) also highlight the importance of social relations, not least because these are frequently aligned with ideas about citizenship. In general, Greek cities, Athens included, prevented extreme differences of wealth through civic ideals which promoted moderation among the elite, an emphasis on principles of political egalitarianism between citizens, and policies which placed greater financial responsibilities on the rich rather than the poor.[6] The organization of public finance in Athens, for example, relied almost solely on wealthier Athenians, and when viewed inter-generationally was burdensome enough to have ensured a high turnover of liable families. This suggests that high levels of wealth accumulation by one sector of the Athenian population were, if not prevented, then certainly moderated.

However, be that as it may, it is difficult to tell the degree to which familial wealth was reduced by spending on liturgical obligations or whether wealth was hidden to avoid performing them. We do see, particularly during the second half of the fourth century, that the already rich were able to consolidate their wealth in ways that they had not so clearly been able to earlier in the century when the gap between rich and poor was smaller. Land-leasing and land sales provided resources for the wealthy at the expense of the rest of the citizen body, public resources were utilized for private economic gains rather than for public goods, and investments in personal properties were increasingly made, thereby demonstrating personal wealth and distinction. These processes ultimately combined, along with other factors of course, to disenfranchise large numbers of Athenians in 322.[7] The capacity of this group to function, therefore, was severely curtailed by these interlinking processes.

[5] These are, of course, limited and context-dependent (see Johnson 2003), but it is necessary to highlight these nonetheless.

[6] On this civic framework and the ways in which civic protectionism prevented accumulation of wealth see Bresson 2015: 216–17.

[7] Diod. 18.18.4–5: the disenfranchised (those not meeting a property qualification of 2,000 dr.) were encouraged to emigrate altogether.

POVERTY AND INEQUALITY IN ATHENS

The picture of the Greek world that has emerged over the past decade is one not of endemic poverty but of economic efflorescence.[8] It is one in which large numbers of people were not living at subsistence levels but had higher standards of living; it is a world with long-term sustained economic growth rather than one of stagnation or decline, with, in comparative perspective at least, relatively low levels of income- or wealth-inequality. I have suggested throughout this book that—at the very least—this picture needs to be viewed side by side with discussion of the processes through which poverty was created, ameliorated, and reproduced, as well as an examination of the well-being of those who are categorized as poor. The questions that follow, therefore, are these. If overall levels of income inequality were comparatively low in Athens, what does this mean for an understanding of Athenian poverty? Were the poor in Athens, as a result, in a better situation than those elsewhere?

On the one hand, we might emphasize that higher proportions of the Athenian population were living above subsistence than previously thought. Simply put, in comparison with other times and places economic inequality in Athens appears to have been less severe than elsewhere. Classical Athens, with its participatory democratic institutions, dense social networks rich in both strong and weak ties, and high wages compares well when juxtaposed with the second-century CE Roman Empire (as well with other historical societies).[9] Increases in trade in the archaic and classical periods, and the labour specialization we see clearly in our source material, suggest that being a *penes* might well have been profitable, especially in certain industries, and this allowed some *penetes* at least to accumulate resources. In addition, technological innovations freed up time for other activities. Bresson, for example, argues that new milling tools created opportunities, particularly for women, to devote more time to household tasks that generated a surplus (such as textile production), rather than those which simply kept the family alive.[10] All of these arguments implicitly assume that the *penetes* benefited from the sustained economic growth that brought with it long-term improvements in

[8] See Chapter 1, n. 7.
[9] Milanovic, Lindert, and Williamson 2011; Kron 2014.
[10] Bresson 2015: 191, 195–7, 210–11.

standards of living and better nutrition for more people. It is this economic growth that is primarily seen as the mechanism that lifted greater numbers of people out of subsistence lifestyles over time.

However, economic growth may be one thing, equitable economic growth is quite another, as the contrasting models of Athens and Rome in Chapter 3 attest. What is more, relatively low levels of inequality between (some) households obscures the high levels of inequality within them, and arguably deflects attention away from the gaps between the rich and the poor. We must be extremely cautious, therefore, about arguments which assume, rather than seek to demonstrate, that economic growth benefited the poor.[11] The fact is that for each of the indicators just mentioned—and many others besides—we can also identify related processes which gave rise to poverty, hardship, and marginalization. For example, median house sizes might well have increased over the long term, but concurrently with this development we also see the poorest in Greek societies being increasingly characterized by their itineracy and by their dependency—they are expressly without *oikos*. These are not the people whose living spaces got larger, but those who were dependent on others for their shelter and sustenance, whether through begging, debt-bondage, or slavery. Similarly, the growth in median house sizes tells us little about the living conditions of those within those houses as outlined in Chapter 6.

To a large degree, Foxhall is correct in pointing out that 'the difference between . . . an Alkibiades on the one hand and a Dikaiopolis . . . on the other might have looked very much greater from a perspective within classical Athens than it does from a modern point of view, from outside and with the benefits of a wider comparative perspective'.[12] Whilst it is important to note that citizen poverty in Athens was probably not as severe as, say, poverty within the Roman Empire, if we stop at this point we do a disservice to those who experienced poverty in both of these societies, because we fail to shine a light on these experiences and the strategies people actively developed to function, subsist, or even prosper.

Economic growth does not necessarily mean that poverty is alleviated or that it is no longer present in a society. Instead it demands that

[11] See the fractious—and politically charged—debate in development studies on this question; e.g. Dollar and Kraay 2002; Sumner 2004; Kanbur 2005.

[12] Foxhall 2007: 32.

we look harder at those structures, institutions, and processes that reproduced poverty and evaluate who were the winners and who were the losers. Some institutions, particularly those of the participatory democracy, certainly did play a role in maintaining the (citizen) poor, but others served simply to maintain poverty. Athens might well have been increasingly affluent in the late fourth century, but this is also the time when we can clearly see the consolidation of wealth by the rich.

Similarly, whilst innovation may have freed up time for more surplus-producing activities, the capacity to invest in innovation is shaped by, as well as reproduces, wealth and poverty: it is more difficult, if not impossible, for those with few financial resources to spare, or limited social capital to draw on, to do so. As Bresson acknowledges, fields cannot be left fallow if that land is needed to grow this year's crop, and resources cannot be diverted to specialize in (for example) product differentiation if a craftsman has very little to spare. Capital cannot be produced within the home through the labour of weaving women if they have other immediate household duties to perform or cannot afford to invest in a loom. Indeed, the innovations in milling technologies that occurred over the course of antiquity are difficult to apply to fourth-century Athens. The technologically advanced rotary mill did not appear until the hellenistic period, whereas the hopper-rubber mill (or Olynthos mill), known elsewhere in the Greek world in the fifth century, is barely found in Athens until the Roman period.[13] This means that here the more labour-intensive saddle quern appears to have been the norm, and the labour-saving arguments that Bresson makes cannot be easily applied to Athens without further evidence.

In most of the discussion of economic growth the emphasis is placed on the improved living standards of the increasingly large 'middling' population rather than those living at or below subsistence. But we need also to recognize how the processes that gave rise to the proposed efflorescence also created, modified, and reinforced poverty. Some groups might well have benefited from economic growth,

[13] Foxhall 2007: 202–4. Frankel 2003: 4 cites three locations from Athens and Attica where hopper-rubbers are found, but two of these are in Laurion, which Jones 1984: 122 explicitly links to ore- rather than grain-crushing, whereas those from the Agora are (with one exception: ST 144) exclusively late hellenistic or Roman: Runnels 1981: 122, 296.

but this needs to be argued for rather than assumed, because large numbers of people demonstrably did not. The processes of economic change during the second half of the fourth century actively favoured the already wealthy rather than Athenians as a whole, as can be seen by the eventual dissolution of democracy. Given that fears of falling into poverty are pervasive in our evidence, it might suggest that the boundary between 'subsistence' and 'middling' (or poor and non-poor?) was more permeable than we can easily detect. Long-term processes, therefore, might obscure the day-to-day realities of poverty.

We cannot escape the fact that Athenians, despite the multiple discussions about poverty in our sources, were not particularly concerned to reduce it for their fellow citizens in any direct way, and were not in the slightest concerned to alleviate the deprivation of the (at least) 40% of the population who were non-citizens. The mechanisms that did help to ameliorate various aspects of poverty—participatory democracy with political pay, a densely networked society rich in strong and weak ties, regular distribution of protein-rich meat, widespread access to credit—did so indirectly, never with the expressed aim of poverty relief, and with access as closely guarded as citizenship. The poverty of non-citizens in Athens, therefore, was much more readily tolerated than the poverty of citizen men. Rarely do discussions about poverty acknowledge non-citizen groups, except in regard to their relationships to citizen husbands, sons, or masters. Poverty was conceptualized as a citizen issue, and only then insofar as it detracted from the ability of those citizens to perform their civic duties properly. It was therefore primarily a question of civic unity rather than one of economic deprivation.

That economic inequality appears relatively low within the body of citizens is, however, an important conclusion, and we should not deny that citizens in Athens had (comparatively speaking) significant capabilities. We might even want to tie this conclusion to specific features of Athenian life: participatory democracy is likely to be a key factor here.[14] However, it also serves to highlight that citizens were a relatively privileged group who should be juxtaposed with the other members of their households—the slaves, women, children, or elderly—as well as others with whom they interacted in public spaces. Economic growth may have been a factor in expanding capabilities

[14] On the relationship between participatory democracy and improved well-being see Touchton and Wampler 2014.

for some, but for others it reinforced existing inequalities, and for yet more it created new ones. The factors which expanded the capabilities of citizens, therefore, constrained them for other groups. As I have argued throughout this book, poverty is not just a matter of wealth or income distribution, but a matter of social relations and well-being. Inequality should likewise be seen in this context; we must be careful, therefore, when we create theories about the ancient economy that we do not further marginalize those who are socially excluded in one way or another. That is, we need to be wary of reproducing, rather than criticizing, the categorizations and discourses of poverty we find in our sources and those which permeate our own assumptions of poverty.

Our final word must rest, as we began, with Dionysios the cobbler (Fig. 1.1), as his dedication represents the value in viewing poverty in terms of well-being, but also shows the complexity of discussing *penia* in Athens. Although we know nothing about his life outside the fact of his dedication, his experience of *penia* was shaped by close family ties, of children trained in the workshop to continue his business, of belonging to a religious community, of desiring, or perhaps wishing for, wealth and happy health. Let us hope he received it.

APPENDIX 1

Testing the Models of Ober and Kron

What has to change in the models of Ober or Kron to falsify the picture of income or wealth distribution presented in Chapter 3? There are a number of questions we could ask.

First, given that the profile of Athenian poverty in Chapter 3 appears strikingly different from that of Rome, how pessimistic do we have to be to make Athens look more like Rome? The answer to this question is 'tremendously'. The headcount measure of poverty (P_0) for Rome (see Appendix 2 for details of calculations), based on Scheidel and Friesen 2009, is 91–94% (Table 3.10); to move the Athenian figure into this range (P_0 = 92) would produce a profile in which 92% of the population had a household income of, at most, three-quarters of a drachma (4½ obols) per day, and where an income of 1 drachma per day or above was attainable by only 8% of the population. Of course, some Athenians did have such an income, but given that regular Assembly meetings paid 1 drachma (and 1½ drachmas for *kyria* Assembly meetings), and rates of pay for work done on the Erechtheion building inscriptions average to approximately 1 drachma per day, it seems untenable that only 8% of them did. We have to be seriously pessimistic (in a way that contradicts almost everything we know about the Athenian economy) to make the Athenian headcount poverty rate approach that of the Roman model.

Second, it might be the case that Ober is too optimistic about the average stability of income which would make his subsistence-to-middling groups (levels 1–6) appear better off than they were (and therefore the gap between rich and poor smaller than it was): he models 300 days per year of income-generation for each group, which might be considered generous (see Chapter 3, n. 36 for relevant bibliography). However, even if this is reduced to a pessimistic 200 days per year only for the subsistence and lowest middling categories, whilst remaining at 300 for everyone else, the Athenian figures are still better than the Roman ones in every measure except P_s, which now becomes 0.319–0.440 from 0.184–0.253 (compare Rome at 0.242–0.250). Note, though, that this metric is deliberately weighted to those furthest away from z (i.e. the poorest and the distribution of their income). How significant is this? It might be the case that although wages were relatively high compared to the cost of living, incomes were by contrast very insecure; this is frequently a feature of poverty in the modern world.

Sixty drachma per year (0.3 dr. × 200 days) might feed an individual for the year (albeit poorly), but as an annual household income it seems well below subsistence. Based on Markle's calculations of the cost of barley meal for a family of four (1.65 obols per day), that family would need more like 100 drachmas per year (for barley meal alone).[1] We may wish in the future to model in more categories of subsistence, middling, and elite than Ober does in his 2010 and 2015 models to capture this variation, but the effects of being more pessimistic on the days-worked variable are pretty minimal here.

Third, is Ober's model too optimistic about median income? That is, is his median income figure (1½ drachmas per day) too high? (The outcome of this is that it makes *z* artificially high). It could be argued that because lower wages, particularly those around half a drachma per day, are more frequently attested than those that are higher, that Ober's 1½ drachmas is overly optimistic. But the fact that some (or lots) of people earned less than the median is not an argument for discarding the median—on the contrary, it is entirely expected. This is not a question of typicality, but one of examining how one part of an income/wealth distribution (the bottom) relates to another (the top). The median provides a way of assessing this. Be that as it may, all poverty-line measurements that are based on distance from the median are, of course, sensitive to that median—raising or lowering the median would change these measurements. However, if we reduce *z* to 3 obols per day (following the line of argument that suggests Ober is too optimistic), the conclusions in Chapter 3 barely change: Athens still appears considerably more equal than Rome, though P_0 is reduced (which, arguably, minimizes poverty; that is, it has the opposite effect of that which it intends).

Fourth, are Ober and Kron's assumptions about a large middling population correct? If we assume that the majority of the Athenian population were not living above, but mostly at, subsistence, what changes? If we halve the size of Ober's middling category from 42–58% of the population to 21% and distribute these people into the subsistence and elite categories, we can create a distribution with a much higher Gini score (0.60), i.e. more in the range of van Wees' calculations (though note his are wealth, not income, distributions). On this model, $P_0 = 64$, $P_i = 0.198$, $P_s = 0.285$, i.e. Athens still performs favourably compared with Rome. Kron's model shows a similar response: if we raise the median wealth, more Athenians would of course fall under *z*, but we would have to more than double it to make much of a difference. Broadly speaking, then, for our purposes here Ober and Kron's assumptions seem reasonable to think with.

Whilst all models (as all hypotheses and all discursive arguments) can surely be refined and nuanced, this suggests that the conclusions in Chapter 3

[1] Markle 1985: 280.

can stand. That being said, Ober's model follows Davies 1981 in assuming that there are only 400 citizen men counted as 'elite' (i.e. with a liturgical fortune of 3–4 talents or above).[2] However, as noted in Chapter 3, Gabrielsen 1994 argues that a larger body of liturgists must have existed if the system were to function (see pp. 71–3). I have, therefore, amended Ober's model in Table 3.12 to reflect this, assuming 1,200–1,500 citizen men. I have kept Ober's assumptions in Table 3.11; however, if we assume a total 'elite' group of between 4,000 and 6,000 in the late fourth century (changing also the other chronological periods accordingly), by assuming (i) each male citizen is married to a woman of equivalent fortune and they have at least one child, and (ii) there were approximately 900 metics (men, women, and children) of this level of wealth, very little actually changes: see the bracketed figures in Table 3.14. Whichever position on the number of elite we follow, the long-term trends shown in Figures 3.4 and 3.5 are not significantly affected, and the poverty statistics in Table 3.14 only very mildly so (see Table 3.14 for summaries). In conclusion, then, we would have to change these models considerably (i.e. in ways that do not seem to fit the evidence any better) in order to alter the conclusions of Chapter 3.

[2] Ober 2010: 280.

APPENDIX 2

Measuring Poverty

Headcount measurements of poverty (P_0) are the easiest to understand, and the Gini index (G) has been used frequently within ancient history over the past decade or so; both have advantages and drawbacks, as discussed in Chapter 3. This appendix outlines some of the other statistical tests of poverty used in that chapter.

Throughout the poverty line, (z) is defined at or below half of median income, a relative cut-off point frequently used by economists. As mentioned in Chapter 3, this is a reasonable but essentially arbitrary line which can, of course, be adapted or changed (see pp. 85–6). For discussion of whether constructing a poverty line is a good idea at all, see pp. 124–5.

Income Gap

The income gap (or poverty gap, P_1) measures the overall distance of the incomes of the poor from the poverty line (z). It is:

$$P_1 = \left(\frac{z - \mu_p}{z}\right)$$

where z is the 'poverty line' (here, half of median income) and μ_p is the mean income of the poor population.

Multiplying by the median of the whole population provides the average shortfall of those below the poverty line.[1]

The income-gap ratio is a depth figure and does not account for the number of people below z. However, it does not assume the dichotomous either–or of the headcount measure (one is either poor or non-poor); it is, rather, a continuous variable.

Poverty-Severity Index

The income gap is an aggregate measure and is not sensitive to the varying distribution of income among the poor. In order to give more weight to the

[1] See Sen 1973: 168–70.

poorest within the distribution, the poverty-severity index (P_2) simply squares the income-gap figure. The advantage is that this is an easy calculation, but has been criticized for being difficult to interpret.

All of the above indices belong to the Foster–Greer–Thorbecke (*FGT*) class of poverty measures.[2] They are considered useful because they are easy to compute, are decomposable (i.e. can be disaggregated from one another), and therefore can be used to identify how much each population subgroup contributes to the total poverty in that population.

Poverty Intensity

Poverty intensity (P_i) combines the headcount and income-gap ratio in order to assess both the quantity and depth of poverty in one metric. It is an interval measure which treats poverty as a continuum (rather than a headcount measure which dichotomizes a sample into poor and non-poor) and therefore expresses the idea that poverty is not a discrete condition.[3] It is calculated by multiplying the headcount by the income-gap ratio (and therefore is always lower than, and not comparable to, the headcount):

$$P_i = P_0 \times P_1$$

where P_0 = headcount, P_1 = income-gap ratio.

The intensity measure is simple to derive, and useful because it allows comparison across time and place. Larger values denote greater poverty, but it does not show whether this is due to a larger number of poor people or larger income shortfalls or inequality within those income shortfalls.[4]

Ordinal Index

Sen argued that—in addition to the number of poor and the depth of their poverty—poverty measurements need to be weighted to take greater account of the poorest of the poor.[5] By using the Gini index to measure distribution of income among the poor, he was able to satisfy a number of criteria which have since become orthodoxy in poverty measurement (see, for example, the *FGT* class of measures): that a reduction of income of the poor increases the measure of poverty (monotonicity); that income transfers from a richer poor person to a poorer poor person leads to a reduction of poverty (the weak transfer condition); and that the poverty measure does not depend on (i.e. is

2 Foster, Greer, and Thorbecke 1984.
3 Atkinson 1987: 754–5; Brady 2003: 727–8; 2009: 41–2.
4 Osberg and Xu 2000: 55–6.
5 Sen 1973: 170–87.

treated separately from) the income of the rich (the focus axiom).[6] The measure is not, however, decomposable (so cannot be used to compare subgroups in a population), and because it isolates the poor it places a high significance on the poverty line (i.e. changing *z* can change the outcome).[7]

Whilst there are mathematically more complex ways of calculating P_s, using the coefficient of variation (*CV*) rather than the Gini index produces the same result.[8] It is therefore calculated here as follows:

$$P_s = P_i(1 - CV)$$

The advantage of this measure is that it combines the number of the poor, the distribution of their income, and the depth of their poverty, and is therefore sensitive to the pattern of income distribution of the poor.[9] Because it gives greater weight to the lower end of this distribution it assumes that the poorest are more important than those closer to *z*. This is reasonable, but is a judgement about what one wants the data to do.[10] Larger values denote greater poverty intensity.

Theil's T

Theil's T is a statistic which, like the Gini index, can be used for measuring inequality. It is particularly good for measuring increases or decreases in inequality within aggregated data: since we do not know, for example, the exact income of each individual within our population groups, but instead suggest a plausible average, arguably Theil's T is a more appropriate measure. It is particularly useful for tracing changes over time.

However, it is more difficult to compute, and because it is an entropy measure—that is, it measures distance from 'order' (which is here conceptualized as perfect inequality, so perfect equality is therefore maximum entropy)—it has been criticized for being unintuitive.[11] Although Theil's T offers something that the Gini coefficient cannot, it may be that the Gini index is, on balance, a more useful measurement. In fact, there is little change in the pattern of inequality over time shown in Figure 3.5 if the Gini index is used. Like the Gini index, lower scores reflect lower inequality.

[6] In addition there are mathematical axioms: symmetry, replication invariance, and scale invariance.

[7] Modifications of Sen's measurement have introduced decomposability: the Sen–Shorrock–Thon index does just this (*SST*). See Osberg and Xu 1999 for discussion and examples.

[8] See Brady 2009: 212, n. 102 and literature cited there.

[9] Sen 1976.

[10] See discussion by Brady 2009: 42–3.

[11] Sen 1973: 34–6.

Theil's T is calculated as follows:

$$T = \sum_{i=1}^{m} \left\{ \left(\frac{p_i}{P}\right) \times \left(\frac{y_i}{\mu}\right) \times \ln\left(\frac{y_i}{\mu}\right) \right\}$$

where i indexes the groups, P_i is the population of the group, P is the total population, y_i is the mean income in group i, and μ is the mean income across the entire population.

The following assumptions are used. (These can of course be modified, but would have to be modified considerably to change the pattern in Fig. 3.5).

The 'mid-fifth century' models pre-Peloponnesian War conditions; that is, pay for serving on a jury or holding office was available for citizens, but pay for Assembly attendance was not. During this period jury service was restricted to a panel of 6,000 citizens aged 30 and over, who may or may not have been picked on any day during their year of service, and certain offices were restricted to those with defined levels of property.

Being young, poor, or not being able to foresee economic hardship a year in advance would have had a detrimental effect on those trying to subsist (regardless of the characterization of Aristophanes' *Wasps*). That is, although political pay provided an important financial resource for members of the demos (and members of the demos alone), neither sitting on a jury nor holding office provided *easy* access to resources for those in immediate dire need. (In contrast, Assembly pay did: there were no age restrictions, meetings were frequent and required little skill or forward planning for attendance, but did not exist at this time.)[12] For these reasons it is likely that there were more people living at (or under) subsistence than in the fourth century when such pay was more readily available.

Rowing in the fleet was, of course, an option for many (citizen and non-citizen), some citizens were resettled overseas (*IG* I³ 46 specifically makes provisions for thetes and *zeugitai*), and large-scale construction projects in the 440s no doubt allowed others to move out of subsistence living, partially offsetting this, but it is likely that those at the very bottom of the income distribution were worse off during the fifth century than in the fourth.

[12] Assembly meetings took place forty times a year in the fourth century, so approximately every nine days (*Ath. Pol.* 43.4–6). Although less frequent than the law courts, this regularity must have provided some measure of security—if a citizen attended, he would get paid. In contrast, there was a danger of being sent home from jury service because of the complexities of jury selection (*Ath. Pol.* 63–5; even though *Ath. Pol.* describes a more complex system than would have existed in the fifth century, not being chosen for service was a distinct possibility at the earlier date too). As the current debate surrounding zero-hours contracts shows, predictability of income is an important factor in negotiating poverty.

Conversely, the resources of empire appear to have been disproportionately accessed by the wealthy, something which is reflected in the anxieties of fifth-century comic poets.[13] The model assumes a total citizen population of approximately 60,000, that service as a hoplite was possible for all those in the 'middling' categories, and that there were between 18,000 and 46,000 potential hoplites in Athens, 1,000 of whom would be considered 'elite'.[14] This is not likely to underestimate the gap between rich and poor: it would have been large.

The 'later Peloponnesian War and aftermath' models conditions in the late fifth and early fourth centuries to reflect the demographic changes discussed in Chapter 3. I assume a reduction of population to approximately 250,000, with 30,000 male citizens. Given that Thucydides complains that 'those who previously had nothing' now came into inheritance, and that despite the turmoil of these years there was a consistent commitment to providing political pay (jury pay, *diobelia*, Assembly pay), I assume an increase in the number of citizens in the 'middling' levels (note that 'middling' assumes an average income of 1 drachma per day, which was within reach of many). The number of elite is reduced to reflect the loss of empire in 403 and the complaints of the wealthy in the late fifth and early fourth century discussed in Chapter 3 (which brings it into line with Gabrielsen's estimate for the minimum size of the liturgical class at the end of the fifth century: i.e. 1,200).[15] We would have to add thousands of extra men in this group to make the trends in Figure 3.5 disappear, something that the evidence does not support.

The 'late fourth century (pre-322)' model is that of Ober 2010, with modification of his 'citizen elite' group to reflect the larger numbers of liturgists that must have been needed (Gabrielsen 1994: 180).[16] There is no evidence that the size of the population changed significantly during the fourth century (i.e. at least until after 322).

The 'late fourth century (post-322)' follows van Wees' 2011 distribution model. Note that this is a model of wealth rather than income distribution, so is likely to provide an overestimation, especially in the headcount metric (in this sense it compares better with Kron's model of wealth distribution), but given that political pay was abolished during this period perhaps this is not a gross overestimation.[17] Following van Wees, I assume a citizen population in

[13] See, for example, Kratinos *Ploutoi* F 171–1a.

[14] Number of hoplites: at least 18,000: van Wees 2001. As many as 50,000: Akrigg 2005.

[15] Gabrielsen 1994: 180.

[16] Ober 2010: 264 envisages his 'elite' category to be coterminous with payers of liturgies and wealth of 3–4 talents, but follows Davies 1981: 34 with the 'low' figure of 200–400. I modify this to 1,200–1,500.

[17] For this reason I have excluded the post-322 category from Figure 3.4.

the region of 27,000–30,000, 25% of whom had less than 500 drachmas (and were disenfranchised in 322 and again in 317 by Demetrios of Phaleron). These men can be considered poor. According to his Table 1, 2,000 citizens had properties worth 1 talent or more. Together with those who owned over 2,000 drachmas, the group comprised approximately 9,000 men. In addition, 13,500 fell below this line but had more than 500 drachmas. In Table 2, van Wees assumes a smaller (1,200) but richer (3 talents minimum) elite (i.e. a level of wealth comparable to Ober's 'elite' category), with several thousands more in the 1–3 talent bracket, bringing the size of this group as a whole to 4,500. See van Wees 2011: Tables 1 and 2 for detailed population breakdowns.

Bibliography

Acton, P. H. (2014). *Poiesis: Manufacturing in Classical Athens*. Oxford.

Addison, T., Hulme, D., and Kanbur, R. (2009a). 'Poverty dynamics: measurement and understanding from an interdisciplinary perspective', in T. Addison, D. Hulme, and R. Kanbur (eds.), *Poverty Dynamics: Interdisciplinary Perspectives*. Oxford, 3-26.

Addison, T., Hulme, D., and Kanbur, R. (eds.) (2009b). *Poverty Dynamics: Interdisciplinary Perspectives*. Oxford.

Akrigg, B. (2005). 'The demography and economy of Athens, 432–c.380 BC', unpublished PhD thesis, University of Cambridge.

Akrigg, B. (2007). 'The nature and implications of Athens' changed social structure and economy', in R. Osborne (ed.), *The Anatomy of Cultural Revolution. Athens 430–380 BC*. Cambridge, 27–43.

Akrigg, B. (2011). 'Demography and classical Athens', in C. Holleran and A. Pudsey (eds.), *Demography and the Graeco-Roman World: New Insights and Approaches*. Cambridge, 84–132.

Alexandri, O. (1967). '*Γ' Ἐφορεία Κλασσικῶν Ἀρχαιοτήτων: Ἀθῆναι-Ἀττικη*', *Archaiologikon Deltion* 22: 37–130.

Alexandri, O. (1968). '*Γ' Ἐφορεία Κλασσικῶν Ἀρχαιοτήτων: Ἀθῆναι-Ἀττικη*', *Archaiologikon Deltion* 23: 33–109.

Alexandri, O. (1969). '*Γ' Ἐφορεία Κλασσικῶν Ἀρχαιοτήτων: Ἀθῆναι-Ἀττικη*', *Archaiologikon Deltion* 24: 25–88.

Alkire, S. (2005). *Valuing Freedoms: Sen's Capability Approach and Poverty Reduction*. Oxford.

Allen, P. (ed.) (2009). *Preaching Poverty in Late Antiquity: Perceptions and Realities*. Leipzig.

Allen, P. and Sitzler, S. (2009). 'Introduction', in P. Allen (ed.), *Preaching Poverty in Late Antiquity: Perceptions and Realities*. Leipzig, 15–33.

Allen, R. (2009). 'How prosperous were the Romans? Evidence from Diocletian's Price Edict (AD 301)', in A. K. Bowman and A. Wilson (eds.), *Quantifying the Roman Economy: Methods and Problems*. Oxford, 327–45.

Amyx, D. A. and Pritchett, W. K. (1958). 'The Attic stelai: Part III. Vases and other containers', *Hesperia* 27: 255–310.

Andreyev, V. N. (1974). 'Some aspects of agrarian conditions in Attica in the fifth to third centuries B.C.', *Eirene* 12: 5–46.

Anetakis, M., Syrianou, E., Kontopanagou, M., Petrou, A., Palaiokosta, E., Dovinou, I., and Vlachodemetropoulou, V. (2009). '*Νεκροταφεία και ταφικοί περίβολοι, χθόνιο ιερό και κτίριο με ανδρώνα στην Μερέντα*', in

V. Vasilopoulou and S. Katsarou-Tzeveleke (eds.), *Από τα Μεσόγεια στον Αργοσαρωνικό: Β' Εφορεία Προϊστορικών και Κλασικών Αρχαιοτήτων. Το έργο μιας δεκαετίας, 1994–2003*. Markopoulou, 189–204.

Arnaoutoglou, I. (1994a). 'Associations and patronage in ancient Athens', *Ancient Society* 25: 5–17.

Arnaoutoglou, I. (1994b). 'Ἀρχερανιστής and its meaning in inscriptions', *Zeitschrift für Papyrologie und Epigraphik* 104: 107–10.

Arnaoutoglou, I. (2003). *Thusias heneka kai sunousias: Private Religious Associations in Hellenistic Athens*. Athens.

Atkins, E. M. and Osborne, R. (2006). *Poverty in the Roman World*. Cambridge.

Atkinson, A. B. (1987). 'On the measurement of poverty', *Econometrica* 55.4: 749–64.

Ault, B. A. (2005). 'Housing the poor and homeless in ancient Greece', in B. A. Ault and L. C. Nevett (eds.), *Ancient Greek Houses and Households: Chronological, Regional, and Social Diversity*. Philadelphia, 140–59.

Austin, M. M. and Vidal-Naquet, P. (1977). *Economic and Social History of Ancient Greece: An Introduction*. Berkeley.

Bäbler, B. (1998). *Fleissige Thrakerinnen und wehrhafte Skythen. Nichtgriechen im klassischen Athen und ihre Archäologische Hinterlassenschaft*. Stuttgart.

Bäbler, B. (2005). 'Fremde Frauen im Athen. Thrakische Ammen und athenische Kinder', in U. Riemer and P. Riemer (eds.), *Xenophobie-Philoxenie. Vom Umgang mit Fremden in der Antike*. Stuttgart, 65–88.

Bagnall, R. S. (1992). 'Landholding in Late Roman Egypt: the distribution of wealth', *Journal of Roman Studies* 82: 128–49.

Bain, D. (1994). '*?ΒΟ.ΤΙΑΔΕΣ Ο ΠΡΩΚΤΟΣ*: an abusive graffito from Thorikos', *Zeitschrift für Papyrologie und Epigraphik* 104: 33–5.

Baird, J. A. (2015). 'On reading the material culture of ancient sexual labor', *Helios* 42.1: 163–75.

Baird, J. A. and Taylor, C. (2011). 'Introduction: ancient graffiti in context', in J. A. Baird and C. Taylor (eds.), *Ancient Graffiti in Context*. London, 1–17.

Bakola, E. (2010). *Cratinus and the Art of Comedy*. Oxford.

Balme, M. (1984). 'Attitudes to work and leisure in ancient Greece', *Greece and Rome* 31: 140–52.

Balot, R. K. (2004). 'Courage in the democratic polis', *Classical Quarterly* 54.2: 406–23.

Balot, R. K. (2014). *Courage in the Democratic Polis: Ideology and Critique in Classical Athens*. Oxford.

Barnes, J. A. (2011). 'Land rich and cash poor: the materiality of poverty in Appalachia', *Historical Archaeology* 45.3: 26–40.

Barrett, C. B., Carter, M. R., and Little, P. D. (2006). 'Understanding and reducing persistent poverty in Africa: Introduction to a special issue', *Journal of Development Studies* 42.2: 167–77.

Baslez, M.-F. and Briquel-Chatonnet, F. (1991). 'Un exemple d'intégration phénicienne au monde grec: Les Sidoniens à Pirée à la fin du IVe siècle', in E. Acquaro (ed.), *Atti del II Congresso internazionale di studi fenici e punici: Roma, 9–14 novembre 1987 (Collezione di studi fenici 30)*. Rome, 229–40.

Bastiaensen, J., de Herdt, T., and D'Exelle, B. (2005). 'Poverty reduction as a local institutional process', *World Development* 33: 979–93.

Baumer, L. E. (2014). '"Où le paysan faisait une pause pour offrir quelque modeste don". Les sanctuaires ruraux en Grèce: entre pauvreté romantique et réalité archéologique', in E. Galbois and S. Rougier-Blanc (eds.), *La pauvreté en Grèce ancienne: formes, représentations, enjeux*. Bordeaux, 97–104.

Baxter, J. E. (2005). *The Archaeology of Childhood: Children, Gender and Material Culture*. Walnut Creek.

Becq, J. (2010). 'Theatre figures', in V. Jeammet (ed.), *Tanagras. Figurines for Life and Eternity: The Musée du Louvre's Collection of Greek Figurines*. Valencia, 70–5.

Beier, A. L. (2008). '"A new serfdom". Labor laws, vagrancy statutes, and labor discipline in England, 1350–1800', in A. L. Beier and P. Ocobock (eds.), *Cast Out: Vagrancy and Homelessness in Global and Historical Perspective*. Athens, Ohio, 35–63.

Bérard, V. (1888). 'Inscription du Laurium', *Bulletin de correspondance hellénique* 12: 246–8.

Bergemann, J. (1997). *Demos und Thanatos. Untersuchungen zum Wertsystem der Polis im Spiegel der attischen Grabreliefs des 4. Jhdts. v. Chr. und zur der gleichzeitigen Grabbauten*. Munich.

Besques, S. (1954). *Musée du Louvre. Catalogue raisonné des figurines et reliefs en terre-cuite grecs, étrusques et romains*. Paris.

Bisel, S. C. (1990). 'Anthropologische Untersuchungen', in W. Kovacsovics (ed.), *Kerameikos XII: Die Eckterrasse an der Gräberstraße des Kerameikos*. Berlin, 151–60.

Bissa, E. M. A. (2008). 'Investment patterns in the Laurion mining industry in the fourth century BCE', *Historia* 57: 263–73.

Blok, J. H. and Lambert, S. D. (2009). 'The appointment of priests in Attic *gene*', *Zeitschrift für Papyrologie und Epigraphik* 169: 95–121.

Bonfante, L. (1997). 'Nursing mothers in classical art', in A. O. Koloski-Ostrow and C. L. Lyons (eds.), *Naked Truths: Women, Sexuality, and Gender in Classical Art and Archaeology*. London, 174–96.

Bourdieu, P. (1984). *Distinction: A Social Critique of the Judgment of Taste*. London.

Bradley, K. (1986). 'Wet-nursing at Rome: a study in social relations', in B. Rawson (ed.), *The Family in Ancient Rome: New Perspectives*. London, 201–29.

Bradley, M. (2002). '"It all comes out in the wash": looking harder at the Roman *fullonica*', *Journal of Roman Archaeology* 15: 20–44.

Brady, D. (2003). 'Rethinking the sociological measurement of poverty', *Social Forces* 81.3: 715–51.

Brady, D. (2009). *Rich Democracies, Poor People: How Politics Explain Poverty*. Oxford.

Brandolini, A. and Smeeding, T. M. (2009). 'Income inequality in richer and OECD countries', in W. Salverda, B. Nolan, and T. M. Smeeding (eds.), *The Oxford Handbook of Economic Inequality*. Oxford, 71–100.

Braund, D. and Tsetskhladze, G. R. (1989). 'The export of slaves from Colchis', *Classical Quarterly* 39: 114–25.

Bresson, A. (2015). *The Making of the Ancient Greek Economy: Institutions, Markets, and Growth in the City-States*. Princeton.

Brock, R. (1994). 'The labour of women in classical Athens', *Classical Quarterly* 44: 336–46.

Brouskari, M. S. (2002). *Οἱ ἀνασκαφὲς νοτίως τῆς Ἀκροπόλεως. Τὰ γλυπτά*. Athens.

Brown, P. R. L. (2002). *Poverty and Leadership in the Later Roman Empire*. Hanover.

Buikstra, J. and Lagia, A. (2009). 'Bioarchaeological approaches to Aegean archaeology', in L. A. Schepartz, S. C. Fox, and C. Bourbou (eds.), *New Directions in the Skeletal Biology of Greece*. Princeton, 7–30.

Burford, A. (1972). *Craftsmen in Greek and Roman Society*. London.

Burford, A. (1993). *Land and Labor in the Greek World*. Baltimore.

Burke, E. M. (2010). 'Finances and the operation of the Athenian democracy in the "Lycurgan Era"', *American Journal of Philology* 131.3: 393–423.

Burn, L. and Higgins, R. (2001). *Catalogue of Greek Terracottas in the British Museum, Volume III*. London.

Burnyeat, M. (1977). 'Socratic midwifery, Platonic imagination', *Bulletin of the Institute of Classical Studies* 24: 7–16.

Cahill, N. D. (2005). 'Household industry in Greece and Anatolia', in B. A. Ault and L. C. Nevett (eds.), *Ancient Greek Houses and Households. Chronological, Regional, and Social Diversity*. Philadelphia, 54–66.

Camp, J. (1986). *The Athenian Agora. Excavations in the Heart of Classical Athens*. London.

Carey, C. (1990). 'Structure and strategy in Lysias XXIV', *Greece and Rome* 37.1: 44–51.

Carnevali, F. (2011). 'Social capital and trade associations in America, *c*. 1860–1914: a microhistory approach', *Economic History Review* 64.3: 905–28.

Carter, M. R. and Barrett, C. B. (2006). 'The economics of poverty traps and persistent poverty: an asset-based approach', *Journal of Development Studies* 42.2: 178–99.

Cartledge, P. (1996). 'Comparatively equal', in J. Ober and C. W. Hedrick (eds.), *Demokratia: A Conversation on Democracies, Ancient and Modern*. Princeton, 175–85.

Cartledge, P. (1998). 'The machismo of the Athenian Empire—or the reign of the *phaulus*?', in L. Foxhall and J. B. Salmon (eds.), *When Men Were Men: Masculinity, Power and Identity in Classical Antiquity*. London, 54–67.

Cartledge, P. (2002). *Sparta and Lakonia: A Regional History, 1300 to 362 BC*. 2nd edn. London.

Cartledge, P. (2009). *Ancient Greek Political Thought in Practice*. Cambridge.

Cawkwell, G. L. (1963). 'Eubulus', *Journal of Hellenic Studies* 83: 47–67.

Cecchet, L. (2013). 'Poverty as argument in Athenian forensic speeches', *Ktema* 38: 53–66.

Cecchet, L. (2014). 'Giving to the poor in ancient Greece: a form of social aid?', in F. Carlà and M. Gori (eds.), *Gift Giving and the 'Embedded' Economy in the Ancient World*. Heidelberg, 157–80.

Chaniotis, A. (1996). 'Conflicting authorities. *Asylia* between secular and divine law in the classical and hellenistic poleis', *Kernos* 9: 65–86.

Chaniotis, A. (2011). 'Graffiti in Aphrodisias', in J. A. Baird and C. Taylor (eds.), *Ancient Graffiti in Context*. London, 191–207.

Charlesworth, S. J. (2000). *A Phenomenology of Working Class Experience*. Cambridge.

Chicone, S. J. (2011a). 'Respectable rags: working-class poverty and the 1913–14 Southern Colorado coal strike', *International Journal of Historical Archaeology* 15.1: 51–81.

Chicone, S. J. (2011b). 'From goats to gardens: feeding Southern Colorado's working-class poor', *Historical Archaeology* 45.3: 121–39.

Christensen, K. A. (1984). 'The Theseion: a slave refuge at Athens', *American Journal of Ancient History* 9: 23–32.

Christesen, P. (2013). 'Sport and democratization in Ancient Greece (with an excursus on athletic nudity)', in P. Christesen and D. G. Kyle (eds.), *A Companion to Sport and Spectacle in Greek and Roman Antiquity*. Oxford, 209–35.

Christ, M. R. (1990). 'Liturgy avoidance and *antidosis* in classical Athens', *Transactions of the American Philological Association* 120: 147–69.

Christ, M. R. (2001). 'Conscription of hoplites in classical Athens', *Classical Quarterly* 51: 398–422.

Christ, M. R. (2007). 'The evolution of the *eisphora* in classical Athens', *Classical Quarterly* 57: 53–69.

Christ, M. R. (2010). 'Helping behavior in classical Athens', *Phoenix* 64.3/4: 254–90.

Clairmont, C. W. (1970). *Gravestone and Epigram: Greek Memorials from the Archaic and Classical Period*. Mainz.

Clark, D. A. (2005). 'Sen's capability approach and the many spaces of human well-being', *Journal of Development Studies* 41.8: 1339–68.

Cleaver, F. (2005). 'The inequality of social capital and the reproduction of poverty', *World Development* 33: 893–906.

Cleland, L. (2005). *The Brauron Clothing Catalogues: Text, Analysis, Glossary and Translation*. Oxford.

Closterman, W. E. (2007). 'Family ideology and family history: the function of funerary markers in classical Attic *peribolos* tombs', *American Journal of Archaeology* 111: 633–52.

Cohen, D. (1998). 'Women, property and status in Demosthenes 41 and 57', *Dike* 1: 53–61.

Cohen, E. E. (1974). *Ancient Athenian Maritime Courts*. Princeton.

Cohen, E. E. (1992). *Athenian Economy and Society: A Banking Perspective*. Princeton.

Cohen, E. E. (1998). 'The wealthy slaves of Athens: legal rights, economic obligations', in H. Jones (ed.), *Le monde antique et les droits de l'homme: actes de la 50e session de la Société internationale Fernand De Visscher pour l'histoire des droits de l'antiquité, Bruxelles, 16–19 septembre 1996*. Brussels, 105–23.

Cohen, R. (1996). *Theories of Migration*. Cheltenham.

Coin-Longeray, S. (2014a). 'Pénès et Ptôchos: le pauvre et le mendiant. Deux figures de la pauvreté dans la poésie grecque ancienne', in E. Galbois and S. Rougier-Blanc (eds.), *La pauvreté en Grèce ancienne: Formes, représentations, enjeux*. Bordeaux, 45–65.

Coin-Longeray, S. (2014b). *Poésie de la richesse et de la pauvreté: étude du vocabulaire de la richesse et de la pauvreté dans la poésie grecque antique, d'Homère à Aristophane*. Saint-Étienne.

Comella, A. (2002). *I rilievi votivi greci di periodo arcaico e classico: diffusione, ideologia, committenza*. Bari.

Connelly, J. M. (2007). *Portrait of a Priestess: Women and Ritual in Ancient Greece*. Princeton.

Conophagos, C. E. (1980). *Le Laurium antique et la technique grecque de la production de l'argent*. Athens.

Corner, S. (2013a). 'The politics of the parasite (Part 1)', *Phoenix* 67.1/2: 43–80.

Corner, S. (2013b). 'The politics of the parasite (Part 2)', *Phoenix* 67.3/4: 223–36.

Coulié, A. (1998). 'Nouvelles inscriptions érotiques à Thasos', *Bulletin de correspondance hellénique* 122: 445–53.

Coulter, P. B. (1989). *Measuring Inequality: A Methodological Handbook*. Boulder.

Cox, C. A. (1998). *Household Interests: Property, Marriage Strategies, and Family Dynamics in Ancient Athens*. Princeton.

Cuomo, S. (2007). *Technology and Culture in Greek and Roman Antiquity*. Cambridge.

Daly, M. (1992). 'Europe's poor women? Gender in research on poverty', *European Sociological Review* 8: 1–12.

Daux, G. (1972). 'Stèles funéraires et épigrammes', *Bulletin de correspondance hellénique* 96.1: 503–66.

Davidson, J. (1997). *Courtesans and Fishcakes: The Consuming Passions of Classical Athens*. London.

Davies, J. K. (1971). *Athenian Propertied Families, 600–300 BC*. Oxford.

Davies, J. K. (1981). *Wealth and the Power of Wealth in Classical Athens*. New York.

Davies, J. K. (2015). 'Retrospect and prospect', in C. Taylor and K. Vlassopoulos (eds.), *Communities and Networks in the Ancient Greek World*. Oxford, 239–56.

Davis, G. (2014). 'Mining money in late archaic Athens', *Historia* 63.3: 257–77.

de Callataÿ, F. (2014). 'Long-term quantification in ancient history: a historical perspective', in F. de Callataÿ (ed.), *Quantifying the Greco-Roman Economy and Beyond*. Bari, 13–27.

Demand, N. H. (1994). *Birth, Death, and Motherhood in Classical Greece*. Baltimore.

Demand, N. H. (1995). 'Monuments, midwives and gynecology', in P. van der Eijk, H. F. J. Horstmannshoff, and P. H. Schrijvers (eds.), *Ancient Medicine in its Socio-Cultural Context: Papers Read at the Congress held at Leiden University 13–15 April 1992*. Amsterdam, 275–90.

Desmond, W. D. (2006). *The Greek Praise of Poverty: Origins of Ancient Cynicism*. Notre Dame.

Dickie, M. W. (2001). *Magic and Magicians in the Greco-Roman World*. London.

Dillon, M. (1995). 'Payments for the disabled at Athens: social justice or fear of aristocratic patronage?', *Ancient Society* 26: 27–57.

Distilo, N. (2012). *Commento critico-testuale all'Elettra di Euripide*. Padua.

Dollar, D. and Kraay, A. (2002). 'Growth is good for the poor', *Journal of Economic Growth* 7: 195–225.

Douglas, M. and Ney, S. (1998). *Missing Persons: A Critique of the Social Sciences*. Berkeley.

Dover, K. J. (1974). *Greek Popular Morality in the Time of Plato and Aristotle*. Oxford.

DuBois, P. (2008). *Slaves and other Objects*. Chicago.

Duplouy, A. (2006). *Le prestige des élites: recherches sur les modes de reconnaissance sociale en Grèce entre les Xe et Ve siècles avant J.-C.* Paris.

du Toit, A. (2009). 'Poverty measurement blues: beyond "Q-Squared" approaches to understanding chronic poverty in South Africa', in T. Addison, D. Hulme, and R. Kanbur (eds.), *Poverty Dynamics: Interdisciplinary Perspectives*. Oxford, 225–46.

Edwards, C. M. (1985). 'Greek votive reliefs to Pan and the Nymphs', unpublished PhD thesis, New York University.

Edwards, M. and Usher, S. (1985). *Greek Orators I: Antiphon and Lysias*. Warminster.

Eleutheratou, S. (2001). '*Ανασκαφή οικοπέδου Μακρυγιάννη για την ανέγερση του Νέου Μουσείου Ακροπόλεως*', *Archaiologikon Deltion* 56–59: 147–52.

Faraguna, M. (1992). *Atene nell'età di Alessandro: problemi politici, economici, finanziari*. Rome.

Fawcett, P. W. (2016). '"When I squeeze you with *eisphorai*": taxes and tax policy in Classical Athens', *Hesperia* 85.1: 153–99.

Ferguson, W. S. (1944). 'The Attic *orgeones*', *Harvard Theological Review* 37: 61–140.

Ferguson, J. (2010). 'The uses of neoliberalism', *Antipode* 41: 166–84.

Feyel, C. (2006). *Les artisans dans les sanctuaires grecs aux époques classique et hellénistique à travers la documentation financière en Grèce*. Athens.

Fine, B. (2010). *Theories of Social Capital: Researchers Behaving Badly*. London.

Finley, M. I. (1985). *Studies in Land and Credit in Ancient Athens, 500–200 BC*. New Brunswick.

Finn, R. D. (2006). *Almsgiving in the Later Roman Empire: Christian Promotion and Practice (313–450)*. Oxford.

Fisher, N. R. E. (1998). 'Gymnastic behaviour and the democratic values of leisure in Athens', in P. Cartledge, P. Millett, and S. von Reden (eds.), *Kosmos: Order, Individuality and the Community in Classical Athens*. Cambridge, 84–104.

Fisher, N. R. E. (2000). 'Symposiasts, fish-eaters and flatterers: social mobility and moral concerns in Old Comedy', in D. Harvey and J. Wilkins (eds.), *The Rivals of Aristophanes: Studies in Athenian Old Comedy*. Swansea: 355–96.

Fisher, N. R. E. (2001). *Aeschines: Against Timarchos. Introduction, Translation and Commentary*. Oxford.

Fiszbein, A. and Schady, N. R. (2009). *Conditional Cash Transfers: Policy Research Reports*. Washington, DC.

Fontaine, L. (2014). *The Moral Economy: Poverty, Credit, and Trust in Early Modern Europe*. Cambridge.

Forsdyke, S. (2012). *Slaves Tell Tales and Other Episodes in the Politics of Popular Culture in Ancient Greece*. Princeton.

Fortenbaugh, W. W. (2011). *Theophrastus of Eresus. Commentary, Volume 6.1: Sources on Ethics*. Leiden.

Fortenbaugh, W. W., Huby, P. M., Sharples, R. W., and Gutas, D. (1992). *Theophrastus of Eresus. Sources for his Life, Writings, Thought and Influence*. Leiden.

Foster, J., Greer, J., and Thorbecke, E. (1984). 'A class of decomposable poverty measures', *Econometrica* 52.3: 761–6.

Foxhall, L. (1989). 'Household, gender and property in classical Athens', *Classical Quarterly* 39: 22–44.

Foxhall, L. (1992). 'The control of the Attic landscape', in B. Wells (ed.), *Agriculture in Ancient Greece. Proceedings of the Seventh International Symposium at the Swedish Institute at Athens, 16–17th May 1990*. Stockholm, 155–9.

Foxhall, L. (1997). 'A view from the top. Evaluating the Solonian property classes', in L. G. Mitchell and P. J. Rhodes (eds.), *The Development of the Polis in Archaic Greece*. London, 113–36.

Foxhall, L. (2003). 'Pandora unbound: a feminist critique of Foucault's *History of Sexuality*', in M. Golden and P. Toohey (eds.), *Sex and Difference in Ancient Greece and Rome*. Edinburgh, 167–82.

Foxhall, L. (2007). *Olive Cultivation in Ancient Greece: Seeking the Ancient Economy*. Oxford.

Foxhall, L. and Forbes, H. A. (1982). '*Sitometreia*: the role of grain as a staple food in classical antiquity', *Chiron* 12: 14–90.

Frankel, R. (2003). 'The Olynthus mill, its origin, and diffusion: typology and distribution', *American Journal of Archaeology* 107.1: 1–21.

Frey, B. S. and Stutzer, A. (2000). 'Happiness, economy and institutions', *Economic Journal* 110: 918–38.

Fuks, A. (1951). '*Kolonos misthios*: labour exchange in classical Athens', *Eranos* 49: 171–3.

Fuks, A. (1974). 'Patterns and types of social-economic revolution in Greece from the fourth to the second century BC', *Ancient Society* 5: 51–81.

Fuks, A. (1977). 'Plato and the social question: the problem of poverty and riches in the *Republic*', *Ancient Society* 8: 49–83.

Fuks, A. (1979). 'Plato and the social question: the problem of poverty and riches in the *Laws*', *Ancient Society* 10: 33–78.

Gabrielsen, V. (1994). *Financing the Athenian Fleet*. Baltimore.

Gabrielsen, V. (2007). 'Brotherhoods of faith and provident planning: the non-public associations of the Greek world', *Mediterranean Historical Review* 22: 183–210.

Gabrielsen, V. (2015). 'Naval and grain networks in fourth-century Athens', in C. Taylor and K. Vlassopoulos (eds.), *Communities and Networks in the Ancient Greek World*. Oxford, 177–212.

Gaggio, D. (2004). 'Do social historians need social capital?', *Social History* 29.4: 499–513.

Gaggio, D. (2007). *In Gold we Trust: Social Capital and Economic Change in the Italian Jewelry Towns*. Princeton.

Galbois, E. and Rougier-Blanc, S. (2014a). 'La pauvreté en Grèce ancienne, un faux sujet de recherche?', in E. Galbois and S. Rougier-Blanc (eds.), *La pauvreté en Grèce ancienne: Formes, représentations, enjeux*. Bordeaux, 13–23.

Galbois, E. and Rougier-Blanc, S. (2014b). 'Les mots de la pauvreté. Définitions et concepts: Introduction de la 1ère partie', in E. Galbois and S. Rougier-Blanc (eds.), *La pauvreté en Grèce ancienne: Formes, représentations, enjeux*. Bordeaux, 37–44.

Galbois, E. and Rougier-Blanc, S. (eds.) (2014c). *La pauvreté en Grèce ancienne: Formes, représentations, enjeux*. Bordeaux.

Gallant, T. W. (1991). *Risk and Survival in Ancient Greece. Reconstructing the Rural Domestic Economy*. Cambridge.

Garlan, Y. and Masson, O. (1982). 'Les acclamations pédérastiques de Kalami (Thasos)', *Bulletin de correspondance hellénique* 106: 3–22.

Garland, R. (1992). *Introducing New Gods: The Politics of Athenian Religion*. Ithaca, NY.

Garnsey, P. (1988). *Famine and Food-Supply in the Graeco-Roman World: Responses to Risk and Crisis*. Cambridge.

Garnsey, P. (1998). *Cities, Peasants, and Food in Classical Antiquity: Essays in Social and Economic History*. Cambridge.

Gauthier, P. (1976). *Un commentaire historique des Poroi de Xénophon*. Paris.

Gauthier, P. (2010). 'Xenophon's programme in the *Poroi*', in V. Gray (ed.), *Xenophon*. Oxford, 113–36.

Glazebrook, A. (2011). '*Porneion*: prostitution in Athenian civic space', in A. Glazebrook and M. M. Henry (eds.), *Greek Prostitutes in the Ancient Mediterranean, 800 BCE–200 CE*. Madison, 34–59.

Goette, H. R. (2000). *Ὁ ἀξιόλογος δῆμος Σούνιον. Landeskundliche Studien in Südost-Attika*. Rahden.

Golden, M. (1990). *Children and Childhood in Classical Athens*. Baltimore.

Golden, M. (2011). 'Slavery and the Greek family', in K. Bradley and P. Cartledge (eds.), *The Cambridge World History of Slavery. Volume 1: The Ancient Mediterranean World*. Cambridge, 134–52.

Gottesman, A. (2014). *Politics and the Street in Democratic Athens*. Cambridge.

Graham, J. W. (1974). 'Houses of classical Athens', *Phoenix* 28: 45–54.

Granovetter, M. (1973). 'The strength of weak ties', *American Journal of Sociology* 78: 1360–80.

Granovetter, M. (1983). 'The strength of weak ties: a network theory revisited', *Sociological Theory* 1: 203–33.

Gray, V. (1998). *The Framing of Socrates: The Literary Interpretation of Xenophon's Memorabilia*. Stuttgart.

Graziosi, B. (2002). *Inventing Homer: The Early Reception of Epic*. Cambridge.

Green, M. (2007). 'Representing poverty and attacking representations: perspectives on poverty from social anthropology', in D. Hulme and J. Toye (eds.), *Understanding Poverty and Well-Being: Bridging the Disciplines*. London, 24–45.

Green, M. (2009). 'The social distribution of sanctioned harm: thinking through chronic poverty, durable poverty, and destitution', in T. Addison, D. Hulme, and R. Kanbur (eds.), *Poverty Dynamics: Interdisciplinary Perspectives*. Oxford, 309–27.

Green, M. and Hulme, D. (2005). 'From correlates and characteristics to causes: thinking about poverty from a chronic poverty perspective', *World Development* 33: 867–79.

Greenwood, E. (2006). *Thucydides and the Shaping of History*. London.

Güntner, G. (1994). *Göttervereine und Götterversammlungen auf attischen Weihreliefs: Untersuchungen zur Typologie und Bedeutung*. Würzburg.

Hadjú, I. (2002). *Kommentar zur 4. Philippischen Rede des Demosthenes*. Berlin.

Hagemajer Allen, K. (2003). 'Becoming the "Other": attitudes and practices at Attic cemeteries', in C. Dougherty and L. Kurke (eds.), *The Cultures within Ancient Greek Culture: Contact, Conflict, Collaboration*. Cambridge, 207–36.

Hall, E. (1989). *Inventing the Barbarian: Greek Self-Definition through Tragedy*. Oxford.

Halperin, D. M. (1990). *One Hundred Years of Homosexuality and Other Essays on Greek Love*. New York.

Hands, A. R. (1968). *Charities and Social Aid in Greece and Rome*. London.

Hansen, M. H. (1975). *Eisangelia: The Sovereignty of the People's Court in Athens in the Fourth Century* BC *and the Impeachment of Generals and Politicians*. Odense.

Hansen, M. H. (1985). *Demography and Democracy. The Number of Athenian Citizens in the Fourth Century* BC. Herning.

Hansen, M. H. (1990). 'Athenian democracy: review of J. Ober, *Mass and Elite in Democratic Athens: Rhetoric, Ideology, and the Power of the People*, Princeton, 1989', *Classical Review* 40: 348–56.

Hansen, M. H. (2006). *The Shotgun Method: The Demography of the Ancient Greek City-State Culture*. Columbia.

Hansen, M. H. (2014). '*Misthos* for magistrates in fourth-century Athens?', *Greek, Roman, and Byzantine Studies* 54.3: 404–19.

Hanson, A. E. (1996). 'Phaenarete: mother and Maia', in R. Wittern and P. Pellegrin (eds.), *Hippokratische Medizin und antike Philosophie:*

Verhandlungen des VIII. Internationalen Hippokrates-Kolloquiums in Kloster Banz/Staffelstein vom 23. bis 28. September 1993. Hildesheim, 159–81.

Harris, E. M. (1992). 'Women and lending in Athenian society: a "horos" re-examined', *Phoenix* 46: 309–21.

Harris, E. M. (1993). '*Apotimema*: Athenian terminology for real security in leases and dowry agreements', *Classical Quarterly* 43: 73–95.

Harris, E. M. (1995). *Aeschines and Athenian Politics*. Oxford.

Harris, E. M. (1996). 'Demosthenes and the theoric fund', in R. W. Wallace and E. M. Harris (eds.), *Transitions to Empire: Essays in Greco-Roman History 360–146* BC *in Honor of E. Badian*. London, 70–4.

Harris, E. M. (2002a). 'Workshop, marketplace and household: the nature of technical specialisation in classical Athens and its influence on economy and society', in P. Cartledge, E. E. Cohen, and L. Foxhall (eds.), *Money, Labour and Land: Approaches to the Economies of Ancient Greece*. London, 67–99.

Harris, E. M. (2002b). 'Did Solon abolish debt-bondage?', *Classical Quarterly* 52: 415–30.

Harris, E. M. (2013). 'Finley's "Studies in Land and Credit" sixty years later', *Dike* 16.0: 123–46.

Harris, R. (1995). *Signs of Writing*. London.

Harris, R. (2000). *Rethinking Writing*. London.

Harriss, J. (2009). 'Bringing politics back into poverty analysis. Why understanding of social relations matters more for policy on chronic poverty than measurement', in T. Addison, D. Hulme, and R. Kanbur (eds.), *Poverty Dynamics: Interdisciplinary Perspectives*. Oxford, 205–24.

Harriss-White, B. (2005). 'Destitution and the poverty of its politics: with special reference to South Asia', *World Development* 33: 881–91.

Harvey, F. D. (1965). 'Two kinds of equality', *Classica et Mediaevalia* 26: 101–46.

Higgens, R. A. (1967). *Greek Terracottas*. London.

Hintzen-Bohlen, B. (1997). *Die Kulturpolitik des Eubolos und des Lykurg: Die Denkmäler- und Bauprojekte in Athen zwischen 355 und 322 v. Chr.* Berlin.

Hodkinson, S. (1992). 'Imperialist democracy and market-oriented pastoral production in classical Athens', *Anthropozoologica* 16: 53–60.

Hodkinson, S. (2000). *Property and Wealth in Classical Sparta*. London.

Holleran, C. and Pudsey, A. (2011). 'Introduction: Studies in ancient historical demography', in C. Holleran and A. Pudsey (eds.), *Demography and the Graeco-Roman World: New Insights and Approaches*. Cambridge, 1–13.

Hopper, R. J. (1953). 'The Attic silver mines in the fourth century BC', *Annual of the British School at Athens* 48: 200–54.

Humphreys, S. C. (1993). 'Family tombs and tomb cult in ancient Athens: tradition or traditionalism?', in *The Family, Women and Death. Comparative Studies*. Ann Arbor, 79–134.

Humphreys, S. C. (2004). 'A sense of agency: religion in the Attic demes', in S. C. Humphreys (ed.), *The Strangeness of Gods: Historical Perspectives on the Interpretation of Athenian Religion*. Oxford, 130–96.

Hunter, V. (2000). 'Policing public debtors in classical Athens', *Phoenix* 54: 21–38.

Hunt, P. (1998). *Slaves, Warfare, Ideology in the Greek Historians*. Cambridge.

Hunt, P. (2001). 'The slaves and the generals of Arginusae', *American Journal of Philology* 122: 359–80.

Hunt, P. (2015). 'Trojan slaves in classical Athens: ethnic identity among Athenian slaves', in C. Taylor and K. Vlassopoulos (eds.), *Communities and Networks in the Ancient Greek World*. Oxford, 128–54.

Jackson, C. (1998). 'Women and poverty or gender and well-being?', *Journal of International Affairs* 52: 67–81.

Jackson, W. A. (2005). 'Capabilities, culture and social structure', *Review of Social Economy* 63: 101–24.

Jacquemin, A. (2013). 'D'une condition sociale à un statut politique, les ambiguïtés du thète', *Ktema* 38: 7–13.

Jacquet-Rimassa, P. (2014). '"Cherchez le pauvre!" Quelques réflexions sur la pauvreté dans l'imagerie attique (VI–V^{e} a.C)', in E. Galbois and S. Rougier-Blanc (eds.), *La pauvreté en Grèce ancienne: Formes, représentations, enjeux*. Bordeaux, 179–88.

Jeammet, V. (2010). 'The origin of the Tanagras: fourth century BC Athens', in V. Jeammet (ed.), *Tanagras: Figurines for Life and Eternity. The Musée du Louvre's Collection of Greek Figurines*. Valencia, 62–9.

Johansson, S. R. (1994). 'Food for thought: rhetoric and reality in modern mortality history', *Historical Methods* 27: 101–25.

Johnson, W. (2003). 'On agency', *Journal of Social History* 37.1: 113–24.

Johnstone, S. (2003). 'Women, property and surveillance in classical Athens', *Classical Antiquity* 22: 247–74.

Johnstone, S. (2010). 'Virtuous toil, vicious work: Xenophon on aristocratic style', in V. Gray (ed.), *Xenophon*. Oxford, 137–66.

Jones, A. H. M. (1957). *Athenian Democracy*. Baltimore.

Jones, C. P. (2008). 'Hypereides and the sale of slave families', *Zeitschrift für Papyrologie und Epigraphik* 164: 19–20.

Jones, J. E. (1975). 'Town and country houses of Attica in classical times', in H. F. Mussche, P. Spitaels, and F. Goemaere-de Poerck (eds.), *Thorikos and Laurion in Archaic and Classical Times*. Ghent, 63–140.

Jones, J. E. (1984). 'Laurion: Agrileza, 1977–1983: Excavations at a silver mine site', *Archaeological Reports* 31: 106–23.

Jones, J. E. (2007). '"Living above the shop": domestic aspects of the ancient industrial workshops of the Laurion area of Attica', in R. Westgate, N. Fisher, and J. Whitley (eds.), *Building Communities: House, Settlement and Society in the Aegean and Beyond*. London, 267–80.

Jones, J. E., Graham, A. J., and Sackett, L. H. (1973). 'An Attic country house below the Cave of Pan at Vari', *Annual of the British School at Athens* 68: 355–452.

Jones, J. E., Sackett, L. H., and Graham, A. J. (1962). 'The Dema House in Attica', *Annual of the British School at Athens* 57: 75–114.

Jones, N. (1999). *The Associations of Classical Athens*. Princeton.

Jones, O. (2011). *Chavs: The Demonization of the Working Class*. London.

Jones, O. (2014). '*Benefits Street*: A healthy media would stand up to the powerful and wealthy. Ours targets the poor and voiceless', *The Independent*, 8 January.

Jongman, W. (2007). 'The early Roman Empire: consumption', in W. Scheidel, I. Morris, and R. Saller (eds.), *The Cambridge Economic History of the Greco-Roman World*. Cambridge, 592–618.

Jongman, W. (2012). 'Roman economic change and the Antonine plague: endogenous, exogeneous or what?', in E. Lo Cascio (ed.), *L'impatto della 'peste antonina'*. Bari, 253–64.

Kaiser, B. A. (2007). 'The Athenian trierarchy: mechanism design for the private provision of public goods', *Journal of Economic History* 67.2: 445–80.

Kakavogianni, O. (2000). '*Αττική οδός*', *Archaiologikon Deltion* 55: 133–6.

Kakavogianni, O. (2001). '*Ανασκαφικές Εργασίες* 2001: *Μεσογεία*', *Archaiologikon Deltion* 56–59: 320–7.

Kakavogianni, O. and Galiatsatou, P. (2009). '*Από τα αρχαία νεκροταφεία στα Μεσόγεια. Ο αρχαίος δήμος της Όης*', in V. Vasilopoulou and S. Katsarou-Tzeveleke (eds.), *Από τα Μεσόγεια στον Αργοσαρωνικό: Β' Εφορεία Προϊστορικών και Κλασικών Αρχαιοτήτων. Το έργο μιας δεκαετίας, 1994-2003*. Markopoulou, 399–422.

Kalcyk, H. (1982). *Untersuchungen zum attischen Silberbergbau. Gebietsstruktur, Geschichte, Technik*. Frankfurt.

Kanbur, R. (2005). 'Growth, inequality and poverty: some hard questions', *Journal of International Affairs* 58.2: 223–32.

Karanika, A. (2014). *Voices at Work: Women, Performance, and Labor in Ancient Greece*. Baltimore.

Karydas, H. P. (1998). *Eurykleia and Her Successors: Female Figures of Authority in Greek Poetics*. Lanham.

Keaney, J. J. and Szegedy-Maszak, A. (1976). 'Theophrastus' *De Eligendis Magistratibus*: Vat. Gr. 2306, fragment B', *Transactions of the American Philological Association* 106: 227–40.

Keister, L. A. (2000). *Wealth in America: Trends in Wealth Inequality*. Cambridge.

Keister, L. A. and Moller, S. (2000). 'Wealth inequality in the United States', *American Review of Sociology* 26: 63–81.

Kennedy, R. F. (2014). *Immigrant Women in Athens: Gender, Ethnicity, and Citizenship in the Classical City*. London.

Keyt, D. (1999). *Aristotle's Politics Books V and VI, Translated with a Commentary*. Oxford.

King, H. (1998). *Hippocrates' Woman: Reading the Female Body in Ancient Greece*. London.

Kloft, H. (1988). 'Gedanken zum Ptochos', in I. Weiler and H. Grassl (eds.), *Soziale Randgruppen und Aussenseiter im Altertum: Referate vom Symposion 'Soziale Randgruppen und Antike Sozialpolitik' in Graz (21. bis 23. September 1987)*. Graz, 81–106.

Kloppenborg, J. S. and Ascough, R. S. (2011). *Greco-Roman Associations: Texts, Translations and Commentary. Volume I: Attica, Central Greece, Macedonia, Thrace*. Berlin.

Knoch, S. (2010). 'Beobachtungen zu Armut und Armen bei Platon und Aristoteles, Cicero und Seneca', *Klio* 92: 305–30.

Kosmopoulou, A. (2001). '"Working women": female professionals on classical Attic gravestones', *Annual of the British School at Athens* 96: 281–319.

Kovacsovics, W. (1990). *Kerameikos XII: Die Eckterrasse an der Gräberstraße des Kerameikos*. Berlin.

Kovaleinen, A. (2004). 'Rethinking the revival of social capital and trust in social theory: possibilities for feminist analyses of social capital and trust', in B. L. Marshall and A. M. Witz (eds.), *Engendering the Social: Feminist Encounters with Sociological Theory*. Maidenhead and New York, 155–70.

Krishna, A. (ed.) (2008). *Poverty, Participation, and Democracy: A Global Perspective*. New York.

Kron, G. (2005). 'Anthropometry, physical anthropology, and the reconstruction of ancient health nutrition and living standards', *Historia* 54: 68–83.

Kron, G. (2011). 'The distribution of wealth in Athens in comparative perspective', *Zeitschrift für Papyrologie und Epigraphik* 179: 129–38.

Kron, G. (2012). 'Nutrition, hygiene and mortality: setting parameters for Roman life expectancy consistent with our comparative evidence', in E. Lo Cascio (ed.), *L'impatto della 'peste antonina'*. Bari, 193–252.

Kron, G. (2014). 'Comparative evidence and the reconstruction of the ancient economy: Greco-Roman housing and the level and distribution of wealth and income', in F. de Callataÿ (ed.), *Quantifying the Greco-Roman Economy and Beyond*. Bari, 123–46.

Kusmer, K. L. (2001). *Down and Out, On the Road: The Homeless in American History*. Oxford.

Kwok, C. S. and Keenleyside, A. (2015). 'Stable isotope evidence for infant feeding practices in the Greek colony of Apollonia Pontica', in A. Papathanasiou, M. P. Richards, and S. C. Fox (eds.), *Archaeodiet in the Greek World: Dietary Reconstruction from Stable Isotope Analysis* (Hesperia Supplement 49). Princeton, 119–45.

Lacey, W. K. (1980). 'The family of Euxitheus (Demosthenes LVII)', *Classical Quarterly* 30: 57–61.

Laderchi, C. R., Saith, R., and Stewart, F. (2003). 'Does it matter that we do not agree on the definition of poverty? A comparison of four approaches', *Oxford Development Studies* 31.3: 243–74.

Laes, C. (2011). 'Midwives in Greek inscriptions in hellenistic and Roman antiquity', *Zeitschrift für Papyrologie und Epigraphik* 176: 154–62.

Lagia, A. (2007a). 'Notions of childhood in the classical polis: evidence from the bioarchaeological record', in A. Cohen and J. B. Rutter (eds.), *Constructions of Childhood in Ancient Greece and Italy*. Princeton, 293–306.

Lagia, A. (2007b). 'The human skeletal remains', in F. Ruppenstein (ed.), *Kerameikos XVIII: Die submykenische Nekropole: Neufunde und Neuberwertung*. Berlin, 273–81.

Lagia, A. (2014). 'Health inequalities in the classical city: a biocultural approach to socioeconomic differentials in the polis of Athens during the classical, hellenistic, and imperial Roman periods', in A.-C. Gillis (ed.), *Corps, travail et statut social. L'apport de la paléoanthropologie funéraire aux sciences historiques*. Lille, 95–115.

Lagia, A. (2015a). 'Diet and the polis: an isotopic study of diet in Athens and Laurion during the classical, hellenistic, and early Roman periods', in A. Papathanasiou, M. P. Richards, and S. C. Fox (eds.), *Archaeodiet in the Greek World: Dietary Reconstruction from Stable Isotope Analysis* (Hesperia Supplement 49). Princeton, 119–45.

Lagia, A. (2015b). 'The potential and limitations of bioarchaeological investigations in classical contexts: an example from the polis in Athens', in D. C. Haggis and C. M. Antonaccio (eds.), *Classical Archaeology in Context: Theory and Practice in Excavation in the Greek World*. Berlin, 149–76.

Lambert, S. D. (1997). *Rationes Centesimarum. Sales of Public Land in Lykourgan Athens*. Amsterdam.

Lambert, S. D. (1998). *The Phratries of Attica*, 2nd edn. Ann Arbor.

Lambert, S. D. (2002a). 'The sacrificial calendar of Athens', *Annual of the British School at Athens* 97: 353–99.

Lambert, S. D. (2002b). 'Fish, low fares and *IG* II^2 283', *Zeitschrift für Papyrologie und Epigraphik* 140: 73–9.

Langdon, M. (1985). 'Hymettiana I', *Hesperia* 54: 257–70.

Langdon, M. (2004). 'Hymettiana V: A willing *katapygon*', *Zeitschrift für Papyrologie und Epigraphik* 148: 201–6.

Langdon, M. (2005). 'A new Greek abecedarium', *Kadmos* 44: 175–82.

Langdon, M. and Watrous, L. V. (1977). 'The farm of Timesios: rock-cut inscriptions in south Attica', *Hesperia* 46: 162–77.

Lape, S. (2004). *Reproducing Athens: Menander's Comedy, Democratic Culture, and the Hellenistic City*. Princeton.

Laskaris, J. (2008). 'Nursing mothers in Greek and Roman medicine', *American Journal of Archaeology* 112: 459–64.

Lauffer, S. (1979). *Die Bergwerkssklaven von Laureion*. Wiesbaden.

Leader, R. E. (1997). 'In death not divided: gender, family and state on classical Athenian grave stelae', *American Journal of Archaeology* 101: 683–99.

Lenfant, D. (2013). 'Intégrés ou dénoncés: la place faite aux pauvres dans les discours grecs sur la démocratie', *Ktema* 38: 37–51.

Lévy, E. (1997). 'Richesse et pauvreté dans le Ploutos', *Ktema* 22: 201–12.

Liddel, P. (2007). *Civic Obligation and Individual Liberty in Ancient Athens*. Oxford.

Lister, R. (2004). *Poverty*. London.

Livi-Bacci, M. (1991). *Population and Nutrition: An Essay on European Demographic History*. Cambridge.

Lohmann, H. (1992). 'Agriculture and country life in classical Attica', in B. Wells (ed.), *Agriculture in Ancient Greece: Proceedings of the Seventh International Symposium at the Swedish Institute at Athens, 16–17th May 1990*. Stockholm, 29–60.

Lohmann, H. (1993). *Atene. Forschungen zu Siedlungs- und Wirtschaftsstruktur des klassischen Attika*. Cologne and Vienna.

Löhr, C. (2000). *Griechische Familienweihungen: Untersuchungen einer Repräsentationsform von ihre Anfängen bis zum Ende des 4. Jhs. v. Chr.* Rahden/Westf.

Loizos, P. (2000). 'Are refugees social capitalists?', in S. Baron, J. Field, and T. Schuller (eds.), *Social Capital. Critical Perspectives*. Oxford, 124–41.

Loomis, W. T. (1998). *Wages, Welfare Costs and Inflation in Classical Athens*. Ann Arbor.

Loraux, N. (2002). *The Divided City: On Memory and Forgetting in Ancient Athens*. New York.

Lowndes, V. (2000). 'Women and social capital: a comment on Hall's "Social Capital in Britain"', *British Journal of Political Science* 30: 533–7.

Lupu, E. (2001). 'The sacred law from the Cave of Pan at Marathon (*SEG* 36 267)', *Zeitschrift für Papyrologie und Epigraphik* 137: 119–24.

MacDowell, D. M. (1986). 'The law of Periandros about symmories', *Classical Quarterly* 36: 438–49.

MacKinnon, M. (2014). 'Animals, economics, and culture in the Athenian Agora: comparative zooarchaeological investigations', *Hesperia* 83.2: 189–255.

Marchiandi, D. (2011). *I periboli funerari nell'Attica classica: lo specchio di una 'borghesia'*. Athens.

Markle, M. M. (1985). 'Jury pay and Assembly pay at Athens', in P. Cartledge and F. D. Harvey (eds.), *Crux: Essays Presented to G. E. M. de Ste Croix on his 75th Birthday*. London and Exeter, 265–97.

Markle, M. M. (1990). 'Participation of farmers in Athenian juries and assemblies', *Ancient Society* 21: 149–65.

Martin, R. (2001). 'Just like a woman: enigmas of the lyric voice', in A. P. M. H. Lardinois and L. McClure (eds.), *Making Silence Speak: Women's Voices in Greek Literature and Society*. Princeton, 55–74.

Masciadri, M. M. and Montevecchi, O. (1984). *I contratti di baliatico*. Milan.

Masson, O. (1961). *Les inscriptions chypriotes syllabiques; recueil critique et commenté*. Paris.

Mastronarde, D. J. (2010). *The Art of Euripides: Dramatic Technique and Social Context*. Cambridge.

Mattingly, H. B. (1996). *The Athenian Empire Restored: Epigraphic and Historical Studies*. Ann Arbor.

Menon, N. (2002). 'Universalism without foundations?', *Economy and Society* 31.1: 152–69.

Meyer, E. A. (1993). 'Epitaphs and citizenship in classical Athens', *Journal of Hellenic Studies* 113: 99–121.

Meyer, E. A. (2010). *Metics and the Athenian Phialai-Inscriptions: A Study in Athenian Epigraphy and Law*. Stuttgart.

Meyer, M. (1989). 'Exkurs zum Grabrelief des Sosinos', *Mitteilungen des Deutschen Archäologischen Instituts, Athenische Abteilung* 104: 79–82.

Mikalson, J. D. (1998). *Religion in Hellenistic Athens*. Berkeley.

Milanovic, B. (2006). 'An estimate of average income and inequality in Byzantium around year 1000', *Review of Income and Wealth* 52: 449–70.

Milanovic, B., Lindert, P. H., and Williamson, J. G. (2011). 'Pre-industrial inequality', *Economic Journal* 121: 255–72.

Millett, P. (1989). 'Patronage and its avoidance in classical Athens', in A. Wallace-Hadrill (ed.), *Patronage in Ancient Society*. London, 15–48.

Millett, P. (1991). *Lending and Borrowing in Ancient Athens*. Cambridge.

Misturelli, F. and Heffernan, C. (2010). 'The concept of poverty: a synchronic perspective', *Progress in Development Studies* 10: 35–58.

Mitsopoulos-Leon, V. (2009). *Vrauron: die Tonstatuetten aus dem Heiligtum der Artemis Brauronia: die frühen Statuetten 7. bis 5. Jh. v. Chr.* Athens.

Molyneux, M. (2002). 'Gender and the silences of social capital: lessons from Latin America', *Development and Change* 33: 167–8.

Moreno, A. (2007). *Feeding the Democracy: The Athenian Grain Supply in the Fifth and Fourth Centuries BC*. Oxford.

Morgan, J. (2010). *The Classical Greek House*. Exeter.

Morley, N. (2006). 'The poor in the city of Rome', in M. Atkins and R. Osborne (eds.), *Poverty in the Roman World*. Cambridge, 21–39.

Morley, N. (2011). 'Demography and development in classical antiquity', in C. Holleran and A. Pudsey (eds.), *Demography and the Graeco-Roman World: New Insights and Approaches*. Cambridge, 39–83.

Morley, N. (2014). 'Orders of magnitude, margins of error', in F. de Callataÿ (ed.), *Quantifying the Greco-Roman Economy and Beyond*. Bari, 29–42.

Morris, I. (1992). *Death-Ritual and Social Structure in Classical Antiquity*. Cambridge.

Morris, I. (1996). 'The strong principle of equality and the archaic origins of Greek democracy', in J. Ober and C. Hedrick (eds.), *Demokratia: A Conversation on Democracies Ancient and Modern*. Princeton, 19–48.

Morris, I. (2000). *Archaeology as Cultural History: Words and Things in Iron Age Greece*. Oxford.

Morris, I. (2004). 'Economic growth in ancient Greece', *Journal of Institutional and Theoretical Economics* 160: 709–42.

Morris, I. (2005). 'Archaeology, standards of living, and Greek economic history', in J. G. Manning and I. Morris (eds.), *The Ancient Economy: Evidence and Models*. Stanford, 91–126.

Morris, I. (2011). 'Archaeology and Greek slavery', in K. Bradley and P. Cartledge (eds.), *The Cambridge World History of Slavery. Vol. 1: The Ancient Mediterranean World*. Cambridge, 176–93.

Morris, I. (2014). *War! What is it Good For? Conflict and the Progress of Civilization from Primates to Robots*. New York.

Morris, S. P. and Papadopoulos, J. K. (2005). 'Greek towers and slaves: an archaeology of exploitation', *American Journal of Archaeology* 109: 155–225.

Mussche, H. F. (1974). *Thorikos: A Guide to the Excavations*. Brussels.

Mussche, H. F. (1998). *Thorikos: A Mining Town in Ancient Attica*. Ghent.

Mussche, H. F., Bingen, J., Jones, J. E., and Waelkens, M. (1990). *Thorikos IX. 1977/1982*. Ghent.

Narayan, D., Patel, R., Schafft, K., Rademacher, A., and Kock-Schulte, S. (2000). *Voices of the Poor*: vol. 1, *Can Anyone Hear Us?* New York.

Nelson, F. (2014). '*Benefits Street*: the real scandal', *Daily Telegraph*, 17 January.

Nevett, L. C. (2000). 'A real estate "market" in classical Greece? The example of town housing', *Annual of the British School at Athens* 95: 329–44.

Nielsen, T. H., Bjertrup, L., Hansen, M. H., Rubinstein, L., and Vestergaard, T. (1989). 'Athenian grave monuments and social-class', *Greek, Roman and Byzantine Studies* 30: 411–20.

Nussbaum, M. C. (1988). 'Nature, function, and capability: Aristotle on political distribution', in J. Annas and R. Grimm (eds.), *Oxford Studies in Ancient Philosophy Supplementary Volume*. Oxford, 173–84.

Nussbaum, M. C. (2000a). 'Aristotle, politics, and human capabilities: a response to Antony, Arneson, Charlesworth, and Mulgan', *Ethics* 111: 102–40.

Nussbaum, M. C. (2000b). *Women and Human Development: The Capabilities Approach*. Cambridge.

Nussbaum, M. C. (2003). 'Capabilities and fundamental entitlements: Sen and social justice', *Feminist Economics* 9: 33–59.

Ober, J. (1989). *Mass and Elite in Democratic Athens: Rhetoric, Ideology, and the Power of the People*. Princeton.

Ober, J. (1998). 'Revolution matters: democracy as demotic action. (A response to Kurt A. Raaflaub)', in I. Morris and K. Raaflaub (eds.), *Democracy 2500? Questions and Challenges*. Dubuque, 67–86.

Ober, J. (2008). *Democracy and Knowledge: Innovation and Learning in Classical Athens*. Princeton.

Ober, J. (2010). 'Wealthy Hellas', *Transactions of the American Philological Association* 140: 241–86.

Ober, J. (2014). 'Greek economic performance, 800–300 BCE: a comparison case', in F. de Callataÿ (ed.), *Quantifying the Greco-Roman Economy and Beyond*. Bari, 103–22.

Ober, J. (2015). *The Rise and Fall of Classical Greece*. Princeton.

Ogilvie, S., Küpker, M., and Maegraith, J. (2012). 'Household debt in early modern Germany: evidence from personal inventories', *Journal of Economic History* 72.01: 134–67.

Oikonomakou, M. (1993). '*Ὅρος προικώου ἀποτιμήματος*', *Archaiologike Ephemeris* 132: 211–14.

Oikonomakou, M. (1997). '*Ανασκαφικές Εργασίες: Λαυρεωτική*', *Archaiologikon Deltion* 52: 84–90.

Oikonomakou, M. (1998). '*Ανασκαφικές Εργασίες: Λαυρεωτική*', *Archaiologikon Deltion* 53: 83–4.

Oikonomakou, M. (2001a). '*Ανασκαφικές Εργασίες* 2001–2004: *Λαυρεωτική*', *Archaiologikon Deltion* 56–59: 356–67.

Oikonomakou, M. (2001b). '*Ανασκαφικές Εργασίες* 2001–2004: *Μαραθώνας*', *Archaiologikon Deltion* 56–59: 372–88.

Oikonomakou, M. (2004). '*Οἱ ἀνασκαφὲς στὸ Μεγάλο Ἕλος τοῦ Μαραθῶνος*', *Archaiologike Ephemeris* 143: 81–177.

Oliver, G. J. (2000). 'Athenian funerary monuments: style, grandeur, and cost', in G. J. Oliver (ed.), *The Epigraphy of Death: Studies in the History and Society of Greece and Rome*. Liverpool, 59–80.

Oliver, G. J. (2007). *War, Food, and Politics in Early Hellenistic Athens*. Oxford.

Olson, S. (1990). 'Economics and ideology in Aristophanes' *Wealth*', *Harvard Studies in Classical Philology* 93: 223–42.

O'Neill, B. and Gidengil, E. (eds.) (2006). *Gender and Social Capital*. New York.

Orser, C. E. (2011a). 'Beneath the surface of tenement life: the dialectics of race and poverty during America's First Gilded Age', *Historical Archaeology* 45.3: 151–65.

Orser, C. E. (2011b). 'The archaeology of poverty and the poverty of archaeology', *International Journal of Historical Archaeology* 15.4: 533–43.

Osberg, L. and Xu, K. (1999). 'Poverty intensity: how well do Canadian Provinces compare?', *Canadian Public Policy /Analyse de Politiques* 25.2: 179–95.

Osberg, L. and Xu, K. (2000). 'International comparisons of poverty intensity: index decomposition and bootstrap inference', *Journal of Human Resources* 35.1: 51–81.

Osborne, M. (1981). *Naturalization in Athens*. Brussels.

Osborne, R. (1985). *Demos: The Discovery of Classical Attika*. Cambridge.

Osborne, R. (1988). 'Social and economic implications of the leasing of land and property in classical and hellenistic Greece', *Chiron* 18: 225–70.

Osborne, R. (1991). 'The potential mobility of human populations', *Oxford Journal of Archaeology* 10: 231–52.

Osborne, R. (1992). '"Is it a farm?" The definition of agricultural sites and settlements in ancient Greece', in B. Wells (ed.), *Agriculture in Ancient Greece: Proceedings of the Seventh International Symposium at the Swedish Institute at Athens, 16–17th May 1990*. Stockholm, 21–7.

Osborne, R. (2011). *The History Written on the Classical Greek Body*. Cambridge.

Pache, C. O. (2001). 'Barbarian bond: Thracian Bendis among the Athenians', in S. R. Asirvatham, C. O. Pache, and J. Watrous (eds.), *Between Magic and Religion: Interdisciplinary Studies in Ancient Mediterranean Religion and Society*. Lanham, 3–11.

Papademitriou, I. (1957). '*Ὁ θεῖος τοῦ Αἰσχίνου Κλεόβουλος ὁ μάντις*', *Platon* 9: 154–63.

Papagrigorakis, M. J., Yapijakis, C., Synodinos, P. N., and Batziotopoulou-Valavani, E. (2006). 'DNA examination of ancient dental pulp incriminates typhoid fever as a probable cause of the Plague of Athens', *International Journal of Infectious Diseases* 10: 206–14.

Papazarkadas, N. (2011). *Sacred and Public Land in Ancient Athens*. Oxford.

Parker Pearson, M. (1982). 'Mortuary practices, society and ideology: an ethnoarchaeological study', in I. Hodder (ed.), *Symbolic and Structural Archaeology*. Cambridge, 99–113.

Parker, R. (1996). *Athenian Religion: A History*. Oxford.

Parker, R. (2005). *Polytheism and Society at Athens*. Oxford.

Parker, R. (2010). 'New problems in Athenian religion: the "Sacred Law" from Aixone', in J. Dijkstra, J. Kroeson, and Y. Kuiper (eds.), *Myths, Martyrs, and Modernity: Studies in the History of Religions in Honour of Jan N. Bremmer*. Leiden, 193–208.

Parkin, A. (2006). '"You do him no service": an exploration of pagan almsgiving', in M. Atkins and R. Osborne (eds.), *Poverty in the Roman World*. Cambridge, 60–82.

Parlama, L. and Stampolidis, N. C. (2000). *Athens: The City Beneath the City. Antiquities from the Metropolitan Railway Excavations*. Athens.

Patlagean, E. (1977). *Pauvreté économique et pauvreté sociale à Byzance, 4e–7e siècles*. Paris.

Patlagean, E. (1997). 'The poor', in G. Cavallo (ed.), *The Byzantines*. Chicago, 15–42.

Patterson, C. (1981). *Pericles' Citizenship Law of 451/0 BC*. New York.

Patterson, C. (1998). *The Family in Greek History*. Cambridge.

Patterson, O. (1982). *Slavery and Social Death*. Cambridge.

Pébarthe, C. (2014). 'Les sophistes, les philosophes et la pauvreté', in E. Galbois and S. Rougier-Blanc (eds.), *La pauvreté en Grèce ancienne: Formes, représentations, enjeux*. Bordeaux, 223–36.

Perdrizet, P. P. (1889). 'Mèn', *Bulletin de correspondance hellénique* 20: 55–106.

Petritaki, M. (1997). '*Πειραιάς*', *Archaiologikon Deltion* 52: 71–82.

Pfisterer-Haas, S. (1989). *Darstellungen alter Frauen in der griechischen Kunst*. Frankfurt.

Piketty, T. (2014). *Capital in the Twenty-First Century*. Cambridge.

Pipili, M. (2000). 'Wearing the other hat: workmen in town and country', in B. Cohen (ed.), *Not the Classical Ideal: Athens and the Construction of the Other in Greek Art*. Leiden, 150–79.

Planeaux, C. (2000). 'The date of Bendis' entry into Attica', *Classical Journal* 96: 165–92.

Platonos-Giota, M. (2004). *Αχαρναί: ιστορική και τοπογραφική επισκόπηση των αρχαίων Αχαρνών, των γειτονικών δήμων και των οχυρώσεων της Πάρνηθας*. Athens.

Podes, S. (1993). 'Pay and political participation in classical Athens: an empirical application of rational choice theory', *Journal of Institutional and Theoretical Economics* 149: 495–515.

Podes, S. (1995). 'Bezahlung für politische Partizipation im klassichen Athen. Die Diäten als sozialstaatliche Institution?', *Ancient Society* 26: 5–25.

Pomeroy, S. (1977). 'Technikai kai mousikai', *American Journal of Ancient History* 2: 58–60.

Pomeroy, S. (1978). 'Plato and the female physician (*Republic* 454d2)', *American Journal of Philology* 99: 496–500.

Portes, A. (1998). 'Social capital: its origins and applications in modern sociology', *Annual Review of Sociology* 24: 1–24.
Pritchard, D. M. (2013). 'The public payment of magistrates in fourth-century Athens', *Greek, Roman, and Byzantine Studies* 54.1: 1–16.
Pritchett, W. K. (1953). 'The Attic Stelai: I', *Hesperia* 22: 225–99.
Pritchett, W. K. (1956). 'The Attic Stelai II', *Hesperia* 25: 178–328.
Putnam, R. D. (1993). *Making Democracy Work: Civic Traditions in Modern Italy*. Princeton.
Putnam, R. D. (2000). *Bowling Alone: The Collapse and Revival of American Community*. New York.
Raaflaub, K. A. (1996). 'Equalities and inequalities in Athenian democracy', in J. Ober and C. Hedrick (eds.), *Demokratia. A Conversation on Democracies, Ancient and Modern*. Princeton, 139–74.
Raffeiner, H. (1977). *Sklaven und Freigelassene: eine soziologische Studie auf der Grundlage des griechischen Grabepigramms*. Innsbruck.
Randall, R. H. (1953). 'The Erechtheum workmen', *American Journal of Archaeology* 57: 199–210.
Rathbone, D. (2009). 'Earnings and costs: living standards and the Roman economy', in A. K. Bowman and A. Wilson (eds.), *Quantifying the Roman Economy: Methods and Problems*. Oxford, 299–326.
Raubitschek, A. E. (1949). *Dedications on the Athenian Acropolis*. London.
Razavi, S. (1999). 'Gendered poverty and well-being: introduction', *Development and Change* 30: 409–33.
Rhodes, P. J. (1982). 'Problems in Athenian *eisphora* and liturgies', *American Journal of Ancient History* 7: 1–19.
Rhodes, P. J. (1993). *A Commentary on the Aristotelian 'Athenaion Politeia'*. Oxford.
Rhodes, P. J. (2008). 'After the three-bar "sigma" controversy: the history of Athenian imperialism reassessed', *Classical Quarterly* 58: 500–6.
Richard, F. G. (2011). 'Materializing poverty: archaeological reflections from the postcolony', *Historical Archaeology* 45.3: 166–82.
Rihll, T. (2010). 'Skilled slaves and the economy: the silver mines of Laurion', in H. Heinen (ed.), *Antike Sklaverei: Rückblick und Ausblick. Neue Beiträge zur Forschungsgeschichte und zur Erschließung der Archäologischen Zeugnisse*. Stuttgart, 203–20.
Roberts, J. T. (1983). *Accountability in Athenian Government*. Madison.
Robertson, M. (1975). *A History of Greek Art*. Cambridge.
Robertson, N. (1983). 'Greek ritual begging in aid of women's fertility and childbirth', *Transactions of the American Philological Association* 113: 143–69.
Robeyns, I. (2005). 'The capability approach: a theoretical framework', *Journal of Human Development* 6: 93–114.

Roselli, D. K. (2005). 'Vegetable-hawking mom and fortunate son: Euripides, tragic style, and reception', *Phoenix* 59: 1–49.

Roselli, D. K. (2009). '*Theorika* in fifth-century Athens', *Greek, Roman and Byzantine Studies* 49: 5–30.

Rosenbloom, D. S. (2002). 'From *poneros* to *pharmakos*: theater, social drama and revolution at Athens', *Classical Antiquity* 21: 283–346.

Rosenbloom, D. S. (2004a). '*Poneroi* vs. *chrestoi*: the ostracism of Hyperbolos and the struggle for hegemony in Athens after the death of Perikles, Part 1', *Transactions of the American Philological Association* 134: 55–105.

Rosenbloom, D. S. (2004b). '*Poneroi* vs. *chrestoi*: the ostracism of Hyperbolos and the struggle for hegemony in Athens after the death of Perikles, Part 2', *Transactions of the American Philological Association* 134: 323–58.

Rosen, R. M. (2012). 'Timocles fr. 6 K-A and the parody of Greek literary theory', in C. W. Marshall and G. Kovacs (eds.), *No Laughing Matter: Studies in Athenian Comedy*. London, 177–86.

Rosivach, V. J. (1989). '*Talasiourgoi* and *paidia* in *IG* II^2 1553–78: a note on Athenian social history', *Historia* 38: 365–70.

Rosivach, V. J. (1991). 'Some Athenian presuppositions about "the poor"', *Greece and Rome* 38: 189–98.

Rosivach, V. J. (1994). *The System of Public Sacrifice in Fourth-Century Athens*. Atlanta.

Rosivach, V. J. (2002a). '*Zeugitai* and hoplites', *Ancient History Bulletin* 16: 33–43.

Rosivach, V. J. (2002b). 'The requirements for the Solonic classes in Aristotle, *AP* 7.4', *Hermes* 130: 36–47.

Rosivach, V. J. (2011). 'State pay as war relief in Peloponnesian-War Athens', *Greece and Rome* 58: 176–83.

Rosivach, V. J. (2012). 'The meaning of ζευγίτης', *Classical Philology* 107.2: 146–50.

Rotroff, S. I. (1997). *The Athenian Agora XXIX: Hellenistic Pottery: Athenian and Imported Wheelmade Table Ware and Related Material*. Part 1: Text, Part 2: Illustrations. Princeton.

Roubineau, J.-M. (2010). 'Sources littéraires et histoire sociale: être riche, être pauvre selon Xénophon', in L. Capdetrey and Y. Lafond (eds.), *La cité et ses élites. Pratiques et représentation des formes de domination et de contrôle social dans les cités grecques*. Bordeaux, 211–24.

Roubineau, J.-M. (2012). 'La cité égoïste? Cité athénienne et action sociale', in K. Konuk (ed.), *Stephanèphoros. De l'économie antique à l'asie mineure. Hommages à Raymond Descat*. Bordeaux, 165–78.

Roubineau, J.-M. (2013). 'Mendicité, déchéance et indignité sociale dans les cités grecques', *Ktema* 38: 15–36.

Roubineau, J.-M. (2014). 'Pauvreté, rationalité économique et abandon d'enfants dans les cités grecques', in E. Galbois and S. Rougier-Blanc (eds.), *La pauvreté en Grèce ancienne: Formes, représentations, enjeux*. Bordeaux, 145–64.

Rougier-Blanc, S. (2014). 'Architecture et/ou espaces de la pauvreté? Habitats modestes, cabanes et "squats" en Grèce ancienne', in E. Galbois and S. Rougier-Blanc (eds.), *La pauvreté en Grèce ancienne: Formes, représentations, enjeux*. Bordeaux, 105–35.

Rowlandson, J. (1998). *Women and Society in Greek and Roman Egypt: A Sourcebook*. Cambridge.

Rubinstein, L. (1993). *Adoption in Fourth-Century Athens*. Copenhagen.

Rubinstein, L. (2013). 'Evoking anger through pity: portraits of the vulnerable and defenceless in Attic oratory', in P. Ducrey and A. Chaniotis (eds.), *Unveiling Emotions II: Emotions in Greece and Rome: Texts, Images, Material Culture*. Stuttgart, 135–65.

Runnels, C. N. (1981). 'A diachronic study and economic analysis of millstones from the Argolid, Greece', unpublished PhD thesis, Indiana University.

Ruschenbusch, E. (1978). 'Die athenischen Symmorien des 4. Jh v. Chr.' *Zeitschrift für Papyrologie und Epigraphik* 31: 275–84.

Sallares, R. (1991). *The Ecology of the Ancient Greek World*. London.

Saller, R. (2005). 'Framing the debate over economic growth in the ancient economy', in J. G. Manning and I. Morris (eds.), *The Ancient Economy. Evidence and Models*. Stanford, 223–38.

Salliora-Oikonomakou, M. (1985). '*Αρχαίο νεκροταφείο στην περιοχή Λαυρίου*', *Archaiologikon Deltion* 40: 90–132.

Salliora-Oikonomakou, M. (1996). '*Δύο αρχαία εργαστήρια στην περιοχή του Θορικού*', *Archaiologikon Deltion* 51–52: 125–40.

Salliora-Oikonomakou, M. (2004). *Ο αρχαίος Δήμος του Σουνίου. Ιστορική και τοπογραφική επισκόπηση*. Athens.

Salzmann, D. (1982). *Untersuchungen zu den antiken Kieselmosaiken: von den Anfängen bis zum Beginn der Tesseratechnik*. Berlin.

Schaps, D. M. (1977). 'The woman least mentioned: etiquette and women's names', *Classical Quarterly* 27.2: 323–30.

Scheidel, W. (1995). 'The most silent women of Greece and Rome: rural labour and women's life in the ancient world. Part 1', *Greece and Rome* 42: 202–17.

Scheidel, W. (1996). 'The most silent women of Greece and Rome: rural labour and women's life in the ancient world. Part 2', *Greece and Rome* 43: 1–10.

Scheidel, W. (1999). 'Emperors, aristocrats, and the Grim Reaper: towards a demographic profile of the Roman elite', *Classical Quarterly* 49: 254–81.

Scheidel, W. (2009). 'New ways of studying incomes in the Roman economy', in A. K. Bowman and A. Wilson (eds.), *Quantifying the Roman Economy: Methods and Problems*. Oxford, 346–52.

Scheidel, W. (2010). 'Real wages in early economies: evidence for living standards from 1800 BCE to 1300 CE', *Journal of the Economic and Social History of the Orient* 53: 425–62.

Scheidel, W. and Friesen, S. J. (2009). 'The size of the economy and the distribution of income in the Roman Empire', *Journal of Roman Studies* 99: 61–91.

Scholl, A. (1994). '*Πολυτάλαντα μνημεῖα*: Zur literarischen und monumentalen Überlieferung aufwendiger Grabmäler im spätklassichen Athen', *Jahrbuch des Deutschen Archäologischen Instituts* 109: 239–71.

Scholl, A. (1996). *Die attischen Bildfeldstelen des 4. Jhs. v. Chr. Untersuchungen zu den kleinformatigen Grabreliefs im spätklassichen Athen*. Berlin.

Schörner, G. and Goette, H. R. (2004). *Die Pan-Grotte von Vari*. Mainz.

Schulze, H. (1988). *Ammen und Pädagogen. Sklavinnen und Sklaven als Erzieher in der antiken Kunst und Gesellschaft*. Mainz.

Schumacher, L. (2001). *Sklaverei in der Antike: Alltag und Schicksal der Unfreien*. Munich.

Scott, J. (1994). *Poverty and Wealth: Citizenship, Deprivation and Privilege*. London.

Sears, M. A. (2013). *Athens, Thrace, and the Shaping of Athenian Leadership*. Cambridge.

Sen, A. (1973). *On Economic Inequality*. Oxford.

Sen, A. (1976). 'Poverty: an ordinal approach to measurement', *Econometrica* 44.2: 219–31.

Sen, A. (1987). *The Standard of Living: The Tanner Lectures, Clare Hall, Cambridge, 1985*. Cambridge.

Sen, A. (1991). 'Capability and well-being', in M. Nussbaum and A. Sen (eds.), *The Quality of Life*. Oxford, 30–53.

Sen, A. (1999a). *Commodities and Capabilities*. Oxford.

Sen, A. (1999b). *Development as Freedom*. New York.

Sen, A. (2000). *Social Exclusion: Concept, Application, Scrutiny*. Manila.

Shapiro, B., Rambaut, A., and Gilbert, M. T. P. (2006). 'No proof that typhoid caused the Plague of Athens (a reply to Papagrigorakis et al.)', *International Journal of Infectious Diseases* 10.4: 334–5.

Shear Jr., T. L. (1973). 'The Athenian Agora: excavations of 1971', *Hesperia* 42: 121–79.

Shipton, K. (2000). *Leasing and Lending: The Cash Economy in Fourth-Century BC Athens*. London.

Silver, H. (1994). 'Social exclusion and social solidarity: three paradigms', *International Labour Review* 133.5/6: 531.

Simms, R. R. (1988). 'The cult of the Thracian goddess Bendis in Athens and Attica', *Ancient World* 18: 59–76.

Sinclair, R. K. (1988). *Democracy and Participation in Athens*. Cambridge.

Sklavos, M., Tselepe, E., Anetakis, M., and Markou, S. (2009). '*Αγροικίες και άλλα οικοδομικά συγκροτήματα στη Μερέντα*', in V. Vasilopoulou and S. Katsarou-Tzeveleke (eds.), *Από τα Μεσόγεια στον Αργοσαρωνικό: Β' Εφορεία Προϊστορικών και Κλασικών Αρχαιοτήτων. Το έργο μιας δεκαετίας, 1994–2003*. Markopoulou, 79–92.

Sobak, R. (2015). 'Sokrates among the shoemakers', *Hesperia* 84.4: 669–712.

Sommerstein, A. H. (1984). 'Aristophanes and the demon poverty', *Classical Quarterly* 34: 314–33.

Sommerstein, A. H. (2001). *The Comedies of Aristophanes*, Vol. 11: *Wealth*. Warminster.

Sommerstein, A. H. (2005). *The Comedies of Aristophanes*, Vol. 5: *Peace*. Warminster.

Spencer-Wood, S. M. (2011). 'Commentary: how feminist theory increases our understanding of the archaeology of poverty', *Historical Archaeology* 45.3: 183–93.

Stager, J. M. S. (2005). '"Let no one wonder at this image": a Phoenician funerary stele in Athens', *Hesperia* 74: 427–49.

Stanton, G. R. (1996). 'Some inscriptions in Attic demes', *Annual of the British School at Athens* 91: 341–64.

Stears, K. (2000). 'The times they are a'changing: developments in fifth-century funerary sculpture', in G. J. Oliver (ed.), *The Epigraphy of Death: Studies in the History and Society of Greece and Rome*. Liverpool, 25–58.

Ste. Croix, G. E. M. de (1953). 'Demosthenes' *τίμημα* and the Athenian *eisphora* in the fourth century BC', *Classica et Mediaevalia* 14: 30–70.

Ste. Croix, G. E. M. de (1954). 'The character of the Athenian empire', *Historia* 3: 1–41.

Ste. Croix, G. E. M. de (1970). 'Some observations on the property rights of Athenian women', *Classical Review* 20: 273–8.

Ste. Croix, G. E. M. de (1981). *The Class Struggle in the Ancient Greek World from the Archaic Age to the Arab Conquests*. London.

Ste. Croix, G. E. M. de (2004). 'The Solonian census classes and the qualifications for cavalry and hoplite service', in D. Harvey and R. Parker (eds.), *Athenian Democratic Origins and Other Essays*. Oxford, 5–72.

Steinhauer, G. (1994). '*Παρατηρήσεις στην οικιστική μορφή των αττικών δήμων*', in W. D. E. Coulson, O. Palagia, T. L. Shear Jr, H. A. Shapiro, and F. J. Frost (eds.), *The Archaeology of Athens and Attica under the Democracy*. Oxford, 175–89.

Stekel, R. H. (2005). 'Health and nutrition in the pre-industrial era: insights from a millennium of average heights in Northern Europe', in R. C. Allen, T. Bengtsson, and M. Dribe (eds.), *Living Standards in the Past, New Perspectives on Well-Being in Asia and Europe*. Oxford, 227–53.

Stewart, A. and Gray, C. (2000). 'Confronting the Other: childbirth, aging and death on an Attic tombstone at Harvard', in B. Cohen (ed.), *Not the*

Classical Ideal: Athens and the Construction of the Other in Greek Art. Leiden, 248–74.

Stewart, F. (2005). 'Groups and capabilities', *Journal of Human Development* 6: 185–204.

Strauss, B. (1986). *Athens After the Peloponnesian War: Class, Faction and Policy 403–386 BC*. London.

Strauss, B. (1996). 'The Athenian trireme, school of democracy', in J. Ober and C. Hedrick (eds.), *Demokratia: A Conversation on Democracies, Ancient and Modern*. Princeton, 313–26.

Stroszeck, J. (2014). 'Water management in classical Athens: cisterns of the classical bathhouse on the Kerameikos road in front of the Dipylon.', in I. K. Kalavroutsiotis and A. N. Angelakis (eds.), *International Water Association Regional Symposium on Water, Wastewater and Environment: Traditions and Culture. Patras (Greece), 22–24 March 2014*. Patras, 499–507.

Stroud, R. (1998). *The Athenian Grain-Tax Law of 374/3 BC* (Hesperia Supplement 29). Princeton.

Sumner, A. (2004). 'Epistemology and "evidence" in development studies: a review of Dollar and Kraay', *Third World Quarterly* 25.6: 1167–77.

Tarlow, S. (1999). *Bereavement and Commemoration: An Archaeology of Mortality*. Oxford.

Tarrant, H. (1988). 'Midwifery and *The Clouds*', *Classical Quarterly* 38: 116–22.

Taylor, C. (2007a). 'A new political world', in R. Osborne (ed.), *Debating the Athenian Cultural Revolution*. Cambridge, 72–90.

Taylor, C. (2007b). 'From the whole citizen body? The sociology of election and lot in the Athenian democracy', *Hesperia* 76: 323–45.

Taylor, C. (2011a). 'Graffiti and the epigraphic habit: creating communities and writing alternate histories in classical Attica', in J. A. Baird and C. Taylor (eds.), *Ancient Graffiti in Context*. London, 90–109.

Taylor, C. (2011b). 'Migration and the demes of Attica', in C. Holleran and A. Pudsey (eds.), *Demography and the Graeco-Roman World: New Insights and Approaches*. Cambridge, 117–34.

Taylor, C. (2011c). 'Women's social networks and female friendship in the Greek city', *Gender & History* 23: 704–21.

Taylor, C. (2015). 'Social networks and social mobility in fourth-century Athens', in C. Taylor and K. Vlassopoulos (eds.), *Communities and Networks in the Ancient Greek World*. Oxford, 35–53.

Taylor, C. (2016). 'Social dynamics in fourth-century Athens: poverty and standards of living', in C. Tiersch (ed.), *Athenische Demokratie im 4. Jh.: zwischen Modernisierung und Tradition*. Stuttgart, 237–53.

Taylor, C. and Vlassopoulos, K. (2015a). 'Introduction: an agenda for the study of Greek history', in C. Taylor and K. Vlassopoulos (eds.), *Communities and Networks in the Ancient Greek World*. Oxford, 1–31.

Taylor, C. and Vlassopoulos, K. (eds.) (2015b). *Communities and Networks in the Ancient Greek World*. Oxford.

Thompson, D. B. (1966). 'The origin of Tanagras', *American Journal of Archaeology* 70: 51–63.

Thompson, H. A. and Wycherley, R. E. (1977). *The Athenian Agora XIV: The History, Shape and Uses of an Ancient City Center*. Princeton.

Thomsen, C. A. (2014). 'The *eranistai* of classical Athens', *Greek, Roman, and Byzantine Studies* 55.1: 154–75.

Thorp, R., Stewart, F., and Heyer, A. (2005). 'When and how far is group formation a route out of chronic poverty?', *World Development* 33: 907–20.

Tilly, C. (2007). 'Poverty and the politics of exclusion', in D. Narayan and P. Petesch (eds.), *Moving out of Poverty*, Volume 1: *Cross-Disciplinary Perspectives on Mobility*. Washington, 45–75.

Todd, S. C. (1990). 'Lady Chatterley's Lover and the Attic orators: the social composition of the Athenian jury', *Journal of Hellenic Studies* 110: 146–73.

Todd, S. C. (1993). *The Shape of Athenian Law*. Oxford.

Todd, S. C. (2000). *The Oratory of Classical Greece*, Vol. 2: *Lysias*. Austin.

Tod, M. N. (1951). 'Laudatory epithets in Greek epitaphs', *Annual of the British School at Athens* 46: 182–90.

Tomin, J. (1987). 'Socratic midwifery', *Classical Quarterly* 37: 97–102.

Too, Y. L. (2008). *A Commentary on Isocrates' Antidosis*. Oxford.

Totelin, L. M. V. (2009). *Hippocratic Recipes: Oral and Written Transmission of Pharmacological Knowledge in Fifth- and Fourth-Century Greece*. Leiden.

Touchton, M. and Wampler, B. (2014). 'Improving social well-being through new democratic institutions', *Comparative Political Studies* 47.10: 1442–69.

Townsend, P. (1979). *Poverty in the United Kingdom: A Survey of Household Resources and Standards of Living*. London.

Travlos, J. (1971). *Pictorial Dictionary of Ancient Athens*. London.

Trümper, M. (2013). 'Urban context of Greek public baths', in S. K. Lucore and M. Trümper (eds.), *Greek Baths and Bathing Culture: New Discoveries and Approaches*. Leuven, 33–72.

Tsagalis, C. C. (2008). *Inscribing Sorrow: Fourth-Century Attic Funerary Epigrams*. Berlin.

Tsaimou, I. (1979). '*Ο ανδρώνας του Πλυντηρίου Σίμου στη Σούρεζα της Λαυρεωτικής*', *Athens Annals of Archaeology* 12: 15–23.

Tsakirgis, B. (2016). 'Whole cloth: exploring the question of self-sufficiency through the evidence for textile manufacture and purchase in Greek houses', in E. M. Harris, D. M. Lewis, and M. Woolmer (eds.), *The Ancient Greek Economy: Markets, Households and City-States*. New York, 166–86.

Tsaravopoulos, A. (2001). '*Ανασκαφικές Εργασίες* 2001–2004: *Καλύβια Θορικού*', *Archaiologikon Deltion* 56–59: 370–1.

Tsoukala, V. (2009). 'Honorary shares of sacrificial meat in Attic vase painting: visual signs of distinction and civic identity', *Hesperia* 78: 1–40.

Vanderpool, E. (1962). 'Some Attic inscriptions', *Hesperia* 31: 399–403.

Vanhove, D. (1994). 'The Laurion revisited', in H. F. Mussche (ed.), *Studies in South Attica II*. Ghent, 30–75.

van Liefferinge, K. (2013). 'Water use and management in the Classical and Early Hellenistic silver industry of Thorikos and the Laurion', *Babesch* 88: 109–26.

van Liefferinge, K., van den Berg, M., Stal, C., Docter, R., de Wulf, A., and Verhoest, N. E. C. (2014). 'Reconsidering the role of Thorikos within the Laurion silver mining area (Attica, Greece) through hydrological analyses', *Journal of Archaeological Science* 41: 272–84.

van Wees, H. (2001). 'The myth of the middle class army: military and social status in ancient Athens', in T. Bekker-Nielsen and L. Hannestad (eds.), *War as a Cultural and Social Force: Essays on Warfare in Antiquity*. Copenhagen, 45–71.

van Wees, H. (2009). 'The economy', in K. A. Raaflaub and H. van Wees (eds.), *A Companion to Archaic Greece*. Oxford, 444–67.

van Wees, H. (2011). 'Demetrius and Draco: Athens' property classes and population in and before 317 BC', *Journal of Hellenic Studies* 131: 95–114.

Vedder, U. (1988). 'Frauentod - Kriegertod im Spiegel der attischen Grabkunst des 4. Jhdts. v. Chr', *Mitteilungen des deutschen archäologischen Instituts, Athenische Abteilung* 103: 161–91.

Vernon, J. (2007). *Hunger: A Modern History*. Cambridge.

Vestergaard, T. (2000). 'Milesian immigrants in late hellenistic and Roman Athens', in G. J. Oliver (ed.), *The Epigraphy of Death: Studies in the History and Society of Greece and Rome*. Liverpool, 81–110.

Viciano, J., Alemán, I., D'Anastasio, R., Capasso, L., and Botella, M. C. (2011). 'Odontometric sex discrimination in the Herculaneum sample (79 AD, Naples, Italy), with application to juveniles', *American Journal of Physical Anthropology* 145: 97–106.

Vierneisel-Schlörb, B. (1997). *Kerameikos XV: Die figurlichen Terrakotten*. Munich.

Villanueva-Puig, M.-C. (2013). 'La pauvreté dans la culture visuelle des Grecs anciens', *Ktema* 38: 89–115.

Vlassopoulos, K. (2007a). 'Beyond and below the polis: networks, associations and the writing of Greek history', *Mediterranean Historical Review* 22: 11–22.

Vlassopoulos, K. (2007b). 'Free spaces: identity, experience, and democracy in classical Athens', *Classical Quarterly* 57: 33–52.

Vlassopoulos, K. (2007c). *Unthinking the Greek Polis: Ancient Greek History beyond Eurocentrism*. Cambridge.

Vlassopoulos, K. (2009). 'Slavery, freedom and citizenship in classical Athens: beyond a legalistic approach', *European Review of History/Revue européenne d'histoire* 16: 347–63.

Vlassopoulos, K. (2010). 'Athenian slave names and Athenian social history', *Zeitschrift für Papyrologie und Epigraphik* 175: 113–44.

Vlassopoulos, K. (2011a). 'Greek slavery: from domination to property and back again', *Journal of Hellenic Studies* 131: 115–30.

Vlassopoulos, K. (2011b). 'Review of Elizabeth A. Meyer, *Metics and the Athenian Phialai-Inscriptions: A Study in Athenian Epigraphy and Law*. Wiesbaden: Steiner, 2009', *Bryn Mawr Classical Review* 2011.02.48.

Vlassopoulos, K. (2015). 'Plotting strategies, networks and communities in classical Athens: the evidence of names', in C. Taylor and K. Vlassopoulos (eds.), *Communities and Networks in the Ancient Greek World*. Oxford, 101–27.

von Eickstedt, K. V. (1991). *Beiträge zur Topographie des antiken Piräus*. Athens.

von Reden, S. (1992). 'Arbeit und Zivilisation. Kriterien der Selbstdefinition im antiken Athen', *Münsterische Beiträge zur antiken Handelsgeschichte* 11: 1–31.

von Reden, S. (2007). 'Classical Greece: consumption', in W. Scheidel, I. Morris, and R. Saller (eds.), *The Cambridge Economic History of the Greco-Roman World*. Cambridge, 385–406.

Wallace, R. W. (1989). 'The Athenian *proeispherontes*', *Hesperia* 58: 473–90.

Walter-Karydi, E. (1994). *Die Nobilitierung des Wohnhauses: Lebensform und Architektur im spätklassischen Griechenland*. Konstanz.

Webster, J. (2008). 'Less beloved: Roman archaeology, slavery and the failure to compare', *Archaeological Dialogues* 15: 103–23.

Webster, T. B. L. (1969). *Monuments Illustrating New Comedy*. London.

Westgate, R. (1998). 'Greek mosaics in their architectural and social context', *Bulletin of the Institute of Classical Studies* 42: 93–115.

Whitehead, D. (1977). *The Ideology of the Athenian Metic*. Cambridge.

Whitehead, D. (1986). *The Demes of Attica, 508/7–ca.250 BC*. Princeton.

Wilhelm, A. (1902). 'Inschrift aus dem Peiraieus', *Jahreshefte des Österreiches Archäologischen Instituts in Wien* 5: 127–39.

Wilhelm, A. (1978). 'Bemerkungen zu den attischen Grabinschriften *I.G.*II^2', *Zeitschrift für Papyrologie und Epigraphik* 29: 57–90.

Wilson, P. J. (1997). 'Leading the tragic *khoros*: tragic prestige in the democratic city', in C. B. R. Pelling (ed.), *Greek Tragedy and the Historian*. Oxford, 81–108.

Wolpert, A. (2002). *Remembering Defeat: Civil War and Civic Memory in Ancient Athens*. Baltimore.

Xagorari-Gleißner, M. (2009). 'Attische bilingue Grabreliefs des 4. Jhs. v. Chr.', *Archäologischer Anzeiger* 113–27.

Young, J. (1956). 'Studies in south Attica: country estates at Sounion', *Hesperia* 25: 122–46.

Zachariadou, O. and Kyriakou, D. (1988). '*Πλατεία Κοτζιά*', *Archaiologikon Deltion* 43: 22–9.

Zelnick-Abramovitz, R. (2002). 'Ploutos, the god of the oligarchs', *Scripta Classica Israelica* 21: 27–44.

Zelnick-Abramowitz, R. (2005). *Not Wholly Free: The Concept of Manumission and the Status of Manumitted Slaves in the Ancient Greek World*. Leiden.

Index Locorum

Index

Page numbers in italics refer to information contained in Figures and Tables

The manufacturer's authorised representative in the EU for product
safety is Oxford University Press España S.A. of El Parque Empresarial
San Fernando de Henares, Avenida de Castilla, 2 - 28830 Madrid
(www.oup.es/en or product.safety@oup.com). OUP España S.A. also acts
as importer into Spain of products made by the manufacturer.
Printed and bound by CPI Group (UK) Ltd, Croydon, CR0 4YY
14/09/2026
02216307-0001